The Insecure American

How We Got Here and What We Should Do about It

Edited by
Hugh Gusterson
and Catherine Besteman

Foreword by Barbara Ehrenreich

UNIVERSITY OF CALIFORNIA PRESS

Berkeley   Los Angeles   London

University of California Press, one of the most distinguished university presses in the United States, enriches lives around the world by advancing scholarship in the humanities, social sciences, and natural sciences. Its activities are supported by the UC Press Foundation and by philanthropic contributions from individuals and institutions. For more information, visit www.ucpress.edu.

University of California Press
Berkeley and Los Angeles, California

University of California Press, Ltd.
London, England

Every effort has been made to identify and locate the rightful copyright holders of all material not specifically commissioned for use in this publication and to secure permission, where applicable, for reuse of all such material. Credit, if and as available, has been provided for all borrowed material either on-page, on the copyright page, or in an acknowledgment section of the book. Errors, omissions, or failure to obtain authorization with respect to material copyrighted by other sources has been either unavoidable or unintentional. The author and publisher welcome any information that would allow them to correct future reprints.

Library of Congress Cataloging-in-Publication Data

The insecure American / edited by Hugh Gusterson and Catherine Besteman.
    p.   cm.
    Includes bibliographical references and index.
    ISBN 978-0-520-25969-0 (cloth : alk. paper)—ISBN 978-0-520-25971-3 (pbk. : alk. paper)
    1. United States—Politics and government—21st century. 2. United States—Social conditions—21st century. 3. Security (Psychology)—United States. 4. Nationalism—United States. I. Gusterson, Hugh. II. Besteman, Catherine Lowe.
    JK275.I57   2010
    973.93—dc22   2009015363

Manufactured in the United States of America

19 18 17 16 15 14 13 12 11 10
10 9 8 7 6 5 4 3 2 1

This book is printed on Cascades Enviro 100, a 100% post consumer waste, recycled, de-inked fiber. FSC recycled certified and processed chlorine free. It is acid free, Ecologo certified, and manufactured by BioGas energy.

To Stanley Ann Dunham

CONTENTS

FOREWORD

Fifty or sixty years ago, the word *insecurity* most commonly referred to a psychological condition. Some people suffered from "insecurities"; otherwise, though, Americans were self-confident to the point of cockiness. Public intellectuals worried over the "problem" of affluence, which was believed to be making us too soft and contented. They held forums to consider the growing challenge of leisure, never imagining that their own children and grandchildren would become accustomed to ten-hour workdays. Yes, there remained a few "social problems" for sociologists to study—poverty, which was "discovered" by the nonpoor in the early sixties, and racial inequality—but it was believed that these would yield easily to enlightened policies. We were so self-confident that Earth itself no longer seemed to offer sufficient outlets for our energy and ambition. We embarked on the exploration of space.

It was at some point in the late 1960s or early 1970s that Americans began their decline from intrepid to insecure. The year 1969 brought the revelation of the massacre at My Lai and the certainty that the Vietnam War would end in disgrace as well as defeat. At the same time, the war was draining federal funds from Lyndon Johnson's Great Society programs, vitiating health services and hundreds of community development projects. Then 1970 saw the first national observance of Earth Day and the dawning awareness that our environmental problems went beyond scattered cases of "pollution." For the first time since Malthus, the possibility was raised that we might someday exhaust the resources required to maintain America's profligate consumer culture.

American business, beginning with the auto industry, woke up, in the 1970s, to the threat of international competition and initiated its long campaign to reduce both wages and the number of American workers. By the 1980s, big business had started the dismantling of American manufacturing—sending the factories overseas and destroying millions of unionized blue-collar jobs. The white-collar workforce discovered that even they were no longer safe from the corporate winnowing process. In the old version of the American dream, a college graduate was more or less guaranteed a middle-class lifestyle. In the emerging version, there were no guarantees at all. People were encouraged to abandon the idea of job security and take on the project of "reinventing" themselves over and over, as the fickle job market required—to see themselves as perpetual salespeople, marketing "the brand called you."

Meanwhile, under both Ronald Reagan and Bill Clinton, the old confidence that we could mobilize collectively to solve social problems like poverty and racial exclusion was replaced by a growing mean-spiritedness toward the unlucky, the underpaid, and the unwanted. The war on poverty gave way to a war on crime, and when there were not enough crimes to justify this massive punitive enterprise, the authorities invented new ones—like the "crime" of drug possession and use. America achieved the embarrassing distinction of having the highest proportion of its citizenry incarcerated, surpassing both Russia and South Africa under apartheid.

Even into the new millennium, which brought the threat of terrorism and the certainty of global warming, we held our insecurities at bay with a combination of scapegoating, distraction, and delusion. Gays and illegal immigrants became our designated scapegoats, regularly excoriated by evangelists and cable news anchormen. War was at least a temporary distraction, even though it was the greatest non sequitur in military history: attacked by a group consisting largely of Saudi Arabians, the United States invaded Iraq. And then, at the personal level, there was the illusion of affluence offered by easy credit. If our jobs no longer paid enough to finance anything resembling the American dream of home ownership and college for the children, we could always borrow—take on a dodgy mortgage, refinance the house, sign up for more credit cards.

But distraction and delusion are not long-term cures for underlying anxiety. This book comes out at a time when more and more Americans are tumbling from insecurity into insolvency—bankrupted by medical debts, made homeless by foreclosure, ousted from their jobs by layoffs. The credit crisis that began in 2007, combined with stunning increases in the cost of fuel and ever-growing economic inequality, has created challenges not seen since the eve of the Great Depression. As I write this, the overwhelming majority of Americans believe that the country is "headed in the wrong direction" and fear that they will be the first generation to see their children live in more straitened circumstances than they have known.

The Insecure American would have been essential reading at any time in the last few years, but today it is indispensable. For the most part, we confront problems and issues only as they arise in the news cycle, taking them from sources usually short on facts and devoid of analysis. In contrast, the contributors to this book have been researching and thinking about their subjects—from militarism to health care, from foreign policy to poverty—for years. Many are academics who teach as well as write, and here they offer a powerful overarching lesson in clear and down-to-earth prose: that we can understand the forces that have robbed us of security, and—through understanding, combined with a renewed commitment to collective action—overcome them.

Barbara Ehrenreich

ACKNOWLEDGMENTS

The remarkable group of contributors to this volume share a vision of anthropology's powerful perspective on contemporary social issues. Nevertheless, a book of this nature demands a lot from contributors, who must submit themselves to the vision of editors and attune themselves to the writing of their coauthors. We thank the contributors to this book for the good humor with which they wrote, rewrote, then rewrote some more as we sought to harmonize their essays into a single book. Surely the authors of the essays in this volume will be relieved to no longer find e-mails from us in their inboxes requesting yet another revision!

Books are always indebted to far more people than those whose names appear in the table of contents. The initial form of this book was envisioned at a 2006 workshop at MIT. We are grateful to MIT, and especially to Susan Silbey, for funding the workshop, and to Nancy Boyce for superintending the administrative details of the workshop. Our workshop discussants offered excellent comments; many thanks to Lee Baker (who became a contributor subsequently), Debbora Battaglia, Carol Cohn, Jeanne Guillemin, Angelique Haugerud, Arthur Kleinman, Jeff Maskovsky, and Heather Paxson. We are also grateful to the following people for attending the workshop and offering their thoughts: Natalie Bormann, Nick Buchanan, Candis Callison, Catherine Dolan, Mike Fischer, Matthew Gutmann, Stefan Helmreich, Jean Jackson, David Jones, Wen Hua Kuo, Philip Loring, Ann Pollock, Aslihan Sanal, Stefan Sperling, Mary Steedly, Ajantha Subramanian, Will Taggart, Livia Wick, and Anya Zilberstein.

We especially want to express our appreciation to Bill Beeman and Mark Pedelty for their participation in this project.

Many of the chapters in this book were presented at a standing-room-only panel at the 2007 meetings of the American Anthropological Association. Our thanks to the discussants (Rob Borofsky, Derrick Jackson of the *Boston Globe,* Barbara Ehrenreich, and Eugene Robinson of the *Washington Post*) for their fine comments in the best extemporaneous fashion. (It was particularly brave of the journalist discussants to accept our invitation, given that our previous book was titled *Why America's Top Pundits Are Wrong.*) Thanks also to the audience for their attentive enthusiasm in an undersized stuffy room.

Roberto Gonzalez and David Price were excellent reviewers for the University of California Press. We thank them for reviewing the manuscript so quickly and for making suggestions that improved the essays in this book still further. We're grateful to Barbara Ehrenreich for her pithy, sharp preface.

It has been a pleasure to work again with Naomi Schneider, our editor at University of California Press. We thank her for her sustained commitment to this project. Thanks as well to our agent, Regula Noetzli. We're grateful to Rob Gehl for his cheerful assistance with formatting the manuscript.

Finally, we are more indebted than we can say to our spouses, Allison Macfarlane and Jorge Acero, for supporting us through another collaboration.

Introduction

Catherine Besteman and Hugh Gusterson

It was a bad year for Steve and Sarah Schober.

Steve Schober had worked as an industrial designer for Maytag in Iowa for twenty-five years. He had several patents to his name. Earning in the low six figures, he lived in an expansive Tudor-style home with his wife, Sarah, and his two teenage children. Then Maytag was bought by Whirlpool. Maytag's unionized plant in Iowa was closed, and the jobs moved to plants with lower wages in Mexico and Ohio. That was when Steve Schober, at fifty-two years old, found himself looking for a new job.

Steve considered taking a job with the post office, largely for the benefits, but eventually decided to start his own industrial design consulting business. His annual income promptly dropped over 75 percent to $25,000, half of which went to pay for a health insurance policy that cost over $800 a month. As Steve told the *New York Times,* "Health insurance was one of those invisible benefits of working for a corporation. You didn't even have to think about it."[1] To help make ends meet, Steve and Sarah also work on weekends, earning $10 an hour doing menial tasks at an auto speedway.

Less than a decade earlier the Iowa Maytag plant had employed 1,200 white-collar workers and 2,500 blue-collar workers. Its best-paid blue-collar workers could earn over $20 an hour, and this put pressure on other local employers to pay their workers well too. Now $12 to $13 an hour is thought to be a good local wage. The shift came when Whirlpool, realizing it would be more efficient to have one company with two plants than two companies with three plants, bought Maytag and moved a thousand jobs to nonunionized facilities in Mexico and Ohio. The plant manager in Ohio noted that, although his plant paid maybe $3 an hour less than the Iowa plant, "whenever we advertise for employment, it is not difficult finding folks." Meanwhile, although those laid off in the merger received severance packages, they lost their pensions. A few hundred, kept on temporarily to help move the Iowa plant to Ohio, considered themselves lucky to at least have a little extra time to seek new work. As one laid-off electrician, Guy Winchell, put it, "I really don't know what I am going to do. I've thought about applying to hospitals because they have health insurance." Like the more affluent Steve Schober, Winchell dreaded needing to use a health care system that seems to be designed for other people.

Most Americans know, or know of, someone like Steve and Sarah Schober or Guy Winchell. They are Insecure Americans. They are the archetypal character of our age in the same way that the immigrant worker was archetypal for the early 1900s and the newly prosperous Levittown resident has come to personify the 1950s. The Schobers' story of downward mobility and collapsing support systems is the nightmare scenario that haunts millions of insecure Americans.

THE NEW ECONOMY

In recent years stories like the Schobers' have become increasingly common in the U.S. middle class. This is new and has dramatically accelerated since the 2008 economic crisis. Until recently middle-class Americans assumed that employment and rising incomes were inherent to American society. The social order created by the New Deal and the Great Society granted most Americans an expectation of shared economic risk, a rising standard of living, and an opportunity for upward mobility. This social order was anchored by the GI Bill, tax deductions for mortgage payments, high levels of defense spending that juiced up the economy, cheap energy, employer-subsidized health insurance, unemployment insurance to protect against periods of economic turbulence, and Social Security and Medicare for old age. Middle-class Americans were vaguely aware of an economic abyss on the other side of which lay chronic job insecurity, hunger, inadequate health care, and substandard housing in neighborhoods pockmarked by drugs and crime. They assumed that this life was reserved for what Michael Harrington famously called "the other America"[2]—the urban and rural underclass that was disproportionately nonwhite and was unable to transcend both the prejudice of mainstream society and its own lack of cultural capital. And even these people had a rudimentary safety net assembled under the Great Society programs—though a safety net with far more holes than was the case in the welfare states of Europe.

Until recently U.S. society was described by sociologists and economists as pear-shaped. The underclass at the bottom and the class of super-rich at the top were relatively small, and there was a great bulging middle that accommodated everyone from plumbers and production-line workers to college professors and middle managers. The years of economic growth between World War II and the 1970s had benefited everyone relatively equally, ensuring that wages for average workers grew at the same pace as wages for executives and profits for investors. The basic employment structure of those years grew out of a compact that has come to be known as "Fordism." (It is named after Henry Ford, who pioneered a new American model of prosperity by giving his auto workers high wages and a forty-hour week in exchange for high levels of productivity. In turn workers' high wages and guaranteed leisure time enabled the consumerism that completed the circuitry of prosperity.)[3] The Fordist compact was based on a three-way understanding between employers, workers, and government. The government ensured a Keynesian fiscal policy designed to smooth out the business cycle, together with subsidies for education, housing, and retirement, while companies and their employees worked out a collective expectation of stable employment and employee benefits and an understanding that workers as well as managers would get a cut of the wealth created by rising productivity, in return for which labor unions would forswear industrial action, except in extremis.

By the 1980s the Fordist compact was clearly falling apart. At the top of the economic pecking order CEO salaries soared into the stratosphere. *Forbes* magazine reports that the top twenty private equity and hedge fund managers in 2006 were paid an average salary of $675 million[4]—sums that would have been unthinkable as recently as the 1970s. Meanwhile workers found themselves falling further behind. Today the archetypical American company is no longer Ford but Wal-Mart. As Jane Collins argues in this volume, if Henry Ford paid his workers well so they could afford to buy his cars, Wal-Mart pays its employees so badly that they can afford to shop only at Wal-Mart. Where Ford deferred to labor union seniority systems, creating job security and company loyalty, Wal-Mart prefers a revolving door for its employees: as a Wal-Mart executive noted in a 2005 memo, "The cost of an associate with seven years of tenure is almost 55 percent more than the cost of an associate with one year of tenure, yet there is no difference in his or her productivity."[5] Where Ford gave generous health benefits, Wal-Mart pays its employees so poorly that they often qualify for state medical assistance. And while Ford created a widening circle of regional and national prosperity by buying American parts for its products, Wal-Mart outsources as much of its production as possible to China, where a ruthless feudal-industrial regime ensures a reliable supply of well-disciplined cheap labor.[6] And now, in an era where wages for most Americans are stagnant or declining and everyone from computer programmers to radiologists lives in fear of seeing his or her job outsourced to Asia, the Wal-Mart effect is radiating upwards. Instead of wealth trickling down, as we were promised in the Reagan years when "supply-side economics" came into vogue, insecurity is trickling up the social ladder. No wonder Barbara Ehrenreich, writing on "the inner life of the middle class," titled her book *Fear of Falling.*[7]

The bottom of the old middle class is increasingly morphing into what sociologists Katherine Newman and Victor Tan Chan call "the missing class"—a class of about fifty million who "are neither officially destitute nor comfortably middle class" but are "near poor" despite being employed. Newman says they are "truly one paycheck, one lost job, one divorce or one sick child away from falling below the poverty line." They are "missing" in the sense that they have no place on old class maps of the United States and because they are largely ignored by politicians.[8] Their lives of precarious neopoverty, lived in fear of falling through the trapdoor into real poverty, are the leading edge of the new economic order. They are particularly vulnerable in economic downturns like the one that hit the global economy in 2008.

This is life under neoliberalism[9]—the aggressive, increasingly unregulated form of capitalism that has produced insecurity for a growing majority around the world in the contemporary era of globalization and high technology. While David Graeber provides an elegant and pithy primer on neoliberalism later in this volume, a few preliminary words are in order. The neoliberal order was forged under Ronald Reagan and Margaret Thatcher, when financial markets were deregulated and the bargaining power of labor unions began to decline in the face of offshoring and deindustrialization. This new economic order hardened in the 1990s with the end of the Cold War, the collapse of socialism as an alternative to capitalism, and the intensification of globalization. The computer revolution made it easier to automate certain kinds of work, to move billions of dollars across the world in thirty seconds, to outsource work to other countries, to build new kinds of delivery systems for manufactured products, and to create new kinds of financial instruments that brought extraordinary wealth to a burgeoning class of analysts and brokers to reward them for devising cunning new ways of squeezing liquidity out of the fabulously complex flows of capital that undergirded globalized capitalism.

These fundamental realignments have been under way for over two decades, although until the 2008 economic meltdown the mainstream media were slow to grasp their full extent. In the last few years, as a pervasive sense of economic insecurity infiltrated the majority of American households, the media began to recognize in the growing concentration of wealth a new "gilded age"—and for good reason. Some numbers tell the story of great wealth concentrating at the top while everyone else struggled to hold on to what they had. While the U.S. GDP grew by 160 percent since 1973 and the productivity of U.S. workers increased by 80 percent, the average wage of 90 percent of Americans *fell* by 11 percent when adjusted for inflation. But at the same time that incomes for the majority of Americans were stagnating or falling, according to the *Economist,* the incomes of the top 1 percent *grew* by 200 percent.[10] By 2001 the top 1 percent of U.S. society claimed a fifth of the nation's income and a third of all net worth—their largest share since 1929.[11] The top 20 percent went from earning thirty times what the bottom 20 percent earned in 1960 to earning seventy-five times as much by 2006. For the elite of the elite the discrepancy was even more spectacular: where the top hundred executives averaged thirty times the income of the average worker in 1960, in 2006 it was one thousand times.[12]

No wonder the *New York Times* titled one 2006 article "Very Rich Are Leaving the Merely Rich Behind," and published a front-page story on the inconvenience caused the "very rich" by the vexatious shortage of $20 million apartments and Ferraris in Manhattan.[13] In his book *Richistan: A Journey through the American Wealth Boom and the Lives of the New Rich,* Robert Frank tells the story of an eleven-year-old pleading with his parents to fly commercial for once, instead of on the family private jet, so he could see how the other 99 percent lived.[14]

A new, more pyramidal social structure has replaced the old pear-shaped social structure within which each generation expected to do better than its predecessor. George Will calls the new order a "plutonomy."[15] The *Economist* suggests that "Americans may be sorting themselves into two more stable groups, the haves and have-nots."[16] A 2007 study by the Economic Mobility Project (funded in part by the American Enterprise Institute and the Heritage Foundation) found that a new generation of Americans is increasingly unable to fulfill the traditional expectation of doing better than its parents and that "only 6 percent of children born to parents with family income at the very bottom move to the very top"—a lower rate of mobility than in supposedly class-bound Britain.[17] As avenues of upward mobility closed down,[18] many middle-class Americans found themselves clinging to their class status in increasingly tenuous ways: by working longer hours, by sinking deeper into credit card debt, by borrowing against housing equity in the bubble market that preceded the real estate collapse, by relying on the cheap labor of illegal immigrants, and by replacing American-made consumer durables with less expensive imports from China. In the words of *Washington Post* columnist Harold Meyerson, "These are epochal shifts of epochal significance. The American middle class has toppled into a world of temporary employment, jobs without benefits, retirement without security"[19]—changes that would only be exacerbated by the liquidity crisis that struck the global financial system in 2008.

In this era of declining average wages, the average American family has managed to increase its income by 16 percent between 1973 and 2005 (years in which corporate profits reached their highest level ever as a proportion of national income) only by increasing the number of family members in the workforce and by working longer hours—an extra 533 hours a year per family compared to the previous generation.[20] More than ever before, families depend on multiple wage earners—whether that means more women entering the workforce or single people having to live with their parents or other relatives. The result is that, while Americans and Europeans worked roughly the same number of hours until the 1970s, now "on average, Americans work 205 hours more per year than the Italians, 270 more than the French, 371 more than the Germans, and an incredible 473 more than the Norwegians."[21] Part of the reason for this, of course, is that the United States is the only wealthy country that does not mandate paid vacation and paid sick days by law. One-quarter of Americans take no vacation at all.[22] Unlike 163 other countries, it also does not guarantee paid maternity leave, putting extreme stress on families with young children.[23] Thus, as sociologist Arlie Hochschild and economist Juliet Schor argue in their respective books, *The Time Bind* and *The Overworked American*, contemporary families feel afflicted not only by a shortage of income but by a chronic shortage of time—time to work and get household chores done, time to spend with children and aging parents, time to get a full night's sleep.[24] In this situation, according to one recent news story, "Lack of sleep [is] America's top health problem."[25]

These figures indicate a dramatic transformation in American society over the past three decades. Inequality has expanded at an unprecedented rate, as has the concentration of wealth in the hands of a privileged few. Social analysts write with alarm about the consequences for our democracy of such massive economic inequality. "Money is choking democracy to death," warns Bill Moyers in a speech about the dangers of a political system where wealth buys political influence and the consolidation of corporate control of the media has changed the media industry "from one of independently owned operators into something akin to a chain store," stifling critical reporting and instituting an informational culture of blandness.[26] Moyers repeats the much-quoted former Supreme Court Justice Louis Brandeis's admonishment that "you can have wealth concentrated in the hands of a few, or democracy, but you cannot have both."

Americans sense that something is terribly amiss, even if the full picture is not entirely clear. Downsizing has devastated communities across America, replacing stable unionized jobs with low-wage insecure service sector jobs. The 2008 real estate crash and stock market collapse wiped out home equity and retirement savings while increasing unemployment, thus exerting further downward pressure on wages. But Americans have lost more than wages and equity during these last few decades; a more equitable division of risk among all income categories has been lost as well. In the decades after World War II, Americans could expect support from their employers and their government for managing the risks of illness, unemployment, and retirement, but since the 1980s, responsibility for managing these risks has been shifted onto the shoulders of American families. This "Great Risk Shift," says Yale political scientist Jacob Hacker, is "the defining economic transformation of our times."[27] The number of employees who receive health care benefits, defined-benefit retirement pensions, and benefits from unemployment insurance has plummeted over the past few decades. Whereas in most other industrialized countries the government provides benefit security, American families are left on their own as employers have withdrawn coverage. Americans are feeling insecure because they are.

In the face of such rising insecurity, younger Americans are loading themselves up with debt to pay for their educations. In the words of Barbara Ehrenreich, "For years now, we've had a solution, or at least a substitute, for low wages and unreliable jobs: easy credit."[28] Between 1996 and 2006, the debt of the average college graduate increased by a staggering 50 percent.[29] Given that real wages have declined marginally since the 1970s for almost all Americans, these graduates are going further into debt than their parents did, only to fall further behind.

Americans have also been going deeper into debt to buy their homes in a kind of collective pyramid scheme that started to crash in 2006. As house prices climbed ever higher between 1995 and 2005, buyers found it harder to qualify for mortgages to buy them. In an atmosphere of fevered speculation, deregulated lenders accommodated developers, realtors, and buyers by relaxing their lending standards and allowing some buyers to borrow hundreds of thousands of dollars with no money down, no verification of their incomes, and much higher debt loads or lower incomes than would have been thought safe ten years earlier. Many of these mortgages had low teaser rates that, after a few years, left borrowers with payments that suddenly escalated by as much as $2,000 a month. When the crash came, as house prices hit their ceiling in 2006 and interest rate adjustments began to kick in, many home owners desperate to avoid foreclosure found that they could not sell because their homes were worth less than they had borrowed to buy them. When they tried to negotiate with the banks that had helped dig them into this financial hole, they found that their loans had been sliced into a thousand pieces and scattered across global financial markets. Instead of being able to talk to bank managers on Main Street, they found themselves confronted with impersonal financial bureaucracies that had turned them from customers into fragments of collateralized debt obligations and seemed set on autopilot to foreclose. In the ensuing meltdown, home owners lost not just their homes but their life savings, renters were evicted as banks took over their landlords' houses, banks were forced to write off hundreds of billions of dollars in losses, failing banks dragged down other industries with them, and the economic slowdown cost hundreds of thousands of jobs. The "irrational exuberance" in the housing and lending markets, to borrow Alan Greenspan's phrase, led to mass insecurity that affected everyone in the United States. The effects of the real estate and banking collapse of 2008 will be felt for decades.

Debt is an essential feature of neoliberal society. It greases the wheels of consumerism by enabling Americans to stretch to the edge of their means; it is also an apparatus for transferring wealth, via foreclosures and interest payments, from those who need money to those who already have more; and by squeezing more work out of the indebted it enforces social discipline. It is a major instrument of insecurity in the contemporary United States, both for individual Americans and for the country as a whole. (The national debt is almost $11 trillion at the time of this writing, while the U.S. trade deficit is currently at the highest level ever. The U.S. trade deficit with China alone is the highest imbalance ever recorded with any country.)[30]

Given its importance in the new social order, it is worth taking a moment to look more closely at one corner of the American debt machinery—the credit card industry—to see how its terms shifted against the average consumer in the era of neoliberalism and how it produced economic insecurity under the guise of facilitating the convenience of consumers. The credit card industry is the most lucrative sector of the U.S. banking industry—so much so that before its insolvency in 2009 Citibank was more profitable than Microsoft. In the 1990s, like much else, the credit card industry was deregulated so that it could charge whatever interest rates and late fees "the market" would bear. Although general interest rates are near historic lows, interest rates on credit card debt average around 30 percent. Some cards charge as much as 40 percent. At the same time, late fees have risen from $5 to $10 to around $30, and credit card companies have learned tricks such as short payment windows, payments due on Sundays, and so on, to increase the likelihood that people will have to pay such late fees. In 1996 the Supreme Court, in *Smiley v. Citibank*, ruled that credit card companies were free to set these late fees as high as they wanted. While increasing people's credit limits and lowering their minimum payments so they would go deeper into debt, the credit card industry also had this clever idea: get customers to open new accounts with teaser rates of 0 percent, then increase their interest rates to 30 percent if they are even a single day late on a payment— even if that payment was on another company's card. (This is permissible under a legal doctrine called "universal default," which allows your Visa company to classify you a bad debtor if you are a day late paying Mastercard, or vice versa.)[31] The result is a situation where the average American family is paying interest rates of 30 percent on a credit card debt of $8,000 that has become a semipermanent part of its financial scenery—on top of payments it may have to make on car loans and on the equity lines of credit that have become increasingly popular in the last decade. As of August 2007, Americans' credit card debt totaled "a whopping $900 billion," according to economist Joseph Stiglitz.[32] By 2007 the average American family was spending almost 20 percent of its income on debt payments, and "one in seven families is dealing with a debt collector. Children today are more likely to live through their parents' bankruptcy than their parents' divorce."[33] The resulting predicament is captured in the titles of recent books such as *Strapped: Why America's 20- and 30-Somethings Can't Get Ahead* and *The Two-Income Trap: Why Middle Class Mothers and Fathers Are Going Broke.*[34]

THE MOST VULNERABLE

If the middle class is increasingly pinched, things are even worse in the financial underworld of the poor. Offshoring, union busting, the rising use of undocumented workers, the transition from a manufacturing to a service economy, and the delinking of corporate profit from employee compensation have pushed rising numbers of Americans into poverty and created an increasingly insecure world for the working class, the working poor, and the very poor. Offshoring and the deindustrialization of the American economy have cost the American economy three million manufacturing jobs since 2000. Christine Walley's chapter in this book offers a close-up, personal perspective on this loss by describing the devastating emotional and financial effects of downsizing on her father, his fellow steelworkers, and their families in Chicago's hardworking South Side during her childhood.

Collins's chapter on Wal-Mart, America's top employer, explains how the service economy that has replaced secure manufacturing jobs translates into chronic poverty. Before the 2008 financial crisis, thirty-seven million Americans, 12 percent, were officially classified as poor. This was an increase of five million since 2000. The number of Americans living in severe poverty (defined as a family of four with an annual income under $9,903) grew 26 percent from 2000 to 2005.[35] One in six American children lives below the poverty line (up from the one in seven when the war on poverty was getting under way in the late 1960s). Three and a half million of the Americans below the official poverty line work full time, but, as the *New York Times*'s Bob Herbert observes, "One of the biggest problems is the simple fact that full-time, year-round employment is not enough to raise a family out of poverty."[36] A recent Harvard study found that "a family with only one full-time minimum-wage earner can't afford a standard two-bedroom apartment anywhere in the country. While many languish on waiting lists for Section 8 housing, "For every new affordable housing unit constructed, two are demolished, abandoned, or become condominiums or expensive rentals."[37] According to government statistics, which almost certainly understate the problem, by 2007, 754,000 Americans were homeless.[38]

The Moody's economist Mark Zandi says, "Lower-income households have balance sheets about as bad as I've ever seen them—complete tatters. These households are on the financial edge, and if there's any slight disruption, like a car breaking down, it can be a real disaster for them financially."[39] In her best-selling book *Nickel and Dimed*, writer Barbara Ehrenreich describes the desperate efforts to stay solvent by those she befriended when she tried to experience the world of the working poor by entering the service economy as a waitress, a housecleaner, and a Wal-Mart employee. She finds people going without health care because they have no health insurance, sleeping in cars because they cannot scrape together the security deposit to rent an apartment, and sending their children to stay with relatives because they cannot afford to look after them. She turns her own efforts to make ends meet on the salaries she earned from these jobs into a vivid and riveting indictment of the conditions under which millions of Americans struggle for economic security through full-time, exhausting, demeaning, poorly compensated jobs.

Brett Williams's essay in this volume explores life on the edge of this financial precipice. She shows in particular how the poor have been forced to turn to predatory lenders and pawnshops for loans that both enable them to stagger from pay-check to paycheck and keep them on a treadmill of debt, paying usurious rates of interest that make the credit card companies look generous. (In some cases, if the interest on short-term payday loans were calculated on an annualized basis, it would be over 400 percent!) The exploding, largely unregulated industry of payday loan companies and pawnshops colonizing poor neighborhoods takes advantage of res-idents' needs for immediate cash to deal with family crises, offering fast credit to people whose neighborhoods are shunned by leading banks, and then financially destroying the borrowers and confiscating their property with devastating interest rates and repossessions. A clearer picture of how those better off benefit from the insecurity of poverty is hard to find.

Except perhaps in the health care industry. In a society where income distribu-tion is increasingly bifurcated and risks are unequally shared, the American health care system produces two very different kinds of insecurity—one for the poor and one for the rich. At the bottom end of the social ladder, in a society where lack of insurance increases a child's risk of dying before his or her first birthday by 50 per-cent, thirty-eight million adults and nine million children lack insurance.[40] The number of full-time workers who lack health insurance continues to rise as well—to twenty-two million in 2006—as employers withdraw coverage. Uninsured fam-ilies tend to defer treatment as long as possible—often until an illness has become more expensive to treat and harder to cure. The substandard quality of health care for the poor helps explain why, despite spending twice as much as the average de-veloped country on health care, the United States is ranked forty-second in life ex-pectancy. According to a 2005 UN report, the United States had the same infant mortality rate as Malaysia, although it was four times as wealthy as that country.[41] A disproportionate number of these children at risk are, of course, black and His-panic. African Americans can expect, on average, to die five years younger than white Americans. The scandalous undertreatment of African Americans was trag-ically dramatized in 2007 by the death of Deamonte Driver—a twelve-year-old African American boy from Maryland whose infected tooth turned into a brain in-fection that killed him after his mother was unable to find a dentist who would treat him as a Medicaid patient. Follow-up investigations in Congress and the media found that local government lists of dentists who accepted Medicaid were hope-lessly inaccurate or out-of-date and that poor minorities seeking subsidized health care faced a wall of indifferent bureaucrats and health care providers.[42]

Even those who do have health insurance increasingly find themselves being eaten by a system that is supposed to take care of them. Since 2001 the average fam-ily health insurance premium has gone from $1,800 per year to $3,300, and, in an era of increasing co-payments and deductibles, the portion of family income go-ing to health care has increased 12 percent. In 1970 the average family spent 6 per-cent of its income on health care. The number is now 16 percent.[43] The *New York*

Times observes that "medical catastrophes are the leading cause of bankruptcy, and most of those are people who have some insurance, clinging to the fraying edge of the middle class."[44] As the popular documentary film *Sicko* dramatizes, health care plans can deny reimbursement for treatment that is not preauthorized (even if it involves emergency treatment for an unconscious crash victim), for treatment at a hospital outside its preferred network of health care providers, for "experimental" treatment, and for any condition it deems "preexisting" in the patient's body. Perversely, doctors employed by the insurance companies to screen claims receive bonuses for denying reimbursement to patients who may sicken or die as a result. (So much for "Do no harm"!)

And, when care is given, it may have a dehumanizing quality, as anyone knows who has spent interminable amounts of time pressing 1 for this and 2 for that in the automated phone systems of hospitals and health insurance companies. In particular, the American health care system has difficulty in enabling patients to die with dignity. While Americans are notoriously anxious about aging, they are especially worried about how they will die, and an American death increasingly has become something to dread. In a now classic article in anthropology, Paul Farmer and Arthur Kleinman compare two deaths from AIDS: that of Robert, a well-off white man in Boston, and that of Anita, a poor Haitian girl. While Anita receives no meaningful medical treatment, she is touched that her family buys her a soft wool blanket, and she dies surrounded by those who love her as she tells her life's short story. Robert dies in one of the best hospitals in the United States. When he asks to be left to die quietly, the doctors decide he must have AIDS dementia, and they order painful and intrusive tests against his wishes. He dies angry, isolated, and defeated, hooked up to the machines that cannot save him.[45]

In a heartrending essay in this volume about her mother's death in a nursing home, Nancy Scheper-Hughes laments the dehumanizing care too often inflicted on Americans in their twilight years. Her mother is treated more as a body to be dealt with—a nuisance and an accounting issue—than as a loved human being to be cared for. In a perversely ironic twist, our medical system struggles to keep our elderly alive by treating them as objects of undignified medical intervention and indifferent bureaucratic domination. One and a half million Americans now live in nursing homes. A 2002 government study found that half of these nursing homes "are understaffed at levels that harm residents." In one case "an 88-year-old woman was found with ants crawling all over her body. Another went without food for a week before being transferred to the hospital, where she died." No wonder "thirty percent of seriously ill elders surveyed have told researchers that they would rather die than go to a nursing home."[46]

The combined pressures of rising financial insecurity and increasing numbers of people without health insurance have produced a particularly appalling outcome for America's most vulnerable citizens, the mentally ill and addicted homeless. In this book T. M. Luhrmann and Philippe Bourgois take us deeply into the worlds of homeless Americans to show how support structures for the poorest of the poor have been shredded. For mentally ill homeless women in Chicago Luhrmann argues the problem is not so much one of inadequate spending by government agencies as the dysfunctional ways in which these resources are deployed. Bourgois reveals the cruel and absurd cycle between emergency care and incarceration that ensnares many homeless addicts. People whose social value is challenged by mental instability and substance abuse are pushed to the very margins of care, subjected to a demeaning and complicated barrage of rules and requirements when they seek assistance and support. It is hard to imagine a less humane system of care than the one they describe.

While the costs of health care and health insurance continue to rise, along with the numbers of uninsured, the profits flowing to the health care industry have skyrocketed. Pharmaceutical companies, in particular, report staggering profits—$10 billion by Johnson and Johnson, $8 billion by Pfizer in 2005, for example.[47] Joseph Dumit, an anthropologist who studies the pharmaceutical industry, shows in his chapter how the pharmaceutical industry increases sales by defining Americans as "prediseased" or as afflicted by various psychological syndromes and therefore in need of permanent medication for chronic conditions. When, in the era of deregulation, the United States became one of only two countries in the world to allow pharmaceutical companies to advertise directly to consumers, Americans were flooded with advertising suggestions about possible ailments and their cures. Americans are increasingly worried that they are afflicted by such problems as depression, shyness, attention deficit disorder, sleeplessness, premenstrual syndrome, psychological compulsions, erectile dysfunction, restless leg syndrome, or high blood pressure—problems for which the solution is a pill. No wonder that, as the former *New England Journal of Medicine* editor Marcia Angell shows in her blockbuster critique of the industry, *The Truth about the Drug Companies,* the pharmaceutical industry was the most profitable in the country at the turn of the century.[48]

Dumit's essay speaks to the way that American society co-produces health and psychological insecurities by treating health care as a commodity to be bought and sold rather than as a public responsibility. Commoditizing everything intensifies the consumerism that is the engine of economic profit and growth, pushing us toward a system in which we are encouraged to believe that the market, for a price, can meet all our needs and desires. In her revealing chapter on the commodification of childhood, Juliet Schor shows how advertising companies are increasingly directing advertisements at children, the members of society least able to resist them, to develop a new and increasingly powerful subpopulation of consumers.

In the meantime, even as our society encourages consumers to get hooked on the drugs produced by pharmaceutical companies, it has cut treatment resources for those struggling with addictions to street drugs—one of the great scourges of our time, as the essays by Luhrmann and Bourgois make clear. Instead of the kind of resources for treatment one finds in many other industrialized countries, the United States now offers mandatory minimum jail sentences. Perversely, as Eric Schlosser shows in his book *Reefer Madness,* these sentences often fall disproportionately on petty dealers and users, since they have little information to trade with prosecutors in return for a reduced sentence.[49] The result is that the number of Americans incarcerated for drug offenses has risen from forty thousand in 1980 to half a million today, and those incarcerated are disproportionately poor and black.[50]

The United States also incarcerates people for petty offenses that would not draw a prison sentence in most other countries, giving it the highest incarceration rate of any country in the world—higher even than China's. With 2.3 million of its citizens behind bars, the United States accounts for 25 percent of the world's prisoners but only 5 percent of the world's population.[51] Roger Lancaster's chapter in this book exposes the vast extent of this catastrophic system of massive imprisonment. The flow of people into our prisons has not stopped the flow of drugs into our country, but it has created a flood of money into the prison complex, now often run by private contractors, and the specter of years behind bars is yet another source of insecurity for those at the bottom of society. Lancaster argues that a justice system that has created a felon class of thirteen million, that has devastated the African American population, that has redirected millions of dollars from schools to prisons, and that locks up more children for life than any other country on earth makes a mockery of democracy.

THE INSECURE AMERICAN

There have been earlier attempts by social scientists to characterize the zeitgeist of American society. We are thinking of, among others, such books as William Whyte's *Organization Man,* David Riesman's *The Lonely Crowd,* Philip Slater's *The Pursuit of Loneliness,* and Robert Bellah et al.'s *Habits of the Heart.* Whyte, Riesman, and Slater wrote in the era of high Fordism. They were concerned that, in an era where large bureaucratic corporations were colonizing the economic landscape, American life was increasingly dominated by a comfortable conformism that, paradoxically, eviscerated community, creating a sort of social herd that was fundamentally lonely—what Riesman called "the lonely crowd." (A century earlier, De Tocqueville had also been troubled by this potential for conformism in American society.) By the early 1980s, as the Fordist compact was crumbling and a sort of consumerism on steroids was emerging, Bellah et al. worried that, for middle-class Americans in particular, processes of social atomization were eroding community still further, leading Americans to treat relationships as contracts to be entered into and dissolved when convenient. They worried about the implications of this for marriage in particular, and they deplored the narcissistic underside of a therapeutic popular culture that encouraged Americans to put "self-actualization" above duty, family, and community. They expressed concern about the ways in which individualism might undermine the social contract, creating a kind of existential insecurity, but they were not concerned—as we are—with the ways in which the international system, and U.S. military and economic policy within that system, are also generating insecurity that is felt as both collective and individual.

We argue that currently the dominant theme in American culture is insecurity. The conformism that worried earlier sociologists certainly finds ample expression in contemporary consumer and advertising culture and in some kinds of nationalist responses to the "war on terror." The willingness to treat other human beings instrumentally and discard them when convenient that disturbed Bellah and his collaborators is one of the hallmarks now not so much of marriage as of the neoliberal American workplace, where employees can be ruthlessly discarded if cheaper replacements are found elsewhere or if the wizards of Wall Street see a way to squeeze further profit out of a company by closing a factory or laying off thousands of workers. Walley's essay on deindustrialization in Chicago reminds us that the maximization of profit by corporate bean counters and investors also wrecks human lives and eviscerates communities. It is, in fact, a mechanism for transmuting derailed lives into profit. We are often told that "globalization" is the culprit, but the essays in this book point instead to the consolidation of corporate control and the aggressive drive to maximize corporate profit regardless of the human consequences.

The same neoliberal model that has so transformed the American economic landscape has had an even greater impact abroad. Peddled by international financial institutions and American foreign policy, and powered by financial deregulation and the rise of new forms of communications technology, neoliberal reforms on a global scale have wreaked havoc in the lives of poor and middle-class citizens across the globe, even while producing a small international class of cosmopolitan jet-setting elites. The rising inequality that seems apparent in the United States is magnified on the global scale, distancing the class of transnational elites from the concerns of ordinary citizens struggling to make ends meet. Neoliberal policies implemented throughout the world by the World Trade Organization, the International Monetary Fund, and the World Bank have succeeded in impoverishing farmers and workers and shredding social services like health care, education, and pensions, forcing many to leave home to find a way to survive. Yet, while trying to seal its borders against those impoverished by these harmful U.S.-supported economic policies, the United States offers comparatively miniscule levels of foreign aid. At just 0.16 percent of the GNP, the U.S. contribution is the lowest of all industrialized donors. Meanwhile, other donors pledged in recent years to raise their aid to 0.7 percent of the GNP, a figure that represents one-seventh of the U.S. military budget for 2005 and one-third of George W. Bush's tax cuts during his first term.[52]

It is no surprise that many people impoverished by a changing global economy are moving to cities and, illegally, crossing national borders to wealthier countries in search of jobs. It is now estimated that there are twelve million undocumented immigrants in the United States, and their presence provokes virulent debates about the alleged threats such people pose to the economic, physical, and cultural security of American citizens. Peter Kwong's chapter in this volume reviews the history of increasingly repressive legislation targeting undocumented immigrants, defined in popular and legal arenas as "criminals" because of their lack of papers. A number of local communities around the country have been discussing measures that would direct local police to search for them, deny them drivers' licenses, prevent their access to social services such as health and education, and even in some cases make it illegal to rent apartments to them. As Setha Low's chapter shows, native-born white Americans are retreating to gated communities in ever greater numbers, motivated in part by their fear of foreigners. Anyone who listens to talk radio will know how angry many Americans are about the growing swell of undocumented workers in the United States.

In this book, Peter Kwong argues that, although much of the political debate casts illegal immigrants as a security risk, the stakes are much more about economic profit than security. Illegal immigrants are used by employers to break worker solidarity, undermine wages, and heighten profits. By threatening undocumented employees with deportation, employers can avoid complying with labor and wage laws and repress worker dissent. The presence of this exploitable docile workforce has contributed to the economic pressure on middle-class Americans and the waning power of unions. Given the ever-growing number of undocumented immigrants living in the United States (from around three million at the end of Reagan's term to over twelve million today), that pressure continues to grow. Because these workers are constantly threatened by their vulnerability in the workplace, the possibility of raids by the Immigration and Naturalization Service and Immigration and Customs Enforcement, Border Patrol surveillance, and police harassment, immigrants are among the most insecure Americans. Proposals for a guest worker program would seem to offer employers a stable supply of carefully controlled, domestically unattached, politically impotent workers. But the drive to maximize employer profit, particularly in the manufacturing, construction, and the service industries, comes at a substantial cost. Not only does it move us closer to a system in which workers are stripped of their humanity and treated as commodities to be moved around by employers and governments, but it also undermines the responsibilities of employers to the communities in which they are located and creates frictions between those fighting for the crumbs at the bottom of society. Lee D. Baker's chapter in this book investigates the impact of undocumented workers on employment opportunities for African American workers and the tensions between African Americans and undocumented workers from south of the border. His revealing essay shows the enduring power of the color line in the United States, demonstrating that although

Americans have elected an African American president and many African Americans have now secured middle-class status, lower down the economic ladder employers often prefer hiring undocumented foreign workers to hiring local African Americans, even if it means breaking the law. His chapter is a remarkable testament to the ongoing force and shifting dynamics of racism in contemporary America, showing that the powerful insecurities provoked by foreigners are surpassed by the even more deeply rooted insecurities white Americans have about African Americans, especially poor African Americans.

Fear of racial or foreign others has fueled a growing fortress mentality among the American public and the government. In a visible, although controversial, symbol of its claim to providing security, the American government has contracted with private firms to build seven hundred miles of fence across the country's border with Mexico. (The predictable result has been tunnels, a growing industry in forged ID documents, and more bodies in the desert than ever.) Massive investments in surveillance technologies and legal reforms to facilitate surveillance suggest a new American view that no price is too high for security. Selling security—or an image of security—is the newest big business. Remarking on the American trade-off of democracy for surveillance, journalist Naomi Klein ruefully muses: "Security is the new prosperity. Surveillance is the new democracy."[53] The obsessive focus on securitizing the landscape means turning American neighborhoods, schools, transportation centers, shopping malls, public spaces, and government buildings into fortresses surrounded by walls and monitored by surveillance systems.

In this book Setha Low takes a look at the explosive growth of gated communities, into which sixteen million Americans have now withdrawn. These middle- and upper-middle-class citizens imagine the gates will offer them and their children protection in an increasingly dangerous world. But what many residents find, Low reports, is alienation and a disturbing deterioration of democratic participation and community. Drawing out the fear of immigrants and minorities that often underlies the decision to move to a gated community, Low explores the irony that so many who live in gated communities depend upon immigrant workers to meet their needs for child care, housekeeping, maintenance, yard work, and even security patrols. The ineradicable presence of such people, even within gated communities, signals the impossibility of the social withdrawal that gated communities embody as fantasy. The gated community offers a disturbing microcosm of American society, surrounding itself by walls to keep out foreigners while depending on foreign workers to maintain the lifestyle inside the fortress. Residents within gated communities speak of this tension to Low, explaining why they use home alarm systems to ensure multiple forms of protection against foreign and ethnic outsiders. Taken together, the chapters by Low, Kwong, and Baker reveal how scared many Americans are about "foreign," "ethnic," and racial others. Few other aspects of American society generate such emotion and vehemence.

Except the specter of terrorism. In addition to the economic sources of the pervasive insecurity felt by Americans today, it hardly needs saying that, following 9/11, Americans have also felt deeply insecure about possible military (or, rather, paramilitary) threats emanating from other parts of the world. This sense of insecurity has raised the American military budget, at well over $500 billion a year excluding those parts of the budget that are not classified, to record highs. The wars in Iraq and Afghanistan add $130 billion a year more.

The years of Fordism were also, for the most part, the years of the Cold War, when Americans learned to routinize the possibility of extinction in a nuclear war. In those years a pervasive insecurity about nuclear war found expression in such films as *Dr. Strangelove, War Games, The Day After, Failsafe,* and *On the Beach.* The threat of large-scale nuclear war between the superpowers has now receded somewhat—although enough nuclear weapons remain in the stockpiles of the world to create devastation on an unfathomable scale. Instead Americans now fear apocalyptic climate change scenarios and terrorist attacks—including the ultimate fear, terrorist attack with nuclear weapons—from shadowy, unknown others who originate in far-off lands with which we are indissolubly linked by the forces of globalization. As in the Cold War there is a fear that these faraway others have taken advantage of our openness by emplacing a fifth column—now Muslims rather than communists—in our own society, so insecurity finds expression not only in the accumulation of weaponry and military intervention abroad but in increasingly paranoid routines of surveillance at home, where the inability to find internal enemies only feeds suspicion that they are so well hidden that we must search harder for them.

Alarmist scenarios of doom also circulate in a religious key among American Christians—the subject of Susan Harding's essay in this volume. In recent years it has become increasingly common for American Christians to believe that these are the final days prophesied in the book of Revelation. Many American Christians believe that true believers will be "raptured" into heaven just before the world ends at Armageddon, and they wonder if the "war on terror" portends the imminence of this denouement. Christian end-timers may be mocked by liberal elites, but they are hardly marginal in American society today. The *Left Behind* series, about a Romanian Antichrist who becomes UN secretary-general just before the Rapture, has sold forty-three million copies. The three movies spun off from the books have grossed well over $100 million. Still, as Harding shows in her subtle and carefully argued essay, American Christianity is more divided and pluralistic than its secular critics see. In an essay largely focused on Christian beliefs about social mores, Harding argues that the Christian community is balanced on a knife's edge between those who cloak a politics of scapegoating in the language of God and those who see the gospel as a regenerative text that might reconstruct a society torn asunder by the cultures of economic, political, and personal insecurity.

The rise of economic insecurity at home and the fear of terrorist threats from abroad are causally entangled with one another. The same neoliberal processes of globalization that are offshoring jobs, upending blue-collar communities, and rewriting the rules of financial accumulation are also driving corporate expansion into poorer countries and the oil extraction processes (and ancillary military interventions) that are so disrupting the Middle East whence many terrorist threats originate. Despite the efforts of such pundits as Samuel Huntington to persuade American readers that we are witnessing a clash of preformed civilizations and that terrorism emanates from the inherent violence of a defective Islam, it is clear that many of our current security threats are intertwined with disruptions provoked by Western military and economic intervention in the rest of the world.[54]

Following World War II, the United States worked with its allies to construct an international legal structure built on multilateral political and economic organizations, treaties, and conventions on human rights issues. The 9/11 attacks tried to strike a blow against this multilateral system of alliances. Unfortunately, under George W. Bush the U.S. government confounded many of its allies by pursuing a course of unilateralism and scoffing at international agencies and conventions. In rejecting or ignoring treaties and chastising allies as insufficiently militaristic, the go-it-alone approach cost the United States its place at the heart of an international network carefully constructed before 9/11. It was left to the Obama administration to try to reclaim this place.

As part of its war on terror, the United States has dramatically shifted resources toward militarization, both at home and abroad, although much of the rest of the world views the American turn to unilateral militarism with alarm. Survey after survey indicates that citizens of other countries often see the United States as a threat to their security. A British survey showed that Britons believed George Bush to be more dangerous than Kim Jong-Il.[55] From 2000 to 2007 anti-American sentiment spread among moderate Muslims throughout the world, according to the largest survey ever of Muslims.[56]

Catherine Lutz's chapter in this book tallies the toll of American militarism on U.S. values, prosperity, democracy, and relations with the rest of the world. It is a sobering portrait in both the short and long term. The Nobel Prize—winning economist Joseph Stiglitz estimates that the current cost of the wars in Iraq and Afghanistan is $3 trillion,[57] a mind-boggling amount that will saddle future generations with staggering debt.[58] Apart from the wars in Iraq and Afghanistan, the Pentagon's 2005 inventory lists over seven hundred U.S. military bases overseas. The U.S. military employs three million workers, and maintains troops, civilian employees, spies, and their dependents on bases in over 130 countries.[59] Lutz documents how, ironically and tragically, the pervasive militarization of American life and the growing presence of American militarism abroad create rather than alleviate insecurities in both arenas.

Blowback is a term coined by the CIA to describe the unintended and deleterious consequences of U.S. military and intelligence operations. Chalmers Johnson has borrowed the term to title a book analyzing the consequences of U.S. militarism abroad, especially covert acts of violence, terrorism, assassination, coups, massacres, and election rigging carried out by U.S. forces without the knowledge of the American public. Covert American support for right-wing military dictatorships during the Cold War (including Indonesia, Uruguay, Brazil, Paraguay, Haiti, the Philippines, Guatemala, El Salvador, and Chile, as well as ruthless governments in apartheid South Africa, Somalia, and Zaire), leading to the deaths of hundreds of thousands, is a well-known story in those locations even if unknown to many Americans. But many have seen the Bush era of U.S. foreign policy as even more arrogant and dismissive of international law, as well as of civil liberties at home. Even with the international goodwill that met the inauguration of Barack Obama, it will be hard to reverse the poisonous effects on international public opinion that are the legacy of Guantánamo, Abu Ghraib, extraordinary rendition, and a unilateral war waged on what turned out to be a false premise.

Janine Wedel's chapter traces the personal and professional networks that have bound together the neoconservative core members of the Bush administration for the past several decades. Calling them a "flex group" because of their ability to step between public and private roles while collectively pursuing a uniform set of policies in America's domestic and foreign realms, Wedel shows how the concentration of power in the hands of a very small group of tightly connected men stifled critical discussion, political debate, and, most fundamentally, democratic processes.

The consequences to America's reputation abroad and democracy at home have been grave. Chalmers Johnson reminds us that maintaining an empire abroad inevitably damages democracy at home: "We are on the brink of losing our democracy for the sake of keeping our empire."[60] In this book, Susan Hirsch turns our attention to the ways in which the American government has wielded the justice system as a weapon in the "war on terror" since 9/11. Hirsch, who lost her husband in the al Qaeda terrorist bombings in Tanzania, offers a cautionary tale about the consequences of substituting vengeance for justice. Manipulating the law into a tool of war rather than a tool of justice, she argues, undermines democracy and destroys the possibility of justice.

Americans' preoccupations with security have enabled a concentration of power and wealth in the hands of a few, a withering of civil liberties for the many, a withdrawal of public support and compassion for our most vulnerable, and a turn to quick fixes of consumerist pleasure and self-imprisonment behind walls and surveillance technology. The basis of economic security—enabling access to productive resources for all, ensuring a support system for the mentally and physically challenged, providing a high-quality education for all our children, and safeguarding our physical environment for the pleasure and health of future generations—has suffered gravely from the redirection of billions to militarism and incarceration and from neoliberal deregulations that have enabled a massive concentration of corporate profit at the expense of working Americans. The basis of political security—working with a strong core of trusted allies, adhering to international conventions on the treatment of human beings, supporting a strong legal system devoted to fair, impartial justice—has suffered gravely from American unilateralism in the international arena and from the redirection of our legal system toward punitive repression rather than security and justice. The result is a social, political, and economic environment that makes us all less secure. By exposing and analyzing the policies that have produced our present state of insecurity, the essays in this book offer a corrective of past mistakes and a vision for a better way forward.

NOTES

1. Louis Uchitelle, "Is There (Middle Class) Life after Maytag?" *New York Times*, August 26, 2007, business section, 1.

2. Michael Harrington, *The Other America* (New York: Macmillan, 1962).

3. On Fordism and post-Fordism, see David Harvey, *The Condition of Postmodernity* (New York: Blackwell, 1989).

4. Steve McGookin, "More in a Day Than a Year," Forbes.com, August 29, 2007, www.forbes.com/leadership/2007/08/29/ceo-executive-compensation-lead-comp-cx_sm_0829pay.html.

5. Harold Meyerson, "A Dream Short-Circuited," *Washington Post*, April 11, 2007, 15. Meyerson notes that Circuit City, another company following the Wal-Mart business model, had just laid off 3,400 salespeople so they could be replaced by new employees earning a starting salary. "One can only imagine," says Meyerson, "the effect of Circuit City's announcement on the morale of workers who didn't get fired. The remaining salesclerks can only conclude: Do a good job, get promoted, and you're outta here." Despite its ruthless employment practices, Circuit City went bankrupt in 2009.

6. Seventy percent of the products on Wal-Mart's shelves were made in China, according to Paul Craig Roberts, "One Big Reason Markets Are Plunging: China's Threat to the Dollar Is Real," Counter-Punch, August 9, 2007, www.counterpunch.org/roberts08102007.html.

7. Barbara Ehrenreich, *Fear of Falling: The Inner Life of the Middle Class* (New York: Pantheon, 1989). See also Katherine Newman, *Falling from Grace: Downward Mobility in the Age of Affluence* (Berkeley: University of California Press, 1999).

8. Katherine S. Newman and Victor Tan Chan, *The Missing Class: The Near Poor in America* (Boston: Beacon Press, 2007); Eyal Press, "The Missing Class," *Nation*, August 13–20, 2007, 22–23.

9. David Harvey, *A Brief History of Neoliberalism* (Oxford: Oxford University Press, 2006). See also Robert Reich, *Supercapitalism: The Transformation of Business, Democracy, and Everyday Life* (New York: Vintage, 2008).

10. Meyerson, "Dream Short-Circuited," 15; Heather Boushey and Joshua Holland, "If This Is Such a Rich Country, Why Are We Getting Squeezed?" Alternet, July 18, 2007, www.truthout.org/issues_06/071807LB.shtml; "Middle of the Class," *Economist*, July 16, 2005. Statistics show that, for 90 percent of Americans, 1973 was their peak year for earnings: adjusted for inflation, individual Americans earned $4,000 a year more than they did in 2005. See Bob Herbert, "Good Jobs Are Where the Money Is," *New York Times*, January 19, 2008; and David Cay Johnston, *Free Lunch: How the Wealthiest Americans Enrich Themselves at Government Expense (and Stick You with the Bill)* (New York: Portfolio Books, 2007).

11. "Ever Higher Society, Ever Harder to Ascend—Meritocracy in America," *Economist*, January 1, 2005; "The Missing Rungs on the Ladder: America's Great Sorting Out," *Economist*, July 16, 2005.

12. Bill Moyers, "Restoring the Public Trust," TomPaine.com, February 24, 2006, www.tompaine.com/articles/2006/02/24/restoring_the_public_trust.php.

13. "Very Rich Are Leaving the Merely Rich Behind," *New York Times*, November 27, 2006, A1; Jenny Anderson, "Wall St. Bonuses: So Much Money, So Few Ferraris," *New York Times*, December 25, 2006, A1.

14. Robert Frank, *Richistan: A Journey through the American Wealth Boom and the Lives of the New Rich* (New York: Crown, 2007).

15. George Will, "A Lexus in Every Garage," *Washington Post*, October 11, 2007, A19.

16. "Middle of the Class."

17. Economic Mobility Project, "The Economic Mobility of Families across Generations," November 2007, www.economicmobility.org/assets/pdfs/EMP_Across_Generations_ES.pdf. See also Eugene Robinson, "Tattered Dream," *Washington Post*, November 23, 2007, A39.

18. See, for example, "Ever Higher Society."

19. Harold Meyerson, "The Rise of the Have-Nots," *Washington Post*, September 27, 2007, A25.

20. Paul Krugman, "Progress or Regress?" *New York Times*, September 15, 2006, A23; "Distract and Disenfranchise," *New York Times*, April 2, 2007, A27; "Another Economic Disconnect," *New York Times*, April 30, 2007, A23; Boushey and Holland, "If This Is Such a Rich Country."

21. Thaddeus Russell, "Bob the Workaholic," *Boston Globe*, April 16, 2004, D2; David Moberg, "What Vacation Days?" *In These Times*, June 18, 2007.

22. Timothy Egan, "A National Gut-Check: Who Lives Better," *New York Times*, July 5, 2007, A15.

23. Martha Burk, "Paid Family Leave—It's About Time," *Ms.*, July 18, 2007.

24. Arlie Hochschild, *The Time Bind* (New York: Metropolitan Books, 1997); Juliet Schor, *The Overworked American* (New York: Basic Books, 1992).

25. "Lack of Sleep America's Top Health Problem, Doctors Say," March 17, 1997, www.cnn.com/HEALTH/9703/17/nfm/sleep.deprivation/index.html.

26. Bill Moyers, "Message to West Point," speech delivered at West Point, November 29, 2006; Anthony DeBarros, "Consolidation Changes Face of Radio," *USA Today*, July 17, 1998, quoted in Eric Klinenberg, *Fighting for Air: The Battle to Control America's Media* (New York: Metropolitan Books, 2007), 28.

27. Jacob Hacker, "The Privatization of Risk and the Growing Economic Insecurity of Americans," Social Science Research Council forum, "The Privatization of Risk," http://privatizationofrisk.ssrc.org/Hacker/; see also Jacob Hacker, *The Great Risk Shift: The Assault on American Jobs, Families, Health Care and Retirement (And How You Can Fight Back)* (New York: Oxford University Press, 2006).

28. Barbara Ehrenreich, "The Boom Was a Bust for Ordinary People," *Washington Post*, February 3, 2008, B1.

29. Jon Gertner, "Forgive Us Our Student Debts," *New York Times Magazine*, June 11, 2006, 60–68.

30. Chalmers Johnson, "Empire v. Democracy: Why Nemesis Is at Our Door," CommonDreams.org, January 31, 2007, www.commondreams.org/views07/0131-27.htm. The latest figures for the national debt can be seen at "U.S. National Debt Clock," www.brillig.com/debt_clock.

31. David Rummel, dir., "Secret History of the Credit Card," documentary, *Frontline*, November 23, 2004, PBS.

32. Joseph Stiglitz, "Reckoning: The Economic Consequences of Mr. Bush," *Vanity Fair*, November 24, 2007.

33. Ray Boshara and Phillip Longman, "Forget Easy Money. Try Saving a Few Bucks," *Washington Post*, October 7, 2007, B3; Steven Greenhouse, "Borrowers We Be," *New York Times*, September 3, 2006, Week in Review, 12.

34. Tamara Draut, *Strapped: Why America's 20- and 30-Somethings Can't Get Ahead* (New York: Anchor Books, 2007); Elizabeth Warren, *The Two-Income Trap: Why Middle-Class Mothers and Fathers Are Going Broke* (New York: Basic Books, 2003).

35. Tony Pugh, "US Economy Leaving Record Numbers in Severe Poverty," McClatchy Newspapers, February 23, 2007, www.commondreams.org/headlines07/0223-09.htm.

36. Thomas Z. Freedman, "How to Really Help Low-Wage Workers," *Washington Post*, February 2, 2007, A15; Paul Krugman, "Helping the Poor, the British Way," *New York Times*, December 25, 2006, A23; Bob Herbert, "The Millions Left Out," *New York Times*, May 12, 2007, A25.

37. Tony Pugh, "Nation's Poor Hit by Housing Crunch," McClatchy Newspapers, July 13, 2007, www.commondreams.org/archive/2007/07/13/2485.

38. Bill Brubaker, "HUD Study of Homeless Quantified the Problem," *Washington Post*, March 1, 2007, A63. According to this study, 19 percent of the homeless were military veterans, and 45 percent were black. A third had children. The National Law Center on Homelessness and Poverty has a much higher estimate of the number of homeless: 2.3 to 3.5 million; see their *2007 Annual Report: Changing Laws, Changing Lives*, http://nlchp.org/content/pubs/2007_Annual_Report2.pdf.

39. Quoted in Greenhouse, "Borrowers We Be."

40. Editorial, "The Next Big Health Care Battle," *New York Times*, March 12, 2007; Editorial, "A Sobering Census Report: Bleak Findings on Health Insurance," *New York Times*, September 25, 2007.

41. Paul Vallely, "UN Hits Back at US in Report Saying Parts of America Are as Poor as Third World," *Independent*, September 8, 2005; Lindsey Tanner, "US Newborn Survival Rate Ranks Low," Associated Press, May 9, 2006; Associated Press, "People in 41 Nations Are Living Longer Than Americans," August 12, 2007, www.truthout.org/issues_06/081407HA.shtml.

42. Mary Otto, "Hearing on Md. Child's Death Explores Dearth of Dental Care," *Washington Post*, May 3, 2007, B1.

43. Reed Abelson and Milt Freudenheim, "Even the Insured Feel the Strain of Health Costs," *New York Times*, May 4, 2008, A1.

44. Egan, "National Gut-Check."

45. Paul Farmer and Arthur Kleinman, "AIDS as Human Suffering," *Daedalus* 118 (Spring 1989): 135–62.

46. Marie-Therese Connolly, "A Hidden Crime," *Washington Post*, January 27, 2008, B1.

47. Adrienne Appel, "Health Care Crisis: Number of Uninsured Soars, Along with Pharma Profits," Interpress Service, April 6, 2007, www.commondreams.org/archive/2007/04/06/343.

48. Marcia Angel, *The Truth about the Drug Companies: How They Deceive Us and What to Do about It* (New York: Random House, 2004).

49. Eric Schlosser, *Reefer Madness: Sex, Drugs, and Cheap Labor in the American Black Market* (Boston: Houghton Mifflin, 2003).

50. Adam Liptak, "Inmate Count in U.S. Dwarfs Other Nations,'" *New York Times*, April 4, 2008, A1. Although African Americans account for 13 percent of the U.S. population, 53 percent of those serving time for drug offenses are African American. Black men are almost twelve times as likely to be imprisoned for drug offenses as white men. See Erik Eckholm, "Reports Find Persistent Racial Gap in Drug Arrests," *New York Times*, May 6, 2008, A21.

51. Liptak, "Inmate Count." According to Liptak, the United States incarcerates 751 per 100,000 population. The incarceration rate in England is 151 per 100,000; in Germany, 88 per 100,000; in Japan 63 per 100,000. The median rate for all nations is 125 per 100,000.

52. Jeffrey Sachs, "The US Fight against Poverty," *Financial Times/UK*, September 13, 2005.

53. Naomi Klein, "Big Brother Democracy: The Security State as Infotainment," *Nation*, August 24, 2007.

54. Catherine Besteman and Hugh Gusterson, eds., *Why America's Top Pundits Are Wrong* (Berkeley: University of California Press).

55. J. Glover, "British Believe Bush Is More Dangerous Than Kim Jong-Il," *Guardian,* November 3, 2006.

56. Ruth Gledhill, "Anti-American Feelings Soar as Muslim Society Is Radicalized by War on Terror," *Times/UK,* February 21, 2007.

57. Joseph Stiglitz, *The Three Trillion Dollar War: The True Cost of the Iraq Conflict* (New York: W. W. Norton, 2008).

58. Writing in the *Baltimore Sun,* Thomas Schaller estimates that figure equals $20 billion per state for new school facilities and resources ("How Failure in the War Has Meant Success for Conservatism," February 27, 2007).

59. Johnson, "Empire v. Democracy."

60. Ibid.

PART ONE

Fortress America

A Nation of Gated Communities

Setha M. Low

PROLOGUE

On our first visit to my sister's new home in San Antonio, Texas, my husband, Joel, and I are amazed to find two corral gates blocking the entrance to her development. I push an intercom button on the visitors' side. Getting no response, I hit the button repeatedly, finally rousing a disembodied voice that asks whom we want to see. I shout Anna and Bob's last name. The entrance gate swings open, and we accelerate through onto a divided drive enclosed by a six-foot wall covered with bougainvillea and heavenly bamboo.

Inside, large homes loom beside small vacant lots with "for sale" signs. The houses are mostly southwestern stucco painted Santa Fe colors with terra cotta tile roofs. There is a sprinkling of brick colonials with slate shingles and wood trim. Uniformly attractive with neat lawns and matching foundation planting, they look like a scene from the movie *Pleasantville*. It is not just peaceful, wealthy, and secure but unreal, like a doll's house or a planned development in Sim City.[1] Everything looks perfect.

Even before we see men playing golf, we are jolted by speed bumps announcing a right-of-way, and we stop as two twelve-year-old kids cross in their shiny red golf cart. We drive up and park in front of an enormous Scottsdale-style house, sea foam green with a dark tile roof and two-story, glass entrance hall. Anna and my niece, Alexandra, stand dwarfed by the scale of the building.

"I am so glad you are finally here," Alexandra says, pulling away from her mother and throwing her small arms around my neck. She takes my hand and starts dragging me toward the door. "Come and see my room."

Inside, the bright sunshine filters through the closed shutters. My boot heels clatter on the marble floors and echo down the long hallway. I see the green slate kitchen floor from the landing as I walk up the white carpeted stairs to the guest room. Everything is huge and out of scale, giving the impression that I have stepped into a five-star hotel complete with a guest suite, master bath, and walk-in closet. Each room is more spacious than the next, with tall windows, ten-foot ceilings, wide hallways, and long vistas from one part of the house to the other, and on the second floor a view of the golf course and cottonwoods beyond. A stucco wall encircles the house, blocking views from the first floor.

The next morning I get up early to have a cup of tea. I go downstairs to the kitchen and start water on a glowing glass-covered burner. Shimmering sunshine draws me to the window, through which I can see a brick patio with a wrought-iron table and chairs surrounded by a high wall. Imagining how pleasant it would be to sit outside, I unlock the French doors and slowly push them open. With no warning, a harsh wailing disrupts my tranquillity. For a moment I panic, wondering what I have done, and then realize it is the burglar alarm.

Anna comes running from her bedroom. "What are you trying to do?" She shuts off the alarm. "Trying to wake the neighbors and call the cops?"

"I wanted to enjoy the morning air," I protest. "It never occurred to me that you leave the alarm on when you are home. Why do you need it living in a gated community?"

"You don't understand," she says.

"You're right, I don't," I reply.

Ever since that visit I have been fascinated by why Anna and her family want to live behind gates with a guard who watches them enter on a video camera, in a place where they are regulated by a thick book of rules dictating everything from the color of Christmas tree lights to the size of their trash can. This chapter draws upon ethnographic research that I undertook to answer this question.

UNDERSTANDING GATED COMMUNITIES

This chapter examines the dramatic increase in the number of Americans moving to secured residential enclaves—sixteen million people, or about 6 percent of all households.[2] Gated communities now include high-rise apartment complexes for the working and lower-middle classes; townhouses and garden apartments for the middle class; retrofitted housing projects for urban poor; and single-family enclaves for the upper-middle class.[3]

To understand the allure of gated communities, I spent ten years studying six gated communities in the city and suburbs of New York City and San Antonio, Texas. I identified gated housing developments located approximately thirty to forty minutes' drive from their respective downtown city center. Each has its own regional style and distinctive design features, but all are enclosed by a five- to six-foot masonry wall or iron fence broken only by entry gates and monitored by a guard or video camera from a central station. The gated developments included apartment complexes in Queens, New York; townhouse developments in San Antonio and on the border of New York City; and large single-family homes in the San Antonio northern suburbs and suburban Long Island.

I found that people move to gated communities for safety, security, "niceness," and community; they talk about a fear of crime and other people and express a deep-seated sense of insecurity about the world and their everyday life. These issues are not new, but in this American dream with a twist security is gained by excluding others and providing services privately. This version of the dream embodies a politics of fear that justifies gating as well as private governance, increased social controls, and surveillance. Gated community architecture and its accompanying politics threaten the viability of public spaces through increasing enclosure and separation of people in a rapidly globalizing world.

Unfortunately, people are not necessarily safer in gated developments, nor do they enjoy any greater sense of community there. And while residents say they feel safer and happier in their secured enclaves, they worry about having a "false sense of security." There are also many negative repercussions: children may feel more afraid of people outside the walls, greater costs are involved in maintaining the infrastructure, taxpayers' costs soar when the development is turned over to the municipality, residents surrender their freedom of speech through private contracts, and outsiders to the community see the walls and gates as insular and threatening.

STARTING THE RESEARCH

I climb into Felicia's Volvo station wagon, carefully setting my tape recorder on the dashboard. Outside, the twisted junipers and gray-green cottonwoods of San Antonio flash by. The six-lane highway posts a seventy mile per hour speed limit, but we are doing eighty. New gated developments with partially constructed houses and bulldozers leveling wild grass fields stretch as far as I can see. Then they suddenly disappear, leaving countryside that looks untouched for the past hundred years. The small town past contrasts with the suburban present as we speed north.

Felicia is a tall, thin woman in her mid-forties who sits straight upright in the driver's seat. Her long fingers clutch the steering wheel as she drives, telling me about her college and graduate degrees. Despite her educational qualifications, she decided to stay home to take care of her seven-year-old daughter. She and her husband moved from California because of her husband's job and the opportunity to have a more comfortable life with a bigger house. They now live on an attractive cul-de-sac in a two-story, four-thousand-square-foot Scottsdale model located within a gated subdivision on the northern edge of the city.

She is articulate and gets right to the point. When she and her husband were shopping for a house, they did not look specifically for gated residences; school district and aesthetics were the important considerations in their decision making. In fact, she had some reservations about living in a gated community because it would have only one exit if there was a fire. But now they feel good about their choice because they feel safe when their child goes outside to play; as Felicia puts it: "We're near San Antonio, and I believe the whole country knows how many child-nappings we've had. And I believe that my husband would not ever allow her outside to play without direct adult supervision unless we were gated." Their choice of residence allows them the freedom to walk around the neighborhood at night, and their daughter and her friends from nongated neighborhoods can ride their bicycles safely.

Yet Felicia also thinks that the gated community produces a false sense of safety. The guards aren't "Johnny-on-the-spot," and anybody who wanted to could jump the gate. Residents could be lulled into a false sense of security "if there was ever an attack." For instance, when she walks in the community, she does not look to see who is coming out of a driveway, as she would on an open city street or in another suburban area. "You don't rely on your own resources so much," she adds.

The development is made up of people who are retired and don't want to maintain large yards, or people who want to raise families in a more protected environment. There is a lot of "fear flight": people who have moved in the last couple of years as the crime rate, or the reporting of crime, has become such a prominent part of the news. She knows people who are moving in because they want to get out of their exclusive subdivisions that don't have gates, and she mentions one family that was shopping for a house in her community because they had been robbed many times.

Her neighbors are upper middle and middle class, white, Christian (apart from one Jewish family), and quite homogeneous—mostly businessmen and doctors, with stay-at-home wives who have no college educations. On their street, she and her husband know everyone by sight and visit with neighbors who have children, but they no longer have a party when new people move in. The houses are "very pretty," architecturally designed and custom built, though she worries the new ones will not be as tasteful or beautiful.

Felicia feels safe inside the community but expresses considerable anxiety about living in San Antonio:

> When I leave the area entirely and go downtown, I feel quite threatened just being out in normal urban areas, unrestricted urban areas. Please let me explain. The north central part of San Antonio by and large is middle class to upper middle class. Period. There are very few pockets of poverty. Very few. And therefore if you go to any store, you will look around and most of the clientele will be middle class as you are yourself. So you are somewhat insulated. But if you go downtown, which is much more mixed, where everybody goes, I feel much more threatened.

Felicia's daughter was four years old when they first moved, and I wonder about the psychological impact of moving from a rambling, unfenced Californian suburb to a gated community. Felicia says her daughter feels threatened when she sees poor people because she hasn't had enough exposure: "We were driving next to a truck with some day laborers and equipment in the back, and we stopped beside them at the light. She [her daughter] wanted to move because she was afraid those people were going to come and get her. They looked scary to her. I explained that they were workmen, they're the 'backbone of our country,' they're coming from work, you know, but . . . "

So living in a secured enclave may heighten a child's fear of others. It is unclear, though, whether Felicia's observation reflects many children's experience of growing up in a gated community or simply her daughter's idiosyncrasy and modeling of her mother's anxiety.

Felicia and her husband wanted to buy the nicest house in the best school district, while providing a safe environment for their daughter, one where they could be cloistered from class differences. They consider the neighborhood as "a real community" where you know your neighbors, although they say it is not as friendly as where they used to live. For them, the gated community provides a haven in a socially and culturally diverse world, offering a protected setting for their upper-middle-class lifestyle.

Desires for safety, security, community, and "niceness," as well as the desire to live near people like oneself because of a fear of "others" and of crime, are not unique to this family but are expressed by most residents of gated communities.[4] The emergence of a fortress mentality and its phenomenal success are surprising in the United States, where most people live in open and unguarded neighborhoods. Thus the rapid increase in the numbers of Americans moving to secured residential enclaves invites a more complex account of their motives and values. While to a large extent they want the same things that other middle-class Americans want, the seemingly self-evident explanations for their choice of residence encompass deeper meanings and concerns.

Living in a gated community represents a new version of the middle-class American dream precisely because it temporarily suppresses and masks, even denies and fuses, the inherent anxieties and conflicting social values of modern urban and suburban life. It transforms Americans' dilemma of how to protect themselves, their homes, and their families from danger, crime, and unknown others while still living in open, friendly neighborhoods and comfortable homes. It reinforces the norms of a middle-class lifestyle in a time when everyday events and news media exacerbate fears of violence and terrorism. Thus residents cite their "need" for gated communities to provide a safe and secure home in the face of a lack of other societal alternatives.

Gated residential communities, however, are not safer than nongated suburban neighborhoods; they merely intensify the social segregation, racism, and exclusionary land use practices already in place in most of the United States. Residents acknowledge their misgivings about the possible false security provided by the gates and guards, but at the same time gating satisfies their desire for a sense of security associated with childhood and neighborhoods where they grew up. In many ways gating resolves middle-class neighborhood tensions concerning individuality and conformity, independence and community, and freedom and security, yet it also produces unintended problems. The contradictions in what residents think, feel, and talk about provide an opportunity to understand the psychological and social meaning-making processes they use to order their lives.

This chapter reviews the consequences of living in a gated community, drawing on resident interviews, behavioral mapping, and participant observation field notes. I begin with a history of gating and then use ethnographic examples to explore gating's psychological, social, economic, legal, and political consequences. I conclude with a discussion of "community" as it is being reconceived in the United States through private governance and gating and outline what we can do to ameliorate its negative aspects.

HISTORY OF THE GATED COMMUNITY

A gated community is a residential development whose houses, streets, sidewalks, and other amenities are entirely enclosed by walls, fences, or earth banks covered with bushes and shrubs. Access to the community is regulated via a secured entrance, usually a gate operated by a guard, key, or electronic card, though in some cases protection is provided by inaccessible land, such as a nature reserve, or even by a guarded bridge. Often a neighborhood watch organization or professional security personnel patrol on foot and by automobile inside the development.

Gated residential communities in the United States originated for year-round living on family estates and in wealthy communities, such as Llewellyn Park in Eagle Ridge, New Jersey, built during the 1850s, and in resorts, such as New York's Tuxedo Park, which was developed in 1886 as a hunting and fishing retreat and was enclosed by a barbed-wire fence eight feet high and twenty-four miles long. Another early resort was Sea Gate in Brooklyn, established with its own private police force in 1899. Between 1867 and 1905 the architect and real estate developer Julius Pitman designed the majority of St. Louis's private streets, borrowing from the English private square to create exclusive residential enclaves for the business elite.[5]

But planned retirement communities such as Leisure World in Seal Beach, Southern California, built in the late 1950s and 1960s, were the first places where middle-class Americans walled themselves off. Gates then spread to resort and country club developments and finally to suburban developments. In the 1980s, real estate speculation accelerated the building of gated communities around golf courses designed for exclusivity, prestige, and leisure.

Gated communities first appeared in California, Texas, and Arizona, drawing retirees attracted to the weather. One-third of all new communities in Southern California are gated, and the percentage is similar around Phoenix, Arizona, the suburbs of Washington, D.C., and parts of Florida. In areas such as Tampa, Florida, gated communities account for four out of five home sales of $300,000 or more. Since the late 1980s gates have become ubiquitous, and by the 1990s they were common even in the northeastern United States. Gated communities on Long Island, New York, were rare in the 1980s, but by the early 1990s almost every condominium development of more than fifty units had a guardhouse.[6] The number of people estimated to be living in gated communities in the United States rapidly increased from four million in 1995 to eight million in 1997. Two new questions on gating and controlled access were added to the 2001 American Housing Survey,[7] establishing that seven million or 5.9 percent of all households currently live in secured residential developments.

PRIVATIZATION AND SOCIAL SEGREGATION

Urban and suburban spatial separation based on race has a long history in the United States. Cities continue to experience high levels of residential segregation based on discriminatory real estate practices and mortgage structures designed to insulate whites from blacks.[8] Middle-class and upper-middle-class suburban neighborhoods also exhibit a pattern of class segregation as people build fences, cut off relationships with neighbors, and move out in response to internal problems and conflicts. Meanwhile governments have expanded their regulatory role through zoning laws, local police departments, ordinances about dogs, quiet laws, and laws against domestic and interpersonal violence that facilitate a new kind of segregation of family and neighborhood life.[9]

The creation of common interest developments (CIDs) provided a legal framework for consolidating these forms of residential segregation. A CID is "a community in which the residents own or control common areas or shared amenities" and one that "carries with it reciprocal rights and obligations enforced by a private governing body."[10] Specialized covenants, contracts, and deed restrictions that extend forms of collective private land tenure while privatizing government were adapted by the lawyer and planner Charles Stern Ascher to create the modern institution of the home owners' association (HOA).[11]

Robert Nelson points out that "[in] 1970 only one percent of American housing units were located in a homeowner association, condominium or cooperative—the three main instruments of collective private ownership of housing. By 1998, this figure had risen to 15 percent. In major metropolitan areas, 50 percent of new housing units are being built and sold as part of a collective housing regime," with the number of HOAs being more than 250,000 in 2005.[12] This increase is a revolution in governance, with private organizations responsible for collecting trash, providing security, and maintaining common property.

THE CONSEQUENCES OF GATING

People decide to move to a gated community for various reasons. At a societal level, people say they move because of their fear of crime and others. They move to find a neighborhood that is stable, to ensure that their home will retain its resale value, and to have control over their environment and the environment of those who live nearby. Residents in rapidly growing areas want to live in a private community for the services. Retirees and residents who travel a lot particularly want the low maintenance and lack of responsibility that comes with living in a well-maintained and easy-to-care-for environment.

At a personal level, though, residents are also searching for the sense of security and safety that they associate with their childhood. The gates are used symbolically to ward off many of life's unknowns, including unemployment, loss of loved ones, and downward mobility; but of course gates cannot deliver all that is promised.

Psychological Consequences: Insecurity and Social Splitting

Most gated community residents say that they moved there because of their fear of crime, but they also express a more pervasive sense of insecurity regarding life in America. As one resident explained, "I think with the gate thing, there is an increasing sense of insecurity all over the place. I think people are beginning to realize they are not really safe anywhere, in middle America. We have had so much violence occurring, the school shootings, you know. That could be part of it." But this is a psychological fear for which there is no physical or technological solution. Policing, video surveillance, gating, walls, and guards do not work because they do not address what is an emotional reaction. The psychological allure of defended space becomes even more enticing when the news media chronicle daily murders, rapes, drive-by shootings, drug busts, and kidnappings—often with excessive coverage. Not surprisingly, then, fear of crime has increased since the mid-1960s, even though there has been a decline in all violent crime since 1990.[13] As Michael Moore points out in his film *Bowling for Columbine,* this sense of insecurity is not entirely new, but it has intensified with increasing globalization, declining economic conditions, and the insecurity of capitalism. 9/11 and Homeland Security warnings have exacerbated it, and the gates and guards, rather than banishing it, perpetuate it by continually reminding residents of their vulnerability.

The gated lifestyle can also have a negative impact on children. All children have fears, but in the United States younger children are experiencing more fear about being harmed by other people than ever before. Living behind gates reinforces the perception that people who live outside are dangerous or bad. This social splitting has always existed, but the walls and gates exacerbate social distinctions.

The dualistic thinking that social splitting exemplifies is used by individuals to cope with anxiety and fear and with contradictory and conflicting feelings. It fuses cultural definitions and social expectations that differentiate self from other, "us" from "them," regardless of whether the contrast is between Anglo and "Mexican," native born and immigrant, or white and black.[14] For example, Donna implicitly contrasts community residents, with whom her child is safe, to "people out there," who might hurt her child, and specifically mentions "Mexicans" (ironically, those who come into the gated community as hired workers) as a source of threat:

> *Donna:* You know, he's always so scared. . . . It has made a world of difference in him since we've been out here.
>
> *Setha:* Really?
>
> *Donna:* A world of difference. And it is that sense of security that they don't think people are roaming the neighborhoods and the streets and that there's people out there that can hurt him.
>
> *Setha:* Ah . . . that's incredible.
>
> *Donna:* . . . That's what's been most important to my husband, to get the children out here where they can feel safe, and we feel safe if they could go out in the streets and not worry that someone is going to grab them. . . . We feel so secure and maybe that's wrong too.
>
> *Setha:* In what sense?
>
> *Donna:* You know, we've got [Mexican] workers out here, and we still think, "Oh, they're safe out here." . . . In the other neighborhood I never let him get out of my sight for a minute. Of course they were a little bit younger too, but I just, would never, you know, think of letting them go to the next street over. It would have scared me to death, because you didn't know. There was so much traffic coming in and out, you never knew who was cruising the street and how fast they can grab a child. And I don't feel that way in our area at all . . . ever.

While the architectural features of gated communities, reinforced by guards and video cameras, are perceived as comforting symbols of protection by residents, they are also producing a landscape of fear by reinforcing perceptions, among both residents and outsiders, that only life inside a "fortress" and physical separation from people of other racial, cultural, and economic groups can keep one safe. This truly new type of residential development, which uses walls and gates rather than simply distance and street patterns to physically separate residents from populations of other races and classes, sends the architectural message that people need to protect and differentiate themselves from others.

Residents, however, are aware of the limitations of this protection and often become even more focused on security issues. Linda, a young, divorced mother of two boys, ten and twelve years old, spoke to me about the security of the gated landscape for her and her mother. She had been living in her mother's house since her mother's recent death. Her mother had moved to Pine Hills because she wanted to be in a setting where there would be neighbors close by and to have the safety of the gate.

> Linda (laughing): The security of the gate. Five dollars an hour, when they're asleep. I don't know how much security the gate is worth. Some of the guards just let you fly right in. The others have to strip-search you. It really depends. I guess that has been my experience with coming in. Some of them are okay, others want your fingerprints.
>
> [For my mother,] it was just basically being less isolated on a big piece of property, and a couple of years before that we had something [happen]. There were helicopters flying over this area. I mean, this may be going back ten years, I don't remember specifically when, but some inmate, they were looking for someone who had escaped who had a murder record. That was quite freaky. You would look out in the backyard and there would be woods out there, and you'd wonder who is out there. . . . Because, you know . . . people can come in here on foot. There's a golf course right behind us, and anyone could be wandering around on there and decide to traipse through here.
>
> Setha: So what do you think?
>
> Linda: Honestly, I don't know how useful the gate is. The gate is useful in preventing vehicles from getting in, that is, if the person at the gate is alert and competent. . . . Most of the time I do get a call if somebody's coming. What can I say about the gate? We did have some robberies here some years ago. . . . I'll try to summarize this, [it's] good in preventing robberies whereby, you know, somebody would need a vehicle to load a whole lot of loot into a car or a van or whatever. But as far as preventing people on foot, it's ridiculous. You know, if anyone would have an interest in coming in to this community and causing some kind of havoc or whatever, I think there are many ways they could get in.

Linda told the following story to illustrate her point:

One time, one of my neighbor's boys, the little one, was missing. And this woman, I mean, she was white as a sheet, and she was really going to have a nervous breakdown. And we couldn't find him. He was actually in another neighbor's house with his friend, playing. I had called that house to find out, not realizing they were away, and there was a workman in the house. And these boys didn't know the workman. The workman just walked in there, went into the kid's room and started working. So she wasn't at ease [because it was so easy for the workman to walk in without any adults being home, and that her boy was there with a strange workman].

You know, we are not living in very secure times now. . . . I can tell you that after a couple of robberies some of the older residents here felt comfortable with hiring a security car that was patrolling the grounds. So they did try to do that.

In this story, a workman walks into a house, without anyone even noticing, at a time when a mother is frantically searching for her youngest child. The mother and apparently Linda herself make the workman, an outsider, the focus of fear, even though he had nothing to do with the incident. Just his presence evokes comment and fear in this purified landscape.

In the past, overt racial categorization provided the ideological context for discriminatory deed restrictions and mortgage programs. More recently, racial attributes have been used to justify social prejudice and unfounded fears. Helen highlights how race still plays a dominant role in defining "others" onto whom unfounded fears are projected. She explained to me why she had chosen a gated community: "after seeing that there are so many beautiful neighborhoods that are not [in] a secure area, [and] that's where burglaries and murders take place. It's an open door [saying] to people, come on in. Why should they try anything here when they can go somewhere else first. It's a strong deterrent, needless to say." She went on to illustrate her point by telling me what had happened to a friend who lived "in a lovely community" outside Washington, D.C.:

Helen: She said this fellow came to the door, and she was very intimidated because she was white, and he was black, and you didn't get many blacks in her neighborhood. She only bought it [what he was selling] just to hurry and quick get him away from the door, because she was scared as hell. That's terrible to be put in that situation. I like the idea of having security.

Setha: Are you concerned about crime in Sun Meadow?

Helen: Not here, but in San Antonio. There are gangs. People are overworked, they have families, they are underpaid, the stress is out of control, and they abuse their children. The children go out because they don't like their home life. There's too much violence everywhere. It starts in the city, but then the kids get smart enough and say, "Oh, gee, I need money for x, y, or z, but it's really hot in the city, let's go out and get it some place else." We're the natural target for it. So being in a secure area, I don't have to worry as much as another neighborhood that doesn't have security.

Ironically, Helen's concern with crime developed after she moved into Sun Meadow; living there reinforced her sense of the importance of having gates and guards for personal security. "Crime," in this context, though, is a coded reference to race. Residents were more comfortable talking about crime and "others" than confronting their own racial fears and their desire to separate themselves from people of color.

In this sense, gating is part of a transformation of American class relations through spatial separation and a reworking of the urban and suburban landscape.

Racist fears about the "threat" of a visible minority, whether it is blacks, Mexicans, or Korean Americans, are remarkably similar. This is because many neighborhoods in the United States are racially homogeneous: the physical space of the neighborhood and its racial composition are synonymous. A "racialized" spatial ordering and the identification of a space with a group of people are fundamental to how suburban landscapes reinforce racial prejudice and discrimination, and gating is just the latest phenomenon to maintain and reinforce this ordering.

Yet ironically, gated community residents remain worried about the porous boundaries of their neighborhoods, especially given that racial "others" still enter the community as hired workers. Withdrawal behind gates may even exacerbate racial fears toward those whose presence can never, finally, be avoided in a globalized, multicultural society, and whose labor will always be indispensable to white middle-class families seeking nannies, housekeepers, and gardeners.

Social Consequences: "Niceness," Social Control, and Exclusion

The word *niceness* captures the ways that residents talk about their desire for a socially controlled, middle-class, "white" environment and is central to what residents are searching for. Residents talk about their insecurity and fear, but they also are interested in finding a "nice" house in a "nice" community. *Niceness* is a way to talk about wanting to live in a neighborhood with people who have similar values and who keep their houses and gardens in a particular way. Residents say they are willing to trade personal freedom for rules and regulations to make sure that their neighborhood will not change in some unintended way.

In some cases, the use of the term *nice* reflects the micropolitics of distinguishing oneself from the family who used to live next door. Status anxiety about downward mobility due to declining male wages and family incomes, shrinking job markets, and periodic economic recessions has increased concern that one's own children will not be able to sustain a middle-class lifestyle.[15] Prospective buyers hear assurances that walls and gates will maintain home values and provide some kind of "class" or "distinction" as a partial solution to the problem of upholding their middle- or upper-middle-class position. As Linda, the Pine Hills resident quoted earlier, put it, "This is my theory: Long Island is very prestige minded. And I think the very fact of having a guard at the gate is akin to living in Manhattan in a doorman building versus a three-flight walk-up type of thing. There's a certain 'pass through the gate' type of thing, this is a private community. That actually, sadly enough, may be part of it. You know, other than the safety issue, just a kind of separating ourselves from the great unwashed, shall we say."

This separation from others and the maintenance of "niceness" can take the form of desiring a "stable" neighborhood with the "right" kind of stores and people. For instance, Sharon said that increased neighborhood deterioration had left her feeling uncomfortable in the house where she had lived for over twenty-five years. Even though she had known everyone in her old neighborhood and had enjoyed walking to the corner store, "When Bloomingdale's moved out and K-Mart moved in, it just brought in a different group of people."

Ted and Carol similarly explained that Great Neck, where they had previously lived, had been a great community socially and that the children had attended a good school. "It's almost like living in the city," Carol said, "but better."

> Ted: But it's changing, it's undergoing internal transformations.
>
> Carol: It's ethnic changes.
>
> Ted: It's ethnic changes, that's a very good way of putting it.

Carol added that the changes had started to happen "in the last, probably, seven to eight years." The changing composition of the neighborhood had made them so uncomfortable they had decided to move. They hoped that their new "nice" community would keep those "changes" out.

Economic Consequences: Subsidizing Inequality

Home owners' associations (HOAs), with and without gates, exist throughout the United States as a rapidly growing form of private government that is competing with public governance by municipalities, counties, and townships. In their substitution of private development and provision of services for public governance, HOAs are part of the neoliberal reformulation of economic responsibility. Cities and townships allow private gated communities to be built because they do not have to pay for the expanding infrastructure of new housing developments. For a while residents are able to support their own services, but eventually the gated community turns over its roads and lights to the city, or the city annexes the area[16]—often just as the infrastructure requires substantial reinvestment, the costs of which now fall on the public or get deferred.

Wayne, a resident of the Links, sees annexation as a bad bargain for gated community residents:

A lot of what's happening in these gated communities is that local government continues to annex. As they annex, the level of service goes down, not only for the annexed areas, but also for the inner parts of the city. [The idea is that] we'll get more money and everybody will benefit. [But in fact] they get more taxes and dilute the level or quality of services.

So developers say, "Well, I have got to have my own amenity package, I have to have my own gated community." All that is, is a reflection of the inability of the municipality to deal properly with the problems at hand. They create another level of government: home owners' associations in these gated communities. So the type of development we get is because the city is ambitious in terms of annexation.

> I see problems with gated communities in the future . . . The reality is that when gated communities are annexed, the city does not take responsibility for repairs of streets [and infrastructure]. Home owners' associations will still have to provide that.

Outsiders to the gated community, however, may well see annexation more as a bad bargain for them. Important public space inequalities are created by the expansion of gated developments. Each time the city takes over a privately constructed community, they are spending money maintaining property and houses that are solely in the private domain. Thus gated communities benefit from public subsidies when they are built and then are bailed out by the taxpayers when they cannot keep up their local services. But their public spaces—streets, parks, pools, and jogging paths—remain private, gated off from the public that supports them. Gated communities, in this sense, are residential mini-prototypes for the neoliberal city and suburb, organized by the private sector and governed by a limited membership of home owners.

Legal Consequences: Loss of Rights

Residents of common interest developments also give up their legal rights to freedom of speech and to court adjudication of their personal civil and property rights.[17] They have signed a private contract with a corporation; therefore, any disputes with that corporation or with their neighbors are handled by contractual law.

Residents are often unaware that in such matters their choice of residence has left them with little to no legal recourse. Yusef, for example, had neighbors who persisted in making excessive noise, but when he went to the board about it he was upset to discover that they would not consider his case: they showed no interest, he said, and merely gave him the address of the local mediation center. "We decided to take them there [to mediation] after it had been proven that they didn't comply with the rules. They knew that they didn't have to go. It's not obligated for you to go to mediation, you can refuse to go. But if they took you to court it would count against you. It seems that you are the aggressor really because you didn't want to make peace when it was offered."

In mediation the neighbor made concessions about the noise but then didn't follow through on them. Yusef, returning to the HOA board, found that even at this point the board would not do anything. I asked Yusef it he would recommend this community to others. He responded, "I would recommend [it only to] those that I know very well. Those that I think are not going to find the rules and regulations very unacceptable. Those people who want a quiet life, who understand that they have to pay a price somehow, to live a quiet life, will enjoy being in a gated community. If you are going to have a place that is secure, then you have to have people who are controlling entry. But some people may not like that they are controlled, and [yet] the same people are asking for security."

Political Consequences: Moral Minimalism

At least half the people I spoke to said they were looking for an old-fashioned neighborhood where they knew and saw their neighbors. But gated communities do not necessarily create community. In fact, the corporate nature of governance in some cases creates more "moral minimalism" than community spirit. As described by M. P. Baumgartner in his *Moral Order of the Suburb,* this ethic, based on an aversion to conflict and confrontation and a valuing of restraint and avoidance, would make the morally correct response to a grievance ignoring it or, if absolutely necessary, calling in a third party to handle the matter.[18] If there is conflict between neighbors, as in Yusef's case, they want it handled by the HOA board, not by themselves.

Yet some residents complain about how HOAs are excessively controlled by a few people and how all decisions are displaced onto an independent body. They are upset about the numerous restrictions placed on their own actions, though at the same time they want restrictions to ensure that others in the community will not harm their property values. Laurel, for example, complained to me about how she couldn't even garden without first getting the HOA to approve her planting choices: "I asked the manager of her development and he said, 'Well, you know, we have a committee, and you have to tell them what you want to do.'"

Her husband, George, who had been to several committee meetings, said that not enough people attended them to give an adequate sense of the consensus of the community. "It's totally ridiculous, especially if you want to make a rule. The committee that's going to run the development, who decides things like whose house gets painted, or what color, you know [does not represent the community]. I think it should be whatever you do in your own backyard, it's your business, but in front it has to meet certain requirements." The couple told me that the committee had even given them trouble about putting up a television satellite dish and colorful curtains when they moved in. To my question of whether the community allowed pets, Laurel replied that they would not have moved in if pets were prohibited. But the committee has put in some rules about pets, since some people let their animals run everywhere and do not pick up after them. Some gated developments are more restrictive and do not allow pets even to visit.

The recent trend of building fake gated communities in Simi Valley, Southern California, for the upper middle and middle classes—communities whose gates are never closed or locked, or whose guard shacks are never staffed, or whose guards have no authority to keep anyone out—dramatizes the point that "gates" are about deeper psychological and social concerns. They do not reduce crime or keep "others" out; they merely offer an illusion of physical safety and security that does not require the "hardware" of guards and real locks. Fake gating as much as real gating enables home owners to feel better about their social status and place in the world in a period of social and economic transition. This evolution of fake gating from the "real" thing substantiates how profoundly gating permeates American culture, replacing and reconstructing notions of "community" and "the American dream."

What is wrong with gated communities is that while residents use gates to create the community they are searching for, their personal housing decisions have unintended negative consequences. Most importantly, they disrupt other people's ability to experience "community": community in the sense of mutual openness of suburb and city, community in terms of access to public open space, and even community within the American tradition of integration and social justice.

Architecture and the layout of towns and suburbs provide concrete anchoring points in people's everyday lives. These anchoring points reinforce ideas about society at large. Gated communities and the social segregation and exclusion they represent are symptomatic of problems Americans have with race, class, and gender inequality and social discrimination. The gated community contributes to a geography of social relations that produces fear and anxiety simply by locating a person's home and place identity in a secured enclave, gated, guarded, and locked.[19]

Some policies and planning and design interventions can ameliorate gated communities' negative impact. For example, it is important to communicate to prospective residents that gated communities may not be safer or protect housing values— the two main reasons that most residents choose to live there. Also, efforts should be made both locally and statewide to increase public education and provide legal information about the limitations of CIDs, including contractual restrictions on residents' right to legal remedy. Further, residents need to understand how an HOA functions, the HOA board's decision-making process, and the covenants, rules, and regulations that will regulate their home and landscape.

Architects and planners as well as the builders and construction companies who design and build gated developments should be encouraged to search for alternatives that deliver the safety and security that residents desire without the enclosure of open space and the use of physical walls and gates to create a sense of community. Advertisers and real estate agents should also reconsider their emphasis on security and exclusivity as strategies for attracting home owners and renters or for selling community as a neighborhood within walls.

Finally, local and state government officials should be required to evaluate the financing of gated communities for the long term. They need to resist the lure of short-term gains that place a future burden on taxpayers to rescue private communities that are unable to support their own aging infrastructure. At the national level, we need debate about the impact of gating on the development of children, social segregation, and community integration. As a society, we must ask the hard question of how we can provide a safe, clean, supportive environment for everyone so that families will not need gating to have the neighborhood and cohesive community that so many Americans only dream about.

NOTES

This chapter includes material previously published in *Behind the Gates: Life, Security and the Pursuit of Happiness in Fortress America* (Routledge, 2003), and many of the sections on the consequences of gating are adapted from "The Politics of Fear," which appeared in 2005 in a special issue of *Soziale Welt* (Baden-Baden) entitled "The Reality of Cities" (ed. Helmuth Berking and Martina Loew). I would like to thank Andrew Kirby and Elena Danila for their participation in this project.

1. A computer game that allows the players to create simulated houses, neighborhoods, and cities.

2. Tom Sanchez and Robert L. Lang, *Security versus Status: The Two Worlds of Gated Communities*, Census Note Series 02.02 (Alexandria: Metropolitan Institute at Virginia Tech, 2002).

3. Setha M. Low, *Behind the Gates: Life, Security and the Pursuit of Happiness in Fortress America* (New York: Routledge, 2003).

4. As part of the research, my research assistants and I conducted extensive interviews with fifty gated community residents.

5. Dolores Hayden, *Building American Suburbia: Green Fields and Urban Growth, 1820–2000* (New York: Pantheon Books, 2003).

6. Low, *Behind the Gates*.

7. Sanchez and Lang, *Security versus Status*.

8. D. S. Massey and Nancy Denton, "Suburbanization and Segregation," *American Journal of Sociology* 94, no. 3 (1988): 592–626; Gabriella Modan, "The Struggle for Neighborhood Identity: Discursive Constructions of Community and Place in a U.S. Multi-ethnic Neighborhood" (PhD diss., Georgetown University, 2000); Constance Perin, *Everything in Its Place: Social Order and Land Use in America* (Princeton: Princeton University Press, 1977).

9. Sally Merry, "Mending Walls and Building Fences: Constructing the Private Neighborhood," *Journal of Legal Pluralism* 33 (1993): 71–90.

10. Dennis Judd, "The Rise of New Walled Cities," in *Spatial Practices: Critical Explorations in Social/Spatial Theory*, ed. Helen Liggett and David C. Perry (Thousand Oaks, CA: Sage Publications, 1995), 144–65.

11. Evan McKenzie, *Privatopia: Homeowner Associations and the Rise of Residential Private Government* (New Haven: Yale University Press, 1994).

12. Robert Nelson, *Private Neighborhoods and the Transformation of Local Government* (Washington, DC: Urban Institute Press, 2005).

13. Barry Glassner, *The Culture of Fear* (New York: Basic Books, 1999); Christopher Stone, "Crime and the City," in *Breaking Away: The Future of Cities*, ed. Julia Vitullo-Martin (New York: Twentieth Century Fund Press, 1996), 98–103; Dean Brennan and Al Zelinka, "Safe and Sound," *Planning* 64 (August 1997): 4–10; Karen Colvard, "Crime Is Down? Don't Confuse Us with the Facts," *HFG Review* 2, no. 1 (1997): 19–26.

14. Catherine Silver, "Construction et deconstruction des identités de genre," *Cahier du Genre* 31 (2002): 185–201; Melanie Klein, *Envy and Gratitude and Other Works, 1946–1963* (New York: Delacorte, 1975).

15. Katherine S. Newman, *Declining Fortunes: The Withering of the American Dream* (New York: Basic Books, 1993); Sherry Ortner, "Generation X: Anthropology in a Media-Saturated World," *Cultural Anthropology* 13, no. 3 (1998): 414–40.

16. Annexation is a process by which a town, county, or other governmental unit becomes part of the city, in this case the metropolitan region of San Antonio.

17. However, a recent New Jersey court ruling found, on the basis of the state's reading of civil rights, which is more liberal than the federal constitution's, that CID regulations could not restrict freedom-of-speech rights.

18. M. P. Baumgartner, *The Moral Order of the Suburb* (New York: Oxford University Press, 1988).

19. Doreen Massey, *Space, Place, and Gender* (Minneapolis: University of Minnesota Press, 1994); Michelle Fine, " 'Whiting Out' Social Justice," in *Addressing Cultural Issues in Organizations: Beyond the Corporate Context,* ed. Robert T. Carter (Thousand Oaks, CA: Sage Publications, 2000), 35–50.

2

Warmaking as the American Way of Life

Catherine Lutz

Sometimes a people's problems are as visible as their rivers coughing up multitudes of dead fish, or homeless women and men lying on sidewalks like trash. Other troubles are more deeply hidden and so likely to persist without names or solutions. So it is with America's permanent and massive mobilization for war. Long before 9/11, nearly every aspect of the American way of life began to depend on, entwine with, or suffer from a massive investment in arms and armies. The evolution from a nation that enshrined its suspicion of the militarist states of eighteenth-century Europe in its constitution to a nation in which war readiness is a way of life was mainly a twentieth-century phenomenon and even more one that emerged during and beyond World War II.

How massive has this investment been? Looking back in time and across the world today, no military has come close to rivaling the global scale of the U.S. military's reach and the lethality of its weapons—not the Roman, the British, the Ottoman, the Soviet, or the Chinese. As of 2008, the U.S. military budget is almost as large as that of every other major and middling military in the world combined and six times larger than any other rival or ally.[1] The Department of Defense (DoD) has millions of employees, thousands of bases established in every state and each corner of the globe, recruiters trawling for young people in every school and mall in America and its territories, and people writing reams each day on nuances of strategic thought, planning interventions for virtually every nation on earth, and creating new weapons. For decades, U.S. civilian and military planners have dreamed of and executed a plan to establish an unconquerable empire of bases overseas and a national industrial and educational policy centered on the production of advanced weaponry.

Many Americans will immediately ask, What is wrong with that? Isn't the scale of our military made necessary by a dangerous world and easily possible by our affluence, and isn't that military a force for good both domestically and abroad? I argue that the evidence is that the massive and long-term mobilization for war in the United States has misshaped cultural values; increased various forms of inequality, most importantly those of race, class, gender, and sexuality; served as a massively antidemocratic force by accelerating the corporatization of government and legitimating secrecy and violation of the rule of law; and exported violence, toxins, and authoritarianism abroad. Since 2003, for example, one hundred thousand Iraqis and thousands of Americans have died in the war begun with the U.S. invasion.[2] Each year, PCBs and greenhouse gases from military and military-industrial operations have poured into the world's air and water supply, and scientific talent has been massively detoured from the task of producing medical cures or teaching. And while affluence may be both cause and effect of the large U.S. military, many thinkers from across the political spectrum note that the decline of American power is ongoing and the result of overinvestment in military matters.

This chapter does three things: it describes the scale and uses of the U.S. military; outlines its broad social, economic, and political impact, especially within the United States; and then asks what beliefs and social processes contribute to our inability to see the gargantuan U.S. military as a massive and enduring problem.

THE SCALE AND USES OF THE U.S. MILITARY

The United States has the largest budget for the production of violence of any government, anywhere, ever. The wealth involved is staggering, with over one *trillion* dollars the estimated cost of the military in 2008. When the official DoD budget is released each year, the figure is far smaller than this. But the true number is much larger because one must include separate congressional allocations for the wars in Iraq and Afghanistan, military spending buried in other areas of the federal budget such as the Department of Energy and Department of State, interest payments on the debt for past and current wars, and Department of Veterans Affairs spending.

Despite the size of this figure, it represents only a fraction of the actual drain of military spending on the nation, as Joseph Stiglitz and Linda Bilmes demonstrated in their 2008 study of the eventual total costs of the Iraq war.[3] They put the price tag for that war alone at $3 trillion. Their total is so much higher than the official budget figures because they include macroeconomic effects such as the higher oil prices that the war prompted, as well as more local costs such as lifetime disability payments to veterans wounded in the war, the economic costs of withdrawal of the civilian labor of the National Guard and Reserve, the costs in lost economic productivity of those who died (the notorious VSL or "value of statistical life"), and the health care costs for the tens of thousands of soldiers with such serious injuries as brain damage, blindness, burns, nerve damage, facial deformation, and mental breakdown.[4] The long Cold War was even pricier: the nuclear arsenal the United States built during those years is estimated to have been $5.5 trillion, and the likely cost of cleaning up U.S. nuclear weapons facilities will come close to matching those of making the weapons in the first place.[5]

The U.S. military is far and away the country's largest employer, leaving Wal-Mart, the Post Office, and General Motors in the dust. It has 3 million workers, 2.3 million of them soldiers and 700,000 of them civilians. Approximately 1.4 million soldiers are permanent employees, and the rest, in the Reserves and National Guard, are temp workers of a sort, called up only when needed. The Pentagon pays the wages of millions more Americans through weapons and other contracts, with the overall result that the military's direct and indirect employees constitute about 5 percent of the U.S. workforce. Other militaries have claimed larger percentages of their nation's workers: the relatively modest size of the U.S. direct military workforce has to do with the preference for capital-intensive investment in advanced weaponry over labor-intensive investment in personnel.

For much of the twentieth century, military dollars have gone to hire industrial, scientific, and technical workers who design and produce weapons. The funding stream is so massive that fully one-quarter of the scientists and technicians in the United States now work on military contracts.[6] To generate the needed workforce, the military has had an intimate and shaping relationship with U.S. universities. There, it provides 41 percent of all federal funds for engineering research and 45 percent of all federally funded support to graduate students in computer science. To take an example of one research project, fifteen universities, particularly the University of Alaska, have received funds since 1993 from the air force and navy to work on the High-Frequency Active Auroral Research Program (HAARP), a project investigating how to control upper-atmosphere processes in order to enhance the military's ability to control enemy communications and conduct surveillance. In 2000, the University of California system received over $147 million in DoD research contracts. As a result of their deep dependence on the Pentagon, the University of California and other universities now actively lobby Congress for increases in military spending. While the assumption is that this research is "basic" rather than applied and devolves to the good of society as a whole, Pentagon spending on research is oriented to the needs of warmaking rather than prioritizing knowledge needed to solve pressing social problems. Because DoD research monies are so significant, they help set the direction of scholarly research more generally and direct young people who apprentice on professors' military contracts into military work.

Increasingly, the DoD also subcontracts out work formerly done only by men and women in uniform. At least three dozen private military companies are currently working for the Pentagon. Between 1994 and 2002, the Pentagon entered into over three thousand contracts with such firms valued at over $300 billion.[7] The rise of these "private warriors" is a recent development that is both the outcome of privatization efforts during the 1990s in efforts to restructure the military along neoliberal lines and the result of lobbying by military corporations for ever larger chunks of the budget. These companies, including KBR (Kellogg, Brown & Root), Vinnel, DynCorp, and Blackwater USA, play roles once belonging to people in uniform, including base construction and logistics, the training of foreign soldiers, and the provision of security details for bases and officials (such as the forty DynCorp gunmen who guard Hamid Karzai in Afghanistan). The DoD counted 129,000 contract employees in Iraq in 2007. These workers, some poorly compensated migrant workers from the global South, others more richly paid U.S. citizens, bring great profit for the corporations that sell their services to the Pentagon. Massive contract fraud has been uncovered in this additional war-for-profit set of operations since the war in Iraq began.[8]

The U.S. arsenal consists of a baroque array of weapons and other technologies. At the pinnacle are 2,700 actively deployed nuclear warheads.[9] Then there are highly sophisticated and expensive missiles of a bewildering variety, including AIM-120 AMRAAM missiles, which cost $386,000 apiece, and the air force's newest fighter aircraft, the F-22A Raptor, which "possesses a sophisticated sensor suite allowing the pilot to track, identify, shoot and kill air-to-air threats before being detected."[10] Other especially controversial components of the arsenal are cluster bombs that rain many small bomblets across an area as large as three football fields. They are "triple threats" in the sense that they can explode in the air, on impact, or later on the ground when disturbed even years later. While the United States has appeared to be adhering to most provisions of the international ban on chemical and biological weapons, the Pentagon has admitted to using white phosphorus in Iraq; further, it continues research on other such banned weapons and maintains the capacity to reintroduce them to the arsenal. The United States is also one of only a handful of countries that have refused to sign the Ottawa Treaty, the international treaty banning land mines, other weapons of mass destruction that have killed or maimed millions.

This arsenal is produced by some of the nation's largest and most profitable corporations, including Lockheed Martin, Boeing, Northrop Grumman, Honeywell International, and United Technologies. Their profit margins consistently have topped the list of American companies. With their R&D costs and infrastructure costs subsidized and other business risks socialized, they have had almost double the return on equity compared with other manufacturing corporations.[11] Their products are expensive: the Hughes Missile Systems Company of Tucson, for example, makes the Tomahawk Cruise Missile, a 3,200-pound submarine-launched missile that can carry conventional or nuclear warheads. Hughes has produced 4,170 of these missiles, at a cost of $1.4 million each.

The Pentagon's investment in weapons research and promotion of the interests of weapons makers together make the United States the world's largest arms producer and dealer. U.S. arms sales agreements from 1999 to 2006 totaled $124 billion and increased radically after 2001, with arms sales to the top twenty-five recipient countries increasing fourfold in the five years after that date in comparison with the previous five. Arms sales totaled $51 billion in just the two years 2007 and 2008. Other countries can order U.S. weapons direct from the factory or can buy them on government credit.[12]

It matters far too little to the sellers whether those who buy weapons ultimately use them on their own people or in eventual combat against the United States or U.S. interests. When the UN held a vote in 2006 on starting to negotiate a treaty regulating international conventional arms transfers, the United States was the only country that voted against it. Despite some domestic attempts to enforce codes of conduct for arms dealing, abuse is widespread. Turkey, for example, has received extensive military arms and other forms of aid from the United States, which it has used to fight a long-term war against its Kurdish minority. More than thirty thousand have died in that war, and between 650,000 and two million Kurds were made refugees in the 1980s. Common as well is what is known as blowback, the most infamous recent example being Osama bin Laden himself, trained by the CIA in the proxy war the United States fought against the Soviet Union in Afghanistan.[13]

What makes the U.S. military stand out in world historical context as well is its imperial structuring and reach: that is, the fact that it is the world's first and only truly global empire. (While the British could claim to be so in the first half of the twentieth century, they did not have military presence in and surveillance of nearly as many places.) There are currently 325,000 U.S. troops overseas, stationed at 909 official bases, with one thousand or more the likely actual number of bases, in forty-six countries and territories. They are housed in facilities worth over $146 billion on the 795,000 overseas acres the U.S. military owns or rents. There it stores extensive amounts of weaponry, including nuclear bombs and missiles whose presence in any particular country it refuses to acknowledge.[14]

The U.S. military also engages in extensive training of other militaries through the International Military Education and Training (IMET) and the Foreign Military Financing (FMF) programs. These put U.S. soldiers, sailors, airmen/women, and marines in an estimated 130 (out of the world's 192) countries. As is the case with arms deals, human rights concerns and the laws of warfare have often taken a back seat to strategic and opportunistic thinking. While claiming to professionalize other militaries, U.S. trainers sometimes train in assassination and torture techniques. Exposure of the official nature of these practices occurred in 1996 when School of the Americas torture manuals were released to the public.[15] Not isolated abuses but systematic patterns of training proxy militaries to "do the dirty work" are well documented, most recently in Colombia, where the United States supports security forces that have massacred civilians suspected of supporting the guerrillas.[16] The goal of the IMET program, as well, is to create in foreign militaries a sense of shared identity of interests with and obligation to the United States. Finally, the U.S. program of "extraordinary rendition," which has expanded during the war on terror, shows how the United States has often engaged other militaries to conduct interrogations for it as a way of outsourcing the responsibility for human rights abuses.[17]

THE DOMESTIC SOCIAL IMPACT OF THE
U.S. MILITARY: THE WAGES OF WAR

The $15 trillion of federal spending on military equipment, personnel, and operations over the period since 1945 has been the United States' largest public works and public employment effort since at least 1947, and as such, those dollars have had profound effects. These include (1) increasing levels of class and race inequality, given how the Pentagon budget redistributes wealth around the country; (2) increasing gender inequality through the hypercitizenship that soldiering, long and still an overwhelmingly male occupation, culturally bestows, and through the support it gives to a militarized, violent version of masculinity; (3) severe erosion in the quality of democratic processes; (4) massive environmental damage from military production and operations; and (5) cultural changes that include the rise of values such as ethnocentrism and belligerence.

How does the military affect levels of race and class equality? To judge by the advertising and the numbers of people of color who join, the effect must be very positive: in 2002, blacks made up 22 percent of the enlisted armed forces while constituting only 13 percent of civilians of comparable age. The military advertises itself as an equal-opportunity employer and has numerous antibias programs, at least since it was forced to desegregate in 1947 and to rely on volunteers since 1973. Many poor and African American and Latino youth do achieve individual advancement through their choice of military work.

The overall statistics, however, are much more mixed and demonstrate how wrong it is to use individual stories to tell institutional ones. "Returns to service" is a commonly used economic measure of whether social mobility results from soldiering. These returns vary by historical cohort, military occupational specialty, gender, and other factors, with the experience of the World War II–era and Korea-era veterans being generally positive. Vietnam-era and post-Vietnam-era veterans, however, generally earn less than demographically comparable nonveterans of all racial groups. The earnings gap between young veterans and nonveterans is greater, however, for whites than for African Americans. In other words, black youth do less poorly than white youth, but the unemployment rate for black and minority vets as a whole remains higher than it is for white veterans.[18] Training in a select group of military jobs, including especially electronics and equipment repair, does bring positive returns to service. These are fields in which minorities have been under-represented because of bias, however; in addition, civilian training programs in the same fields give people even higher rates of return in terms of their longer-term wages. These facts have had a hard time making headway against the belief that military service provides discipline and life skills that improve one's employment prospects or will eventually bring higher wages.

Moreover, the impact of enlistment on college attendance of African American young men has been a subject of great controversy, with many college admissions officers arguing that the military diverts many from college who would otherwise go. In fact, African American recruits have often and increasingly come from a wealthier segment of the black population than white recruits in relation to the white population. The stronger presence of the Junior Reserve Officer Training Corps (JROTC) and recruiters and the greater exposure to military advertising in black schools have meant that the military wins out in competition with colleges for many black youth.

More important even than these effects of military recruitment are the effects of the procurement budget, which is much larger than that for personnel. Tax money that goes into weapons contracts is money that disproportionately benefits male middle- and upper-class whites who dominate the management of the corporations that get Pentagon contracts. These are also the people who are disproportionately the technical, engineering, and scientific workers who dominate in today's high-tech weapons industries.

Nonetheless, a job in the peacetime military has been a much better choice than a job at Wal-Mart for the short term. Many people with families choose military work in order to have health care for their children. In wartime, the trade-offs change radically, though, and political opposition to the current war and the danger of grave bodily harm have caused black enlistment rates to plummet from 24 percent of new recruits in 2000 to 14 percent in 2005.

How does having a military of the sort the United States does affect gender equality? Women currently make up 15 percent of the armed forces, having been recruited primarily in response to a shortage of male recruits. As a group, women receive a negative return to service: that is, they make less after being in the military than do a comparable group of civilian women.[19] Moreover, in the thirty labor markets in the United States with a large military presence, women in the civilian sector were more likely to be unemployed and to earn less than comparable men.[20]

Much harder to measure but even more devastating is the amount of sexual assault and harassment within an institution that still defines masculinity for many Americans. By one estimate, there are approximately fourteen thousand sexual assaults or attempted assaults in the military each year.[21] Two out of three women in a DoD survey reported harassment in the previous year, with fully 15 percent reporting pressure for sexual favors and 5 percent rape or attempted rape. In addition, abortions are prohibited in military hospitals, something particularly difficult for deployed women. Even harder to assess but fundamentally important is the shaping of American masculinity by the notion that to be a man is to be ready to fight to defend a nation construed as a nation of women and children. One of the intangible returns to service that brings young people to the recruiting office is the promise that they will be seen and rewarded as "supercitizens" and real men. Higher rates of domestic violence in military families is one index of the problems with the violent notion of masculinity that military work engenders.

A third impact of having a large military in the United States over the last sixty years has been the erosion of democratic process. The military has provided a massive wedge for the expansion of government secrecy and the notion of the exemption from law on the grounds of national security. The Pentagon classified budget, or "black budget," was $30 billion in 2007, up about 50 percent since 9/11, and the intelligence agencies take billions more without open oversight. The problem of militarization undermining democracy was visible to Eisenhower in the 1950s when he famously identified the new "conjunction of an immense military establishment and a large arms industry . . . [whose] total influence—economic, political, even spiritual—is felt in every city, every State house, every office of the Federal government," entailing "potential for the disastrous rise of misplaced power." The cumulative result of fifty more years of military and military-industrial influence has been huge sections of the federal budget that no longer conform to Article 1 of the Constitution, which requires all Treasury monies to be publicly decided upon and publicly published and accounted for. Long gone as well is enforcement of its requirement that Congress, not the executive, declares war. It is also assumed that the president can use nuclear weapons on his own sole initiative, given the assumption that he would not have time to consult congressional leaders were the United States to come under nuclear attack.

At the local level, democracy has also suffered in the hundreds of military base communities whose governments negotiate on steeply uneven playing fields with base commanders over such things as the behavior of troops in the community. The tax base of these communities is also deeply impoverished since the base is federal property and so tax exempt, but the town retains the financial burdens of supporting the large base and civilian population with public services.

Fourth, the military has been a major unacknowledged contributor to environmental decline in the United States and globally. This occurs in the process of manufacturing weapons; during training, maneuvers, and operations; and with the disposal of old or used weapons. Like civilian industrial concerns, these operations have environmental costs in water and air pollution and the heavy use of fossil fuels that contribute to global warming and resource depletion. In the military as compared to the civilian sector, however, national security justifications, secrecy, and legal exemptions have allowed toxins to flow much more freely into local water and air. Military operations have astounding rates of use of fossil fuels and so contribute even more than other government operations to global warming. The military consumes 2 to 5 percent of the total electricity consumed annually in the United States and more aluminum, copper, nickel, and platinum than many countries' total demand for these materials. Tens of thousands of military vehicles, in constant use, guzzle gasoline; the F-16 consumes nine hundred gallons of fuel per hour; and a carrier battle group consumes ten thousand barrels of oil a day when under way, as numerous groups are each day around the world's oceans. In the 1980s, the Pentagon consumed an average of thirty-seven million barrels of oil annually, enough to run the entire U.S. urban mass transit system for fourteen years. And it has released fully one-third of the global total of ozone-depleting CFC-113 into the atmosphere (the rest of the world's militaries are responsible for another third).[22] Many of the thousands of current and formerly used defense sites around the country have been declared unfit for other human use but continue to cause illness in those exposed to their effects in underground water supplies and air.[23] The Department of Energy has spent $22 billion on environmental cleanup at Hanford—which made plutonium until 1989—and has barely made a dent in the problem. The cleanup is expected to continue at least through 2039.[24]

Finally, the building of a large and imperial military has also created fundamental cultural changes in the United States beyond those entailed by the social changes just mentioned. The military has been able, as Katherine Ferguson and Phyllis Turnbull have noted, to win monumental struggles over the meaning of "America."[25] Making incursions into every facet of American life and identity, it has helped define true manhood and true womanhood and has suggested that certain values that are championed in the military—discipline, loyalty, courage, respect for authority among them—are ultimately American values and superior to other kinds. Less explicitly, warmaking has promoted belligerence and ethnocentrism as quintessential American values. Ironically, the frequency of war and the nation's origin in wars of aggression against Native Americans have had a compensatory response in the development of the idea of the United States as a "peace-loving nation": as Tom Engelhardt notes in *The End of Victory Culture*, Americans see themselves as simply and only responding to mortal threats, rather than pursuing interests through violence.[26] The favored American war story is that the United States has fought only defensive wars, responding to attack from a duplicitous and racialized other. The unpopularity of the preemptive Iraq War hinged on its violation of that story, although the administration's initial attempt was to claim that an attack by Iraq on the United States with WMDs was imminent.

The scale and depth of cultural militarization of the United States are indexed by the simultaneous growth and blurring of the boundary between the "civilian" and the "soldier." While the all-volunteer force that replaced the draft in 1973 has meant that the military has increasingly been demographically and politically different from the rest of the U.S. population—more Republican, more working class, and more often from a second- or third-generation military family—this has deceptively suggested a growing gap between civilian and military worlds. On the one hand, this is true—fewer people and families now than thirty or sixty years ago have intimate experience with military life. More importantly, however, the militarization of everyday life has grown significantly in this same period, meaning that civilians are much more likely to have positive views about the military, to have paid significant parts of their federal and even local taxes to support the military, and to consume media products and political discourse that could have or might as well have emerged from within the public relations arms of military institutions. The idea of civilian control of the military, central to the democratic design of the nation, is made increasingly meaningless when what C. Wright Mills called, at the beginning of the Cold War's militarizing momentum in the 1950s, "a military definition of the situation" reigns in all corners of society.

AMERICA'S MENTAL ARMOR: BELIEFS AND PRACTICES THAT SUPPORT MILITARIZATION

When historians look back in one hundred years at the United States of today, how will they judge the fact that warmaking by the most powerful military ever assembled is at the venerated core of this country? Will they see it, as I think they should, as an unforgivable violence foisted on the world and the nation itself? Will they categorize the United States of today with the militarizing Japan, Germany, and Soviet Union of the 1930s and 1940s or the Argentina and Guatemala of the 1970s and 1980s? One indication that they might is in the evaluation of many of the world's people today, who tell interviewers that they distrust the United States, see its policies as having made the world less safe from terrorism, and increasingly see it as having a negative influence on the world.[27]

But such comparisons to other militarist states are seen as over the top at best in the contemporary United States, disqualifying one from serious discussion. Why is that so? How can a nation's view of itself be so far from the facts as seen by most of humanity, and how can it be so hostile to confrontation with those facts? A number of conditions make this disjuncture possible, and at best their effect is to restrict public debate in the United States to a narrow range of options about when, where, and how to deploy the military and how to size it properly for the job. At worst they silence discussion all together.

The military and its vast size and noxious uses have been deeply and pervasively normalized. Cordoned off by secrecy and political belligerence, the military has been designed to operate outside many aspects of the law that govern everyday life and has been Teflon-coated by cultural veneration. The respect accorded the military needs first mention.

There is no institution that is more revered than the military and whose financial and moral support is thought more unquestionable in the halls of Congress, over the media airwaves, and at the backyard barbeque. We know this from polls showing that even religious institutions garner less respect and that the other institutions of our common governance are in the basement of popular affections. This has simply made it impossible to criticize the military as an institution or to argue that less military could mean more security. The criticism of Donald Rumsfeld's reign by a raft of generals in 2006 was not an exception but proof: only these uniformed critics were taken seriously, and they were passing judgment on their civilian master. Reverence for the military is a relatively recent phenomenon (officers of a certain rank have always merited high status, but the vast bulk of the institution and the uses to which it is put have not), but it has now reached the point that the one tenet that unites people across the widest range of the political spectrum on the war in Iraq is the idea of "supporting," or endorsing the sacrifice and needs of, soldiers (or at least the enlistees, and therein lies a tale of class submerged, with popular films feeling free to take shots at puffy-chested generals and the occasional lower ranked officer-sadist but mostly treating enlistees as victims, survivors, or heroes). The veneration is also seen in widespread mimicry: military drag is now a common component of political spectacle, as when John Kerry began his acceptance speech at the Democratic National Convention in 2004 with a military salute and the announcement that he was "reporting for duty!" and when George Bush made his 2003 aircraft carrier appearance costumed in a military flight suit.

This is not to say that everyone is perfectly content with the military. To many Americans on the right, the complaint is that it does not get enough money, softens its standards for women recruits, allows itself to be drawn into the orbit of UN peacekeeping missions, or has had its strength siphoned off for domestic purposes. To the more left-leaning citizen, the problem is that the military has been tasked with inappropriate jobs, such as the invasion of Iraq, that its budget needs "trimming," or that corruption sometimes erupts within its procurement process.

Behind these differences, there is an utterly thorough agreement that the United States needs a large military, that it should and can use it to do good in the world, and that the one it has is selfless and honorable. In this consensus, soldiering expresses a love for the community greater than any other form of work and deserves commemoration at sporting events, school graduations, and multiple national holidays. In the terms of this consensus, the military is inevitable, even good, because war is in human nature and violence has the power to get things done. These hegemonic cultural ideas matter deeply, squashing debate about the military and legitimating the system as it is.

How can this consensus have emerged when the core of the military's business is killing? (And if this bald statement grates, it may be because, as Elaine Scarry notes in *The Body in Pain*, war's central bloody bodily fact is often conflated with war's ostensible purposes. It may also be because the Pentagon has been working to rename many of its coercive operations humanitarian or nation-building efforts.) How can this consensus exist when profits and self-interest are central to when and where the military is deployed and how it spends its budget, and when its effects are so broad and devastating for those on both ends of the rifle? To understand this phenomenon is to understand the legitimation of war and empire and to begin to understand how warmaking has become the American way of life, as much as the malls and television shows and highways and families at play that are its more visible face and self-image.

When I teach courses on war, I find my students deeply attached to a number of ideas about war and about the U.S. military that solidify its hold on the U.S. budget, foreign policy, and cultural terrain. They represent widespread American beliefs that serve as key supports for people's faith in the naturalness and necessity of the military as it exists. These cultural ideas matter deeply, as they prop up the system and substitute for other, more helpful ways of thinking about violence and the state. A number of sociological factors also play into the normalization and veneration of the military, including the advertising used to raise a volunteer army and the cumulative effect of the nation's twenty-five million veterans, many well organized to act politically on questions of military budget and policy, but here I focus on the cultural narratives that have emerged in response to these and other factors.

They include, first, the notion that the military is an essential and necessary institution because war is deeply coded in human nature, biologically conceived, and therefore inevitable. Humans are territorial, greedy, and aggressive by nature, and war runs on such human instincts and motives. This is widely believed even though social science, including military science, has repeatedly demonstrated that it is untrue: by rough estimate, a mere fraction of 1 percent of humans throughout history have gone into battle, and when they do, they require extensive, extreme resocialization to kill.

Almost as central to American belief and certainly as ill conceived is the idea that violence is an economical and effective way to get things done, the assumption that, as Carol Cohn has suggested, "violence works," that other ways of creating social change take much more time, money, and patience and have uncertain outcomes in comparison. This belief in the efficacy of violence flies in the face of the evidence too, and even of some U.S. military doctrine emphasizing the importance of restraint in the use of violence. We know that, particularly in the second half of the twentieth century, political will and collaborative nonviolent direct action have often achieved goals where violence failed and that violence has often accomplished no more than others' resentful and temporary compliance. Jonathan Schell identifies the fall of the Soviet Union as "the most sweeping demonstration so far of the power of 'politics' without violence." In a discussion of the Solidarity movement, he quotes Havel's assertion that, by operating within the confines of a violent system, "individuals confirm the system, fulfill the system, make the system, *are* the system." In addition, he addresses the success of what he calls "nonviolence from the top down," particularly Gorbachev's policies of perestroika and glasnost.[28]

A caveat: the dominance of pragmatism in American worldviews has meant that winning becomes the measure of many things. When the military is thought to be winning a fight, that war is supported. When things stop working, the military is called to withdraw. This exemplifies not so much a moral vacuum as a morality with a difference: if something works, the reasoning goes, it must be right. The nation's power, by definition, makes its people and their military and warmaking right.

Another of the tenets that supports the normalization of a gigantic military in the United States is the idea that war and soldiering have brought benefits to the nation and to individuals. It is thought to produce unity, discipline, and patriotism in its participants, and military research into new technologies of war is widely believed to have generated spin-offs both concrete, such as sophisticated computing or advances in emergency medicine, and economic, such as preventing recession and providing jobs. Wars, it is believed, are "good for the economy." Again, this assumption contradicts the evidence. Military spending creates far fewer jobs than equivalent amounts of spending for education or health care.[29] Further, the long-term economic harm of war-generated deficit spending and the diversion of research and development into other domains has been demonstrated by economists: for example, Ann Markusen and Joel Yudken highlight the deterioration of the U.S. auto, steel, and consumer electronics industries as R&D resources were diverted to the military, and the decline in investment in public infrastructure such as sewers and mass transit (which fell 21 percent from 1965 to 1977 as military spending skyrocketed).[30]

The invisibility of the role of imperialism in the militarization of the United States has been accomplished through the belief that the military's extensive activities overseas are not only defensive of the United States and its "national interests" but altruistic: that is, the United States is said to "gift" other nations with military security, providing the world's police force free of charge or self-interest. Americans commonly believe that the United States has military bases around the world to defend the countries they are in and ultimately to defend democracy. This is also against the evidence. Bases and military aid were plentiful in the Philippines of Ferdinand Marcos and in South Korea under its several dictatorships, and they are newly proliferating in autocratic states in central Asia and the Middle East. Moreover, the United States has been able to extract significant financial, training, and strategic benefits from this basing. The Japanese, for example, will be paying $10 billion (and by one official estimate the eventual total will be more on the order of $26 billion) to relocate a U.S. Marine base now on Okinawa to Guam.

Another thing that makes it so hard to see militarization and its effects is the hygienic distance Americans are able to keep from the bloody core of war. Unlike uncivilized nations, people continue to believe, this nation does not revel in violence or death but kills reluctantly and surgically, avoiding civilian deaths. This would certainly appear to be the case when the nightly news and mainstream Internet sites are so free of blood or splattered brain matter, with broken bodies displayed at a tasteful distance, if at all. There was public dismay when it became clear that many U.S. soldiers were collecting, displaying, and reveling in gruesome images of war, including horrors and tortures they themselves had produced. The home front response was quickly managed through presentation of these incidents as responses to exceptional circumstances the soldiers were in or as the actions of sick, outlier soldiers.

Finally, the normalization of American militarization has been accomplished through the science of public relations, which strategists recognize as the central fact, strategy, and technique of modern war. Military leaders are deeply committed to the idea that to win a war or to win the battle for funding war preparation requires tactical moves on political and home front terrain. This means winning hearts and minds through advertising or PR spin of everything military, from what its members do each day, to motives for joining, to specific operations around the world. While most of the advertising, portraying proud parents and self-assured, generous-spirited young people in uniform, is directed at convincing the American public to join the military or to support their children in doing so, it has the additional and very important effect of shaping how Americans who have never been in the military see it.

According to a report by the Government Accountability Office, from 2003 to 2005 the DoD spent $1.1 billion on contracts with advertising, public relations, and media firms (an amount on a sharp upswing since the downturn in popular sentiment on Iraq and the war on terror).[31] The military has been engaged in propaganda efforts through its Soldiers News Service, Speakers Service, and other campaigns that place news stories and advertising in U.S. newspapers and on radio and TV. In 2004 and 2005, the Secretary of Defense's office paid a public relations firm to design an "America Supports You" campaign focused on soldier morale that simultaneously encourages Americans to appreciate and respect soldiers. With tag lines like "Nothing Divides Us" and photographs showing heroic backlit soldiers standing sentry, they also encourage viewers to disregard the politics, ethics, and legality of the war being fought.[32] And Pentagon collaboration with Hollywood to present a positive view of the military has been ongoing since the movies became the cultural mythmakers and social imaginary of the United States: when Disney made the film *Pearl Harbor* with major military support, its May 2001 premiere was arranged for the carrier flight deck of the USS *John C. Stennis*.

How will this—the American militarized way of life—all end, or will it end? Despite all the problems just identified and despite the lack of support for the war in

Iraq, the militarized status quo seems to have a firm grip on national hearts and budgets. Dominating Congress is the agenda of a small elite that benefits from a large, interventionist military, directly through the military-industrial complex or indirectly through the unequal global terms of trade that militarization has helped enforce. The United States also has a large middle and working class who believe they benefit from military spending and may even have paychecks that seem to prove it. They may find the rule of the rich somewhat suspicious, but they have been unwilling to risk the level of comfort they have achieved, even if it is built on indebtedness's house of cards.

Like the vast militaries of empires past, though, this one and the military that supports it cannot go on forever. Overinvestment in military power has often been the symptom of an empire whose other forms of power, economic and political, are already in decline. Moreover, military spending and intensified military interventionism only accelerate the descent as those military endeavors—arms sales perhaps to the side—entail underinvestment in other, more economically generative activities. Signs of trouble are on the horizon.

The military is having trouble recruiting youth into the military: when a *Washington Post* columnist suggests offering citizenship to foreign mercenaries willing to fight in place of U.S. youth who will not go, it is clear that business as usual over the last sixty years may be nearing an end.[33] Some of the strongest critiques of militarism have been coming recently from conservatives and libertarians traditionally interested in limiting the state, and they seem ready to make common cause with progressives. Widespread counter-recruitment sentiments and efforts, antiwar political candidates, and appeals to the Golden Age ideal of an America where freedom and democracy were much more robust are all cultural signs that hope for change is available. If these critiques were to expand to consider some of the just-explored attitudes that support militarism, the system itself might more rapidly contract.

The primary pushes for change, though, are going to be transnational and systemic. The collapse of world support for the idea of a United States that dominates the world militarily and economically has already begun, as indicated by the polls and the withdrawal of all but Britain and a handful of surrogate states from serious joint military action with the United States. More importantly, the financial architecture on which the U.S. military and state operate is shaky indeed, with unprecedented levels of personal and national debt and dollar hegemony under threat. Should oil no longer be traded in dollars, should China or other nations call in the massive amount of wealth they have in U.S. Treasury bonds, or should debt-ridden or unemployed U.S. taxpayers fail to pay the bills, there could simply be much less money with which to buy arms and men. Finally, in such a context, the ethical claims and convictions—secular and religious—against violence and imperial hubris might be heard.

NOTES

I would like to thank Anna Christensen for her invaluable assistance with the research for this chapter.

1. Stockholm International Peace Research Institute, "Recent Trends in Military Expenditure," in *SIPRI Yearbook 2008: Armaments, Disarmament and International Security* (Oxford: Oxford University Press, 2008), www.sipri.org/contents/milap/milex/mex_trends.html.

2. The Web site Iraq Body Count (www.iraqbodycount.org/), widely considered authoritative, gives the number of approximately one hundred thousand Iraqi war dead. A Johns Hopkins study published in the *Lancet* (Gilbert Burnham et al., "Mortality after the 2003 Invasion of Iraq: A Cross-Sectional Cluster Sample Survey," *Lancet,* October 11, 2006) reported 655,000 "excess deaths"—deaths that would not have occurred were it not for the invasion—since the beginning of the war in 2003.

3. Joseph E. Stiglitz and Linda Bilmes, *The Three Trillion Dollar War: The True Cost of the Iraq Conflict* (New York: W. W. Norton, 2008).

4. This estimate does not include the costs for a long list of other items, including health care for veterans that is absorbed by families or private insurance, the economic costs that come with oil price volatility, and the costs of tighter monetary policy as a result of the inflationary pressures that war produces.

5. Stephen Schwartz, *Atomic Audit: The Costs and Consequences of U.S. Nuclear Weapons since 1940* (Washington, DC: Brookings Institution, 1998).

6. Lawrence Korb, "The Defense Budget," in *American Defense Annual,* ed. Joseph Kruzel (Lexington, MA: Lexington Books, 1986–87), 41.

7. P. W. Singer, *Corporate Warriors: The Rise of the Privatized Military Industry* (Ithaca, NY: Cornell University Press, 2003).

8. Tim L. O'Brien, "All's Not Quiet on the Military Supply Front," *New York Times,* January 22, 2006; Special Inspector General for Iraq Reconstruction, *Quarterly Report and Semiannual Report to the United States Congress,* January 30, 2009, www.sigir.mil/reports/quarterlyreports/Jan09/Default.aspx.

9. According to the Federation of American Scientists, as of February 2009 the United States maintained, in addition to the 2,700 actively deployed nuclear warheads, 2,500 nuclear warheads in strategic reserve and another 4,200 warheads that were officially retired but not yet dismantled. Hans Kristensen, "United States Reaches Moscow Treaty Warhead Limit Early," February 2009, www.fas.org/blog/ssp/2009/02/sort.php#more-770.

10. U.S. Air Force, "F-22 Raptor," April 2008, www.af.mil/factsheets/factsheet.asp?fsID=199.

11. Sam Marullo, *Ending the Cold War at Home: From Militarism to a More Peaceful World Order* (New York: Lexington Books, 1994).

12. Travis Sharp, "U.S. Arms Sales Agreements Worldwide, 1999–2006," March 4, 2008, Center for Arms Control and Proliferation, www.armscontrolcenter.org/policy/securityspending/articles/arms_sales_99_to_06/; William D. Hartung and Frida Berrigan, "U.S. Weapons at War 2008: Beyond the Bush Legacy," December 2008, New American Foundation, www.newamerica.net/publications/policy/u_s_weapons_war_2008_0.

13. Michael Scheuer, *Imperial Hubris: Why the West Is Losing the War on Terror* (Washington, DC: Potomac Books, 2004), 30.

14. Catherine Lutz, *The Bases of Empire: The Global Struggle against U.S. Military Posts* (London: Pluto Press, 2008).

15. General Accounting Office, *School of the Americas: U.S. Military Training for Latin American Countries* (Washington, DC: General Accounting Office, 1996).

16. Andrew Selsky, "U.S. Green Berets Train Colombians," Associated Press, May 5, 2001.

17. Jane Mayer, *The Dark Side: The Inside Story of How the War on Terror Turned into a War on American Ideals* (New York: Doubleday, 2008).

18. Stephen R. Barley, *Will Military Reductions Create Shortages of Trained Personnel and Harm the*

Career Prospects of American Youth? EQW Working Papers (Philadelphia: National Center on Education Quality of the Workforce, 1994); Richard Bryant and Al Wilhite, "Military Experience and Training Effects on Civilian Wages," *Applied Economics* 22, no. 1 (1990): 69–81; Congressional Budget Office, *Social Representation in the United States Military* (Washington, DC: Congressional Budget Office, 1989); Jon R. Crane and David A. Wise, "Military Service and Civilian Earning of Youths," in *Public Sector Payrolls*, ed. David A. Wise (Chicago: University of Chicago Press, 1987); U.S. Congress and Office of Technology Assessment, *After the Cold War: Living with Lower Defense Spending*, OTA-ITE-524 (Washington, DC: Government Printing Office, 1992).

19. Ann Markusen and Joel Yudken, *Dismantling the Cold War Economy* (New York: Basic Books, 1992), 163–65.

20. J. Brad Schwartz, Lisa L. Wood, and Janet Griffith, "The Impact of Military Life on Spouse Labor Force Outcomes," *Armed Forces and Society* 17, no. 3 (1991): 385–406; Bradford Booth et al., "The Impact of Military Presence in Local Labor Markets on the Employment of Women," *Gender and Society* 14 (April 2000): 318–32.

21. Chalmers Johnson, "America's Empire of Bases," CommonDreams.org NewsCenter, January 15, 2004, www.commondreams.org/views04/0115-08.htm.

22. J. David Singer and Jeffrey Keating, "Military Preparedness, Weapon Systems and the Biosphere: A Preliminary Impact Statement," *New Political Science* 21, no. 3 (1999): 325–43.

23. Examples include areas in and around navy bases in Groton, Connecticut, and Vieques, Puerto Rico, and Otis Air Force Base on Cape Cod. For decades, the navy dumped sulfuric acid, torpedo fuel, waste oil, and incinerator ash in Groton. On Vieques, used as a military bombing range, there are high rates of cancer in surrounding neighborhoods, and fishermen have brought suit against the navy for water pollution. Matt Appuzo, "Base Closings Leave Behind Large Swaths of Pollution," Associated Press, May 31, 2005, www.enn.com/today.html?id=7845; Bridget Dorfman, "Permission to Pollute: The United States Military, Environmental Damage, and Citizens' Constitutional Claims," *Journal of Constitutional Law* 6, no. 3 (2004): 613–14.

24. Blaine Harden, "Nuclear Cleanup Site Has Cities Cleaning Up Financially," *Washington Post*, November 1, 2006.

25. For further discussion, see Katherine Ferguson and Phyllis Turnbull, *Oh Say Can You See: The Semiotics of the Military in Hawaii* (Minneapolis: University of Minnesota Press, 1999), 155–98.

26. Tom Engelhardt, *The End of Victory Culture: Cold War America and the Disillusioning of a Generation*, rev. and expanded ed. (Amherst: University of Massachusetts Press, 2007).

27. The Pew poll, entitled "Islamic Extremism: Common Concern for Muslim and Western Publics," was released on July 14, 2005, and is accessible from http://pewglobal.org/reports/display.php?ReportID=248. The BBC World Service poll, entitled "Views on Iraq," was released on February 28, 2006, and is accessible from http://news.bbc.co.uk/1/shared/bsp/hi/pdfs/27_02_06world_poll.pdf.

28. Jonathan Schell, *The Unconquerable World: Power, Nonviolence, and the Will of the People* (New York: Metropolitan Books, 2003), 186, 196.

29. Marion Anderson, *The Price of the Pentagon* (Lansing, MI: Employment Research Associates, 1982).

30. Ann Markusen and Joel Yudken, *Dismantling the Cold War Economy* (New York: Basic Books, 1992).

31. Government Accountability Office, *Media Contracts: Activities and Financial Obligations to Seven Federal Departments* (Washington, DC: Government Accountability Office, January 2006). The GAO figures are self-reported by each federal agency and are probably lower than actual expenditures. The Pentagon is not alone in the federal public relations purchasing ring, but it is by far the biggest spender, its $1.1 billion representing over two-thirds of the total. The good news is that war and militarization are harder to sell than anything else the federal government does.

32. See the Web site of the Office of the Assistant Secretary of Defense for Public Affairs, Community Relations, www.americasupportsyou.mil, and its Ad Council page providing media outlets with their materials, www.americasupportsyou.mil/americasupportsyou/ad_council.html.

33. Max Boot and Michael O'Hanlon, "A Military Path to Citizenship," *Washington Post*, October 19, 2006.

3

Republic of Fear

The Rise of Punitive Governance in America

Roger N. Lancaster

A number of recent publications take the proper view that something has gone terribly wrong in American society. Public intellectuals and prominent scholars have discerned "the end of America," "the last days of the republic," "the subversion of democracy," and the specter of a new form of totalitarianism.[1] But many of these broadsides incorrectly date the undemocratic turn to the 2000 judicial coup, which stopped the Florida vote recount and thereby installed an unelected president in the White House, or to the days after September 11, 2001, when right-wingers hostile to civil liberties seized the initiative both in drafting new laws and in circumventing existing laws. A dispassionate review of ongoing social trends suggests the need for a longer view. The development of an authoritarian political culture, I argue, has been a long time in the making, and this process has been advanced by Democrats no less than Republicans—by liberals almost as much as by conservatives. Let me sketch here something of this longer view, to offer a more pessimistic appraisal of authoritarian tendencies in America. Fear of crime—which congeals all the familiar racial and sexual anxieties—was undermining democratic norms and fostering a punitive state long before the present "war on terror."

THE RISE OF THE CARCERAL STATE

If one stands only a step back from the periodic changing of the political guard, by far the most impressive trend in post-1960s America has been the rise of what can only be called a carceral state.[2] In plain English, the carceral state is a type of political organization in which two conditions obtain: a bloated prison system supplies the norms for governance in general; moreover, both official bureaucracies and civil society collude to intensify these norms and to keep the prison system growing.[3] A few basic numbers will reveal the gravity of what has happened in American society.

In the 1960s, rates of incarceration in Western democracies generally ranged from 60 to 120 per 100,000 inhabitants. For example, in postfascist Italy, incarceration rates declined from 79 per 100,000 in 1960 to 57 per 100,000 in 1990, before climbing again to 102 per 100,000 in recent estimates. Similar patterns have been posted in other Western European countries. The decline was especially steep in Finland, which began with high crime rates and a penal system built on the Russian model and which, after thirty years of humanitarian and social-democratic reforms, now boasts one of the lowest incarceration rates in Europe. (Not coincidentally, since its prison system is "correctional" in the best sense of the term, not dehumanizing, it provides no breeding ground for anger, resentment, and recidivism. Finland thus also posts one of the lowest crime rates in Europe.) Even after slight increases in the past few years, Finland's rate of imprisonment is 68 per 100,000.

Britain has followed a different course. Under Blair's Labour no less than under Thatcher's Tories, Britain has pursued an increasingly punitive approach to crime. An obvious measure of this punitiveness is the passage of more laws with ever more exacting punishments. Under Tony Blair, the government found 661 new reasons to lock people up, as Nick Cohen derisively described New Labour's overhaul of the criminal code in the *New Statesman*.[4] As a result, the British rate of imprisonment has doubled, from 70 per 100,000 in 1966 to roughly 149 per 100,000 today. Britain's current rate is comparable with U.S. rates in the 1960s.

But even by comparison to the British model, the United States stands out. In less than thirty years we have more than quadrupled the total prison population, and our rate of imprisonment has soared to 751 per 100,000 at latest count. We thus imprison five to ten times more people per capita than do other developed democracies. The United States now ranks first in the world both in both the rate of imprisonment (one in every ninety-nine adult residents is behind bars) and the absolute number of people imprisoned (2.26 million). That's more than China, a strong-arm state with more than four times the population of the United States. It's more than Russia, once the gendarme of Europe, a culture whose fondness for locking people up both predates and postdates the Stalinist period. With 5 percent of the world's population, the United States claims 25 percent of the world's prisoners.[5]

That this remarkable social transition, so inimical to the spirit of a free democratic society, occurred under formally democratic conditions—indeed, was prodded by electoral pressures to "get tough on crime"—would seem to mock any grandiose conception of democracy in America. The most basic facts call to mind the gauge Jean-Paul Sartre and Maurice Merleau-Ponty applied to the loftier claims of Soviet socialism in 1950: "There is no socialism when one out of every 20 citizens is in a camp."[6] If we take the French existentialists' measure as a general guide, then what, plausibly, could be said of the character of American democracy under prevailing conditions? "For an American born [in 1999], the chance of living some part of life in a correction facility is 1 in 20; for black Americans, it is 1 in 4."[7] Twelve percent of African American men between the ages of twenty and thirty-four are currently behind bars; 30 percent of black men in this age range will spend some portion of their lives incarcerated or otherwise entangled in the long reach of the prison system.[8] Such figures have no precedent, not even in the postslavery period (when southern states first organized systems of compulsory prison labor as a substitute for slavery) or during Jim Crow.[9]

We mete out stiffer sentences, longer incarcerations, and more onerous terms of release and surveillance to far, far more people than any of the nations we like to think of as our peers. As a result, a large percentage of people in American prisons today—even many of the inmates serving extremely long sentences—were convicted, not of any violent crime, but only of offenses against public order or morality: they are drug offenders of one sort or another. Many others serve long sentences on property crimes that would have once drawn a short term, a fine, or a suspended sentence. Another expansive class of criminals has been created by legislation raising the age of consent. (Many of the resulting criminals—statutory rapists—are themselves young men, barely adult.) The image of the "repeat offender" looms large in the public imagination, but Bureau of Justice statistics show that the great run-up in the prison population comes as the result of an increase in *first* incarcerations.[10]

Once the system gets its hooks into you, it is loath to let you go: nearly five million Americans are currently on probation or parole. Added to the 2.26 million currently behind bars, this means that one out of every thirty-two adults—3.2 percent of the adult population—is caught up in the carceral state.[11] (This figure does not include some six hundred thousand registered sex offenders.) Extended periods of parole, with their mandatory meetings and drug tests, virtually ensure future infractions. As a result, the number of people in prison today for parole violations alone is the same as the total U.S. prison population in 1980.[12] Many states strip convicts of the right to vote—in a dwindling handful this disenfranchisement remains in effect for life—and bar them from holding work-related business licenses, thus creating a permanent caste of criminal outcasts. Nearly five million Americans have temporarily or permanently lost their right to vote; black men represent 40 percent of this figure.[13] Such numbers have implications for the quality of American democracy. In Florida, Ohio, and other closely contested states, Republicans have used felon disenfranchisement to purge the voter rolls of minority voters and to intimidate other voters. Even assuming a clean count of ballots, this disenfranchisement of black citizens probably made all the difference in the 2000 and 2004 presidential elections.

No legitimate theory of corrections, crime, or social order justifies this approach, which can only be understood as vindictive. This spirit of vindictiveness—the idea that law exists not to correct or balance but to punish—obviously animates the continuing popularity of capital punishment in America. Up until the 5–4 Supreme Court decision in *Roper v. Simmons* in 2005, we even allowed the execution of minors. And although the Supreme Court has barred states from executing the mentally retarded, nothing prevents pro–death penalty states from defining mental retardation more narrowly than less vindictive states.

We joke about these matters: "Book him, Danno!" "Three strikes, you're out!" We compose jingles and ditties celebrating this punitive approach to law: "Don't do the crime if you can't do the time." Everyone knows that race and class disparities pervade, even motivate, this unjust work of the justice system, but many Americans naturalize these monstrous conditions under handy platitudes ("It's because of the breakdown of the family that so many black men are in jail") or attribute responsibility to the final link in a causal chain ("He shouldn't have violated the terms of his parole"). Other than a handful of courageous activists, lawyers, and journalists, no one—least of all the Democratic Party—takes on these questions as a political cause. We perform these and other acts of barbarism because, like every other prefascist society, we adore punishment; we have become obsessed with it, addicted to it. Network police dramas, afternoon programs devoted to courtroom scenarios, and an entire cable channel, Court TV, put the "show" in "show trial" and reinforce this image of law as a punitive spectacle. Among the images endlessly circulated on the Web are police mug shots of celebrities and thumbnail photos in sex offender registries. These serve to stoke the public's appetite for ever more public, ever more humiliating, and ever more stigmatizing forms of retribution.

LAWLESS LAW

I visited the D.C. courthouse early one morning on Martin Luther King Day, 2003, to watch the readings and dismissals of charges resulting from weekend arrests. What transpired there, unrecorded in any official transcript, was an astonishing parody of the occasion: over several distinct periods of the day, dozens, scores of (mostly) Latino and (a few) black men (I calculate upwards of eighty or one hundred in all) were simply released, without any formal reading of any charges, after having been jailed over the weekend. Perhaps a few had been arrested for public drunkenness or for soliciting an undercover cop. But many had committed no crimes or infractions; they had simply been in the wrong neighborhood at the wrong time. They had been caught up in the routine police sweeps we euphemistically call "community policing" (understood by many to be the liberal alternative to repressive policing). The unsavory truth of the matter is that even in one of the most liberal cities in America, any black or Latino man can be detained at any time without any charges on vague suspicions; no questions asked, no Miranda rights read, and no other legal or customary considerations having to do with civil liberties or civil rights need apply. Indeed, to ask too many questions on such an occasion might bring on a beating or charges of "resisting arrest" or interference with police business.

The unpleasant truth, too, is that jail conditions have sunk to a level that approximates the lower thresholds of torture. Whether charged or released without charge, the detainees of MLK Day 2003 told consistent stories of their experiences in jail: no one, save the one white detainee (a gay man arrested outside a club for simple possession of Ecstasy and Viagra), had been allowed the customary phone call. According to both the white gay man and several other informants, every phone call request from black and Latino arrestees was simply refused—usually with bureaucratic techniques that would be admired by officials in any dictatorship: "You can't have a phone call now, because you're just being processed in. Wait." Then, later: "But you should have asked for a phone call when you first came in. You can't have one now, because you've already been processed." Finally, "If I let you make a phone call, then everyone will want to make one." Lawyers sent by families of the arrestees were not allowed to see their clients, who were thus held for an extended period of time without any access to counsel or the outside world. (Defense attorneys tell me that this is not an uncommon practice.) Detainees report that they were served food—a sandwich—once. The only way to keep hunger at bay was to hide half the sandwich under one's cot (in violation of jail rules) and to consume portions of it over the next day and a half. Fresh water was provided only once. Some of the Central American arrestees fended off dehydration by flushing the toilet several times, then drinking the toilet water.

The whole point of such techniques, as I understand them, is to create a sense of isolation and helplessness in the detainee, to thus "soften him up" and break his will. Police officers and prison guards with whom I have spoken understand this principle well enough. Cops and prosecutors use these techniques, strategically and without sanction, to circumvent legal protections against capricious policing. Other, more public aspects of the justice system are similarly coercive: prosecutors strategically "pile on" charges as a substitute for scrupulous investigation. Rather than risk jury conviction on a higher charge, most defendants will plead guilty to the lesser charge. (Ninety-five percent of felony convictions are settled with a plea bargain. This is not, as is often imagined, a sign of leniency but a sign of punitiveness.) Thus the doubly disturbing facts of the notorious case of Tulia, Texas, where a racist and unscrupulous special prosecutor manufactured drug charges against a large percentage of the town's black residents. Submitted to the usual routines of American policing, unable to afford competent legal representation, told that the jig was up and that they might as well cooperate, and unwilling to believe that they would receive a fair trial, a great many of the innocent defendants simply pled guilty to false charges.[14]

Something has gone amiss with American conceptions of law. For thirty-five years now, what Americans have accepted—no, clamored for—is an increasingly lawless law. Overzealous or vindictive prosecutors are almost never brought to heel, even when they conceal exculpatory evidence. Successive revisions to criminal codes everywhere have defined more and more acts as "criminal," while enhancing penalties associated with crime in general, thus codifying sanctions that violate the cardinal rule of law: the idea that punishment should be commensurate with the crime. Policing continues to expand, even in the face of falling crime rates, as do other institutional mechanisms associated with the perpetuation of a police state. Optimistic liberal journalists occasionally produce pieces on the advent of a more rational, less punitive approach to crime, especially drug crimes,[15] but the basic facts remain: the prison population continues to grow; modes of surveillance continue to expand; new laws continue to apply ever broader penalties and sanctions (especially where newly defined sex crimes are concerned); and politicians continue to manipulate fear of crime to win elections. One almost never hears any more what used to be the point of pride of American law, at least in my public high school civics lessons: the idea that it is better to let a few guilty men go free than to imprison a single innocent man. And in the face of gradual erosions, protections against overly aggressive search and seizure embodied in the Bill of Rights seem like relics from happier times.

BUT IS IT PORN YET?
THE PHOTOS FROM ABU GHRAIB

If the war on crime *at home* has taken such a form, then how would you expect American soldiers, cops, rent-a-cops, and mercenaries to make war *abroad,* in some poor and trampled land? Historian Michael Sherry has succinctly shown how the war on terror projects America's thirty-year punitive trend on the international stage, replete with images of tough-talking cowboy sheriffs, "wanted" posters, and steely ultimatums.[16] Beware, world: we're taking our uniquely narcissistic, punitive, and self-righteous act on the road.

The photos from Abu Ghraib, which so inflamed liberal sensibilities, provide graphic postcards of this cruelty on the march: they mark the slippery slope inaugurated by the Bush administration's assorted proclamations and legal memos, which attempted to redefine (so as to allow) torture. They give good insight into how the race/class/sex system works—has always worked—at home. They index ongoing changes in American culture, where fear fosters brutality and inflamed righteousness facilitates extravagant, theatrical cruelties. This becomes especially evident when the photos are read against puritanical narratives purporting to critique the practices they depict.

First, there is the ritual transformation of man into animal. It's not that war releases the "animal" in man (*and* woman, let's be clear here), as some commentators have suggested, but that people at war, and in extreme states of racial, nationalist, or jingoist fervor, symbolically transform other people into animals. This transformation and the violence it predicates support the injured humanity of the torturer: it's how the torturer, the executioner, or the prison guard can look another human being in the face and say, "You had it coming." The visages of the torturers, like those of the lynch mobs of yore, thus reveal mirth, satisfaction. They had it coming— "they" not even being quite human but more like the disobedient dog on a leash whose neck, since one owns it, one might rightly snap. So much is well established in the literature on torture, lynching, and political violence.[17]

Then there is the ritual enactment of American sexual fantasies, via naked prisoners coerced to become a writhing mass. We have made men into animals. Now what would animals do? Thus the conjuring of the *tableau vivant,* at once a spectacle of degradation and fantasy. The role of sex and sexual fantasy in torture, too, is well established. But this is where matters become confused.

A number of observers have commented on the "pornographic" quality of these digital photos—which do seem, at first blush, a very literal enactment of puritanical religious and antisex feminist fantasies: porn as violence and degradation. Susan Sontag thus wonders "how much of the sexual tortures inflicted on the inmates of Abu Ghraib was inspired by the vast repertory of pornographic imagery available on the Internet—and which ordinary people, by sending out Webcasts of themselves, try to emulate."[18] Sontag's query evokes much of the liberal and conservative establishment's reaction to the Abu Ghraib photos: blame it on the Internet.

It is true, and quite obvious, that the use of the digital camera has something to do with the staging of elaborate scenes and posing of inmates depicted in the photos. But the implied scenario, in which people commit evil acts because they imitate the evils they've seen on the Internet, might make one wonder just how torturers managed to do their dirty work (much of it sexual) long before the era of digital representation and communication. (I daresay any bully from my junior high playground pretty much got the gist of sexual humiliation and how it might serve as an effective means of torture.) But the whole point of all the porn I've ever seen is that the participants at least seem to be having a good time. The only film I've ever seen that approaches the sensibility of the scenes from Abu Ghraib is Pasolini's *Salò:* a gay communist's Sade-inspired Catholic fantasy depicting how fascists, given total power, would act. Of course, there is a hitch: Pasolini's leftist passion play is complicated by the director's own adoration of young, well-formed, working-class toughs and subproletarian hustlers, a desire that he fully conveys in every frame of the film. Pasolini concludes his disturbing picture by having the torturers, and the audience, take up the position of spectators: we voyeuristically peer through telescopes at scenes of torture, dismemberment, and mutilation.

The unnerving correspondence between Pasolini's fantasies and those of the tor-

turers at Abu Ghraib, I venture, says a lot. It gets at the tense and volatile relationship between taboo and violence, between attraction and repulsion, between fantasy and power, between the friendly, good-natured demeanor of the co-worker one
might meet at the office and the dreadful perturbations that lurk just beneath the
surface of staid normalcy.[19] It has something to do with the *prurience* of a culture
that meticulously examines and sternly condemns sexual infraction. It says something, too, about the complex motives involved in the rage to punish and about the
conditions under which evil becomes banal. The prison guards whose cheery faces
are caught on film are gardeners, churchgoers, solid citizens—or at any rate, citizens as solid as what the social stratum will admit. (If one hails from the more precarious ranks of the working class, "solidity" is largely about sexual probity—and
about entering jail as a guard rather than an inmate.) But the soldier at war, like the
cop on the beat or the guard in the prison, is allowed a kind of reprieve from everyday existence, with its taboos and conventions. This "reprieve" is internal to structure of violence, not external to it.

MEANWHILE, IN FALLUJA . . .

The photos from Abu Ghraib displaced from the front pages far bigger war crimes:
at Falluja, U.S. operations laid siege to a substantial city and killed, by their own
count, upwards of seven hundred people, mostly civilians. This can only be described
as a "massacre" and as an instance of "collective punishment"—either way, a clear
violation of the Geneva Conventions. And this was only the first sustained assault
on Falluja. In subsequent assaults, U.S. troops cut off water to the city and blocked
food supplies, turning virtually the entire population into refugees; they then razed
the city. Every step in this process meets the strictest definition of a war crime. Liberals didn't beat their chests about how these acts violated international treaties and
agreements to which the U.S. was party. But then, the razing of Falluja didn't involve sex (or its simulation, or its depiction).

HO HUM, ANOTHER WORK
OF EXTRAORDINARY BRUTALITY

Sex and violence—or, if you will, the sexuality of state violence: we can read in these
photos an expression of the American psyche, a Rorschach of lawful lawlessness,
an extension of business as usual in America. For the torture of prisoners of war at
Abu Ghraib, in Afghanistan, and at Guantánamo is only a very slight extension of
the mistreatment of Muslim prisoners in the Brooklyn Detention Center after 9/11.
And *that* episode was only an extension of the everyday indignities (many of them
involving sexual cruelty) heaped on black and brown men in the systematic, worka-
day world of the American prison system.

The torture of Muslim prisoners in New York included mockery, name-calling, beatings, ramming of unresisting prisoners into walls, unnecessary strip searches, and unnecessary cavity searches—one of which involved the insertion of a flashlight up the rectum of a prisoner. Such practices are not entirely exceptional in U.S. prisons, as the intrepid Fox Butterfield has summed up. In some states, "inmates are routinely stripped in front of other inmates before being moved" to a new unit or prison. At the Maricopa County Jail in Phoenix, inmates "are made to wear women's pink underwear as a form of humiliation." At a maximum-security prison in Virginia, inmates have reportedly been "forced to wear black hoods" and report being frequently beaten and forced to crawl on all fours in front of jeering guards. In many states, prison guards allow, effectively oversee, and sometimes even exploit systems of sexual slavery. When George Bush laments that the Iraqi photographs don't represent the "heart" of America, one feels compelled to note that they might at least be at home in the heart of Texas, where prisoner abuse has been especially rampant and where prisons were under a federal consent decree, addressing overcrowding and violence by guards, during the entire time President Bush was governor.[20]

Add to this catalog of American horrors the various forms of sanctioned and unsanctioned human rights abuses documented by Amnesty International and Human Rights Watch. These include beatings and chokings; the unconscionable use of extended solitary confinement in maximum-security and "supermax" prisons; the systematic mistreatment of juvenile and mentally ill detainees; the inhumane use of restraints, electrical devices, and attack dogs against detainees, prisoners, and members of ethnic minorities; and other patterns of police and prison guard brutality.[21] Prison guards in Utah tied one prisoner, a physically slight schizophrenic man, naked to a chair for sixteen hours—because he would not remove a pillowcase from his head. The prisoner died. What, you might ask, is a schizophrenic doing in prison? And what would it matter if he wanted to cover his head (it is said to block out the voices he otherwise heard)? But these are not the questions currently applied to quotidian practices. Torture, endemic in U.S. prisons, spread beyond its usual purview after 9/11, which ushered in a brave new world of secret evidence, secret detentions, vindictive prosecutions, summary deportations, and the extradition of foreign nationals to countries where they face certain (and more extreme forms of) torture.[22] We are outsourcing torture, but we are also practicing it, if one cares to peer inside the increasingly lawless world of law enforcement.

THE ABUSIVENESS OF THE ABUSER
AND THE BULLY AS VICTIM

One might imagine that such acts of violence would find justification in strength, might, or will. In fact, weakness and vulnerability are always asserted. The spontaneous brutalities in New York, shadowy extrajudiciary law enforcement practices, the nauseating business at Abu Ghraib, similar practices at Guantánamo, and the chronic overreaching of presidential power are all fueled by a kind of helpless, inarticulate moral rage at the world: a rage that, if it could be captured in sound, would resemble the noise of barking dogs—or perhaps any six o'clock news crime report. This is the noise of a country that feels "victimized," feels "threatened," and thus construes its acts (which of necessity sometimes will be preemptive) either as righteous self-defense or as the defense of imperiled innocents. An insignia, inscribed by a magic marker on some anonymous prisoner's arm at Abu Ghraib, says it all: "RAPEIST" *(sic)*. Here again rationales turn to sex. The choice of this particular sobriquet is no accident. Pfc. Lynndie England, whose jaunty thumbs-up and bright smiles adorned some of the most sensational photos from Abu Ghraib, told investigators that guards put prisoners on leashes to intimidate them; they were trying to get prisoners to confess to raping a fifteen-year-old boy.[23] What could be more revelatory of converging currents in American culture? Whether a fifteen-year-old boy was actually raped or not is beside the point. Where ongoing sex and crime panics combine with terror panics, the "abusiveness" of the "abuser" becomes a justification for the abuses that flow more and more abundantly from the font of the state. Every bully talks this way. The victimizer will always pose as victim. (Besides, it's not really abuse if you do it to an abuser.)

OF PANIC, PURITANISM, AND PUNITIVENESS

The development of an increasingly paranoid, irrational, narcissistic, and authoritarian political culture (I gloss these four traits from Theodor Adorno's research on fascist psychological and cultural tendencies in America in the 1930s and 1940s) no doubt took a great leap forward after the atrocities of September 11, 2001.[24] But post-9/11 policies have only worked materials already at hand, underscoring victimization narratives, feeding obsessions with infantilized innocence, reinforcing trends toward punitive governance, extending the logic of preemption, and otherwise intensifying notable features of what sociologists call "the culture of fear."[25]

This culture of fear was stoked first by Nixon's "war on crime," the enduring conservative riposte to Johnson's "war on poverty." It has waxed unimpeded since the late 1970s, when modern crime panics got under way in earnest. Fueled by government cutbacks and inept policing strategies, Reagan-era crack wars fostered the perception that white, middle-class Americans were living in a state of emergency, besieged by hardened, incorrigible criminals. Fear-fostered punitiveness accelerated under the Clinton administration: Clinton pointedly refused to reconsider racist drug laws from the Reagan-Bush era (which expressly targeted poor people's drugs for especially draconian enforcement); he moreover consolidated an increasingly irrational and punitive culture of child sex panic. (Megan's Law opened new breaches into civil liberties, creating a new class of pariah-criminals whose sentences can never be fully served.) The so-called "liberal media" have also played their part. Although crime rates have fallen dramatically since the early 1990s, crime reportage has actually risen in inverse proportion: up to 50 percent of local news airtime is now devoted to crime reportage—prurient stories about sex abuse, lurid tales of gang violence, breathless accounts of callous predation. While the news media have profiteered off sensational coverage of this overblown crime beat, right-wing political interests have manipulated it, stoking fear of crime and predation to win elections—and, more enduringly, to reshape the social contract. This new social contract involves ever more "sticks" and ever fewer "carrots." Our current zeal for punishment turns on the perpetual cultivation of outsized fears.

This self-perpetuating culture of fear provides the crucial nexus between punitive governance at home and irrational imperial adventures abroad. America's most intolerable acts—whether dealing with black urban menace, brown border incursions, or far-flung Islamic peril—invariably take shape within a life-world dominated by fear. The uniquely self-righteous posture of her leaders, much noted throughout the world, turns on a familiar Victorian storyline that is likewise grounded in elaborate mechanisms of dread and projection: the infantilized, imperiled innocent always standing in need of rescue. And whether this imagined innocent is fashioned as America's inner child (her true identity) or as the ultimate, suffering Other who commands our attention, the result is much the same: a nation conceived by Puritan revolutionaries is obliged to defend the innocent, to punish evildoers, and to remake the world according to a moral imperative. (Critics of U.S. foreign policy thus have rightly turned a skeptical eye toward the very concept of "humanitarian intervention" but have usually neglected to analyze how deeply rooted its precepts are in American political culture, especially in the dispositions of middle-class progressivism.)

The timing of these cultural trends—which began with a white, family-oriented, middle- and working-class backlash against the civil rights movement, then became a generalized counter-countercultural response to other new social movements, especially the antiwar movement, feminism, and gay liberation—seems anything but coincidental. From the late 1970s on, the politics of fear and punishment sutures a neoconservative political orientation (with its emphasis on policing, surveillance, and punishment) to neoliberal economic policies (deregulation, privatization, laissez-faire). It creates conditions under which a majority not only will tolerate but also will actively embrace ever more punitive forms of governance—allowing, in the process, the accretion of a degree of social inequality not seen since the end of the 1920s.[26]

From the beginning, critics of the neoliberal era noted an apparent irony: as the state got out of the business of regulating the economy, it seemed more and more eager to regulate the *personal* lives of its citizens. The less the state addressed public welfare, the more it talked about private morality. The less it invested in schools and hospitals, the more it invested in prisons and policing. Less generous, it was also less forgiving. So much seems implicit in the rules of the game: unable under post-Keynesian rules to conceive of social problems in social or political-economic terms, state actors could conceive them only in individual terms—as moral shortcomings, bad choices, or criminal trespass. The language of the scold thus becomes the voice of authority, precipitating such distillations as "just say no," "tough love," "three strikes, you're out," and so on. A privatized, downsized, moralized, and decidedly punitive redefinition of "public good" has carried through to the present day: instead of resources, disadvantaged people get surveillance, discipline, and lectures about "personal responsibility."[27] Instead of getting a second chance, those who have run afoul of the law get excessive prison terms and a permanently stigmatized status. Instead of getting a hand up, strugglers get a short, sharp kick down.

Punitive governance is sustained by a symbolic order that equates punishment with justice. This distorted image of justice—which is essentially alien to classical notions of balance, conviviality, and fairness—functions as a theater of cruelty: it cultivates sadism and mean-spiritedness in its audience and coaxes the public to define these traits *as* citizenship. But this unjust justice also serves as a weird, compensatory mirror world of actual social relations. Forbidden to critically contemplate the very real, very high risks associated with neoliberal economic policies—currency crises, job loss, capital flight, reduced health care insurance, underfunded retirement plans, environmental degradation—John and Jane Q. Public are induced to fear instead far less consequential hazards to life and limb; they substitute various forms of pseudopractice (vigilance, show trials) for meaningful social involvement.

Something else no doubt lurks within this dark dreamworld of fear and punishment. Writing at a time when fascism was on the rise, Bertolt Brecht invites audiences to ponder how it is that the middle-class marks fall for the beggars' deceptions: fake stump limbs, made-up injuries. Peachum matter-of-factly explains: because the good bourgeois citizens have to believe that where they have aimed weapons there must be wounds.[28] Fear, it would seem, is a necessary condition of neoliberalism, which eviscerates the state of its social responsibilities while secretly dreading the monster it imagines it has unleashed from the depths of nature.

Neither fear nor puritanism is new in America, but they are stoked in new ways, under new conditions. A simple changing of the political guard will not be sufficient to scale back the republic of fear (which advanced more rapidly during the Clinton era than under Reagan-Bush). Fear has become the basis for social order; the forms of solidarity it predicates are perversions of the concept of social solidarity, the laws it premises are essentially contrary to any reasonable ideal of justice. Punitive governance, I suggest, is the real cultural logic of neoliberalism. What is unclear is how much longer this arrangement can last or what will replace it. The weaknesses of the present system seem glaringly apparent. A public defined by its fears cannot pursue its rational interests. A political system that revolves around fear cannot long remain democratic in any meaningful sense. An empire organized around fear will be predisposed toward disastrous undertakings.

NOTES

1. See Naomi Wolf, *The End of America: Letter of Warning to a Young Patriot* (White River Junction, VT: Chelsea Green, 2007); Chalmers Johnson, *Nemesis: The Last Days of the American Republic* (New York: Holt, 2006); Charlie Savage, *Takeover: The Return of the Imperial Presidency and the Subversion of American Democracy* (New York: Little, Brown, 2007); and Sheldon S. Wolin, *Democracy Incorporated: Managed Democracy and the Specter of Inverted Totalitarianism* (Princeton: Princeton University Press, 2008). See also Joe Conason, *It Can Happen Here: Authoritarian Peril in the Age of Bush* (New York: Thomas Dunne, 2007); Susan Jacoby, *The Age of American Unreason* (New York: Pantheon, 2008); Chris Hedges, *American Fascists: The Christian Right and the War on America* (New York: Free Press, 2007); and John W. Dean, *Broken Government: How Republican Rule Destroyed the Legislative, Executive, and Judicial Branches* (New York: Viking Press, 2007).

2. I draw the term *carceral state* from Foucault's phrase *carceral system*, which is frequently glossed *carceral society*. Michel Foucault, *Discipline and Punish: The Birth of the Prison* (1975; repr., New York: Vintage Books, 1977).

3. On the rise of a carceral state in the United States, see Marie Gottschalk, *The Prison and the Gallows: The Politics of Mass Incarceration in America* (Cambridge: Cambridge University Press, 2006), and Jonathan Simon, *Governing through Crime: How the War on Crime Transformed American Democracy and Created a Culture of Fear* (Oxford: Oxford University Press, 2007).

4. Nick Cohen, "661 New Crimes—and Counting," *New Statesman*, July 7, 2003, 18.

5. On incarceration rates, see the Web site for the International Centre for Prison Studies at King's College London, www.kcl.ac.uk/depsta/rel/icps/ (accessed January 8, 2007); Sentencing Project, "New Incarceration Figures: Thirty-Three Years of Consecutive Growth," www.sentencingproject.org/Default.aspx (accessed January 8, 2007). See also Warren Hoge, "Caught Red-Handed? Let It Be in Finland," *New York Times*, January 2, 2003, A1; Pew Center on the States, "One in 100: Behind Bars in America 2008," February 28, 2008, Pew Center Charitable Trusts, www.pewcenteronthestates.org/report_detail.aspx?id=35904.

6. Maurice Merleau-Ponty, "The USSR and the Camps," in his *Signs*, trans. Richard C. McCleary (1950; repr., Evanston, IL: Northwestern University Press, 1964), 264 (drafted by Merleau-Ponty and endorsed by Sartre, originally published as an editorial in *Les Temps Modernes*).

7. Timothy Egan, "Hard Time: Less Crime, More Criminals," *New York Times*, Week in Review, March 7, 1999; Joel Dyer, *The Perpetual Prisoner Machine: How America Profits from Crime* (Boulder, CO: Westview Press, 2000).

8. Jerome S. Bruner, "Do Not Pass Go," *New York Review of Books*, September 25, 2003; David Garland, *The Culture of Control: Crime and Social Order in Contemporary Society* (Chicago: University of Chicago Press, 2001).

9. Alex Lichtenstein, "The Private and the Public in Penal History: A Commentary on Zimring and Tonry," in *Mass Imprisonment: Social Causes and Consequences*, ed. David Garland (Thousand Oaks, CA: Sage Publications, 2001), 171–78.

10. Bureau of Justice Statistics, "Criminal Offender Statistics," U.S. Department of Justice, www.ojp.usdoj.gov/bjs/crimoff.htm#lifetime (accessed April 10, 2007).

11. "US Prison Population Sets Record," *Washington Post*, December 1, 2006, A03.

12. Jeremy Travis and Sarah Lawrence, "Beyond the Prison Gates: The State of Parole in America," Urban Institute, Justice and Policy Center, November 2002, www.urban.org/publications/900567.html, 24; Jennifer Gonnerman, "A Beaten Path Back to Prison," op-ed, *New York Times*, May 8, 2004.

13. Sentencing Project, "Felony Disenfranchisement Laws in the United States," September 2004, www.sentencingproject.org/pdfs/1046.pdf; Brent Staples, "How Denying the Vote to Ex-offenders Undermines Democracy," editorial, *New York Times*, September 17, 2004.

14. See Samuel R. Gross et al., "Exonerations in the United States, 1989 through 2003," *Journal of Criminal Law and Criminology* 95, no. 2 (2004): 523–60.

15. Chris Suellentrop, "The Right Has a Jailhouse Conversion," *New York Times*, December 24, 2006.

16. Michael Sherry, "Dead or Alive: American Vengeance Goes Global," *Review of International Studies* 31, suppl. S1 (December 2005): 246–63.

17. Elaine Scarry, *The Body in Pain: The Making and Unmaking of the World* (Oxford: Oxford University Press, 1985); Luc Sante, "Tourists and Torturers," op-ed, *New York Times*, May 11, 2004.

18. Susan Sontag, "Regarding the Torture of Others," *New York Times Magazine*, May 23, 2004.

19. Georges Bataille, "The Link between Taboos and Death," in *Eroticism: Death and Sensuality* (San Francisco: City Lights Books, 1986), 40–48.

20. Fox Butterfield, "Mistreatment of Prisoners Is Called Routine in U.S.," *New York Times*, May 8, 2004.

21. Amnesty International, *Amnesty International Report 2002—United States of America*, May 28, 2002, www.unhcr.org/refworld/docid/3cf4bc0510.html, and Amnesty International, *Amnesty International Report 2003—United States of America*, May 28, 2003, www.unhcr.org/refworld/docid/3edb47e21a.html. See also various reports by Human Rights Watch at their site, www.hrw.org.

22. Elaine Cassel, *The War on Civil Liberties: How Bush and Ashcroft Have Dismantled the Bill of Rights* (Chicago: Lawrence Hill Books, 2004).

23. Kate Zernike, "Prison Guard Calls Abuse Routine and Sometimes Amusing," *New York Times*, May 16, 2004.

24. Theodor Adorno, *The Stars Down to Earth and Other Essays on the Irrational in Culture* (New York: Routledge Classics, 2002).

25. I draw the term *punitive governance* from recent work in critical race studies and the sociology of crime and from Sherry's essay, "Dead or Alive," on the punitive turn in American culture. Simon, *Governing through Crime;* Barry Glassner, *The Culture of Fear: Why Americans Are Afraid of the Wrong Things* (New York: Basic Books, 1999).

26. "Plutocracy Reborn," *Nation*, June 30, 2008; Emmanuel Saez, "Striking It Richer: The Evolution of Top Incomes in the United States (Update Using 2006 Preliminary Estimates)," March 15, 2008, http://elsa.berkeley.edu/~saez/saez-UStopincomes-2006prel.pdf.

27. Jane L. Collins, "The Specter of Slavery: Workfare and the Economic Citizenship of Poor Women," in *New Landscapes of Inequality: Neoliberalism and the Erosion of Democracy in America*, ed. Jane L. Collins, Micaela di Leonardo, and Brett Williams (Santa Fe, NM: School for Advanced Research, 2008), 131–51.

28. Bertolt Brecht, *The Threepenny Opera*, trans. Desmond Vesey and Eric Bentley (1928; repr., New York: Grove Press, 1960), 72. See also Bertolt Brecht, *Threepenny Novel*, trans. Desmond Vesey and Christopher Isherwood (1934; repr., New York: Grove Press, 1937), 168.

PART TWO

The New Economy

4

Neoliberalism, or
The Bureaucratization of the World

David Graeber

Americans often find it difficult to talk about politics with people from other parts of the world. Consider three quotes culled, more or less at random, from world newswires around the end of December 2005. In Bolivia, newly elected president Evo Morales declared that in his victory "the people have defeated the neoliberals." "We want to change the neoliberal model," he added. In Germany, Lothar Bisky announced the creation of a new political party that, he hoped, would "contribute to creating a democratic alternative to oppose the damage caused by neoliberalism to social cohesion." Around the same time, a pan-African Web journal announced a special issue whose articles "reflect a growing debate on economic alternatives to neoliberalism from countries as far afield as Mauritius, Swaziland and Mali."[1]

These are just three: I could easily have chosen dozens of them. Across most of the planet, *neoliberalism* is a household word. Arguments about neoliberalism form the stuff of everyday political conversation. Politicians are accused of being neo-liberals or pursuing neoliberal agendas; opposition candidates get elected by run-ning against neoliberalism (then, often as not, are accused by their former supporters of caving in to it). Neoliberalism is seen as the dominant ideological force in the world, an attempt by the United States, as the world's sole remaining superpower, to extend its own social and economic model to the rest of the world. Some say it is inevitable, even desirable; others organize against it. But almost everyone has an opinion on the matter.

In the United States, few have ever heard of it. Mention the word to almost any-one but an academic or international affairs correspondent, and you are likely to be met with empty stares. If you want to talk about the same issues, in fact, you are forced to rely on obvious propaganda terms like *free trade, free-market reforms,* or *globalization.* The bias in the first two is pretty obvious. You don't put the word *free* in front of a name if you're trying to be neutral about it. *Globalization* is only slightly more subtle. When you call something "neoliberalism" you are saying that this is a set of ideas, simply one theory among many about the best way to organize an economy. "Globalization," in contrast, is always treated as something inevitable. There's not much point in having an opinion about whether the sun will rise tomorrow, argues Thomas Friedman, probably the most prominent American advocate of neoliberalism (which of course he never refers to by name): one simply accepts it as reality and tries to make the best of it.[2] Globalization just somehow happened. No one is really responsible. Perhaps it had something to do with the Internet. At any rate, now we all have no choice but to adapt.

From the point of view of those who feel neoliberalism is simply a matter of the United States imposing its own model on the rest of the world, all of this is exactly what one would expect. To be fair, though, there are many more innocent reasons why most Americans would find the term *neoliberalism* confusing. In the United States, political language has developed very differently than it has in the rest of the world. For example, in the nineteenth century, the word *liberal* was applied to people who believed in individual liberty, which they saw as founded on private property rights. These "classical liberals," as they are sometimes called, tended to reject government interference in the economy as much as in personal affairs. This is still what *liberal* implies in most of the world. But in the United States, over the course of the twentieth century, the term was adopted by the moderate Left until it came to mean something like "social democrat." Starting in the 1980s the Right responded by turning the word *liberal* into a term of opprobrium: *liberal* became, in the minds of many working-class Americans, a designator for latte-sipping cultural elitists, "tax-and-spend" politicians, proponents of gay marriage, and similar bête noires. Meanwhile, free-market enthusiasts—the sort of people who elsewhere in the world are referred to as "liberals"—began casting about for a new name. The one they ended up fixing on was *libertarian*—a term they borrowed from the Left. The result is that it is even more difficult for Americans to talk to anyone else about politics, since, in the rest of the world, *libertarian* still largely retains its traditional meaning as a synonym for *anarchist*. In Europe or South America, it is perfectly unremarkable to talk about "libertarian communism"—referring by this to the idea that states should be dismantled and control over economic life placed in the hands of democratically organized communities. Use a term like that in front of the average U.S. citizen, and he will assume that you are one of those annoying people who like to confuse others with intentional oxymorons—or perhaps that you are insane.

It is never a good thing when people cannot talk to each other, and it seems particularly unfortunate right now, when so many Americans seem confused about the widespread anger about their role in the world. In the press, opposition to neoliberalism—particularly in Latin America—is often referred to as "anti-

Americanism," as if neoliberalism really were simply identical to the American way of life. In fact it is nothing of the kind. Indeed, a case could well be made that the majority of Americans reject its core ideas and institutions and that Americans have actually been the first historic victims of neoliberal "reforms"—policies that are the ultimate cause of many of the insecurities described in this volume. Certainly, Americans have also played a prominent role in the growing global movement against neoliberalism.

As the above suggests, I am not making any claim to neutrality here. I think it is fair to say that anyone speaking of the roots of global poverty or the nature of capitalism who claims to be providing an "objective" or "scientific" account is either extraordinarily naive or trying to sell you something. It seems more honest to simply reveal one's biases and let the reader take it from there. For over six years I have been deeply involved in a global movement against neoliberalism, whose overall effects, I feel, have been an unmitigated catastrophe. What follows, then, are a series of efforts to conceptualize the present historical situation, at a time when, across the world, thoughtful people are increasingly trying to imagine a way out.

THE ROOTS OF NEOLIBERALISM

Neoliberalism as an economic and political theory is based on a few relatively simple assumptions. A minimal sketch might run like this:

1. Governments should minimize their engagement in economic planning. Further, they are not competent to run large industrial and commercial enterprises; in fact, private firms operating in pursuit of profit in a market environment can always be expected to do a better job providing public services than public institutions. Government should therefore restrict itself to providing a legal environment in which it is easy for private firms to do this and maintaining necessary infrastructure.

2. Reducing trade barriers is always good and always benefits all parties. Older protectionist policies need to be abandoned; rather than trying to develop autonomously, each nation should pursue its particular "competitive advantage" (whatever this may be: cheap labor, an educated workforce, natural resources) in a single global marketplace.

3. Government spending policies meant to benefit the poor, whether price supports for basic foodstuffs, provision of free medical services, or guaranteed pension funds, are ultimately counterproductive. They should be pared back or eliminated, since they distort the workings of the market. Instead, if governments limit spending so as to maintain balanced budgets to guarantee the stability of their currency, they will create a market environment favorable to foreign investment, and the market itself will provide better solutions to these problems.

Since 1980, almost every country in the world has adopted some version of neoliberal reforms. Only exceptionally, however, did they do so because politicians got
elected by promising to do so. Arguably the first neoliberal experiment was carried
out in the mid-1970s by General Augusto Pinochet in Chile after he had overthrown
an elected government in a military coup. Most reforms, however, were carried out
not by force of arms but by what might be termed fiscal coercion.

The real paradigm here, as David Harvey notes, was New York City's financial
crisis that began in 1975.[3] It is worth considering in some detail. The crisis began
with the city teetering on the edge of fiscal default. After the federal government
refused to provide a bailout and investment bankers refused to roll over the debt,
New York was driven to technical bankruptcy. Creditors then proceeded to form
what they called the Municipal Assistance Corporation, an entity independent of
the city government and hence unaccountable to voters, that as a condition of res-
cuing the city began to remake its political landscape. One must bear in mind that
at the time New York was a kind of enclave of social democracy in America. It had
not only the most extensive rent control in the country but America's most unionized workforce and most extensive public services and even maintained its only free
public university. In the name of balancing the budget, the MAC broke the power
of the municipal unions, slashed services, rolled back pensions and job security, offered enormous tax cuts to business and developers, and began to restructure the
very shape of city government.

Gone first of all was any pretense that city government existed equally for all its
citizens. Rather, the city was a product to be marketed. Logos and jingles were invented (the Big Apple; I Love New York). As the city center was rebuilt as a glittering advertisement for itself, the poor were to be pushed out of sight of potential
tourists and investors. The calculated withdrawal of fire crews allowed peripheral
neighborhoods like the South Bronx and East New York to descend into burnt-out
wastelands; infrastructure like subways, crucial to the working class in the outer
boroughs, was allowed to crumble; CUNY was compelled to charge tuition; at the
same time, city government poured money into supporting gentrification campaigns
and the creation of a new telecommunications infrastructure in the city center aimed
at creating a better "business climate" for investors.

New York in the late 1970s and early 1980s normally evokes images of hedo-
nistic yuppies sniffing cocaine at Studio 54, or, alternately, images of urban decay:
graffiti, crack houses, the epidemic of homelessness that at the time inspired comparisons with Calcutta or Bombay. The increasing divisions between rich and poor
that made these images possible were not, as apologists often claimed, the inevitable
results of deindustrialization and the growth of the communications or service industry. They were the product of policy decisions that New Yorkers as a whole had
not and would never have collectively chosen, that were, effectively, imposed on
them by financiers philosophically opposed to the very idea of public goods. The

gradual result, however, was the emergence of what might be called a neoliberal ethic: simultaneous emphases on personal self-realization for the affluent and "personal responsibility" for the poor. Both seemed to rely on the rejection of any notion that democracy implies some common dedication to a community (let alone that community members should therefore be guaranteed access to those minimal needs, food, shelter, and free time, that would allow them to participate in a community's democratic life). Margaret Thatcher, who was one of the few politicians to state it explicitly, put it most succinctly: "There is no such thing," she said, "as society." There are individuals, and families, and the outcome of their independent self-interested decisions *is* democratic choice. If community was to be evoked, it was—as in the "I Love New York" campaign—just another sales gimmick, since, after all, in the neoliberal universe, reality itself is simply whatever you can sell. The same sense of fragmented individuals left with nothing but their own capacities for self-marketing echoed on every level of the emerging culture of the time, from the savvy postmodernism of New York's art scene to the endless subdivision of consumer identities identified and targeted by its advertising agencies.

Not only does the history of New York show that politicians can rarely get elected running against community;[4] it also shows that, once the process of social triage is already accepted as a fait accompli, politicians can often quite readily win elections on law-and-order tickets, promising to protect middle- and working-class citizens from the chaos and violence that such policies invariably unleash. In New York, the election of Rudy Giuliani in the 1990s was only the culmination of a long degeneration of politics into an obsession with violence and crime—essentially, with cleaning up the mess made in the 1970s. The pattern was to be reproduced worldwide, again and again, in city after city.

In the 1980s, the Third World debt crisis allowed the Reagan regime to begin applying the same model on a global scale. The origins of that debt crisis go back to the Organization of the Petroleum Exporting Countries (OPEC) oil embargo of the late 1970s. Essentially, what happened was that with the spike in oil prices OPEC countries were suddenly awash in so much money that Western banks (in which they invested it) soon ran out of anyone willing to borrow it. The result was a period of "go-go banking," with bank representatives jet-setting about the world aggressively trying to convince Third World leaders to accept high-interest loans based on wild projections of the economic bonanzas that would follow. A large amount of this money was simply stolen; much of the rest was invested in ill-conceived grandiose projects (such as the enormous dams the World Bank became so famous for) that were later used to showcase the foolishness of the very idea of government-sponsored development. Needless to say, within a few years many of the poorer nations themselves teetered on the brink of default. It was at this point that the U.S. Treasury, working closely with the International Monetary Fund (IMF), fixed on a policy that under no circumstances were such debts to be written off.[5] This was, I should note, a major departure from previous economic orthodoxy, which took it for granted that those who lend money are assuming a certain risk. It showcases, in fact, a crucial element of neoliberalism: that, while the poor are to be held accountable for poor economic decisions (real or imagined), the rich must never be. In practical effect, it meant that even if a banker were to lend a hundred million dollars to a corrupt dictator, knowing full well that he was likely to place the sum directly in his personal Swiss bank account, and even if that dictator were to be subsequently ousted by a popular uprising, he could rest assured that the full apparatus of world government and financial institutions would lock into step to insist the money could still be recovered—at generous rates of interest—from the dictator's former victims. If thousands therefore had to starve, so be it.

The innovation was not just insisting on the inviolability of debt but, as in New York, using it as a political instrument.[6] Loans soon became unpayable; the terms had to be refinanced. Before the IMF was willing to do so, however, governments had to agree to undergo what were called "structural adjustment programs" designed by neoliberal economists. Their first priority was always to balance the budget, ostensibly so as to create a stable currency and a favorable climate for investment. This was to be done primarily by slashing social services, most dramatically by the removal of price supports on fuel or basic foodstuffs, or the imposition of "users' fees" for previously free services like health clinics and primary education. This was to be accompanied by selling off public resources and fully opening the local market to foreign trade and investment. As one might imagine, these policies inspired constant rebellions on the part of the urban poor, but governments were able to say they had no choice. They were right. On the few occasions when leaders of poor countries outright refused to sign an IMF agreement—for instance, Madagascar's President Albert Zafy in the early 1990s—they soon discovered that in the absence of one all other countries would shut off foreign aid; without aid, private capital pulled out; without insurance credits, it was not even possible to export products. The effects were—at least in terms of purely economic devastation—roughly comparable to what might have been achieved by a minor nuclear attack.[7]

The 1980s and 1990s were, of course, the very period when, in much of Europe, Africa, and the Americas, dictatorships were being replaced by elected governments. Voters quickly discovered, however, that their choices had next to no effect on economic policy, since the levers of economic decision were simultaneously being removed from the hands of governments and passed to unelected, and unaccountable, neoliberal technocrats. This did not happen just through debt. Another leitmotif of the era has been the passing of jurisdiction over economic matters to bodies meant to enforce trade agreements: the signing of the North American Free Trade Agreement (NAFTA), in 1994, for instance, committed Mexico to make major constitutional changes—notably, abolishing all forms of communal land tenure, including the collective *ejidos* that were one of the main legacies of the revolution—without the matter ever coming up before the electorate.[8] In Europe, European Union agreements played a similar role, forcing governments to eliminate social protections and institute "flexible" labor regimes in the name of balancing the budget, so as to maintain the stability of Europe's new common currency. This was soon followed by the expansion of similar trade agreements—the General Agreement on Tariffs and Trade (GATT), then the World Trade Organization (WTO)—worldwide. In each case appointed bodies of bureaucrats were empowered to strike down laws that were deemed overly protectionist, including laws designed to protect working conditions or the environment.

Perhaps the most dramatic case, though, was that of Eastern and Central Europe. Surveys taken immediately after the fall of communism in 1989 and 1991 revealed that in pretty much every case most citizens preferred to see the creation of some kind of Scandinavian-style social welfare state, with substantial minorities in favor of the maintenance of socialism and almost no one in favor of instituting a pure free-market model. Yet as soon as elected governments were in place, they uniformly began administering "shock therapy" programs designed abroad to institute exactly that, as quickly as possible. It was all the more striking since these states were not, for the most part, burdened with substantial debt. By that time, it had apparently become impossible to fully integrate with the world economy on any other terms.[9]

In fact, by the 1990s one can genuinely speak of a system of global governance operating on neoliberal lines. Imagine it as consisting in a series of tiers. On the top are the money traders. One of the great innovations of recent decades is the enormous efflorescence of finance capital: at this point, over 90 percent of economic transactions in what is called the global marketplace no longer have any immediate connection with manufacturing or trading commodities of any kind but consist simply of currency trading and other forms of financial speculation. This acts as an enormous disciplining mechanism, since the "electronic herd," as Thomas Friedman likes to call them, can instantly pull money out of "emerging markets" seen as betraying neoliberal orthodoxy. The effects of such a currency run can be, again, near-nuclear in their implications. Next are transnational corporations, whose incomes are often far larger than the GDPs of most actual countries. During the 1980s and 1990s, thousands of formerly independent enterprises—from newspapers to department stores to construction companies—have been absorbed into gigantic conglomerates organized on bureaucratic lines. Next are the various trade bureaucracies—the IMF, the WTO, the EU, the Association of Southeast Asian Nations (ASEAN), NAFTA, the various Reserve Banks, and so on, whose economists regularly evoke the threat of the financiers to insist on policies amenable to the transnationals. Finally, one has the endless elaboration of nongovernmental organizations (NGOs), which have come to provide services—from childhood inoculations to the provision of agricultural credits—previously considered the work of national governments.

All of these tiers—including the huge brokerage houses and hedge funds that conduct most of the world's financial trading—together constitute a single huge, de facto, administrative system. It is the first administrative system in human history that actually has the power to enforce decisions on a planetary scale, since, after all, no empire has ever spanned the entire world, and the UN, the first genuinely global institution, never had more than moral authority. There is of course a word for large, hierarchically organized administrative systems. They are called bureaucracies. Certainly, most of those operating within this new administrative system do not like to think of themselves as bureaucrats. And certainly, these organizations tend to operate in a far more decentralized and flexible style than the government bureaucracies they aimed to (largely) supersede.[10] But it is only to be expected that a planetwide trade bureaucracy would be organized differently than those with which we are most familiar. The remarkable thing is that it has been so effective in imposing its dictates that most of those inhabiting the richer countries are effectively unaware of its existence.

THE BALANCE BOOK

Supporters of neoliberal reforms were usually perfectly willing to admit that their prescriptions were, as they often put it, "harsh medicine" or that the effects would, at least initially, be "painful." The justification was—it was Margaret Thatcher again who put it most succinctly—that "there is no alternative." Socialist solutions having failed, and global competition being what it was, there was simply no other way. "Capitalism" (by implication, neoliberal capitalism) had been proven "the only thing that works." The phrase itself is significant, since it shows how thoroughly we have come to see states and societies as business enterprises; it rarely seemed to occur to anyone to ask, "Works to do what?" Nevertheless, even if neoliberalism is judged in its own terms—in which success is measured almost exclusively by economic growth—it has proved, on a global scale, remarkably unsuccessful.

Remember here that "free-market reforms" were supposed to be a reaction to the shortcomings of the state-sponsored development strategies of the 1960s and 1970s. Here numbers are available. In the 1960s and 1970s, global growth rates averaged 3.5 percent and 2.4 percent per year, respectively. During the period of neoliberal reforms in the 1980s that number fell to 1.4 percent, and during the neoliberal "Washington consensus" of the 1990s it fell to 1.1 percent.[11] The effects were even more dramatic in the countries of the developing world, which were supposed to be the greatest beneficiaries of "free trade." If one excludes China,[12] the first two decades saw an overall 3.2 percent per year per capita growth in real domestic product in the global South—higher, in fact, than the global average at that time. During the neoliberal era (1981–99) this fell to 0.7 percent.[13] Many economies actually shrank. What's more, low rates of growth were almost invariably accompanied by increasingly unequal distribution. As national elites established themselves in the glittering metropolises of global cities or locked themselves away in Ethernet-wired gated communities, governments abandoned any commitment to policies once meant to ensure a minimal degree of social protection to all their citizens. The effect was, as in New York, a kind of social triage, with government's role largely to sweep the poor or newly impoverished away and keep them out of sight, while international NGOs attempted to limit the damage. Taken on a world scale, overall social indicators like literacy rates and life expectancy declined dramatically.[14]

If this is not general knowledge, it is partly because proponents of neoliberalism never talk about the big picture. It is in the nature of the global market that there are winners and losers, they say; then they try to demonstrate that the winners are those that followed their advice most closely. Hence Lithuania is doing better than Russia, Uganda than Angola, Chile than Brazil. Even this usually requires a fair amount of cooking the books. In the 1980s, for example, reformers liked to point to the success of the "Asian Tigers" like South Korea and Taiwan. This required soft-pedaling the fact that both had actually relied on heavy tariffs, massive government investment in public education, and even government-directed industrial five-year plans—basically, exactly the opposite of what neoliberals were recommending. In Europe, Great Britain, easily the most assiduous in carrying out free-market reforms, now has living standards lower than Ireland's, while Finland, which of all European countries has the largest share of its economy dedicated to social welfare programs, has, according to the World Economic Forum, now replaced the United States as the most economically competitive nation on earth.[15] At the same time, the two great winners in the world economy during the last decade, the United States and the People's Republic of China, are those in a position to most systematically ignore the advice of the IMF. It is little known in the United States, for example, that every year the IMF chastises the U.S. government for its massive budget deficits and demands the slashing of tariffs and farm subsidies. The government simply ignores it, since in the United States the IMF lacks any means of enforcement.[16] China, as the United States' largest creditor, has also managed to avoid almost all of the "discipline" applied to other developing countries: if it were in the same position as, say, Brazil, it would never have been allowed to maintain policies like extending endless credit for the building of industrial infrastructure, let alone systematically ignoring foreign patents and copyrights—policies that have been, arguably, the keystones of China's spectacular economic success.

IMF economists are of course aware of the disastrous effects that so often seem to follow when countries adopt their policy recommendations. Their reaction is always the same: such countries had not gone far enough. Even harsher medicine is required.

As the Filipino economist Walden Bello remarks, this is at the very least somewhat puzzling. Most of these economists have worked extensively with the private sector. They are aware that if a private firm hires a consultant to recommend an economic strategy, and the strategy recommended fails completely to reach its stated objectives, that consultant can normally expect to be fired. At the very least he will be expected to come up with a different strategy. When those same economists insist that countries like Uruguay or Mali pursue the same policies year after year for decades without seeing any significant positive effects, one has to wonder if the best interests of Uruguay or Mali are really foremost in their minds.[17] Certainly many in Uruguay and Mali concluded from quite early on that this was not the case.

There has been a great deal of speculation on this account. David Harvey has noted that neoliberalism, however ineffective as a strategy for global prosperity, has proved remarkably effective in solidifying class power—a power that had been widely threatened by revolutionary and democratic movements in the 1970s. (To this I would add, the greatest beneficiaries of neoliberal policies have been the staff of the emerging administrative apparatus itself.) Bello himself makes a similar argument, but in geopolitical terms. By the end of the 1970s, countries like Brazil were indeed emerging as significant industrial powers, and the general economic position of the South was advancing so quickly that its political representatives in the nonaligned movement were beginning to demand changes in the very structure of the global economy. The OPEC oil embargo was only the most dramatic manifestation of this general flexing of new economic muscles. If so, structural adjustment has proven extremely effective in blunting the offensive and turning many countries of the South into impoverished suppliants. This perspective, however, raises the intriguing question of the degree to which the United States was, through neoliberal policies, simply postponing the inevitable. This is the view, in turn, of Immanuel Wallerstein, who points out that if one peeks behind the virtual universe of finance capital one discovers that American economic power relative to the rest of the world has been declining continually since at least the 1960s. The main reason, he argues, is low overall productivity. While the United States appears on paper to have the most productive workforce in the world, this is because statistics measure the productivity only of wage laborers—who in the United States are squeezed more than almost anywhere—and never of managers. To put it crudely: in the United States, it takes two or three executives to do the work done by one in Europe or East Asia, and U.S. executives demand to be paid five or six times more. One of the main effects of U.S.-promoted neoliberal reforms around the world, according to Wallerstein, has been to encourage the creation of a similarly parasitical executive class in other countries, with the effect of at least slowing down the rate at which the rest of the world is overtaking it. The rapid rise of India and China suggest this game might soon be up.[18]

NEOLIBERALISM AS PHILOSOPHY

We are left with a paradox. How did a philosophy of radical individualism become the justification for creating the world's first global administrative bureaucracy?

Here I think we have to return to the nineteenth century. If old and new liberalism have anything in common, it is first, that both saw human freedom largely as the ability to enjoy one's personal property, and second, that both nonetheless saw themselves as progressive, even revolutionary forces in human history.

Let us consider briefly the political context of such claims. When, during the Putney debates in 1647, radical factions in Cromwell's army argued that "every man by nature [is] a king, priest and prophet in his own natural circuit and compass," the sole proprietor of his own person and possessions "on which none could trespass," even the government, this was a very radical claim.[19] Two hundred years later, it was distinctly less so. By that time, workers' movements were beginning to level a fundamental challenge against the political power of private wealth. Liberals, on the other hand, were that fraction of the Left most likely to defend private wealth and particularly market economies.

This is not to say that nineteenth-century liberals were not, as they generally claimed, radicals and even leftists. Most were honest opponents of slavery and militarism, proponents of individual rights and universal suffrage. Free-market enthusiasts, they also tended to follow Adam Smith in seeing large chartered companies as government-imposed monopolies and restraints on genuine economic competition. The liberal ideal was of a world of autonomous individuals or small family firms buying and selling their wares on a global market. If most looked with favor on the British Empire of their day, it was because that empire did, to a certain degree, put these ideals into practice. For example, though it used force of arms to open markets, it refused all forms of protectionism at home. Since chartered monopolies like the East India Company had been dismantled at the beginning of the century, British capitalism of that time actually was largely a matter of relatively small family firms. Finally, for all the depredations of the industrial revolution, liberals were able to see even wage labor as progress in the direction of freedom when compared with the slavery, debt peonage, and forced and bonded labor on which capitalists had largely depended up to that point, and on which, globally, to some degree they always have depended and still do depend.

American capitalism began even closer to the liberal ideal than British, but by the 1870s and 1880s it had begun to take a very different direction. Its key innovation was the creation of the modern joint-stock corporation. Corporate charters—which potentially allowed joint-stock companies with thousands of employees to be treated, for legal purposes, as individual persons—had for most of the nineteenth century been considered privileges granted by local governments to local businessmen in a position to afford them some specific public service, such as building a canal or railroad. By the 1880s and 1890s, corporations not only had attained permanent status but had come to dominate the national economy. In the twentieth century, America led the way in creating transnational corporations that effectively spanned the world. As Giovanni Arrighi notes, when the United States replaced Great Britain as the dominant world power, it brought its own, bureaucratic, form of capitalism.[20] The torch was formally passed after World War II, and one of President Roosevelt's first acts at the time was to create the original framework for what I have called the emerging global bureaucracy. These came to be known as the Bretton Woods institutions, after the ski resort in New Hampshire where the conference was held at which they were created: the IMF, the World Bank, and the GATT, ancestor of the WTO. Technically under the legal umbrella of the newly created United Nations, they soon came to overshadow it as an effective system of global administration.[21] Arrighi also notes that unlike Great Britain, the United States at its most powerful was never particularly committed to free trade. It never opened its home markets in the way that England had. Even today, roughly a third of all transactions counted as "international trade" under the American aegis are not trade at all but simply transfers between different branches of corporations that, in their internal organization, are often barely distinguishable from enterprises in the old Soviet Union.[22]

So how does the second wave of liberalism fit in? It seems to me it can be understood only in the light of what Wallerstein calls "the world revolution of 1968." The riots, uprisings, and campus revolts that shook the industrialized world in the late 1960s were rebellions against capitalism but equally against the welfare states with which capitalists were then allied. They also tended to declare a complete break with both the "respectable" Marxist opposition and Leninist regimes of the day. The rebels of May 1968 in Paris wanted nothing to do with the French Communist Party; theirs was a revolt in the name of individual liberation, pleasure, and self-expression against every sort of stifling social convention and bureaucratic constraint. And the same was true of the spirit of 1968 in America as well. It hardly seems coincidental that neoliberalism became the dominant ideology at precisely the moment when the generation that attended college in the late 1960s began to come to institutional power. As an ideology, it appears designed to do exactly what the liberalism of the nineteenth century had done: to recuperate revolutionary energies, ideas, even revolutionary language, for capitalism.

Probably the best example here is the history of the word *capitalism* itself. A key element in neoliberal rhetoric has been the idea that capitalism is, itself, a revolutionary force. This kind of language is actually quite new—at least, coming from capitalists. Capitalists have historically never used the word *capitalism* at all, preferring terms like *free enterprise, entrepreneurialism, private enterprise,* or *economic freedom. Capitalism* was a term employed almost exclusively by its critics to describe what they saw as a sordid economic reality, one where productive wealth was controlled by the few for their own benefit. "Socialism," in turn, was the unrealized ideal of a world where productive wealth would be administered democratically for the common good. One of the most characteristic intellectual moves of the neoliberal era was to flip this around. Capitalism became the unrealized ideal: a utopian dream of a perfectly free, self-regulating market. Socialism was the sordid reality of government regulation. All progress in human happiness and freedom could therefore be attributed to capitalism and everything bad to the lingering effects of socialism.

This was not traditional capitalist rhetoric. It was, rather, a kind of Marxism in reverse. Tellingly, the language was first employed largely by defectors from the other side: most notoriously Russian exile Ayn Rand; her *Capitalism: The Unknown Ideal,* originally published in 1946, was a powerful influence on the young Alan Greenspan, who, as head of the American Federal Reserve between 1987 and 2006, was to become the veritable high priest of neoliberal orthodoxy. What began as the language of the hard Right was soon to be adopted almost everywhere. By the 1980s, the revalidation of the word *capitalism* seems to have been adopted as a special cause by the editors of the supposedly left-leaning *New York Times,* which probably ran at least a hundred different headlines and editorials during that period announcing that some left-wing regime or party had been forced to embrace "capitalism." After the collapse of Marxist regimes, *Times* columnists had become so intoxicated with the idea of capitalism as a radical force that there was a lively debate in its pages on whether Che Guevera, were he alive today, would have become a free-market reformer out of sheer revolutionary enthusiasm.

Only in this context, I think, can we understand how a rhetoric of absolute individualism could ever have become the basis for an emerging bureaucracy. It arrived tumbled breathlessly together with the language of revolution. The problem was that this was not just a language, and the aspects of the revolutionary that it drew on were, mostly, the most disastrous. The essence of the neoliberal position in fact bears stunning similarity to Stalinism—that is, to the very arguments used by Marxist revolutionaries in the 1920s and 1930s to justify the creation of a bureaucratic state. One might summarize it like this: "Science has shown that there is only one possible way forward, and it is the same for any society on earth. There is a scientifically trained elite who understand this and must be given the power to reengineer society appropriately. The economic views of those not trained in this science are irrelevant. So shut up and do what you're told, because, even if in the short run this may cause tremendous pain and dislocation, even starvation and death, somewhere down the line (we're not quite sure when) it will all lead to a paradise of peace and prosperity."

The same line touted by Soviet apparatchiks to Russian peasants in the 1930s is now being touted to just about everyone; the only significant difference is that now historical materialism has been replaced by Milton Friedman–style free-market economics. It is hardly surprising, then, that since 1989 so many actual Stalinist apparatchiks, from Poland to Vietnam, have found it so easy to simply switch from one orthodoxy to the other. It didn't really require much of a fundamental leap.

Obviously, neoliberal global bureaucracies are not nearly so directly hands-on as old communist ones were in trying to impose their utopian vision. But the ultimate ideal, to subject every aspect of life to the logic of the market, is—as defectors like financier George Soros like to point out—if anything just as totalitarian in its ambitions. What's more, many of the effects have been curiously similar. Under Soviet regimes, political life—let alone ideological debate—was outlawed. All political questions were deemed settled; all that remained was the administration of economic affairs—supposedly aimed at eventually creating a consumer paradise. As a result, the only way one could stake a political claim on the center was by playing to some kind of ethnic or cultural identity: for example, if the Khazaks get a nuclear power plant, surely we Uzbeks deserve one too. Identity politics was the only kind the bureaucratic apparatus found acceptable. One result was that when these states dissolved, many instantly descended into ethnic warfare. It is clear that something rather similar is now happening on a global scale. The fall of communism in particular was taken to mean that ideological—in effect, political—debate was over. The result was that identity politics not only were seen as legitimate but were in a very real sense the only sort of politics seen as entirely legitimate. In some cases the link to global bureaucracies is quite clear. Neoliberalism, as I have noted, seeks to eliminate all collective forms of property—the only exception that seems to be allowable is for people classified as "indigenous." One result has been a worldwide outpouring of attempts by groups to claim indigenous status, including many (such as the pastoral Maasai in Kenya) that would never have dreamed of describing themselves as such before. On a broader scale, Samuel Huntington's argument that, now that the age of ideological struggle is over, a "war of civilizations" (i.e., religious and cultural identities) is all that remains is a perfect expression of the logical results of trying to declare an end to any other kind of history.

ALTERNATIVES, OR "WORKS TO DO WHAT?"

Without this Manichean framework, borrowed from the cruder varieties of Marxism, it would be impossible to argue that, since "communism failed," there was no alternative but to strive toward some ideal of pure free-market capitalism—one that has never actually existed anywhere. Otherwise the argument would make about as much sense as the argument of someone who, witnessing the collapse of the Catholic Church after a long struggle with Episcopalianism, concluded that therefore we all had to become Baptists (or maybe Jews). It seems to me that a more sober assessment of history would rather have concluded that the most effective way to win a cold war is through limited social welfare programs combined with massive government military spending to stimulate the economy; that the most effective way for poor countries to play economic catch-up with rich capitalist ones is by combining market forces, protection of key industries, strategic exports, and massive government investment in education and infrastructure; and that if one's aim is to create the richest possible material life and greatest freedom for about 10 percent of the world's population while tossing the bottom third to the wolves, neoliberalism is surely one's best bet. It also seems to me that none of this has any necessary bearing on other questions, such as "What is the most effective way to bring about a world in which ordinary people are secure in their basic needs, and thus free to pursue the things that are most important to them?" or "How do we ensure that the planet is not destroyed?"

Capitalism itself—industrial capitalism at least—has had a very brief historical run. During a mere two hundred years, however, it has nonetheless shown a remarkable ability to come up with threats to the very existence of the species: first nuclear destruction, now global climate change. There are good reasons to believe it is simply not a viable long-term system: most obviously, because it is premised on the need for continual growth, and economic growth cannot continue forever on a planet with finite resources. Capitalism that was not based on the need to continually expand production would simply not be capitalism; its fundamental dynamics would change; it would become something else. Whatever economic system predominates in fifty years, it is very likely to be something other than capitalism. Of course, that something might be even worse. This is why it seems to me this is precisely the wrong time to give up on imagining alternatives to capitalism: that is, to come up with ideas for what might actually be better.

This is why, for me, the movements of resistance against neoliberalism have been so crucially important. These began almost immediately in the 1980s in most parts of the world, largely taking form around grassroots campaigns in defense of one or another form of common property.[23] At first they were largely unconnected. The Zapatista revolt in Chiapas in 1994 was a key moment; it was the Zapatistas, in fact, who sponsored the first international meetings that eventually gave birth to what the media came to call "the antiglobalization" movement—really, a global movement, as the Zapatistas put it, "for humanity and against neoliberalism." The spectacular mass actions during the WTO meetings in Seattle in November 1999, then afterwards in Washington and Prague (versus the IMF), Quebec (versus the Free Trade Agreement of the Americas [FTAA]), and Genoa (versus the Group of Eight), were all intended first and foremost to reveal to the world the undemocratic nature of the bodies that had come to control global economic policy. They served, in other words, to point out the very existence of this new global bureaucracy, on the assumption that most people in the world would draw the obvious conclusions. In this they were strikingly successful: within less than two years' time most of the key tenets of neoliberalism, treated as self-evident truths in the 1990s, had everywhere begun to be called into question. Ambitious plans to expand the WTO and create new trade pacts like the FTAA treaty stopped dead in their tracks.

It is a bit ironic, in fact, that ever since the war on terror began distracting U.S. activists and the U.S. public, no one seems to have noticed that most of the original apparatus of neoliberalism has entered into a crisis. The "Doha round" of the WTO was declared a failure in 2006, and the very existence of the institution is being called into question. The IMF is if anything in even deeper crisis. After the meltdown of the Argentine economy in 2002, and a veritable popular uprising against the entire political class, the social democratic president elected in 2003, Nestor Kirchner, had to make a dramatic move to restore the legitimacy of the very idea of government. So he defaulted on Argentina's foreign debt. This is precisely what the IMF is supposed to ensure never happens, and international bankers urged it to step in and punish the country, but for once it was unable to do so. This was for various reasons (partly the fact that the global movement had rendered it a pariah, partly that everyone knew its disastrous advice was largely responsible for the crisis in Argentina to begin with), but as a result the entire edifice of power-through-debt has begun to crack. Argentina and Brazil paid off their entire IMF debt; soon, with the help of Venezuela's petrodollars, so had the rest of Latin America. (Between 2003 and 2007, Latin America's total debt to the IMF declined by 98.4 percent. They basically owe nothing.) Russia, India, China all followed suit and, along with countries like Korea, Thailand, Malaysia, Indonesia, and the Philippines, now refuse to even talk about new loans. As a result the IMF itself, reduced largely to lording it over Africa, is rapidly itself going bankrupt. The World Bank holds on, but its revenue is radically reduced.

All this seems to be happening under the radar of the U.S. public. Meanwhile, in most of the rest of the world, lively arguments continue on what a different, more humane world economy might actually look like. In the United States, the movement has seen enormous debates between reformist ("anticorporate") and revolutionary ("anticapitalist") approaches. In much of the world, these arguments have come to turn more on the potential role of the state: pitting those that wish to see the creation of new forms of commons (the restoration of rights in land, water, oil, as communal resources) through the aegis of national governments against those that reject the state entirely and dream of a world of what is sometimes called "true globalization," without national borders or government bureaucracies, built on confederations of free communities managing their resources through direct democracy—in effect, through some form of libertarian communism. It is far too early to tell what will emerge from these conversations, whether new democratic forms will actually emerge or whether we will just see a reshuffling of the architecture of global bureaucracy. Neoliberalism is by no means dead: similar reforms are being carried out on a massive scale within newly emerging powers like India and China, where it is much harder to mobilize international opposition. But we might do well to pay attention to the arguments, because they may well prove critical to the future history of humanity.

NOTES

1. The sources are, respectively, Alex Emery, "Bolivia's Morales to Challenge U.S. after Election" (Update 3), Bloomberg Wire Services, December 19, 2005, www.bloomberg.com/apps/news?pid=10000086& sid=aEbMZeNviHPE; "Alternative Left Parties Sign Cooperation Agreement," *Deutsche Welle,* December 11, 2005, www.dw-world.de/dw/article/0,2144,1811746,00.html; George Dor, ed., "Alternatives to Neo-Liberalism," special issue, *Pambazuka News,* no. 234 (December 15, 2005), www.pambazuka.org/en/issue/234.

2. That was a paraphrase. The exact quote reads: "I feel about globalization a lot like I feel about the dawn. Generally speaking, I think it's a good thing that the sun comes up every morning. It does more good than harm . . . . But even if I didn't much care for the dawn there isn't much I could do about it." Thomas Friedman, *The Lexus and the Olive Tree* (New York: Anchor Books, 2000), xxi–xxii.

3. David Harvey, *A Brief History of Neoliberalism* (New York: Oxford University Press, 2005).

4. Thatcher was something of an exception in this regard, though it is to be noted that even she never got more than about a third of the popular vote.

5. Or to be more accurate, interest would not be counted as principal. By the mid-1980s most poor countries had in fact paid out much more than they had ever borrowed. The interest rates, however, were set so high as to make full repayment effectively impossible.

6. The idea of tying debt relief to political reforms was the brainchild of Reagan's secretary of state James Baker and become known as the Baker Plan.

7. The case of Madagascar is all the more telling because Zafy, a surgeon who was placed in power by a nonviolent revolution that replaced former dictator Didier Ratsiraka, had the impertinence to demand that the IMF provide one example of a poor country that had taken their advice and was now rich. After he refused to sign, the economic devastation was such that in the next election he was defeated by Ratsiraka, who vowed to reverse the policy. Five years later Ratsiraka was ousted by another popular uprising, but this time by a neoliberal yogurt magnate.

8. All the more so considering that the government that signed NAFTA had not been honestly elected but had won by fraud.

9. See Janine Wedel's *Collision and Collusion: The Strange Case of Western Aid to Eastern Europe, 1989–1998* (New York: St. Martin's Press, 1998). Wedel was the first anthropologist to tell this remarkable story.

10. The relation of this larger system and national governments has changed in significant ways over the course of the neoliberal period. At first government itself was widely represented as the problem: its simple removal was supposed to lead to the spontaneous emergence of market mechanisms. Investors, however, soon discovered that the open encouragement of greed and disparagement of the very idea of government tended to foster extreme corruption, which got in the way of business, all the more so after "shock therapy" in much of Eastern Europe led not to free markets but to lawless "gangster capitalism." Under Clinton, the emphasis shifted to the idea of "good governance," emphasizing especially the need to maintain an honest legal climate conducive to foreign investment.

11. World Commission on the Social Dimension of Globalization, *A Fair Globalization: Creating Opportunities for All* (Geneva: International Labour Office, 2004); UN Development Program, "Human Development Report," 1999, and "Human Development Report," 2003.

12. China is excluded for several reasons: in the first period, its autarkic policies kept it to a certain degree outside the larger system; in the second, its government dramatically flaunted major principles of neoliberal policy, strategically deploying just the sort of planning, protections, and easy credit arrangements that the rest of the developing world was being forced to abandon.

13. Robert Pollin, *Contours of Descent: U.S. Economic Fractures and the Landscape of Global Austerity* (London: Verso, 2003).

14. If statistics sometimes seem ambiguous, it is largely because many of these figures improved in much of East Asia—usually, in precisely those countries that resisted IMF pressure to pare back or privatize health and education. The declines in Africa and Latin America, where few countries were in a position to resist, were quite dramatic.

15. It has held pride of place since 2004. In the World Economic Forum's 2004–5 rankings, Finland is followed by the United States, then Sweden, Taiwan, Denmark, and Norway. Note that the top six do not include a single country following neoliberal orthodoxy, since the United States itself regularly defies most of the precepts it urges on other governments. For the full report, see World Economic Forum, "Global Competitiveness Report 2004–2005," October 2004, www.weforum.org/en/initiatives/gcp/Global%20Competitiveness%20Report/PastReports/index.htm.

16. One might consider this a perfect example of that hoary piece of economic wisdom: "if you owe the bank a million dollars, the bank owns you. If you owe the bank a hundred million, you own the bank."

17. Walden Bello, *Future in the Balance: Essays on Globalization and Resistance* (Oakland, CA: Food First Books, 2001). See also Walden Bello, *Dark Victory: The United States, Structural Adjustment, and Global Poverty* (Oakland, CA: Institute for Food and Development Policy, 1994).

18. Bello, *Dark Victory;* Harvey, *Brief History of Neoliberalism;* Immanuel Wallerstein, *The Decline of American Power: The U.S. in a Chaotic World* (New York: New Press, 2003).

19. The line is from Richard Overton's *An Arrow against All Tyrants* (Exeter: Rota, 1976). The best discussion of the political theory of possessive individualism is in C. B. MacPherson, *The Political Theory of Possessive Individualism* (Oxford: Oxford University Press, 1962).

20. Giovanni Arrighi, *The Long Twentieth Century: Money, Power, and the Origins of Our Times* (London: Verso, 1994).

21. The fact that the IMF operates under the UN umbrella is particularly ironic when one considers that the UN's Universal Charter of Human Rights specifies that all human beings have a right to food and shelter. It has never shown much ability to enforce such rights. The IMF, however, has intervened quite systematically and effectively against any country that has attempted to enact policies inspired by such principles.

22. The 1980s and 1990s certainly saw more market elements introduced into some of these bureaucracies, particularly with outsourcing of primary production, and new, Asian-inspired "just in time" production strategies. On the other hand it also saw unprecedented concentration of ownership. Few Americans are aware that almost all department stores in the United States, for instance, are now owned by one company, Macy's Retail Holdings. So in effect corporate bureaucracies became more flexible but far larger.

23. The most incisive analysis on the importance of different sorts of "commons" to capitalism has been made by the Midnight Notes Collective: they were the first to emphasize that while capitalists preferred to see a world in which all forms of common property administered by communities for their own collective benefit would be privatized or otherwise eliminated, they also promoted the creation of new forms of commons for their own benefit: for instance, collective responsibilities for research, transport, waste disposal, and new and elaborate security functions. Struggles over the definition and management of collective resources are thus the common theme of global resistance struggles that might otherwise seem to have next to nothing to do with one another, such as those of the Twenty-first Century Socialists in South America and of Islamic movements in the Middle East. See "Midnight Notes Collective," last updated January 4, 2005, www.midnightnotes.org/index2.htl, for the best introduction to this line of thought.

5

The Age of Wal-Mart

Jane L. Collins

PROFITS IN "POORVILLE"

Quarrels about Wal-Mart are everywhere these days, from the *Wall Street Journal* to the smallest local newspaper, on the Internet, in the blogosphere, and in state-houses and local planning commissions across the nation. The debates are fueled by a handful of vociferous watchdog groups, such as Wal-Mart Watch and Wake Up Wal-Mart, whose research supports labor and community battles against the company, and by the firm's own advocacy groups, such as Working Families for Wal-Mart, established to counter public criticism. Wal-Mart's detractors argue that its size, success, and political influence enable it "to rezone our cities, determine the real minimum wage, break trade unions, set the boundaries for popular culture and channel capital throughout the world." They link the firm's competitiveness to "the destruction of all that remains of New Deal social regulation" and its replacement with a "global system that relentlessly squeezes labor . . . from South Carolina to south China."[1] These critics say that, like the Pennsylvania Railroad in the late nineteenth century, U.S. Steel in the early twentieth century, and General Motors in the mid-twentieth century, Wal-Mart has become the template business for world capitalism and that the template it provides contributes to the insecurity of American workers. I will argue in this chapter that these claims understate Wal-Mart's influence.

Historian Nelson Lichtenstein has laid out the template argument in the following way: "Wal-Mart is setting a new standard that other firms have to follow if they hope to compete. . . . It is setting standards for the nation as a whole. It's almost legislating social policy, not in terms of votes and lobbying, but when it does something, it's so large, it's so influential, others follow it."[2] This argument attributes Wal-Mart's dominance to its size and global reach, which have been extensively chronicled in the popular press. Wal-Mart is the largest company in the world. It has over five thousand stores and employs over 1.2 million U.S. workers. With its sales of over $3 billion a year, it does more business than Target, Home Depot, Sears, Safeway, K-Mart, and Kroger combined. With annual profits in the tens of billions of dollars, Sam Walton's heirs are twice as wealthy as Bill Gates. As the largest profit-making enterprise in the world, Wal-Mart has no rival. Clearly market share and profitability are part of the story of Wal-Mart's dominance.[3]

Sociologists Edna Bonacich and Khaleelah Hardie take the idea of the template a bit further when they say that "Wal-Mart lowers labor standards, not just for its workers, but for employees of all competitors and potential competitors." They are suggesting that other firms emulate Wal-Mart, not just because it sets an example of how to be profitable in today's economy, but because if they do not find ways to offer "everyday low prices" they will lose market share. They must copy Wal-Mart's labor practices and logistics to stay in business.[4]

This chapter builds on these understandings but goes further to suggest that Wal-Mart's business practices forge a relationship between poverty and profits that is breathtaking in its implications for the economy as a whole. Wal-Mart is not only actively unraveling mid-twentieth-century bargains among workers, employers, and the state and wrapping its neoliberal assault on labor in nostalgia for the good old days and the flag. It is also *inverting* the mid-twentieth-century relationship between production and consumption that has come to be known as Fordism. This idea was first articulated by journalist Liza Featherstone in a 2005 article for the *Nation*. She said: "In a chilling reversal of Henry Ford's strategy, which was to pay his workers amply so they could buy Ford cars, Wal-Mart's stingy compensation policies contribute to an economy in which workers can only afford to shop at Wal-Mart."[5]

In what follows, I will explore the idea that Wal-Mart's success is built on—actually premised on—the impoverishment of workers, both here and abroad, who lose out in the race to the bottom. Like Featherstone, I will argue that, through payment of poverty-level wages to retail workers in the United States and sweatshop conditions in supplier factories abroad, Wal-Mart is creating consumers whose survival depends on the low prices thus achieved. As Wal-Mart's low wages and harsh labor practices reverberate throughout the economy, they unleash a vicious cycle in which profits, lower consumer prices, and poverty are intertwined. CEO Lee Scott's claim that the company gives consumers "a wage increase every time they shop with us" is frighteningly clear: workers who are paid little enough will have to stretch their wages by shopping at Wal-Mart.

A disclaimer: Wal-Mart has never been the subject of my research. But in recent years I have studied life at the lower end of the labor market in several settings. I have interviewed apparel workers in southern Virginia, central Mexico, and rural

Wisconsin and women transitioning off welfare in the declining industrial centers of Milwaukee and Racine. In every phase of this research I bumped into Wal-Mart in ways that highlighted the relationship between the firm's profits and poverty. Driving into Martinsville, Virginia, in the summer of 1999, I asked a Stop-N-Go clerk for directions to the Tultex apparel factory. "Straight ahead and left at the Wal-Mart," he said. When I drove into Dodgeville, Wisconsin, in 2003 looking for the Lands' End plant, the clerk at McDonald's directed me: "Right up there on the hill, across from Wal-Mart." I noticed, but did not dwell on, Wal-Mart's salient presence in the daily environment of the women I was interviewing.

In her article "Down and Out in Discount America," Liza Featherstone makes the case that Wal-Mart knows that its customer base is low-waged people. She cites evidence that the company takes out ads in poor communities on the days that women receive welfare checks and cites studies showing that 23 percent of Wal-Mart customers live on salaries of less than $25,000 a year and that 20 percent are too poor to even have a bank account. She quotes economists who have found a significant negative relationship between median household income and Wal-Mart's presence in the local labor market. While some upscale retailers worry that Wal-Mart also attracts a share of their more affluent customers, poor people have been and continue to be Wal-Mart's bread and butter. As one of Featherstone's sources noted: "They plant themselves right in the middle of Poorville."[6]

The connection between Wal-Mart's profits and poverty became clearer to me in 2004, when I was collecting the work histories of forty women who were losing access to welfare in Milwaukee and Racine, Wisconsin. Wal-Mart figured prominently in nearly every narrative. A large proportion of the women I spoke with had worked at Wal-Mart at one time or another and told stories about their experiences. Those who had not had often worked for Wal-Mart's competitors under conditions that were similar to and shaped by Wal-Mart's practices. An even larger proportion of the women—virtually all of them—shopped at Wal-Mart. What is more, they saw shopping at Wal-Mart as crucial to making ends meet—the only way they could afford to buy clothing and diapers for the children. As Wal-Mart moved aggressively into the grocery trade, they increasingly felt that way about food as well. These interviews convinced me that there is an integral, intentional, and multifaceted relationship between Wal-Mart and poverty.

HOW POVERTY AND PROFITS ARE RELATED

Perhaps the most thoroughgoing attempts to theorize the connection between production and consumption in an economy have come from regulation theory, a school of economics that arose in France in the 1960s and 1970s. Regulation theorists were concerned with a key paradox of capitalism: how its tendencies toward instability, crisis, and change were balanced by its ability to coalesce and stabilize around institutions, norms, and rules that promote stability. To explain this, regulation theorists developed the concept of regime of accumulation. A regime of accumulation is a relationship between production and consumption in an economy at a given moment. It includes norms governing work and the organization of production; financial rules and practices; rules governing the management of industries and corporations; accepted principles about how income should be shared among wages, profits, and taxes; and norms of consumption and related patterns of demand in the market. Regulation theorists believe that the stability of a regime of accumulation is linked to these formal and informal rules, laws, agreements, habits, and practices.[7]

Here is the story, in very broad strokes, of one regime of accumulation. In 1914, Henry Ford introduced the $5, eight-hour day on the basis of an understanding that mass production was going to require mass consumption and that, for his company to sell cars, workers would need enough income to buy them and enough leisure to use them. He maintained this approach even through the worst of the Depression. During the massive labor mobilizations of the 1930s, this vision of how the fruits of labor should be distributed was a powerful part of workers' ideas about how the world should be organized and what was fair. By the 1940s, as the United States began to recover from the crisis of the Depression, a new era of stability began to grow up around practices of assembly line production pioneered in the auto industry. Ford and General Motors were the template firms of that era. Not only did they pay their workers enough to buy cars and the other household necessities of the day, but they recognized unions and engaged in collective bargaining with their workers. The Treaty of Detroit in 1948 guaranteed that workers' income would increase annually regardless of inflation, recession, or corporate profitability. And increase it did: the real income of auto workers doubled between 1947 and 1973, and the real income of those in the bottom half of the U.S. income distribution rose as rapidly as the income of those in the top 10 percent during that period.[8]

This wage growth represented a new societal consensus about how income should be shared among workers and owners of capital. It was part of a mode of growth in the larger economy that was based on the following interlinked features: mass production, rising productivity based on economies of scale, rising incomes linked to productivity, increasing demand due to rising wages, increased profits based on full utilization of capacity, and increased investment in improved mass production. As Bob Jessop has pointed out, this virtuous cycle relied on separation of ownership and control in large, multidivisional, decentralized corporations; on monopoly pricing; and on union recognition and collective bargaining. It required wages indexed to productivity growth and retail price inflation and monetary credit policies oriented to securing demand.[9] Not all workers and branches of industry participated directly in mass production—racial and gender segregation relegated many to a secondary sector of work that was far less stable and well paid. But the wage bargains struck in companies like Ford and General Motors spread through comparability claims. Integral to these social arrangements, which Antonio Gramsci christened "Fordism," was the consumption of standardized commodities in nuclear family households. The newly emerging Keynesian state played key roles in managing conflict between owners and workers, in providing social benefits to elderly and unemployed white male workers, and in providing collective goods and services.

Beginning in the 1970s, these arrangements became unstable. Many economists argue that this was due to rigidities in the system: the rigidity of fixed investments in large factories, the rigidity of labor contracts and lifelong bargains with workers, and the rigidity of the state's commitments to social programs. The crisis was also linked to the sharp recession and oil shocks of 1973, which caused instability in world financial markets and led to new patterns of global investment. Inflation, excess capacity, and intensifying global competition drove corporations to find ways to roll back their bargains with workers. Through the next three decades, the rise of neoliberal public policy and the erosion of Fordism went hand in hand.

Scholars have spent a great deal of time arguing about how to properly characterize the years since 1973. The approach that has gained most traction argues that we are now in an era of "flexible accumulation." Proponents of this view, which is associated most closely with the work of Michael Piore and Charles Sabel and their book *The Second Industrial Divide*, see large corporations being replaced by new lean firms that subcontract production and services. Piore and Sabel argue that whereas mass production used special-purpose machines and employed semiskilled workers to produce standardized goods, flexible firms use skilled workers to produce small batches of customized goods on a quick-response basis. They argue that these new economic arrangements foster worker participation in decentralized decision making and a culture of cooperation and trust among firms.[10] Other social scientists see the rise of new "flexible" arrangements more critically, noting that it essentially frees firms to reduce wages, increase hours, undercut unions, and demand concessions from workers, taking advantage of uneven development to pit workers in different places and different sectors against each other.[11]

How does Wal-Mart fit into this picture? Sam Walton started Wal-Mart in 1962. During the 1970s, the company expanded out of the South "like molasses spreading through tier after tier of rural and exurban counties." As Lichtenstein has noted, the firm emerged out of a rural southern context "that barely tolerated New Deal social regulation, the civil rights revolution or the feminist [movement]." It promulgated "an ideology of family, faith and small town sentimentality that coexists in strange harmony with a world of transnational commerce, stagnant living standards and a stressful work life."[12] As historian Nancy MacLean argues, these kinds of southern ideas, rooted in the social relations of slavery and white privilege, offered a new and appealing model to nascent neoliberals of the 1980s and 1990s, especially to corporations clamoring for ways to roll back the moral economy of

Fordism.[13] Lichtenstein claims that "Wal-Mart's Christian entrepreneurialism and faux egalitarianism translated Reagan-era conservative populism into tropes that worked to legitimate the firm's hierarchy," such as calling workers "associates."[14] Framing the corporation as a family and a bastion of homespun values masked its stingy wages, harsh work rules, and discriminatory practices. As Bethany Moreton emphasizes, Wal-Mart's cultivated traditionalism is a new creation. Its folksy formulations were not behind the curve in labor relations but ahead of it, shaping the emerging contours of a new regime of accumulation, a new set of patterned relations between production and consumption, and a new (though contested) consensus among workers, employers, and the state.[15]

What gave a retailer emerging out of Bentonville, Arkansas, the power to hijack a regime of accumulation? The model that Wal-Mart was constructing had a sound footing in an entrepreneurial strategy that gave it power and influence unprecedented for a firm in the retail sector. Three features were key. To start with, Wal-Mart was a first mover in adopting four new technologies associated with what has come to be called "lean retailing." These included the use of bar codes and scanning devices, computerized inventory management, automated distribution centers, and electronic data interchange along its supply chain. To quote analysts, the firm emerged as the "undisputed leader of supply chain rationalization" and the "major driver of technology-based productivity gains in the American economy."[16] Second, during the 1980s (ironically the high point of its "Buy American" advertising campaigns), Wal-Mart was establishing relationships with offshore manufacturers, particularly in Asia. By the mid-1980s, almost half of all the merchandise sold in its stores was imported, a figure now closer to 85 percent.[17] Third, by the mid-1980s, Wal-Mart's buying power had grown so large that it gained the upper hand in its relationships with suppliers, allowing the firm not only to dictate the price of an order but to insist that suppliers adopt bar coding, electronic data interchange, and other technologies. In Lichtenstein's words, "For the first time in the history of modern capitalism, the Wal-Mart template has made the retailer king and the manufacturer his vassal."[18]

THE DOUBLE LIFE OF LOW-WAGE WORKERS

In the film *Wal-Mart: The High Cost of Low Price*, a woman leaves Wal-Mart and cashes her paycheck in order to return to Wal-Mart to shop.[19] Liza Featherstone writes of the "solidarity across the check-out counter" that results from this double connection to discount shopping.[20] While Barbara Ehrenreich, in her brief stint working in a Minnesota Wal-Mart, confessed to hating customers she perceived as sloppy, demanding, and obese, the women Featherstone spoke to said things like "I always loved shopping there. . . . That's why I wanted to work there."[21] In the interviews I conducted in Milwaukee, women talked about being able to buy at Wal-

Mart as a benefit of being employed there; they spoke of family members working at the store who brought home sale-priced diapers and clothing purchased with an employee discount. This link between workers and consumers is more important than it might seem at first glance; in fact, the secret of Wal-Mart's success lies in the dense, gendered connection between these two roles.

For the women I interviewed in Milwaukee, shopping at Wal-Mart was both pleasurable and a crucial part of their strategy for making a $628 welfare check or a $750 paycheck last their families for a month. For these women, meeting their children's needs was a constant struggle. As one woman explained: "Everything you face every day, the first thing you're faced with is 'I got to do this by myself.' I got to come up with food by myself. I got to come up with clothes by myself. . . . If they need anything, I got to come up with the money to get it. Everything is just a hardship, from school to the summer. They want summer clothes, so now you got to worry about summer clothes. You got to come up with this stuff." Another told us, "I'd like to do better for them. I wish I could be like, 'Hey guys, it's a Friday night. Here, mom will get you some new shoes, or some new clothes.' I can't do that, and I feel bad." Still another said, "It's either they're bustin' out of their coats or their pants don't fit and you're scrounging up change to get them a new pair of shoes, you know."

Several women saw Wal-Mart's low prices as helping them provide for their children within their budgets. One young single mother of three told me: "When times get bad, I don't mind shopping at Wal-Mart. Wal-Mart is $2.88 on the clearance rack for nice outfits like she's got on here." An older woman explained that because her teenaged son refused to wear Wal-Mart clothes she could get him only one outfit at the beginning of the school year, but because her daughter didn't mind shopping there she "could get her a little bit more." She said, "I told her brother if he didn't like it, he could change his name brand of clothes." A young woman spoke to the pleasure of shopping at Wal-Mart: "I'm a Wal-Mart girl," she said. "Even with my preferred customer card, I spend too much there." A mother of five, after describing the complex budgeting strategy that allowed her to make it through the month, said, "I shop at Wal-Mart because they have nice clothes for all of us." All of the women I talked to relied on Wal-Mart or other discount retailers to obtain diapers or baby formula, reduce their grocery bills, or keep their children in clothing and shoes.

Wal-Mart is aware that its low prices are indispensable to some consumers and appealing to many. Whenever critics point to unfair labor practices or the ways the firm strong-arms local communities over zoning issues, the company responds by pointing to its low prices. The firm's Web site claims to save working families "countless millions on the everyday items they need for daily life"—over $2,300 per household per year. It says that Wal-Mart lowers the grocery bills of families who shop there by 20 percent over competitors' prices. CEO Lee Scott suggests that these savings represent a "wage increase" for the working poor. But unlike money in a pay-check, which can be saved or used for any purpose, this raise can be realized only by shopping at Wal-Mart. The company is so focused on low prices as the hook that guarantees public loyalty that one activist has commented, "Every time we try to talk about quality of life, they bring up the price of underpants."[22]

Like all discount retailers, Wal-Mart can sell at such low prices because of its sales volume. Big box discounters turn product over two to three times faster than traditional department stores, and Wal-Mart is the fastest. Crucial to its formula is keeping labor costs to less than 15 percent of sales, or about half of what they are in most department stores.[23] The key to Wal-Mart's success in delivering on this model, and in continually "rolling back" prices, is its demand that store managers "beat yesterday" by increasing sales and decreasing labor costs in every department over the previous period. The company applies this same dictate to its supplier fac-tories, demanding either higher quality or lower unit price in every product cate-gory for each new contract. Low prices are thus transformed into a relentless force driving down wages and increasing the stress of work both for U.S. retail employ-ees and for factory workers here and abroad.[24]

Wal-Mart's low wages have been well documented. The average hourly starting wage for a sales associate in 2005 was $7.05. For a cashier it was $7.20. A full-time worker would thus bring home between $12,000 and $14,000 a year, far below the federal poverty line of $19,157 or a living wage as calculated anywhere in the coun-try.[25] The media have also begun to pay significant attention to Wal-Mart's stingy benefits. Until recently, full-time employees had to wait six months before they were eligible for any coverage; part-time employees had to wait two years. The insurance provided excluded many important items, such as vaccinations and well-child vis-its, and had deductibles as high as $1,000. The company expected employees to pay one-third of their premium; this share could be as high as $400 a month, often 40 percent of a paycheck or higher. For this reason only 44 percent of Wal-Mart's em-ployees choose coverage under this plan.[26] In response to public criticism, Wal-Mart upgraded its health plan in the fall of 2007, cutting the waiting period from two years to one and offering a wider array of plans. Now workers can pay as little as $250 a year for bare-bones plans with a $4,000 deductible, while better plans with lower deductibles can cost up to $7,000 a year. The company still insures fewer than half of its employees.[27] At the same time, Wal-Mart's workers' compensation poli-cies were drawn into the public spotlight after the State of Washington's Depart-ment of Labor and Industries—in response to the company's repeated refusal to pay claims—seized control of its program, saying, "Wal-Mart has shown itself un-willing or unable to manage its workers compensation program as required by law."[28]

The media have seized on the health care issue because most of the employees who are not covered are eligible for state medical assistance. In Wisconsin, in 2004, the state spent $1.8 million to cover Wal-Mart workers and their children. The state of Tennessee spent $15.3 million and the state of California $32 million. As one woman in Milwaukee told me, the personnel officer at Wal-Mart explained to her "off the record" that with her salary she would still be eligible for state medical assistance and "that might be a better value." In 2005, several states passed "fair share" bills that would require Wal-Mart and other large employers to do better. The most visible campaign was in Maryland, where the legislature passed a measure that obliged all employers with more than ten thousand employees to spend at least 8 percent of their payroll on health benefits or to put the money directly into the state's health program for the poor. As Wal-Mart was the only firm large enough to be affected, the bill became known as the Wal-Mart Bill. Governor Robert Ehrlich vetoed the measure, but the legislature overturned his veto in January 2006. In July 2006, a federal judge struck down the law.[29]

The salaries of many Wal-Mart workers are also low enough that they remain eligible for food stamps, free lunches, and subsidized housing. Wal-Mart employees' participation in these programs cost the state of California $54 million in 2004.[30] As more and more public assistance goes to the working poor, these trends have unleashed public debate about taxpayer subsidies to corporations.

One of the young women we interviewed, who worked at Wal-Mart thirty-six hours a week, vividly illustrated the impact of the company's low wages on her family's standard of living. "I want my kids to have more than what they have," she said, "but financially, it's kind of hard. It makes me sad. I just wish they had more than what they have. Like their own rooms . . . stuff of their own. 'Cause we all sleep in my room and it's crowded. They have the TV there, and their toys."

In addition to low wages and poor benefits, Wal-Mart is facing increasing legal pressure for violating labor and antidiscrimination laws. The company's 2005 annual report listed more than forty pending wage and hour cases currently seeking class action status. These cases allege that the company forced employees to work off the clock or deprived them of breaks. The company has settled lawsuits with sixty-nine thousand workers who claimed that they had been forced to work unpaid hours.[31] One of the Wal-Mart workers I interviewed in Milwaukee started each day at 2:00 p.m. and was supposed to clock out at 10:00 p.m., when the store closed and when the last bus left to return to her neighborhood. Managers told her that she was expected to stay until 11:00 to help clean up the store. When she said that she couldn't because she would not have a way home, they cut her hours back to part time.

In July of 2000, Wal-Mart's own internal audit found tens of thousands of instances of employees working through breaks and meals and over a thousand cases of minors working too late, during school hours, or too many hours a day.[32] Since 1995, the less-than-aggressive Bush-era National Labor Relations Board has issued more than sixty complaints against Wal-Mart.[33] Two of the company's union-busting efforts were sufficiently brazen to make the national and international news: the firm's closure of a store in Quebec after a successful union certification drive and its "phaseout" of in-store meat preparation and packing after meat cutters organized at a store in Texas.[34] In addition, in *Dukes v. Wal-Mart*, the largest class action lawsuit ever mounted, over one million current and former employees charged Wal-Mart with systematic gender discrimination in pay and promotions.[35]

Finally, Wal-Mart has perfected a kind of workplace control that Rosen has called "management by intimidation." She argues that the imperative for managers to reduce costs over the previous year results in deliberate understaffing. Scheduling formulas are devised at Wal-Mart headquarters in Bentonville. Rosen quotes a manager as saying, "There is not a store out there that is allowed to run the kind of hours that are needed." For workers, this generates a constant sense of insufficient time. In addition, Wal-Mart's state-of-the-art information technology systems create stress as managers push employees to work to the speed of the new system.[36] Thomas Adams has described how the layout of Wal-Mart's stores facilitates continuous surveillance.[37] One example of how far the company will go is their practice of locking in workers overnight. In 2004, the national press carried stories of a worker in Corpus Christi, Texas, who was injured by equipment while working in the store at night and could not be reached by an ambulance because workers were locked in. Subsequent investigations revealed that this was a common practice across the country and that other workers had experienced problems getting health care during asthma attacks and had been unable to leave to respond to family crises.[38]

In 2003, all the major media in the United States carried the news that federal agents had raided Wal-Mart headquarters and sixty of their stores in twenty-one states, arresting more than three hundred illegal workers. While the workers were technically employed by firms subcontracted to clean its stores, federal agents alleged that Wal-Mart knew that the contractors were hiring illegal immigrants. A number of immigrants have since filed suit, claiming that Wal-Mart's contractors exploited their immigration status to avoid paying them overtime, filing their taxes, or making required workers' compensation contributions. Wal-Mart agreed to pay a fine and to take internal measures to ensure that illegal immigrant workers would not be hired in the future.

Women in Milwaukee had many stories about harsh management practices. One woman, who had a back injury, was fired for allowing a customer to lift a large bag of water softener salt onto the conveyor belt. Another, who had worked for Wal-Mart for several years and had been promoted to claims manager, said, "I ended up getting fired for taking my break fifteen minutes early because I had to use the restroom. And I was pregnant, mind you. They called it time theft because it wasn't my scheduled time to take my break." These labor practices contribute to Wal-Mart's 40 percent annual turnover in employment. But this extraordinarily high rate—close to that of McDonald's—does not worry Wal-Mart. Secret memos leaked from the company's headquarters in 2005 revealed that it actively sought to push out all employees making more than $10 an hour.

As disturbing as these labor conditions are, they are far better than the situation in the offshore factories Wal-Mart contracts to produce its beach balls and tank tops, lawn furniture and shoes. Because of their imperative to produce at the lowest price, Wal-Mart drives the global "race to the bottom" in wages. While CEO H. Lee Scott made over $17 million in 2004, and the average U.S. Wal-Mart employee made $9.68 per hour, workers in Bangladesh and China made $0.17 an hour, those in Nicaragua $0.23, and those in Indonesia $0.46.[39] Wal-Mart's size and reach result in the extension of its low-wage practices beyond its own contract factories. As STITCH notes: "Wal-Mart is a pricing leader, meaning that once they set an incredibly low price, all other retailers are then expected to offer the same price and must cut costs to do so. Therefore, the practices and policies of Wal-Mart set the retail standard and even more workers are ultimately affected."[40] Because of the scope of Wal-Mart's retail presence, these price pressures affect a wide range of sectors, from electronics, consumer goods, and clothing to agriculture.

The company claims that it bears no responsibility for what happens in these factories, since it is not the direct employer of the workers and since it asks the contract factories to follow a code of conduct. But conditions in factories that produce for Wal-Mart are notoriously harsh. Workers in Dhaka, Bangladesh, report working fifteen hours per day, seven days a week, without proper overtime pay. Women in Guatemala say they have been forced to take illegal pregnancy tests before and during employment. Workers producing for Wal-Mart in Shenzhan, China, have reported working eleven-hour days, with half of their wages deducted for dormitory rent. Women as young as fourteen labor up to fourteen hours a day in Honduran factories. Managers deny them sick leave and closely monitor bathroom breaks. Workers producing for Wal-Mart in Bangladesh make less than $50 a month, and Canadian journalists have documented child labor in Wal-Mart's contract factories there, after the company claimed to have fully implemented its code of conduct.[41]

In its offshore operations, as in the United States and Canada, Wal-Mart is among the most antiunion corporations in the world, and workers who try to unionize in any of its factories face reprisals. For this reason, as well as low wages, the company finds it congenial to operate in China, where state-sponsored unions are an instrument of labor control and other forms of organizing are actively repressed. In 2001, violence against women organizing union drives at Choi Sin and CIMA Textiles factories in Guatemala—where Wal-Mart had contracts—was widely documented. While Liz Claiborne, which also produced in these factories, spoke out against the repression by supervisors and antiunion workers, Wal-Mart did not.

Workers abroad also feel the impact of Wal-Mart's "beat yesterday" policy, which is known to its international suppliers as the "plus one" policy. A Wal-Mart vice president explained, "For each item a factory handles they must either lower the cost or raise the quality" on each order. As one worker suffering from a severe repetitive stress injury reported, "There is always an acceleration. The goals are always increasing but the pay stays the same." Her Korean boss said that Wal-Mart was paying $3 for a shirt—less than last year's price. He said, "I think we have reached the limit."[42] Factory managers in Indonesia tell employees that they cannot pay the legally mandated wage because Wal-Mart does not pay the managers enough per item to cover it.[43]

THE DOWNWARD SPIRAL

What do these interlinked experiences—those of Wal-Mart's customers, its retail associates, and the workers who assemble its merchandise—tell us about its corporate strategy and the effect of that strategy on the U.S. economy as a whole? Liza Featherstone quotes an official of the United Food and Commercial Workers union who explains that appealing to the poor "was Sam Walton's real genius. He figured out how to make money off of poverty. He located his first stores in poor rural areas and discovered a real market. The only problem with the business model is that it really needs to create more poverty to grow."[44]

How does Wal-Mart create more poverty? Not simply by paying its own workers poverty wages and denying them health care. An increasing body of evidence supports what workers have been saying for quite some time: that Wal-Mart's presence in a local labor market depresses wages. Studies in San Diego County, California, associated Wal-Mart's entry into the regional economy with an annual decline in wages and benefits of between $105 and $221 million.[45] A study of three thousand counties nationwide showed that those with more Wal-Mart stores had larger increases in the poverty rate than counties with fewer or no Wal-Marts. It concluded that "the presence of Wal-Mart unequivocally raised poverty rates in U.S. counties in the 1990s relative to places that had no such stores."[46] A third study found that Wal-Mart's incursion into the Southern California grocery market triggered a dynamic in which grocery stores negotiated with workers for reduced compensation in an attempt to relevel the playing field, lowering wages at area grocers by as much as $8 an hour.[47]

Wal-Mart's large shadow, both as a direct employer and as a competitor with low labor costs, creates an impact on the economy so pervasive that in 2005 the independent humor rag the *Onion*, famous for its fake headlines, could quip, "Okie Hears There's Sam's Club Work in New Mexico."[48] What followed was a short story about day laborer Carl Thornton, who was ready to drive his family from the Oklahoma Wal-Mart where they had worked the stockroom for generations to a Sam's Club in Las Cruces where they would unload pallets of toilet paper, baby food, and cans of peaches "so big, you got to use two hands to lift 'em." Not only does the coming of Wal-Mart drive clothing stores, groceries, and hardware outlets out of business, but, to remain competitive, the retailers that remain have to adopt labor practices that look increasingly like Wal-Mart's; soon, Wal-Mart-style labor practices dominate the landscape for the working poor.

The reverse Fordism that Wal-Mart unleashes links the company's growth and profits to the expansion of a low-waged, near-poverty-level population. The firm expands that sector by pushing down wages in its stores and setting the labor cost parameters that its competitors must meet. Thus the virtuous cycle of Fordism is transformed into a vicious downward spiral: downward pressure on wages creates more people who need to shop at Wal-Mart, and the "beat yesterday" policy that allows the firm to continually roll back prices for these consumers unleashes new waves of cost cutting, wage reductions, and hours violations both here and abroad. This relationship between Wal-Mart's everyday low prices and the impoverishment of the workforce gives new meaning to what Herbert Gans once called "the uses of poverty."

Of course, every regime of accumulation generates its own contradictions. Wal-Mart is generating resistance, through watchdog groups that mobilize consumer pressure, through neighborhood associations that question the economic benefits it claims to bring and take issue with the subsidies it receives, and through muckraking journalists, lawsuits, and the emerging strategy of a Wal-Mart employees' association.[49] But there are contradictions within the economy as well.

Many scholars who theorize the end of Fordism argue that, in the 1970s, the U.S. economy reached a point when it needed to throw off the fetters of the Keynesian welfare state and the bargains with a unionized workforce in order to free capital to invest and be productive once again. But the assumption in these accounts was that unfettered capital would create new and better jobs—that cutting spending on social programs and rolling back labor regulation would open new opportunities for growth, not just in profits, but in productivity and well-being. In the scenarios laid out by neoliberal policy makers, a new market-driven economy would harness new technologies and generate new, skilled higher-paying jobs.

Whether we agree with that rosy prediction or not, it is clear that Wal-Mart has hijacked a large portion of the economic activity of this new phase, linking its own growth, not to skilled and lucrative jobs, but to a downward-spiraling relationship between production and consumption. Wal-Mart is not the whole of the economy and never will be. Given the tremendous bifurcation of wealth that is occurring in America, other retailers will make their fortunes purveying high-end goods to the very rich. But with $2.5 billion in sales and a ranking at the top of the Fortune 500, Wal-Mart runs a business model that profits from this growing class schism and contributes to it through its labor practices and retail strategy. This means that for the first time in U.S. history a substantial portion of the retail sector and its associated manufacturing has a material interest, not in increasing consumer incomes, but in perpetuating the poverty that makes shopping at Wal-Mart their best option.

After twenty-five years in which neoliberalism and market fundamentalism gained strength, the years from 2004 to 2006 revealed a growing public debate about where this had brought us. Outspoken voices were asking what it meant that two decades had passed without an increase in the minimum wage, that a significant portion of the U.S. population had no health care, and that corporations had acquired more rights than people. One could sense the emergence of what Karl Polanyi called "a double movement"—a public outcry for measures that would temper the treatment of labor as a simple commodity.[50] Debates over Wal-Mart—attempts to require the firm to provide better benefits, pay living wages, and behave as a better corporate citizen in the communities where it does business—were central to these debates as they played out at mid-decade. Because of the company's size and its role in driving new practices in the retail sector, solving the problem of Wal-Mart will have major implications for the outcome of these debates. It will challenge us to rethink the relationship, not just between firms and their workers, but among corporations, the state, and citizens who both consume and labor within their enterprise.

NOTES

1. Nelson Lichtenstein, ed., *Wal-Mart: The Face of 21st-Century Capitalism* (New York: New Press, 2006), 3–4.

2. Nelson Lichtenstein, "Interview: Is Wal-Mart Good for America?" *Frontline*, November 16, 2004, transcript, Public Broadcasting Service, www.pbs.org/wgbh/pages/frontline/shows/walmart/interviews/lichtenstein.html.

3. Lichtenstein, *Wal-Mart*; Annette Bernhardt, Anmol Chaddha, and Siobhan McGrath, "What Do We Know about Wal-Mart?" (Economic Policy Brief No. 2, Brennan Center for Justice, New York University School of Law, 2005).

4. Edna Bonacich and Khaleelah Hardie, "Wal-Mart and the Logistics Revolution," in Lichtenstein, *Wal-Mart*, 181.

5. Liza Featherstone, "Down and Out in Discount America," *Nation*, January 3, 2005.

6. Ibid.

7. Ash Amin, "Post-Fordism," in *Post-Fordism: A Reader*, ed. Ash Amin (Cambridge: Blackwell, 1994), 1–40.

8. David Harvey, *The Condition of Postmodernity: An Enquiry into the Origins of Cultural Change* (Cambridge: Blackwell, 1989), ch. 8; Nelson Lichtenstein, *State of the Union: A Century of American Labor* (Princeton, NJ: Princeton University Press, 2002), 130–40.

9. Bob Jessop, "Thatcherism and Flexibility," in *The Politics of Flexibility: Restructuring State and Industry in Britain, Germany, and Scandinavia*, ed. Bob Jessop et al. (Aldershot: Edward Elger, 1991), 136–37.

10. Michael J. Piore and Charles F. Sabel, *The Second Industrial Divide: Possibilities for Prosperity* (New York: Basic Books, 1984).

11. Mike Parker and Jane Slaughter, *Choosing Sides: Unions and the Team Concept* (Boston: South End Press, 1988); Harvey, *Condition of Postmodernity*, ch. 9.

12. Lichtenstein, *Wal-Mart*, 20, .3.

13. Nancy MacLean, "Southern Dominance in Borrowed Language," in *New Landscapes of Inequality: Neoliberalism and the Erosion of Democracy in America*, ed. Jane Collins, Micaela di Leonardo, and Brett Williams (Santa Fe, NM: SAR Press, 2008).

14. Lichtenstein, *Wal-Mart*, 17.

15. Bethany E. Moreton, "It Came from Bentonville," in Lichtenstein, *Wal-Mart*, 61, 82.

16. Misha Petrovic and Gary Hamilton, "Making Global Markets," in Lichtenstein, *Wal-Mart*, 137–38.

17. Ibid., 137; and Lichtenstein, "Interview."

18. Lichtenstein, *Wal-Mart*, 45.

19. Robert Greenwald, dir., *Wal-Mart: The High Cost of Low Price* (Brave New Films, 2005).

20. Featherstone, "Down and Out," n.p.

21. Barbara Ehrenreich, *Nickel and Dimed: On (Not) Getting By in America* (New York: Metropolitan Books, 2001), 163; Featherstone, "Down and Out," n.p.

22. Greenwald, *Wal-Mart*.

23. Lichtenstein, *Wal-Mart*, 13.

24. Ellen Rosen, "How to Squeeze More Out of a Penny," in Lichtenstein, *Wal-Mart*, 254.

25. For a family of four, this would be $31,000 in Nebraska and $64,650 in Boston. Elizabeth Cohn, "Wal-Mart: A College Curriculum—The World's Largest Company and Its Impact," December 1, 2005, Center for Community and Corporate Ethics, Wal-Mart Watch, http://walmartwatch.com/docs/walmart-curriculum.pdf), 15.

26. Bernhardt, Chaddha, and McGrath, *What Do We Know?* 2–3.

27. Michael Barbaro and Reed Abelson, "A Health Plan for Wal-Mart: Less Stinginess," *New York Times*, November 13, 2007.

28. Ellen Rosen, "Adding Insult to Injury: Wal-Mart's Workers Compensation Scam," *New Labor Forum* 17, no. 1 (2008): 63.

29. "Maryland Legislature Overrides Veto on 'Wal-Mart Bill,'" *Washington Post*, January 13, 2006.

30. Arindrajit Dube and Ken Jacobs, "Hidden Cost of Wal-Mart Jobs" (briefing paper, Berkeley Labor Center, University of California, August 2, 2004), http://laborcenter.berkeley.edu/retail/walmart.pdf.

31. "Federal Jury Finds Wal-Mart Guilty in Overtime Pay Case," *Chicago Tribune*, December 20, 2003, 3.

32. Steven Greenhouse, "Walmart Forces Workers to Toil Off the Clock," *New York Times*, June 25, 2002, A1.

33. International Confederation of Free Trade Unions, *Internationally Recognized Core Labour Standards in the United States*, Geneva, January 14–16, 2004.

34. Ian Austen, "Quebec Rules against Wal-Mart in Closing of Unionized Store," *New York Times*, September 20, 2005, C7; Constance Hays, "Here's the Beef: So Where's the Butcher?" *New York Times*, February 15, 2003, C1.

35. Liza Featherstone, *Selling Women Short: Gender Inequality on Wall Street* (New York: Basic Books, 2004).

36. Rosen, "How to Squeeze More," 246, 250.

37. Thomas Adams, "Making the New Shop Floor," in Lichtenstein, *Wal-Mart*, 213–30.

38. "Workers Assail Night Lock-Ins by Wal-Mart," *New York Times*, January 18, 2004.

39. Sarah Anderson, "Wal-Mart's Pay Gap," April 15, 2005, Institute for Policy Studies, www.wakeupwalmart.com/facts/Wal-mart-pay-gap.pdf.

40. STITCH, "What Do Wal-Mart's Low Prices Mean for Women Globally," 2006, www.stitchonline.org/archives/womenandwalmart.asp.

41. Anderson, "Wal-Mart's Pay Gap"; "Wal-Mart to Cut Ties with Bangladesh Factories Using Child Labour," CBC News, November 30, 2005, www.cbc.ca/world/story/2005/11/30/walmartbangladesh051130.html; STITCH, "What Do Wal-Mart's Low Prices Mean?"

42. "It's Wal-Mart's Way, or No Way, the World Over," *Los Angeles Times*, January 3, 2003.

43. Anderson, "Wal-Mart's Pay Gap."

44. Featherstone, "Down and Out."

45. David Karjanen, "The Wal-Mart Effect and the New Face of Capitalism," in Lichtenstein, *Wal-Mart*, 143–62.

46. Stephen J. Goetz and Hema Swaminthan, "Wal-Mart and County-Wide Poverty," *Social Science Quarterly* 87, no. 2 (2006): 211–33.

47. Arindrajit Dube, Barry Eidlin, and Bill Lester, "Impact of Wal-Mart Growth on Earnings throughout the Retail Sector" (Working Paper No. 126, University of California, Berkeley, Institute of Industrial Relations, 2005), http://repositories.cdlib.org/iir/iirwps-126-05.

48. "Okie Hears There's Sam's Club Work in New Mexico," *Onion*, November 9, 2005.

49. Wade Rathke, "A Wal-Mart Workers Association?" in Lichtenstein, *Wal-Mart*, 261–84.

50. Karl Polanyi, *The Great Transformation* (1944; repr., New York: Beacon, 2001), 79.

6

Deindustrializing Chicago

A Daughter's Story

Christine J. Walley

When I was fourteen, my world was turned upside down. My mom entered my bedroom and shook my shoulder as I lay sleeping. She said quietly, "Don't worry, it'll be okay. They called the ore boat back, but it'll be all right." I was puzzled why we should be worrying about an "oar boat" but drowsily accepted her reassurances. Only later did I learn that the recall of the ore boat meant that the financial lenders to the Wisconsin Steel Works, where my father worked in a rolling mill, had foreclosed on the property, sending it into bankruptcy. It was a crucial moment of rupture, sharply dividing our lives into a time Before the Mill Went Down and After the Mill Went Down. Wisconsin Steel's collapse in 1980 was also a harbinger of things to come for the Calumet area,[1] once one of the largest steel-producing regions in the world, as well as for the United States as a whole. In the ensuing years, the steel mills in Southeast Chicago would close one by one. As stunned residents strove to assimilate what had happened, some noted bitterly that the situation was even worse than that of the 1930s Great Depression. At least after the Depression, they said, the mills had reopened and people had gone on with their lives. This time, the steel mills were gone for good. Their closing would tear through a social fabric that had sustained generations. Although the midwestern part of the United States may have been hit particularly hard by deindustrialization, what happened in Southeast Chicago is not unique. Over the last quarter-century, variations of such experiences have occurred—and continue to occur—throughout the country, creating a widespread sense of insecurity for countless Americans.

This account of Southeast Chicago and the trauma its residents went through is unabashedly personal. It is a story of my childhood, my family, and the area in which I was raised. Yet I am also writing as an anthropologist. Some might even describe this work as "autoethnography," or what Deborah Reed-Danahay defines as "a form of self-narrative that places the self within a social context."[2] Autobiographies, although focusing on individuals, can be powerful tools to illuminate larger social forces. Yet what I am concerned with here is more particular: the revealing points of awkwardness between the personal stories that we wish to tell and the broader societal narratives through which we are encouraged to make sense of our experiences. Carolyn Steedman's work provides a classic example of what we can learn by paying attention to such tensions.[3] Her raw personal account of growing up working class in post–World War II London shattered romantic, mythical stereotypes of a close-knit British laboring class by pointing to the gap between such assumptions and the experiences of women on the margins such as her mother. Although the stories we tell about ourselves are of necessity built upon, and given meaning through, references to more dominant societal narratives, it is these points of tension and omission that I find most instructive. As we attempt to narrate our lives, where do we feel constrained? What are the discrepancies between our own stories and those that others wish to tell for us? What do such gaps reveal about our social worlds? While autobiography (and the tensions it encapsulates) can illuminate far more than a single life, anthropology can, in return, offer useful tools in the art of self-examination. It does so by encouraging an ethnographic tacking back and forth between the details of personal lives and the collective dynamics that link us, providing greater depth to the stories that we tell about our pasts and our presents, both individually and as a society.

As a kid who thought that Southeast Chicago was the core of the universe, I was almost entirely unaware of outside depictions of my own community. The people who inhabited the TV shows, movies, and books to which I had access seemed to live in a parallel universe that had little to do with me or my family. Consequently, it was an odd sensation to discover later that Southeast Chicago had a certain notoriety, at least among academics. Historically, scholars from the University of Chicago regularly used the nearby working-class or poor neighborhoods on Chicago's South Side for sociological studies of immigrants or racial and ethnic "succession." William Kornblum even conducted research on Wisconsin Steel for his book *Blue Collar Community* during the same period in the 1970s when my father was working as a shearman in the No. 5 rolling mill.[4] Other scholars of deindustrialization have offered accounts of the notoriously shady dealings that contributed to Wisconsin Steel's demise.[5] Nevertheless, the language of social class in academic accounts can, at times, feel distressingly distant from its lived realities,[6] and the kinds of awkward moments with which I am concerned rarely enter the picture. Writing a personal narrative of deindustrialization offers a way to capture what academic accounts often miss and highlights the painful but instructive tensions between individual experience and broader societal understandings.

Although I have wanted to tell this story almost to the point of obsession since

I was a teenager, there are obstacles to speaking about growing up white and working class in the United States. Perhaps this should not be surprising in a country where both rich and poor prefer to locate themselves in an amorphous "middle class" and where class differences are often referenced through other kinds of coded language, including those of race and ethnicity. The difficulties in telling this kind of story are instructive, and I have watched other family members struggle with similar questions: How does one find the confidence to believe that one's story is worth telling and that others should listen? How does one find the language to express such experiences or make the words stick to intended meanings? How does one keep one's meaning from being derailed or appropriated by the accounts of more powerful others? In this attempt to tell my own story and that of my family, I have broken the account into two parts—one suggestive of The World Before the Mills Went Down and the other of The World After. The first part offers a history of Southeast Chicago through the personal stories of my grandparents and great-grandparents. These narratives are classic ones of American immigration and labor that feel almost stereotypical in the telling. Yet they also reveal points of tension that are too significant to ignore. The second part gives an account of deindustrialization through my father's experiences, my relationship with him, and the ways in which the shutdown of Southeast Chicago's steel mills transformed us both. With "USA" emblazoned on his baseball cap and his ever-present flannel shirt, my father in many ways epitomized the archetypal steelworker, once a stereotypical image of the white working class. My own story is easily subsumed by archetypal ideas of upward mobility in the United States. Yet the clichéd assumptions associated with such images fail to convey the bitterness of these stories or the places where more powerful societal narratives have acted to destroy the shoots of alternative accounts. In the end, what these interweaving stories add up to is the role that deindustrialization has played and is playing, not only in transforming class in the United States, but in redefining what it means to be "American" in the twenty-first century.

A WORLD OF IRON AND STEEL: A FAMILY ALBUM

Defined by the steel mills that in the 1870s began drawing generations of immigrants to live near their gates, Southeast Chicago has what might euphemistically be described as a "colorful" history. Al Capone once maintained houses and speakeasies in the area because of its convenient proximity to the Indiana state line. My dad would drive me around the neighborhood when I was a child and point out the brick bungalows rumored to have been Capone's and to still have bulletproof windows. Laughingly, he told stories of how one of my great-uncles quit his job as a night watchman after Capone's men showed up one evening and told him not to report to work the next day. One of the defining events in U.S. labor history, the Memorial Day Massacre of 1937, happened on a plot of land across the street from the local high school that my sisters and I attended. On that Memorial Day, locked-out steelworkers and sympathizers, including my grandfather, massed in protest near Republic Steel, where ten were killed and nearly a hundred wounded by police under the influence of mill management. A federal investigation and subsequent legislation were milestones in allowing U.S. workers the right to unionize. In 1966, Martin Luther King Jr. marched through the streets of Southeast Chicago protesting the deep-seated racial hatred and housing segregation in the area, to the consternation of many of the white working class, including many of my own family members.

What was most striking about growing up in Southeast Chicago, aside from the contentious relationships found among its patchwork of ethnic groups including Scandinavians, Germans, Poles, Slavs, Italians, Greeks, Mexicans, and, later, African Americans, was the neighborhood's dense networks of kinship ties. Many families, like my own, had lived in the mill neighborhoods for generations. When I was growing up, my grandparents lived across the alley from my parents' house, and nearly all my cousins, aunts, and uncles were within walking distance. My sisters and I attended the same grammar school as our parents as well as several of our grandparents and even great-grandparents. At times, the interconnectedness reached near comic proportions. For example, my mother's mother, a widow, eventually married my father's father, a widower, a year before my own parents were married. Despite perplexed looks when I explained that my mother and father had become stepbrother and stepsister as adults, the situation seemed an oddly appropriate expression of the dense social bonds that knit together the mill neighborhoods. At other times, the interconnectedness took on darker overtones. I remember my parents reminiscing about trying to decide as newlyweds whether it was appropriate to attend the funeral of my father's aunt after she was killed by a distant relative on my mother's side, a man who had become mentally unstable after serving in the Korean War and had exploded a bomb in a local department store.

While families were at the root of social life, they also mirrored the divisions found among the white working class more broadly. In many ways, my mother's family approximated the classic immigrant narrative of modest upward mobility, while my father's family reflected the far-less-often-told reality of long-term white poverty. Although the immigrant narrative of my mother's family story was valorized while my father's family's story was swept under the collective national rug, the accounts from relatives on both sides of the family built upon classic American myths of a modern industrial "melting pot" society and, at the same time, regularly contradicted such mythology. The story of my maternal great-grandfather is a prime example. My mother's grandfather, Johan Martinsson, came to Chicago from Sweden in 1910, becoming John Mattson in the process. After his death, my grandmother found hidden in the attic a memoir stuffed in a paper sack that he had written in broken English at the age of seventy-five. The dramatic title *The Strugle* [sic] *for Existence from the Cradle to the Grave* was scrawled across the front. His wanting to tell his story so badly, yet feeling the need to hide it in the attic to be found after his death, has always fascinated me. To me, it suggests not only the ambivalence of wanting to convey—yet being afraid to convey—painful family events but also ambivalence about how to tell a life story that so bitterly contradicted mythic portrayals of immigrants grateful to be on American shores.

John, or, as I knew him, "Big Grandpa," tells a story that both references and contests classic immigrant narratives that were intended to make sense of experiences like his. He recounts how, as a child, he grew up on a farm near Göteborg in Sweden and was apprenticed at the age of eight to a blacksmith. He later alternated odd days of school with hard labor for neighboring farmers. Part of a large and impoverished family of thirteen, he left his community at the age of seventeen along with a group of other Swedes (including the father of his future wife) to find work in America. He worked for a while as a steelworker but was put off by the high death toll of the mills. After receiving a lucky break, he managed to become a carpenter and later, as a union builder and contractor, would help construct buildings throughout South Chicago. Yet in contrast to the mythic accounts of immigration in the United States, he refers to his decision to leave for the United States as a "mistake" and one that "I should never had made if [I] had known what I know today." He continues: "Sweden had peace for 150 years and do not [sic] meddle in another nation's affairs. That's more than I can say for my adopted country where I raised my family and worked hard since 1910. I was drafted in the First World War and had a son in the 2nd World War and now a grandson soon of age for Vietnam. When are [sic] this going to stop?"[7] In addition to expressing his regret that he ever left Sweden, his story dwells in bitter detail upon harsh economic struggles as well as the festering sores of an unhappy marriage. He conveys the hand-to-mouth existence of his early years in the United States, the utter vulnerability and dependency of those like himself who were without resources, and the cruel insecurities of the life of a laborer.

In my childhood memories, I remember my great-grandfather as an enormous, taciturn man who always wore suspenders and occasionally still played the accordion. In old family movies from the 1940s, "Big Grandpa" can be seen riding a paddleboat-like contraption built by his younger brother Gust. Wearing a suit and hat, he stares at the camera from the industrial wetlands amid the steel mills. In contemplating this and other images, I try to locate the inner turmoil revealed in his writing beneath their impenetrable surfaces. Family lore has it that he tried to move back to Sweden in later years but found himself too heavy to ride a bicycle and came back to the United States. In such stories, the bicycle symbolizes the immigrant's inability to go home, the dilemmas of a life transformed unalterably by the journey and caught betwixt and between.

The women in my mother's family left no written records, but it was they who,

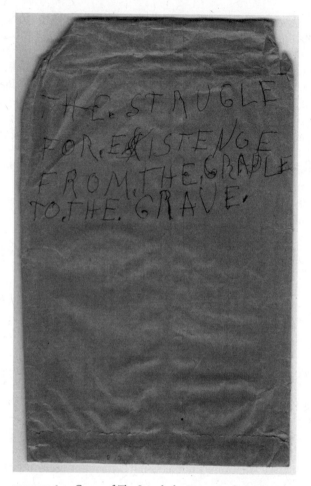

FIGURE 6.1. Cover of *The Strugle for Existence from the Cradle to the Grave*

in my memory, were always at the center of things. In the early years of the steel mill neighborhoods, men vastly outnumbered women. Nevertheless, some women, like my great-aunt Jenny, ran the boardinghouses where steelworkers and other immigrants lived or, like another great-aunt, worked in the mill cafeterias. Others took in laundry, were waitresses, or cleaned houses for others, including the wealthy who lived in the mansions in South Shore. My grandmother did almost all of these at various points in her life and later supported my mother and uncle as a dentist office receptionist after her first husband died at an early age. In contrast to middle-class narratives that stereotypically portray working-class men as sexist and violent

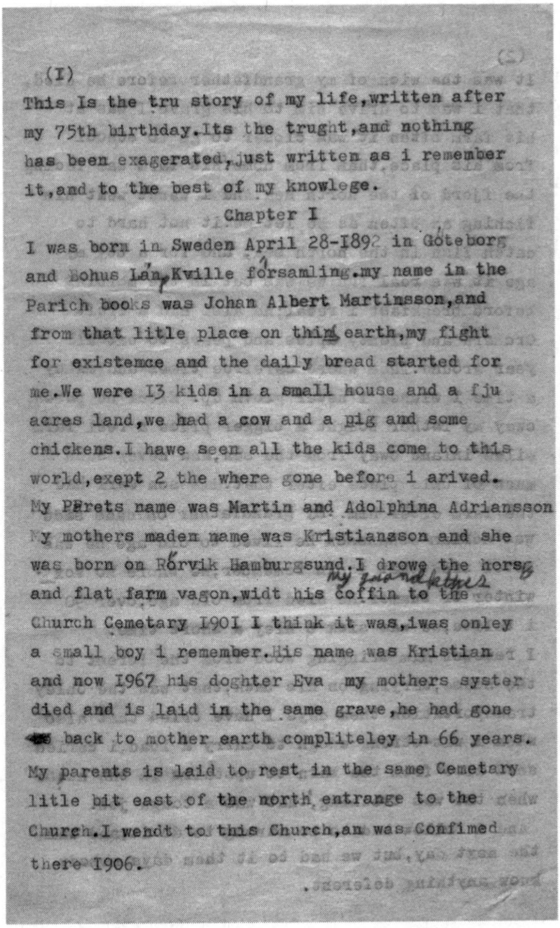

```
(I)                                                    (2)
This Is the tru story of my life,written after
my 75th birthday.Its the trught,and nothing
has been exagerated,just written as i remember
it,and to the best of my knowlege.
              Chapter I
I was born in Sweden April 28-1892 in Göteborg
and Bohus Län,Kville församling.my name in the
Parich books was Johan Albert Martinsson,and
from that litle place on thim earth,my fight
for existemce and the daily bread started for
me.We were 13 kids in a small house and a fju
acres land,we had a cow and a pig and some
chickens.I hawe seen all the kids come to this
world,exept 2 the where gone before i arived.
My Pärets name was Martin and Adolphina Adriansson
my mothers maden name was Kristiansson and she
was born on Rörvik Hamburgsund.I drowe the horse
and flat farm vagon,widt his coffin to the
Church Cemetary 1901 I think it was,iwas onley
a small boy i remember.His name was Kristian
and now 1967 his doghter Eva my mothers syster
died and is laid in the same grave,he had gone
back to mother earth compliteley in 66 years.
My parents is laid to rest in the same Cemetary
litle bit east of the north entrange to the
Church.I wendt to this Church,an was Confimed
there 1906.
```

FIGURE 6.2. Page of text from *The Strugle for Existence from the Cradle to the Grave*

and women and children as their perpetual victims, in my experience it was women who were the powerful beings. They were in charge of the social world that gave life meaning in these mill neighborhoods, binding together kin networks, maintaining churches, schools, and ethnic organizations.[8] While the men in Southeast Chicago might mark ethnic boundaries with belligerence and occasionally violence, the women could draw ethnic boundaries just as real through such acts as making Swedish holiday *glögg* and sausages, managing the Santa Lucia pageants in which we girls dressed up in white robes and silver tinsel, and organizing potlucks for organizations like the Bahus Klubben and the Viking Lodge. Like

Steedman's British working-class mother, who was a Tory and strove for the good things in life, many of the women on my mother's side of the family gravitated toward cultural styles of respectability that they associated with refinement and "classiness." It was this politics of desire for respectability, I believe, that made my utterly apolitical grandmother a Republican in the midst of this quintessential Chicago Democratic machine ward.

While some of my mom's childhood friends married "up" and eventually moved out of the mill neighborhoods to the suburbs, my father's family represented the other side of the white working class. In contrast to the classic immigrant tales of upward striving, they were long-term white poor. Although my father's mother was the child of Czech immigrants from Bohemia, her story is largely missing from the family album. Since it was the women who passed on family histories, her death when my father was barely more than a teenager meant that I grew up knowing almost nothing about her. In one of the few photos we have of her, she is standing next to my grandfather and surrounded by her sons, including my dad, who is positioned on the right. My father's father was—I surmise—originally from Appalachia. Before coming to Chicago to work in the steel mills, his family were tenant farmers and coal miners in southern Illinois. I never knew where they were from before that. When I asked my grandfather (who was known to us as "Little Grandpa" to differentiate him from our maternal great-grandfather), he would answer angrily that we were "American, goddamn it," and tolerate no further questions. Later, I learned that he had asked his own father this same question upon arriving in Chicago and had received the same answer. In a place where nearly everyone was an immigrant from somewhere and in which ethnic affiliations, churches, and organizations were powerful institutions of social life and upward mobility, to be without an ethnic group was a form of deprivation. I only then realized that being "American, goddamn it," was a statement not simply of racism but of the defensiveness of poor whites denigrated as "hillbillies" who were viewed as socially inferior to the incoming immigrant groups and who clung to their Americanness as one of their few badges of status.

In many ways, my grandfather's story is a classic tale of the rise of American labor and the transition from rural origins to the city. A family crisis occurred when his father, ill with "sugar diabetes," was forced off the land in southern Illinois, where he had been a tenant farmer. My great-uncle Arley, then a teenager, rose to the occasion by leading the family to the north in search of opportunities for labor in heavy industry. Arley went first, hitching rides on freight trains and dodging the gun-toting railroad "dicks" (as detectives were then known) to reach Detroit. He then sent the fare for my grandfather, who went to work as a waterboy in the car factories at age sixteen. Most of the family, including my great-grandparents, then relocated to Chicago a few years later. In Chicago, "Little Grandpa" eventually worked for more than forty-five years in an iron foundry, Valley Mould, that sat across the polluted

FIGURE 6.3. "Little Grandpa," my dad, and his mother and brothers

waters of the Calumet River from Wisconsin Steel. Several of his brothers went to work in the other steel mills. Before the unions ameliorated labor conditions, "Little Grandpa" worked twelve-hour shifts, seven days a week, with one day off a month. When someone didn't show up for work, he sometimes worked twenty-four hours straight. One day, a crane operator, who was working twenty-four hours, fell asleep at the controls as my grandfather and his fellow workers were extracting an enormous red-hot casting mold. My grandfather barely managed to scramble out of the way of the swinging tons of hot steel, and he lost part of two fingers of the hand he had thrown up to protect himself. According to my father, my grandfather's severed fingers were placed in a paper sack, and he was given a nickel for the trolley and told to take himself to the hospital. "Can you believe it?" my dad would say, offering this story repeatedly over the years as an archetypal example of how the "little guy" got screwed. Scoffing at this account and reasserting his own respectability, "Little Grandpa" insisted that he had been brought to the hospital in a proper ambulance. Nevertheless, Valley Mould *was* nicknamed "Death Valley" at this time, and my grandfather could tell stories of men he had seen die. One friend of his had fallen when crossing a plank catwalk across an enormous vat of hot sand. The man succeeded in grasping the chain that my grandfather threw down to him but suffocated before they could pull him out. My grandfather said that the man's body shriveled up from the heat. My father said that it had taken a long time for my grandfather to get over it. Not surprisingly, "Little Grandpa" was an ardent supporter of the unions. "You better believe it," he'd say. He even used to take my father, when he was five or six, to meetings at a tavern called Sam's Place where steelworkers from the smaller steel companies and their supporters, who were fighting for the right to unionize, would gather in the days before the Memorial Day Massacre.

Yet "Little Grandpa's" stories were just as challenging to beliefs on the left as my great-grandfather John's were to those on the right that celebrated America as the land of opportunity. While he fought passionately for his scrap of the pie, he had no time for social causes or political ideology that went beyond a decent wage and a measure of respect. Unions were important to him because with the "big guys" in control "you need a little something to show," a statement with an implicit hint of violence. When I tried to get him to talk about the terrible conditions in "Death Valley" that I had been reading about in history articles, however, he impatiently insisted that "it was all right" and took me down to his workroom to proudly show me the gadgets he had forged with scrap metal during his downtime at the foundry. He was far more interested in discussing the intricacies of ingot molds than the social conditions of the mills. My grandfather's stories were also shorn of idealistic notions of bravery and patriotism that laced the mythic narratives of both the Right and the Left in the United States. When I asked my grandfather what he had done on the fateful Memorial Day when the police started shooting at the protesting steelworkers and their supporters, he looked at me as if to determine whether I was a fool and spat, "What d'ya think I did? I turned around and ran like hell!" When I asked him why he hadn't fought in World War II, he boasted that, after receiving an induction letter, he conspired with his superintendent at Valley Mould to get shifted to the job of crane operator, a category of worker for which the superintendent could claim a deferment. "Hell yes!" he snorted. "What would I want to go to any shitting war for?"

Like many in my family, "Little Grandpa" also never lost the profound ethnic and racial hatreds that characterized the mill neighborhoods, and he never privileged the plight of "the working man" over such prejudices. Over Sunday dinner, he banged his silverware and told how in the old days if you were dating a girl whose families were "bohunks" (Bohemians) or "hunkies" (Hungarians) and you strayed over the wrong side of Ewing Avenue, you'd "better watch out, you'd better believe it!" When I went to say good-bye to my grandfather before leaving for a college study abroad program in Greece, his parting words were, "You watch out for those dagos over there." I smart-mouthed back that there were no dagos in Greece. "Dagos, spics, whatever, they'll get you every time," he glared ferociously at me. In a place where ethnic animosities had long been fed by company practices of hiring the most recent immigrant arrivals en masse as strikebreakers or using them to lower the wages of existing millworkers, ethnic divisions were a profound source of contention as well as of identity and support in my childhood world. As is clear from my grandfather's stories, various factions of European immigrant and native workers had fought among each other before they turned on Mexicans and, later, African Americans as the latest entrants into the mill neighborhoods. The bitterness of such divisions is epitomized by my first distinct memory of a black person. I imagine I was about four or five years old at the time and holding my mother's hand. Near the Swedish Lutheran church we attended, two white neighborhood boys were chasing an African American teenager with a pipe; they were clearly intending to beat him senseless for daring to cross neighborhood lines that were as rigidly enforced as any national border. It was the same hatred that in later years would cause a troubled teenage cousin from my father's side to go off into the woods with his biker buddies and machine-gun portraits of Chicago's first black mayor, Harold Washington. How does one talk about such hatreds without resurrecting every stereotype of the white working class? How does one lash together an understanding of a man like my "Little Grandpa," who would both spout vitriolic hatred and watch reruns of *Little House on the Prairie* on television, TV dinner sitting on his lap, tears streaming down his face, transfixed by nostalgic memories of his own rural upbringing?

During college, I valorized the parts of my grandfather that accorded with romantic leftist labor narratives—his work in the foundry, his union activities and presence at the Memorial Day Massacre. I conveniently tried to ignore those aspects that would make my liberal college friends cringe. (Secretly, I doubted whether most of my college friends would actually like "labor" if they met them in person.) Yet I loved talking to my grandfather. It was almost like stepping into a time machine. He often spoke and acted as if it were still the 1930s. And it wasn't simply a sign of old age; from what everyone said, he had been like that his whole life, as if his world had been arrested at some point when he was in his twenties. Once in the 1990s, outside a neighborhood restaurant on one of Southeast Chicago's main drags, he only half-jokingly pushed my future husband into the shadows of a storefront as a police car drove by. "Watch out. It's the flivver squad," he said in an undertone, as if it were still the Al Capone era and they were young punks afraid of the cops chasing them and knocking their heads together. He remained feisty until the end. My mom called me once when "Little Grandpa" was in his eighties and told me in an exasperated voice how he had been banned for life from the local Ace Hardware for pulling a penknife on a smart-mouthed employee. A few days before he died at age ninety-two, he expressed his impatience to see deceased loved ones once again in the afterlife. He irritably instructed my sisters and myself to help him put on his best suit, then lay down on the bed to await his death.

My grandfather's life, like those of many in Southeast Chicago, had revolved around the steel mills and the social worlds the mills had helped to create. The steel industry was the reason everyone had been brought together. Like a domineering family member about whom one feels profoundly ambivalent, the mills were both frightening and something upon which everyone depended. Craning my neck from the backseat of our car as we drove past the mills, I would, as a child, try to catch a glimpse of the fires blazing in their innards. There was a stark, overwhelming beauty to the enormous industrial scale of the mills, with vats the size of houses pouring molten rivers of golden steel while gas jets flared through the nighttime sky. At the same time, it was impossible to escape the sooty air and the less visible toxic waste that seeped from heavy industry into the ground and the surrounding river, wetlands, and lakes where I used to go skinny-dipping as a teenager. The steel mills and the union wages the mills paid after World War II had raised both sides of my family—the respectability-seeking immigrants as well as the hard-scrabble white poor—to a stable, almost "middle-class" prosperity. Even my Big Grandpa, for all his supposed regret about immigrating to the United States, enjoyed a degree of economic security in the second half of his life that contrasted sharply with the hardships he had known as a child. While the stories my relatives told sometimes resonated with and sometimes challenged the dominant societal narratives that threatened to overshadow their own, there was a continuity and stability to this world. There was, in both the Calumet region and in the United States as a whole, a widespread belief in future prosperity for oneself and one's family and a sense that both factory owners and workers were bound in a common enterprise that linked them indelibly to places like Southeast Chicago.

IT ALL CAME TUMBLING DOWN: MY FATHER
AND THE DEMISE OF WISCONSIN STEEL

I associate the destruction of the steel mills with my father's destruction. I had always identified with my dad. I looked like him. I was sensitive like him, and also, like him, I could throw what my husband refers to as "dagger eyes" on those occasions when I become angry. When I was a child, my mother always told me, "You are your father's daughter," her voice laced with exasperation that I wasn't more like her. Continuously told that I was a "Walley," I took a special interest in my father's family, about whom my mother was profoundly ambivalent. I was also fascinated by Wisconsin Steel, the fiery place where my father disappeared while working endless night shifts and where he had to wear long underwear under his work clothes as protection from the heat even in the summertime. In later years, I was annoyed when some fellow feminists assumed that girls primarily identified with their mothers. Paying far less attention to the relationship between daughters and fathers, they assumed that if girls identified with men it was ultimately because males were more powerful. In my own case, it was the opposite. I identified with my father because we were both in some ways rebellious outsiders in a domestic world dominated by the senior women in the family, those whom my father jokingly referred to as the "Swedish Army."

My father's own personality was contradictory. On the surface, he had the macho veneer that easily fit stereotypes of the white working-class men of his generation. Born on the dining room table during a snowstorm in the depths of the Depression, he had been a rowdy but playful neighborhood boy. My grandfather once caught him and my Uncle Bill hiding in ditches in the "prairies" near one of Al Capone's speakeasies, trying to catch a glimpse of the action. When he was a teenager, my mother, who was several years younger, admired him from afar. He hung out at the school playground, where he was known as an ace player at Ping-Pong, then a popular pastime. When they froze the schoolyard, he proved to be a beautiful ice-skater as well. My mother relates that he courted her neighbor, an older girl, and would sit with her on her lawn for long hours "picking four-leaf clovers." Yet he was also a "bad boy" sent to a special high school for "juvenile delinquents" (he insisted it was only for ditching school, although I was never fully convinced). At sixteen, he quit school and went to work pumping gas at one of the gas stations that lined the Indiana state border. He also devoted himself to drinking and being unruly with his friends, most of whom had nicknames like "Peg" (who had lost a leg hopping rails) or "Inky" (who had been put in an incubator as a baby). He hopped freighters himself and sometimes ended up in places like Kentucky with no way to get home. It was on a drinking binge in downtown Chicago with his buddy Big Russ that he got the tattoo that I loved as a child. All my male relatives, most of them steelworkers and nearly all veterans, had tattoos. I liked to admire them when they wore undershirts and smoked cigarettes in kitchens at family parties or on the porch in the summertime. My father's tattoo was of a black panther crawling up his arm, with red drops of dye representing blood dripping from where the claws would have entered his arm. When he was in the hospital with lung cancer at the end of his life, his chemotherapy nurses looked at his sagging panther and teased him about how he "really must have been a thing back in the day!"

Yet underneath the tough-guy exterior he was a sensitive, even fragile man, one wounded in so many places that it was impossible to patch him up. A hard life as well as his own father's harshness had fatally damaged him. After he married my mother, he often chose to stay home during his free time. In a picture taken one Christmas, I can be seen sitting on his lap surrounded by my mother, sister, and an aged "Big Grandpa." As I look at such pictures, I wonder if my father had not always secretly longed for a quiet life; after all, living up to an image of self-assured masculinity was a heavy weight to sustain. As a kid, I tried to extract stories from him of his younger days. His early life seemed glamorous to me, an exciting contrast to the churchgoing respectability of my mother; yet it was a source of embarrassment to him. When I tried to get him to recount thrilling tales of riding the rails, he would instead tell the bitter story of how one time, when he had ended up in Kentucky and phoned his family for help, his father had refused to pay for his fare home. I liked the times when instead of going out to play poker with his brother and in-laws he stayed home and played cards with me and my sisters. It was while playing cards or Ping-Pong in the basement that the joking demeanor of his youth would occasionally reappear. At such times, my sisters and I sometimes managed to extract a good story from him, like how he had lost his corporal's stripe when he was in Germany immediately after World War II. He and a buddy of his had gone AWOL and ended up drinking in a tavern, from which they had to be hauled out by the German police after a fight broke out. At such times, my dad would jokingly intone, "Nicht rauchen in der barren" (No smoking in the bar), the few words of German he had acquired while in the army. Although it was clear that respectability was important to my mother, it was only later that I realized that it was important to my father as well. Perhaps he had seen marrying my mother as a form of upward mobility, an escape from the tumultuous family life of his own relatives. As if to keep us from the fate of the nieces and female cousins on his side of the family, who (shamefully without shame, according to some) became unwed mothers at a young age, he ferociously told us at adolescence that if we got "knocked up" we would be kicked out of the house.

His paycheck from the mills was his source of manhood and self-respect in a world over which he had little control. Going into the mills in the decade after World War II, he never suffered the long hours or low pay that my grandfather had. Instead, he was of a generation that watched the expansion of powerful unions and their representatives with a cynical eye. After the mills went down and newspaper accounts blamed it on U.S. workers wanting "too much" or lacking the work ethic of the Japanese, he made a point of stressing that the average steelworker never made very much money; it was skilled workers who worked long hours of overtime that made the "big money" in the mills. My memories support his contention. A climate of anxiety over money permeates my childhood recollections. When I was about five, I remember my dad coming home from the hospital after a hernia operation from a mill-related injury. I recall drawing him a "get well" card with crayons and taping my own pennies on it in an attempt to prevent him and my mom from fighting over money. Practical and down-to-earth like her own mother, my mom

FIGURE 6.4. Dad, Mom, "Big Grandpa," and me and my sister

was skilled at stretching to make ends meet. But although we had a home, a car, and food, it was never easy for her. I hated the hand-me-down clothes that I was given by a neighbor's grandchild who now lived in the suburbs, and I remember my disappointment at getting a toy guitar Christmas ornament instead of the real one I had asked for—a disappointment she sensed as well. I also hated the fact that my father used his role as male family provider to ground his own authority. I remember him punctuating arguments with my mother with the refrain that since it was he who "paid the bills," he should make the decisions. Although, in retrospect, I recognize his bravado as an attempt to buttress his own losing domestic position, the injustice of it still rankles and has underwritten my own determination never to live without a wage of my own.

Given that his role as family provider was central to his identity, as it was for many men in the area, the closing of the mills devastated my father. Wisconsin Steel was the first mill to close in Southeast Chicago. In some ways, it was the worst closing, certainly the most disorderly. There was a great deal of mystery about what actually happened. After being assured that their jobs were safe, workers, like my father, who were finishing a shift were simply told to go home, the gates were padlocked by armed guards, and they weren't even allowed to clear out their lockers. Later, the preshutdown sale of Wisconsin Steel to a tiny computer company from California would be deemed a "spurious" transaction by the courts. The former owner, International Harvester, had sold the mill to a company with almost no assets in what, some argued, was an attempt to avoid millions of dollars in unfunded pension obligations. Wisconsin Steel itself was used as collateral on the loan to buy the mill, and the new company appeared to strip the mill of assets and treat it like a "cash cow" in its few years of ownership.[9] Although more than a decade later a class action suit filed by steelworker activists would lead to a partial settlement, many workers lost not only their jobs but part or all of their pensions, their health insurance, and other money and benefits, including vacation and severance pay contractually owed to them. Their last three paychecks bounced.

In an area where neat lawns and never going on public assistance were quintessential points of pride, the stigma of being out of work was traumatic. At first, there was hope that the mill would open again. But over time that hope dissipated. Seven months after the March 1980 closing, steelworkers picketed the home of Mayor Jane Byrne at Thanksgiving with signs reading, "Where's our turkeys, Jane?" As time passed, my dad became increasingly depressed and refused to leave the house. Too wounded to show his face to the outside world, he gradually stopped shaving or changing his clothes. He would sit on the couch or at the kitchen table, with a cigarette continuously poised in his fingers, his fingertips dyed orange from the cheap butts. As my mother screamed about the wasted cigarette money and searched for odd change in the sofa cushions, the acrid smoke killed the houseplants and turned the white ceiling orange. Coming home late at night, I'd find him watching the white fuzz on the TV set.

Yet in retrospect our family considered itself lucky. My father was one of three Wisconsin Steel workers who lived on our block; the second became an alcoholic and died a few years later, and the third attempted suicide. In later years, I would read studies that documented the toll of the mill shutdowns in Southeast Chicago, offering painful statistics regarding depression, suicides, illness, and broken families to back up the personal lived experiences of those we knew. The numbers for Wisconsin Steel were staggering. In 1989, the local *Daily Calumet* newspaper reported that in the years since Wisconsin had been shut down nearly 800 out of 3,400 workers had died, mostly from alcohol and stress-related illnesses, compounded by the lack of health care and high suicide rates.[10] While the shutdowns caused untold social devastation, they also caused neighbors to band together. Some said the situation reminded them of how everyone had depended upon each other during the Depression. While the dense social ties and animosities of Southeast Chicago could be stifling and insular, those same ties could be activated in times of trouble, providing a last-ditch social safety net for the working class and poor. The wife of the unemployed Wisconsin steelworker across the street would bring over tomatoes from her backyard; her husband got my dad an off-the-books job for a couple days emptying out a warehouse. Another neighbor, feeling sorry for my mother as she struggled to hold things together, secretly left an envelope with $50 in cash in the mailbox; it was anonymous, so as not to hurt my mother's pride.

Like many other wives of steelworkers, my mom went back to work in order to hold our family together financially. My stomach churns when I imagine the experiences of workers with no other adult wage earner at home to fall back upon, including the handful of women steelworkers who were often single moms with kids. After a number of dark and uncertain days following Wisconsin's shutdown, my mother joined many other women in becoming part of a growing army of temporary workers, a cog in the wheel of the economic logic that David Harvey has referred to as "flexible accumulation."[11] After several anxiety-filled years of bouncing between temporary jobs and scrambling to find friends and family to help with rides when there was no money to fix the family car, she found a permanent "temp" position doing clerical work in the blueprint room of a local oil refinery. (She has now worked twenty-three years at the same "temporary" job, much of that time without benefits for herself or the rest of our family.) Although media accounts presented the movement of women like my mother into wage labor as a "new" development in the traditionally gendered division of labor in Southeast Chicago, the trend was actually more of a "return." Like the older female relatives mentioned earlier, women had often worked for money in both formal and informal economies in the early years of South Chicago's mill neighborhoods. Indeed, it was the post–World War II family wages of unionized steelworkers that allowed wives to stay home and thus to achieve the kind of respectability to which previous generations of working-class women (who had been chastised by turn-of-the-century domestic reformers for neglecting their families) had aspired. In the 1980s, many of the wives of former steelworkers went back to work as waitresses, hairdressers, cashiers, salesclerks, bank tellers, receptionists, and clerical workers. Some worked informally out of their homes, making household crafts, holiday decorations, and cakes for extra cash. Although my mom had enjoyed staying home (for her, in contrast to many middle-class suburban housewives, "home" meant being at the center of dense social and organizational networks built over generations), the chance to "get out" and earn some money increased her self-confidence, even as my father's crumbled.

Over the course of the 1980s and early 1990s, as the other steel mills in the area closed one by one, it sometimes felt as if the entire world were collapsing. While most former steelworkers who weren't already retired were now unemployed, the women and men who worked at the local stores, restaurants, and supplier shops often found themselves out of work as well. During these years, my father found occasional work as a janitor or a security guard. Yet these jobs were never stable, and there was active discrimination against hiring former steelworkers, particularly aging ones.[12] He never held a permanent job again. In general, a cloud of depression and despair seemed to hang over the entire region. While many residents blamed the corporations and government for this social devastation, others, fearful that they had done something wrong, blamed themselves. A few, however, tried to protest. Strikingly, the most cohesively organized steelworkers in Southeast Chicago were African American and Latino. Such individuals were more likely to be supporting extended families, and consequently the loss of their jobs had an even more devastating effect upon their communities. Many were also of a generation that had watched, if not taken part in, the civil rights movement, and some were comfortable with political organizing. Those like my father, who had traded in the fighting spirit of my grandfather's generation for a growing respectability and who came of age disillusioned with the corruption of unions, were often at loose ends. Perhaps protesting seemed too much to them like 1960s-style rabble-rousing. For a region that had sent large numbers of young men to Vietnam and applauded Mayor Daley for cracking together the heads of college "hippies" during the Democratic convention in 1968, there was room for little other than individualized despair and bitterness at being ejected from the American Dream. Years later, my father, apropos of nothing, intoned, "Yeah, we thought we were middle class there for a while. We were almost middle class."

What do I myself remember from this time? I recall local community groups bringing my family and those of other unemployed steelworkers free turkeys and care baskets during the holidays. I remember the inedible government-issue free cheese given to steelworkers after the mills went down, the thought of which, even now, makes me feel nauseated. I remember how, at a time when the waves of deindustrialization hitting the Midwest still seemed unfathomable, a newly elected President Ronald Reagan (a man many steelworkers had voted for) would seek to cut back unemployment benefits, including for the victims of plant closings.[13] When Reagan died in 2004, I was shocked by the resurgence of bitterness that I felt toward the man. It was not the resentment of an adult calculated from an abstract political philosophy, but the painful disillusionment of a fourteen-year-old. I remember thinking at the time, with a sudden realization, like the stab of a knife, that those in power did not care about me or my family: our lives were meaningless to them. It was a brutal lesson that would haunt me in later years. I also remember trying to help relieve my parents' burden of providing by trying to take care of myself. I did odd jobs after school and even went to the local ward boss (a figure who still existed in the steel mill neighborhoods) and asked for an age exemption so that I could work on the government CETA program for poor youngsters. Although my father explained that I might have to distribute political flyers in return for the favor, the summer job helped me buy my own school clothes and supplies. When I later read the literature on deindustrialization, it was easy to recognize myself in the accounts of those children who tried to grow up quickly in an attempt to help shoulder the responsibilities of their careworn parents.

However, I am somewhat ashamed to admit that my most overwhelming reaction was to try to escape. I wanted to run away from the clouds of depression hanging over my father, my parents' home, and Southeast Chicago in general. I turned my long-standing habit of reading and daydreaming to use in searching out escape routes. I sent for a brochure on a girls' boarding school on the East Coast (something unheard of in Southeast Chicago), and I remember staring longingly at photos of rich-looking, well-fed girls in uniforms who sat around reading books on neatly manicured lawns. Then came a moment of freak chance. A friend, the daughter of a local firefighter, had a brother who managed to attend the University of Chicago after graduating from a local Catholic high school. His college roommate told her about a New England prep school called Phillips Exeter Academy. When I decided to apply, my mom humored me by taking me for a required standardized test in downtown Chicago. The test was given in a private school, where I sat intimidated and frightened by the alien environment and wealthy students. Nevertheless, months later, a heavy piece of stationery with official Exeter letterhead informed me that I had been awarded a full scholarship. In retrospect, I am uncomfortably aware that it was my father's fall that unexpectedly made me a candidate for elite schools concerned with diversity.

My parents, however, refused to let me go. The idea of sending a child away to school, much less halfway across the country, seemed like an act of cruelty to many parents in Southeast Chicago. But there were deeper reasons as well. When I yelled at my father, who was then working temporarily as a janitor, and demanded that he tell me why I couldn't go, he responded, almost in tears, "Because when you come back, you'll look down on me for being a janitor!" His words and the pained look on his face are imprinted on my memory. Yet I was determined to make my escape. My mom, convinced that I was simply causing trouble, complained about me to our sympathetic family doctor. Unlike my parents, he knew of Exeter's reputation and demanded that she let me go. At the time, I attributed the fact that my parents finally relented to his intervention. But once again in retrospect, I suspect that the real reason was both more mundane and more troubling. At a point when my parents were fearful of losing their house and openly worried about the possibility of having to send me and my sisters to live with relatives, the brute economic fact that my expenses would be paid for and there would be one mouth less to feed at home was critical. In the days ahead, a couple of my former teachers at the local grammar school took me shopping and bought me some clothes, a new winter jacket, and a portable typewriter. My uncle, whose job was still safe at the local Ford plant, lent my father his blue pickup truck, and the entire family drove me across the country to New Hampshire.

Although I had made my escape almost exactly on my sixteenth birthday, it was a far rockier and more painful trek than I could have imagined or than is commonly found in the American mythology of upward mobility. It left me saddled with life-long feelings of guilt. At a time when my little sister at home was making extra vis-its to my grandparents' house in the hopes of getting something to eat besides the hotdogs that had become my family's daily fare, I was catapulted to the other end of the American class spectrum. I found myself sitting in classes in colonial build-ings of brick and marble with students with names like Getty, Firestone, Packard, and Coors. My euphoria at escaping soon disintegrated into a profound disloca-tion. In a country where race and ethnicity are highly elaborated categories but class is not, there was no recognition that the transition might be difficult for a white working-class girl. If, according to American mythology, all I had previously lacked was opportunity, now that opportunity had presented itself, shouldn't I be fine? The radical disjunctures in this transition—the profound social differences that I had no way to articulate—created an unnamable and painful sense of rupture. It is ironic that when I later traveled outside the country for the first time on a college-year abroad program, I remember feeling no culture shock at all. The people I met in Greece reminded me of my Mediterranean neighbors in Southeast Chicago. Even if I had felt "culture shock," however, it would have been explainable, an acknowl-edgment that cultural and ethnic differences are recognized to exist. Instead, it was the class journey from Southeast Chicago to Exeter that was by far the most pro-foundly dislocating one of my life and the one most difficult to articulate in terms that others would recognize. This state of being betwixt and between, an unac-knowledged class "halfie," to paraphrase Lila Abu-Lughod's terms,[14] would later lead me to try to use anthropology as a means to explain the world to myself.

The sense of dislocation, and at times humiliation, that I felt at Exeter emerged in countless small incidents. In classes, I was startled by the self-confidence of my fellow students, their belief that their words mattered, their relish in articulating abstract ideas in a mode I found foreign. I tried to contribute to class conversations, taking an entire class period to work up the necessary bravery. Red in the face, heart hammering by the time I managed to get something out, I was constantly afraid that I would speak in the ungrammatical diction that was my first language. I re-member sitting one afternoon on the well-tended lawn outside my dorm with my housemates, including a classmate from Greenwich, Connecticut, who was dressed in expensive, preppy clothing. She stared in perplexity at a seemingly unfashion-able, polyester-clad "townie" from the working-class town of Exeter who happened to be walking past (a woman who to me bore a comforting resemblance to my own mother) and wondered aloud, "What is wrong with people in this town?" Trapped in my own insecurities, I cringed inside and said nothing. I remember housemates good-naturedly telling anecdotes of their families, but when I would try to recip-rocate, revealing a bit of what was happening with my family, there would instead be an awkward silence. My story was a "downer" that simply made people feel uncomfortable (and perhaps secretly guilty?); I quickly learned to remain silent. At the end of such days, I would go to the music practice rooms on campus where I was learning to play the harpsichord and would cry in the only truly private space I could find. My sense of dislocation eventually turned to anger. How was it that there could be places where privilege was so utterly taken for granted? By what right did some people enjoy such ease when others' lives were being ripped apart in places like Southeast Chicago? For a while, I even tried to hate my classmates and their parents. After all, weren't their parents among the business elite who made decisions like closing my father's mill? Weren't they the ones who stood to profit as their investment shares rose in the conglomerates that had once owned the steel mills? But it didn't work; I was forced to admit that I liked many of my classmates. When the father of one housemate, a descendent of the wealthy DuPont family, visited and took us out to dinner, I hoped I could despise him. But he was kind and attentive, and I was ashamed of myself.

I tried to protest, to find a voice to tell my own story in other ways. In my creative writing class, I wrote a tale about a man who could barely read, a character whom I can now admit was a melodramatic exaggeration of my father. (Although I never saw my father read a book or write a letter and although my mother euphemistically described his literacy skills as "limited," he obsessively read the tabloid newspapers his entire life.) Painfully aware of the presence of one of the Getty boys in my class, I had written this story in a spirit of defiance, hoping to salve my own pain by surreptitiously pricking at his privilege. (He remained imperturbable.) I was asked to speak to alumni as a scholarship student and wrote out on three-by-five cards a speech that I considered a manifesto. I wrote about Southeast Chicago and stated that the people I grew up with were no less intelligent or worthy than those who went to schools like Exeter. In my mind, it seemed a bold attack, although reading it back years later it instead seems overly timid and polite. On the day I gave the speech, I cried and couldn't get through it. Afterwards, instead of responding to it as the attack I intended, several alumni came up and told me what a good speech I had written and that they were proud of me. Ashamed that I was grateful for their praise even when I had been actively courting their anger, I smiled back in confusion. Later, I came to realize that they could not hear the story of class I wanted to tell—a story of injustice and anger at class inequalities in the United States couched in the self-righteousness of a sixteen-year-old—because it was too readily subsumed by the broader narrative of America as a land of opportunity. For the assembled alumni, my own presence at Exeter merely confirmed this; even better for the liberal-minded, my speech had acknowledged those left behind. I felt trapped by my inability to find an object upon which to vent my rage, trapped by my inability to find my own voice, trapped by an inability to be heard.

As difficult as it was during those two years at Exeter, it was even more difficult to come home. On vacations, my parents never asked me about life at school and pretended that it didn't exist. Like a chameleon, I tried to assimilate into the neighborhood again. When my father angrily told me to stop using such big words, I let my sentences drift back into a semigrammatical form out of fear that I would confirm the worries he had revealed before I went to Exeter. During the summers, I worked multiple jobs, once again including a stint on the government-sponsored CETA program. The tutoring program was housed in the local grammar school I had attended, yet most of the other tutors were African American teenagers bused in from poorer parts of Chicago's South Side. Although we were hired to tutor younger children, the school's Italian American vice principal was clearly afraid of my black teenaged co-workers. In the long downtime in the periods before and after our charges arrived, he would force us to sit in silence with our heads on the desk so we wouldn't cause trouble. I remember sitting there, my head lying on the same wooden desks with holes for inkwells that my parents, grandparents, and great-grandparents had used. I thought about how only a few weeks earlier I had been in the marbled and red-carpeted assembly hall at Exeter being lectured on how I was one of the future leaders of America. Now I was sitting with my head on a desk, an object of distrust, someone to be controlled. I didn't know how the African American teenagers around me could stand it. Here were all the paradoxes. The white working class, including my own family and that of the Italian vice principal, were the victims of class in a way I had never imagined before I left Southeast Chicago. Yet, as one of them, I couldn't comfort myself with romantic platitudes. The respectability, as it were, of the white steel mill neighborhoods was built up by a hatred of those on the next rung below. Victims, in other contexts, can be abusers. Just as when I met my friends' parents at Exeter, the only way I could find to stand such tensions was by an act of dissociation: one had to hate the "thing"—class injustice or racism—without hating the people who embodied it. Otherwise, one could find reasons to hate all of humanity. In later years, anthropology would become my route to try to understand what caused such hateful social realities. It would appeal to me, not only for the insights it offered, but also for the way it leavened such insights with a sense of human sympathy.

At the time, however, I attempted to escape such tensions by running away again. I chose to go to a small liberal arts college in California that I had indifferently picked out of my roommate's guidebook to colleges. It was as far away from both Chicago and New England as I could go. Still, there was no escape. For the twenty-five years between the demise of Wisconsin Steel and my father's death, he and I both remained obsessed by the shutdown of the steel mills and psychologically unable to get past its trauma. We each had difficulty expressing the object of our obsession in our own way. After entering graduate school in anthropology, I decided to write my master's thesis about the deindustrialization of Southeast Chicago, in what I hoped would be an act of catharsis. Yet I found that it was easy to use academic jargon as a way to distance myself from my adolescent anger, a pain that I couldn't leave behind but didn't want to relive. For my thesis, I conducted taped interviews with numerous people in Southeast Chicago, including my dad, mom, sisters, and grandfather. This material, upon which the present account is partially based, contained some surprises.

For a man who talked incessantly and with unmitigated bitterness about how they should have put him in his grave when they shut the mill down, my father had little to say when I interviewed him. He answered in monosyllables or brief sentences with no elaboration. I think he was afraid that putting himself on the record would get him into trouble with some authority, the vague powers-that-be that existed in the world beyond Southeast Chicago, which he respected but which also oppressed him. Yet in retrospect I think he was even more scared that he had nothing of value to say. A man whose self-respect had been pummeled by the mill closings decades before, he had no confidence that his words were worth listening to. This tendency came out even more strongly a few years later when I began making a video documentary about Southeast Chicago with my filmmaker husband. On the occasions when my husband would pull out the camera, my father would at first demur and say he didn't want to be on tape. Then, unbidden, he would start talking to the camera, telling it his story and justifying his view of the mill shutdowns. Perplexed at first, we gradually realized that he liked the feeling of validation that having the camera listen to him gave him but did not have the confidence to make it "official." So we videotaped him with minimal equipment, all of us locked in the pretense that we weren't doing anything. When my father saw a short piece of the video later, he asked to replay the tape and nodded in vigorous agreement with his on-camera persona. It proved to be an odd sort of conversation with himself. It was my husband who spotted the pattern and the irony. Like my great-grandfather who hid his memoir in the attic, my father couldn't escape his own ambivalence about speaking. Neither could I. We all shared both a desire and an inability to speak—fears that could be named and those that escaped naming. Perhaps this struggle to recount my own story—and theirs—is an attempt to break free, at least for a moment, from a history of such fetters.

The neighborhoods of my childhood are now very different. The steel mills of Southeast Chicago are now all closed, some for more than twenty-five years. Even the few mills that have continued across the state line in Indiana have done so with radically fewer workers (and, in a throwback to another time, one has even reinstituted the twelve-hour workday that my grandfather fought so hard against). As a whole, the Calumet region is permeated by a sense of nostalgia for the lost era I knew briefly as a child. It is strange to think that the history of only a few generations of my own family would nearly span the rise and fall of heavy industry in Southeast Chicago, as well as in much of the United States. My immigrant great-grandfather's venture into the mills shortly after the turn of the twentieth century, my grandfather's strug-gles in the early union era, and the deindustrialization suffered by my parents' gen-eration traced the history of an industry and a way of life that would prove far more ephemeral than any could have imagined. In today's Southeast Chicago, toxic brownfields now extend over vast tracts of land in between the increasingly broken-down wooden clapboard houses and brick bungalows of former steelworkers. What sociologists once clinically labeled "urban succession" has continued. As newly arrived Mexican immigrants and African Americans increasingly make their homes in this depressed area, many members of the former white working class have moved over the state line into Indiana. It is instructive that since the demise of the steel mills the Calumet region has been characterized by the growth of two industries: toxic waste dumps and, across the Indiana border, floating gambling casinos. The flashing neon signs of the lakefront casinos that now light up the skyway at night appear as none-too subtle symbols of the emergence of a new form of risk-centered society in the United States, one characterized by levels of insecurity that my fore-bears thought they had long left behind.

The physical absences of the steel mills, not surprisingly, have been paralleled by equally prominent holes in the social fabric of the region. Just as jobs in heavy industry were once the primary means for working-class and poor Americans to enter the expanding post–World War II "middle class," the loss of such jobs has played a central role in the growing levels of social inequality found in the United States. In the postindustrial landscape of the Calumet region, such divisions are ap-parent even among the two branches of my own extended family. While some of my cousins on my father's side have been thrown back into hard-core poverty, liv-ing in trailers, trying to make do, limited to minimum-wage jobs or the informal economy, my cousins on my mother's side have become more suburbanized. Some have used positions as skilled laborers to move up to jobs increasingly dependent on computer technology; one has gone back to college and is now a businessman. Both sides, however, find themselves worried about job security as well as the sky-rocketing costs of health care and housing at the start of a new millennium. In con-trast to the world of diminishing inequalities that my parents' generation had be-lieved in—one in which we would all be middle class—the future now appears as a world of expanding economic disparities with heightened stakes for both success and failure.

As I read over this account, the question of where to attribute blame for the so-cial devastation caused in places like Southeast Chicago looms as large for me as it did while I was at Exeter. I find that as I try to answer this question, my pronouns, almost inevitably, begin to tack back and forth between the "I" of the "autoethno-grapher," the daughter of the steelworker, and the "we" of American society that is the concern of pundits and social analysts. Of course, blue-collar workers and their families debated the larger causes of deindustrialization as much as did journalists and academics. I recall various family members and neighbors during the 1980s and 1990s trying to ascertain where to lay the "blame." Some steelworkers, like my father, vented their ire in equal measure upon the government and the steel companies. During the Cold War and even before, the steel companies had preached ideas of a corporate "family" that promised ongoing commitment to the communities where their factories were located. Yet, some residents charged, hadn't the corporations sold them out for a cold profit when convenient, while politicians failed to defend them? Others turned their worries inward. Perhaps, as the newspapers suggested, they hadn't worked hard enough after all; could this, somehow, have been their own fault? Were they greedy to have wanted to be middle class? Many whites turned their anger on more socially vulnerable others. Some men asked how, after they had fought in world wars, the government could abandon them while it helped welfare moms (read: African Americans) who didn't want to work. Even the working-class African Americans and Latinos I knew joined in a variation on this chorus: Why, they asked, should the United States spend so much money on international aid helping countries "over there" when there was such need at home? But hidden beneath the apparent selfishness of these bitter complaints was a common demand for respect: "We are good citizens; we are human beings; how can we be abandoned as if our lives meant nothing?"

In their most pensive moments, some steelworkers I knew wondered whether the demise of the steel industry wasn't simply inevitable, part of an evolutionary transformation, much as journalists and academics suggested when they used the language of globalization. One neighbor and former U.S. Steel employee followed an angry diatribe against government and corporations with a deflated sigh of resignation. "Was it simply the end of an era," he asked, "like the passing of the steam engines or horses and buggies?" While offering the benefit of a clarity based on historical inevitability, such interpretations failed to acknowledge that particular social groups, with American leaders at the forefront, had played a central role in creating the domestic and international laws, institutions, and market dynamics that would be known in shorthand as "globalization." Elite accounts of this phenomenon held multiple blind spots. When well-off Americans in the 1980s and 1990s celebrated such trends and pondered whether sending factory jobs abroad might bring positive forms of development to other parts of the world, they often downplayed the fact that such shifts would come largely at the expense of one segment of the American population. At the same time that the American working class was being catastrophically undermined, the wealthy in the United States were becoming far wealthier. Such assumptions were problematic for other reasons as well. Although many U.S. steel mills did not so much "run away" to other countries as leave the playing field while their parent companies searched for greater profits elsewhere, the phenomenon of deindustrialization in general demonstrates an insidious logic widely remarked upon by critics. As factory production relocates to wherever labor is cheapest, the factory jobs shipped to Mexico may not stay there but leave for China, while those in China, in turn, leave for Bangladesh and Vietnam. Just as the downward spiral of the search for ever cheaper wages has punched gaping holes in the American Dream in this country, it holds out the possibility, not only of higher standards of living, but of similar traumas of "creative destruction" and heightened inequalities in other locales.

Although it is important to recognize that governments and corporations are not exempt from the exigencies of global economic logics (even as they participate in their creation), the key question is how the United States, as a society, has dealt with these pressures. Have we sought to direct such transformations in ways less destructive to those made vulnerable in the process, or have we instead embraced such transformations and even forced them upon ourselves as well as other parts of the world? Have we paid attention to those whose lives have been battered in their wake? As a college professor and social scientist, I am expected to participate in public conversations about American society and the direction in which it should head. Given my background, I am painfully aware of the class privilege involved in such assumptions and the number of voices that are ignored in such debates. Yet in making the leap from the "I" of the autoethnographer to the "we" of U.S. society, I hope to underscore that the "we" made up of a concerned American citizenry also need to reclaim our ability to speak.

NOTES

This article is dedicated to the memory of my father, Charles William Walley (1931–2005). My deepest thanks to my mother and sisters for their love and for allowing me to share this story. I would also like to thank my other relatives, neighbors, and friends in Southeast Chicago who shared similar experiences. My gratitude also extends to my husband, Chris Boebel, for his perceptiveness in first suggesting the problem of speaking as a central issue in my own family life. It was his idea to use it as a motif in this essay as well as in the documentary film, *Exit Zero*, that we are jointly making about Southeast Chicago. I am grateful to Faye Ginsburg and Owen Lynch, who were supportive advisers for my 1993 master's thesis on this topic in New York University's Anthropology Department. Thanks also to Lila Abu-Lughod, Rod Sellers, and members of the Walley family for their helpful comments on this essay. Finally, I would like to extend my appreciation to Hugh Gusterson and Catherine Besteman for creating the much-desired opportunity to revisit the issue. I am grateful for their insights and encouragement as well as for the stimulating conversation that they and other participants provided in the 2006 "What's Wrong with America" workshop held at MIT as well as the 2007 "Insecure American" panel at the American Anthropological Association meetings.

1. The Calumet is the wetland region near the southern tip of Lake Michigan that surrounds Lake Calumet and includes the Calumet River watershed. It encompasses Southeast Chicago, Northwest Indiana, and some of the south suburbs. While a few "mini-mills" and small portions of some of the older mills continued to operate after the mass shutdowns of the early 1980s, the only sizable steel mills still operating have been located in Northwest Indiana. These include U.S. Steel's historic Gary Works as well as Mittal Steel (later Arcelor-Mittal), which has come to encompass parts of the former Inland, LTV, and Bethlehem steel plants in Burns Harbor and East Chicago, Indiana. The remaining Indiana mills

operate with vastly reduced workforces, the mini-mills are generally nonunion, and Mittal Steel has even reverted to the twelve-hour workday. In addition, the remaining steel companies have fought to limit benefits owed to retirees and to lower their tax rates even during times of profitability for their companies. See Eric Sergio Boria, "Borne in the Industrial Everyday: Reterritorializing Claims-Making in a Global Steel Economy" (PhD diss., Loyola University Chicago, 2006). As a consequence, I would argue that this remaining industry has done little to challenge the larger narrative of the decline of an industrial way of life in the Calumet region (see Boria for a somewhat different perspective).

2. Deborah Reed-Danahay, introduction to *Auto/Ethnography: Rewriting the Self and the Social*, ed. Deborah Reed-Danahay (New York: Berg Press, 1997), 9. For more on "autoethnography," see the other chapters in Reed-Danahay's book. See also the introduction by Mary Louise Pratt in *Imperial Eyes: Travel Writing and Transculturation* (London: Routledge, 1992); Catherine Russell, "Autoethnography: Journeys of the Self," ch. 10 in *Experimental Ethnography* (Durham, NC: Duke University Press, 1999); and Carolyn Ellis's *The Ethnographic I: A Methodological Novel about Autoethnography* (Walnut Creek, CA: Altamira Press, 2004).

3. Carolyn Kay Steedman, *Landscape for a Good Woman: A Story of Two Lives* (New Brunswick, NJ: Rutgers University Press, 1986).

4. William Kornblum, *Blue Collar Community* (Chicago: University of Chicago Press, 1974).

5. David Bensman and Roberta Lynch, *Rusted Dreams: Hard Times in a Steel Community* (Berkeley: University of California Press, 1987); Gordon L. Clark, "Piercing the Corporate Veil: The Closure of Wisconsin Steel in South Chicago," *Regional Studies* 24, no. 5 (1990): 405–20.

6. One exception, however, is Bensman and Lynch's *Rusted Dreams*, which offers a more vivid sense of neighborhood life in Southeast Chicago and the demise of the steel industry than most academic accounts.

7. This quote is converted from the Swedish-inflected spelling (for example, *fju* for "few" and *wendt* for "went") for ease of reading.

8. See also Micaela DiLeonardo, "The Female World of Cards and Holidays: Women, Families and the Work of Kinship," *Signs* 12, no. 3 (1987): 440–53.

9. International Harvester (later renamed Navistar) had wanted to sell the mill but was saddled with $62 million in unfunded pension liabilities. Wisconsin's eventual sale to a tiny company with no assets (a company that was deemed an inappropriate buyer by many in the business world) theoretically insulated Harvester from its pension liabilities. However, the terms of the sale also left Harvester in control over crucial mill assets, and Harvester itself eventually triggered the collapse of the mill. For an overview of the complex—and disturbing—machinations surrounding the collapse of Wisconsin Steel, see Bensman and Lynch, *Rusted Dreams;* Clark, "Piercing the Corporate Veil"; and Thomas Geoghegan, *Which Side Are You On? Trying to Be for Labor When It's Flat on Its Back* (New York: Farrar, Straus and Giroux, 1991).

10. Robert Bergsvik, "Rally Marks 9th Anniversary of Wisconsin Steel's Closing," *Daily Calumet*, March 29, 1989, 1. In the previous year, John F. Wasik put the number at six hundred in "End of the Line at Wisconsin Steel," *Progressive* 52 (October 1988): 15.

11. David Harvey, *The Condition of Postmodernity* (Oxford: Basil Blackwell, 1989).

12. Numerous accounts of deindustrialization in Southeast Chicago noted active discrimination in hiring against former steelworkers. Because they had been unionized and earned relatively high wages, there was a perception by some that they would be "difficult" employees in service positions. For example, see the discussion in Bensman and Lynch, *Rusted Dreams*, and Geoghegan, *Which Side Are You On?*

13. For example, see Martha M. Hamilton, "Jobless Benefits," *Washington Post*, February 19, 1981, A1.

14. Lila Abu-Lughod, "Writing against Culture," in *Recapturing Anthropology*, ed. Richard G. Fox (Santa Fe, NM: School of American Research, 1991), 137–62.

7

Racism, Risk, and the
New Color of Dirty Jobs

Lee D. Baker

Springtime in North Carolina is stunning. In mid-April 2006, I was driving west on I-40 between Raleigh and Durham. It was bright, sunny, and sixty-nine degrees. Various work crews were out along the highway—picking up litter, doing construction, mowing medians, and planting flowers. Of all the states in the Union, North Carolina is second only to Texas in miles of state-maintained highways— each mile is well maintained. As traffic slowed along a narrow strip near Research Triangle Park, I noticed two crews on opposite sides of the highway, each comprising about a dozen men. I distinctly remember how the Day-Glo vest each man wore paled in comparison to the pockets of brilliant-violet redbud tucked in between the equally bright white flowers of the elegant dogwoods that bespeckled that particular stand of loblolly pines. Each crew was working very hard, and each was working for the state of North Carolina; one crew was all black, and the other was all Latino. One crew had "NCDT" (North Carolina Department of Transportation) emblazoned across their vests with bold reflective lettering; the other crew had "INMATE" stamped across their vests. Probably members of the Latino crew were immigrant day laborers whom a contractor had picked up that morning from the throng of young men who milled around the local Lowe's Home Improvement Store. And if that was the case, not one of those hardworking men on either side of the highway had legal rights afforded to employees of the state of North Carolina, and each man was being exploited and sorely underpaid. Innocent or guilty, documented or undocumented, each man labored under a pall of criminality, his status as undocumented or convict forcing him to keep North Carolina highways beautiful. For me, this tale of two crews adds an important dimension to the immigration debate that has been roiling Congress, prompting protests en masse; it demonstrates that any discussion of immigration must be viewed against the gritty background of race and racism. That vivid image of the two work crews has gotten me thinking about the shifting politics of race in the United States such that discussions of race should be linked to immigration and discussions of immigration should be linked to race. Connecting these issues quickly leads to a major question: How is Latino immigration affecting economic opportunities and job security for black American men? Although I do not have an answer, that question structures my analysis.

Immigration is emerging as a defining issue for the first part of the twenty-first century—much as it was at the beginning of the twentieth century. And today, as was the case a century ago, the politics and economics of race, labor, assimilation, and civic belonging are being stretched and contorted as they collide and ricochet off each other to the point where no one can predict exactly what the next iteration of racial formation will look and feel like.

The one proimmigrant argument that seems to resonate across party lines and between social classes is the notion that so-called undocumented workers come to this country and do the work that no other Americans want to perform but that is vital to the health of the economy and the comfort of the middle and upper classes. In testimony to the Senate Judiciary Committee, New York City mayor Michael Bloomberg pushed this line of thought further when he explained that his city has some three million immigrants and is financially dependent on the half-million of those who came to this country illegally. "Although they broke the law by illegally crossing our borders," Bloomberg explained, "our city's economy would be a shell of itself had they not, and it would collapse if they were deported." He emphasized that the "same holds true for the nation."[1]

After all, one cannot outsource construction, janitorial services, or highway maintenance. Employers, however, can "in-source" less expensive and more vulnerable labor in the United States from the pool of undocumented labor that hails from the same countries to which so many manufacturing jobs have been relocated. The very premise of this argument—jobs no one else wants to perform—is fundamentally wrong; if the price is right, hardworking Americans will perform the most demeaning or dangerous jobs.

The Discovery Channel produces two shows that demonstrate this point every week. The first, called *Deadliest Catch,* is a derby-style reality TV show that profiles a half-dozen crab boat captains as they ply the unforgiving waters of the Bering Sea in the hunt for Alaska king and opilio crab. Focusing on each captain's strategy and the crews' tenacity, the producers chronicle the onboard adventure and use a leaderboard to log the number of pounds of crab meat in each ship's cargo hold. Ostensibly a contest to see which boat catches the most crab, the drama is driven by an up-close look at the work and lives of the crew members who brave subfreezing temperatures, forty-foot waves, sleepless nights, and dangerous ice packs as they "set the pots" and haul unwieldy steel cages from the bone-chilling sea. The producers worked hard to create television drama out of dropping, setting, and hauling seven-hundred-pound pots day after day, night after night; sometimes the pots were teeming with crab, often they were not. There is an almost 100 percent injury rate, and 80 percent of the on-the-job fatalities result from drowning; fishing for Alaska king crab is a mind-numbing, miserable, and dangerous job, but a deckhand can earn up to $50,000 in just a few months of work. Despite the rough-and-tumble mix of cowboy and maritime culture on deck and in the galley, it's a job no one wants to do. The reward, however, outweighs the risk of literal life and limb for these working-class men.

The second show, Discovery Channel's *Dirty Jobs,* is hosted by Mike Rowe, the good-natured Hollywood hunk from Baltimore who made his name hawking jewelry on QVC. The show purports to "honor" workers who perform often-unpleasant jobs that "make your everyday life easier, safer—and often cleaner." The hook is the affable host making a fool of himself as he makes a bigger mess out of a dirty job that demands some level of skill and experience. The real hook, however, is the viewer imagining his or herself cleaning blood, guts, and all forms of human remains off the walls and ceilings of crime scenes for a starting salary of $35,000, or performing the task of a full-time Porta Potty cleaner, who can earn up to $50,000 a year. As many game and reality shows attest, Americans will do virtually anything for money—the right amount of money. What is unique about these Discovery Channel broadcasts is that they demonstrate that many Americans will perform dangerous, gross, or demeaning work for the right amount of cash and that there is virtually no job out there that documented workers are unwilling to take on. Although it's obvious, it is worth repeating: like the immigrants before them, undocumented immigrants to the United States today are willing to take jobs no other Americans are willing to do *for such low wages.* This is a complex issue, of course. Immigrants are not necessarily "willing" participants in this process and are forced to take these low-paying jobs, often struggling to survive in the United States while sending remittances to loved ones and dependents. Further complicating this dynamic is the idea that the American worker is entitled to high wages or higher wages than undocumented workers. I do not want to imply that documented workers will work only for high wages or to imply that they will not get off their lazy butts unless they "get paid." Countless people labor hard every day for unfair wages, and many documented and undocumented workers do the jobs no one wants to perform, not because they want to, but because they are forced to perform those jobs for meager wages to survive. Rolling back the hard-fought struggle for safe working conditions and a living wage, employers who desire or need low-wage workers fuel the cycle of insecurity, inequality, and instability of work.

This is a tricky essay. I want to connect the immigration of undocumented workers in the United States to the enduring plight of poor black men without sounding racist, xenophobic, sexist, or reactionary. I want to highlight the facts but also explain an important connection between new forms of immigration, the continued plight of poor black men, and ultimately new constructions of race in the United States. Like those two crews, poor black men and poor undocumented immigrants in the United States may be on different sides of the highway, but they are doing the same work. Both are being used to perpetuate inequality, making the American Dream a nightmare in the United States and enabling all Americans to feel more insecure.

As some of the old men in the barbershop would have it, there is a conspiracy to lock up poor black and brown citizens and recruit illegal aliens to this country to take the few jobs left that poor blacks, Chicanos, and Puerto Ricans performed before most of those jobs went overseas. In North Carolina, they often point to such industries as textiles, chicken processing, and construction, whose workforce was filled by black people but now is largely drawn from relatively new foreign-born Latino immigrants. They bemoan the fact that jail, the military, and Wal-Mart seem to be the only real options available for many black people in America. On the other hand, they are also quick to point to a perception that young black men must take on more responsibility—showing up to a job on time, paying child support, treating women with respect, and not getting caught up in the drama of the streets. This personal-responsibility narrative by these old heads, however, is often tempered with the idea that the legacy of racism is as salient a barrier to success today as it has been in the past.

It is sometimes tough to argue complexity and nuance with these organic intellectuals or barber-pole philosophers. As they see it, the facts and common sense drive interpretation, and some light-skinned professor from Duke University is not going to change their minds. I trust their instinct and observations and value their collective wisdom. These ideas, however, are also held in conjunction with the understanding that the newest population of lower-skilled workers can provide a real opportunity for African Americans. No longer relegated to lowest rungs of the workforce, some black Americans can leverage their proficiency in English, citizenship, and cultural competence—cultural capital—to climb their way up and into more stable livelihoods.

This pattern of upward mobility is particularly apparent among the jobs on Duke's academic campus that do not require a college degree. For example, virtually all of the bus drivers are black men, while the housekeeping staff is made up of mostly black women. The big distinction is with the positions that are contract labor. Some of the food service employees are employees of the university; these are mostly black Americans, the majority of whom are women. On the other hand, even more food service workers are employees of the vendors who have won contracts with the university. The majority of these employees are Latinas. There is a similar pattern with the groundskeeping staff. The university employees are mostly black men who manage the day-to-day keeping of the grounds but serve in a supervisory role when the big landscaping jobs are needed right before alumni weekend and graduation. The university contracts these jobs out, and teams of Spanish-speaking men descend on the campus to pull weeds, mow lawns, plant flowers, and erect the ubiquitous white tents on the manicured lawns of Duke's west campus. With high-fidelity sound systems and high-powered air conditioners, these climate-controlled mobile fundraising units are torn down as fast as they are put up, and the Latino groundskeepers are gone until the next big job.

Even though Duke's hourly wages are notoriously low, the health care, retirement, and college tuition reimbursement plans are generous. Even the old men in the barbershop will concede that a black citizen has a better chance than an undocumented worker of getting an entry-level job at a university, the Transportation Security Administration, or FedEx, or an array of the "good jobs" that have emerged as the service industry has eclipsed the "good jobs" in manufacturing. But they are also quick to point out that individuals have to show up for work, be on time, and learn that being ordered to perform menial tasks for minimum wage is not a form of disrespect. This sentiment echoes the famous words penned by African American labor organizer A. Philip Randolph: "Service is not Servitude." Or is it?

My argument in this essay is that the flow of undocumented immigrants to the United States is a component of globalization that is having a rather large impact on poor, undereducated black men—but most people don't notice. Globalization is changing the shape of racial constructs in the United States. Obviously, it is changing demographics, but it is also changing the terms and conditions of race itself.

The construction of race and the articulation of racism are intentional—not to the point of a conspiracy, but often efforts are concerted or work in concert to orchestrate the way ideological precepts bolster financial interests and partisan politics affect material conditions. Although George Fredrickson turns to biology to help identify these dynamics by explaining that "racism is a scavenger ideology," Derrick Bell is more blunt and simply calls race "an indeterminate social construct that is continually reinvented and manipulated to maintain domination and enhance white privilege."[2] In this essay, I address some of the collateral damage and development or unintended consequences that have affected African American communities in the United States in a post-9/11 era, when the agents of the most virulent and explicit forms of racism in the United States target "Arabs" and "immigrants." Yet African American men have not made meaningful material gains during the last decade, even though new groups have joined the ranks of the most feared in America. There has been a noticeable rise in prejudice and anxiety regarding Latino immigrants, Arab Americans, and gays and lesbians in the United States; according to the *Christian Science Monitor,* an actual increase in violence against members of these groups has coincided with the harsh public discourse around gay marriage, terrorism, and immigration.[3] Nevertheless, black Americans still lead the FBI's hate crime statistics in terms of being targeted for such crimes, and "anti-Jewish" hate crimes are six times higher than are "anti-Muslim" crimes, according to the figures for 2007.[4]

There is a sense, however, within some segments of black communities that African Americans should catch a break because they did not bomb the World Trade Center, the Murrow Federal Building, or Centennial Park. Black people are not responsible for the bombing of abortion clinics, the torching of churches, or the rash of school shootings; and, although John Allen Muhammad and Lee Boyd Malvo, charged with the so-called Beltway sniper attacks, are black, African Americans are rarely, if ever, depraved serial killers. Okay, there was Colin Ferguson too.

This sentiment is perhaps best voiced by the peripatetic comics who work the circuits of comedy clubs that cater to black audiences. In the immediate aftermath of 9/11, ethnographer Lanita Jacobs-Huey engaged in fieldwork at these sites and wrote a provocative article titled "'The Arab Is the New Nigger': African American Comics Confront the Irony and Tragedy of September 11." She captured this peculiar view well:

> The "Arab or Middle Easterner as the new nigger" theme echoed like a riff in many urban comedy rooms. Comic/actor "D.C." Curry remarked at the Ha Ha Café, "It's a good time to be Black. If you ain't got no towel wrapped around your head, your ass is in the game!" Glenn B. speculated that "good things come out of bad things," since racists now deflect their hatred from Blacks to people of Middle Eastern descent. At the Comedy Store, he reported meeting a skinhead in the post office who sought to reassure him by saying, "We don't hate you. We hate the Arabs." Similarly, "A. C." acknowledged that, while the national tragedy was "messed up," it had fortuitous consequences as well. He told a crowd at Mixed Nuts, "I haven't been a nigger for a month! Everyone's like, 'Hey Brother!'"[5]

Although the comedians relished exaggerating this sentiment, they graphically portray how members of one racialized minority might hope for a bounce in the polls as another group falls from grace. A similar situation occurred with Chinese Americans after the government of Japan bombed Pearl Harbor and the United States declared war.

Even before the mass migrations in the 1840s, Chinese people in America were very much despised and persecuted. It got so bad that in 1882 the federal government banned Chinese immigration altogether. Japanese immigrants and their children were often viewed more favorably. After the bombing of Pearl Harbor in 1941, however, Japanese Americans went from model minority to a pariah caste.

Although there was little evidence and no provocation, President Franklin D. Roosevelt succumbed to fear and issued Executive Order 9066, which forced U.S. citizens, against their will and with no formal charges, into fortified but makeshift assembly centers before they were loaded by train and convoy to remote internment camps. Approximately 120,000 men, women, and children were incarcerated with no due process and were forcefully removed from their friends, businesses, and homes. They were first "processed"—tagged, labeled, and contained—and then trucked to various camps. Descendants of Italians and Germans in America, however, did not face a similar fate, nor were they perceived as an imminent threat in the same way. Just as important, Chinese Americans began to be viewed in a more positive light, and in 1943 Congress passed the Magnuson Act, which repealed the Chinese Exclusion Act, creating quotas for Chinese immigrants and making provisions so Chinese immigrants could become citizens. From zero to hero. Black Americans, however, have not received any legislative compensation for their historic suffering and have only witnessed affirmative action programs erode in the post-9/11 era. It appears that the comics' hope for some positive unintended consequences never materialized.

THE BEST AND WORST OF TIMES

In many respects, the cliché about the best of times and the worst of times rings true as black people in the United States experience a new century and as the once-rigid color line, like many postmodern iterations of previously starkly delineated entities, has become blurred, globalized, and, well—more flexible.

Every year, the National Urban League publishes a book-length report titled *The State of Black America*. Chock-full of doomsday statistics tempered by rays of hope, it documents how African Americans are faring compared with their white counterparts. The venerable civil rights organization's team of social scientists compiles various measurements and findings into what they call "The State of Black America's Equality Index," which compares the conditions between blacks and whites in economics, health, education, and social justice. Researchers assign whites a weighted index value of 1, and the index measures the equality gaps or disparities between blacks and whites; or, in the case of civic engagement, it demonstrates that members of African American communities are generally more involved in civic society than whites. Numerous subindexes contribute to this overall index, which in 2006 stood virtually unchanged from previous years at 0.73. The dizzying array of graphs and charts is not broken down by region, but many metrics are broken down by age, educational attainment, and other subcategories in an attempt to identify or capture the disparity within particular segments of black communities. Although it is not the Urban League's intent, one could interpret the myriad of charts in *The State of Black America* to demonstrate that black people generally share a racial identity, a history, a heritage, and a sense of civic responsibility but little else. The report actually documents very different life experiences of black people that too often turn on class and educational attainment. For example, in the category "Labor Force Participation," the Urban League pegged that index for black people at 0.98 overall, but for black people over twenty-five years of age with less than a high school education the number dropped to 0.86. Looking closely at the labor force participation category, which does not account for wage disparity or job channeling, one finds an interesting pattern and a trend that has been gaining traction for years. Educated black people are doing better today than ever, and less educated blacks, especially men, are doing very poorly. According to the Urban League's 2006 report, black high school graduates are indexed at 1.09; those with some college at 1.07; those with an associate's degree at 1.03; and college graduates at 1.06. In short, according to the Urban League, those who graduate from high school can find work and participate in the labor force at a rate equal to, even a hair better than, their white counterparts.[6]

Other positive indicators include home ownership in the black community, which is at an all-time high, though blacks experience twice as many mortgage denials. The number of blacks owning their own businesses is also at an all-time high. The U.S. Department of Commerce announced in April 2006 that between 1997 and 2002 black business ownership was up 45 percent and revenues for the nation's 1.2 million black-owned businesses rose 25 percent to $88.8 billion. It is important to note that 1.1 million black-owned businesses are sole proprietorships with an average annual revenue of $25,000.[7]

While revenues for black business are up, teen pregnancy in black communities is down, way down. The Centers for Disease Control and Prevention (CDC) has reported that its most recent data show a continued decline in the teenage birthrate to historic lows, with the sharpest drop in births for African American teens. Overall in the United States, the teen birthrate declined by 30 percent over the past decade, but the rate for black teens was down by more than 40 percent. For young black teens (fifteen to seventeen years of age), the number of live births was cut in half from 1991 levels.[8]

Although respected studies produced by the Urban Institute and the Manhattan Institute report that there is roughly a fifty-fifty chance that a black student entering high school will receive a regular diploma in four years, the U.S. Census Bureau confidently reported that "the proportion of both Blacks and non-Hispanic Whites who had a high school diploma reached record highs at 80 percent and 89 percent, respectively in 2003" and that the gap between the proportions of whites and blacks who had diplomas was getting smaller and smaller.[9] Echoing these findings, the *Journal of Blacks in Higher Education* (*JBHE*) reported that "the percentage of African Americans ages 20 to 24 who have completed high school or successfully passed a high school equivalency examination is now almost equal to the rate for whites."[10]

The *JBHE* has developed an overall index of racial parity that is very similar to that of the Urban League. The *JBHE* calls it the "Black-White Higher Education Equality Index" and updates it quarterly. For the spring of 2006, the journal reported that its equity index was at its highest level ever—73.6 percent: "An Education Equality Index reading of 100 percent is the JBHE's Holy Grail. This would mean for the most part that blacks had reached parity with whites in all important measures of presence and achievement in higher education."[11] Pushing its index to its highest level ever, the journal reported, were the record numbers of black students enrolling in graduate and professional schools and the record number of blacks who have received a GED or a high school diploma.

Finally, the number of African American homicide victims has also been cut almost in half in the last fifteen years. The FBI reported that in 1991 the number topped at 12,296 but that by 2003 the number had dropped to 6,912.[12] From a variety of different sources and perspectives, it appears that black people have been doing relatively well in recent years, with home ownership, educational attainment, labor force participation, and business revenues going up while teen pregnancies and homicides have been going down.

The Urban League has a specific policy agenda and often highlights the negative to leverage its position to effect much-needed change. In the wake of Hurricanes Katrina and Rita, which laid bare the stark reality of the vulnerable poor, the Urban League focused on the economic disparity that persists between blacks and whites in the United States, noting that the median net worth of black families was $6,166 compared with $67,000 for white families and that median income was $34,369 for black families and $55,768 for white families. When it comes to health and welfare, the state of black America is dire; as reported by the Urban League, a black person is ten times as likely as a white person to have HIV/AIDS, twice as likely to have diabetes, and five times as likely to die of homicide. In the same report, the Urban League invited Marian Wright Edelman, president of the Children's Defense Fund, to help interpret some of the data. Her sobering but eye-opening essay recounted that in 2006 a black boy in kindergarten had a 1 in 3 chance of serving a sentence in prison during his lifetime and that today 580,000 black males are serving prison sentences, whereas fewer than forty thousand black students earn bachelor degrees each year. The homogeneous "black community" or metrics that aggregate data to give a picture of the putative "black family" are dangerous reifications that flatten the cross-cutting ways class, gender, sexual orientation, age, region, occupation, and a myriad of other factors can affect individuals, families, and entire communities.

BEING A BLACK MAN

These types of negative findings documenting the plight of black people have always been grist for news media and foundations. Recently, however, the focus on young black men has eclipsed the more positive findings, as well as the dire straits of the many poor black women, children, and elderly. In March 2006, Erik Eckholm wrote a *New York Times* article entitled "Plight Deepens for Black Men." Eckholm reviewed several recent studies that underscore the grim prospects of undereducated black men between twenty and thirty-nine years of age.[13] Each study, Eckholm explained, paints a grim picture of black men in America and points to the usual suspects—jobs, education, and incarceration. Culling the data, Eckholm reported that in 2000, 65 percent of black male high school dropouts in their twenties were jobless and that by 2004 that number had grown to 72 percent, compared with 34 percent of white and 19 percent of Hispanic dropouts. Although the growth of the black middle class and the shrinking prospects of the "truly disadvantaged" in a deindustrialized economy are not new, they continue to be newsworthy. And as anyone who regularly attends college commencement exercises knows, it is vividly apparent that black women are faring better than black men. The reasons are complicated but rooted in a history of whites' anxieties over threats that they see black men as embodying.

White people have always had more intimate access to black women, their labor, and their bodies, while black men's labor and bodies have been viewed as threatening since Reconstruction. What has changed in the era of Colin Powell and 50 Cent, Barack Obama and LeBron James, is the notion that somehow racism and simply being a black man in America is no longer the barrier to success it used to be. Even if one had it hard growing up, with a little luck and a lot of pluck, one can parlay an up-from-the-ghetto narrative into a successful career as a rap artist, a colorful bad-boy backstory for a successful athlete, or a hard-work-and-determination bio for a politician. The fact that Barack Obama sits in the Oval Office compounds these dynamics, because racial barriers and discrimination are now surmountable and with hard work and determination anyone can become president of the United States. The problem with the luck-and-pluck narrative is that it belies the fact that black boys and black men are systematically discriminated against in school and in the workforce. More important, systemic and institutional racism gives way to individual shortcomings as the main reason black men don't succeed at the rate they should. The problem with the luck-and-pluck narrative is that it belies the fact that black boys and black men are systematically discriminated against in school and in the workforce. I do not want to discount the systemic sexism and racism that continue to be leveled against black women or to downplay the collective triumphs and sorrows that so many black women experience as they stake their claims to the American Dream. But the life chances for young black men and young black women today are quantitatively and qualitatively different; in the words of Ron Dellums, longtime congressional representative and the mayor of Oakland, the schools, low-wage workforce, and prison system are "grinding young men of color up like glass."

In response to the spate of new studies on black men, as well as the widely circulated Eckholm article in the *New York Times,* the *Washington Post* ran a series of articles simply titled "Being a Black Man." To accompany the series, the *Post* launched an interactive Web site and partnered with Harvard University and the Kaiser Family Foundation to conduct a comprehensive survey and host a high-profile forum.

The long-running series detailed the findings of the survey as well as profiling the lives of several black men and boys. One of the most popular articles documented the Herculean efforts of Jachin Leatherman and Wayne Nesbit to become the valedictorian and salutatorian, respectively, of Ballou High School's class of 2006. The *Post* journalist V. Dion Haynes described in detail how these young men successfully navigated the perilous halls of a school "tinged with every headline and grim event that has given it a reputation as one of Washington's worst and most dangerous high schools."[14] In a noble attempt to put a positive spin on grim statistics, the *Post* described how both boys had won scholarships to attend elite private high schools in suburban Maryland but had declined the offers and decided at the end of junior high school to make "a private pact with each other that by the time they graduated from high school, they would have made Ballou a better place to be young, black and male."[15]

To underscore the odds faced by these two handsome kids who excelled in the classroom and on the gridiron, the *Washington Post* trotted out the grim statistics to paint a bleak picture: African American males have the lowest reading and math proficiency levels of any group; black boys represent only 8.7 percent of the nation's public school enrollment, but they make up 23 percent of students suspended and 22 percent of those expelled—the largest for any group; only 45 percent of black boys receive high school diplomas within four years, compared with 70 percent of white boys; and, finally, black boys are overrepresented in special education programs.

What the *Post* did not mention, but the January 30, 2006, cover story of *Newsweek* did, is that "by almost every benchmark, boys across the nation and in every demographic group are falling behind. In elementary school, boys are two times more likely than girls to be diagnosed with learning disabilities and twice as likely to be placed in special-education classes. High school boys are losing ground to girls on standardized writing tests. The number of boys who said they didn't like school rose 71 percent between 1980 and 2001."[16] To properly conceptualize the *Post*'s bleak picture, one must add racism, economic disparity, and failing schools to this troubling overall trend. Additionally, when one considers the high levels of lead, mercury, and other neurotoxins disproportionately contaminating black neighborhoods, it is no wonder that too many black boys begin to fall behind by fourth grade and that many begin a downward spiral toward dropping out of school.

By articulating the all-too-American narrative of triumph in the face of adversity (a running theme throughout the series), the *Post* simultaneously articulated a seductive counternarrative; if these two boys can do it, there must be something wrong with the others who are bedeviled by gang violence, shackled by poverty, or mired in despair. Without the barriers of Jim Crow and explicit racism, the implied narrative goes, these others must have bad brains or bad behavior—and both explanations were routinely referenced in one way or another at that star-studded forum hosted by the *Washington Post* and the Kaiser Family Foundation, where both Wayne Nesbit and Jachin Leatherman were greeted by thunderous applause and received well-deserved accolades from the likes of Bill Cosby, Ron Dellums, and Alvin Poussaint.[17]

Although the bad-brains narrative was muted compared with the bad-behavior discussion, Alvin Poussaint raised the specter of biology. Citing a Yale Child Study Center report, he explained that twice as many black children as white children were expelled from preschool and that nine out of ten of those black children were boys. He posed questions: "Is racial profiling happening at three and four?" "Or, is it something that has to do with the Black family?"[18]

Citing high rates of aggression, violence, attention-deficit disorder, and dyslexia, Alvin Poussaint actually said that many, many more black boys than black girls are "mentally handicapped" or "retarded." "Is something happening prenatally?" he asked, but he quickly turned his attention to the role of single mothers and parenting and focused on high levels of child abuse, neglect, and the overuse of corporal punishment on boys, explaining that research shows the more you beat them, the angrier they get. Downplaying the role of white racism or anything else, he placed the responsibility for what he perceived as an epidemic of bad brains on black women—the mothers—concluding simply that "it is not totally natural for them" to raise boys.[19]

Although the scholars, politicians, and celebrities at the forum often cloaked these easy answers in sophistry, the *Post* readers who responded online were straightforward. For example, Bazeyi Hategekimana concluded that in the absence of "the usefulness, the accuracy, and the scientific value of IQ theory, What I can say is: 'Give me a break.'"[20] He implied what many people think: the success or failure of young black men is the personal responsibility of each individual, and each individual has the capacity to achieve and be meritorious. This popular luck-and-pluck line of thought, however, does not account for the complicated racism generated at the intersection of American desire for conspicuous consumption, the low-wage workforce, failing schools, thriving prisons, crippling poverty, and the disrespect that comes from systematic and debilitating racial discrimination.

Although most of the reader responses to the *Washington Post* complimented the editors for addressing such a thorny problem head-on, many people tried their hand at armchair sociology and amateur anthropology, sharing their own explanations for the dire conditions confronting black men. As on many other interactive blogs, some posts were very sophisticated, while others were just banal. In the collective effort to identify cause and effect, one of the most popular approaches was to give a nod to racism, yet employ the rhetoric about an individual's personal responsibility to engage in good behavior and suffer the consequences of bad decisions.

An interesting theme, however, emerged within these posts: whites' belief that their own situation was as bad as blacks' or worse. G. Butler summed up this line of thought: "THE SAME CRAP HAPPENS TO EVERY MAN IN AMERICA." One anonymous reader complained, "I may stop reading the *Washington Post* for the remainder of the year since I'm tired of pity parties from black Americans." She continued: "If I had as many incentives as a middle-class white girl that a single black (unwed) mother or father receives, I'd be living the high life and not struggling. And yes, I have a college degree. Where in the hell has it gotten me? Now, if I was black with/or without children, I'd be actively recruited for jobs, internships, etc, etc. etc. The worst thing you can be in today's world is white and middle class. You will not get anywhere!"

Although some readers claimed that America was a meritocracy and that mediocrity was not a racial characteristic, it is important to note that not one of the scores of readers responding to the series resorted to the idea that lower IQ or a higher incidence of "bad brains" explained the *Post's* depiction of black men's dire straits; ten years ago, in the wake of the best-selling *The Bell Curve: Intelligence and Class Structure in American Life*,[21] that explanation was getting quite a bit of consideration. And while opinions were evenly split, explaining the situation as the result of white racism or the sum total of poor individual decisions, another popular narrative emerged: bad behavior was the result of bad culture. This variant emerged as a result of two distinct themes, one coming mainly from the black middle class and the other coming from people of Caribbean descent. For example, R. Warren commented:

> As a Black Woman in Washington, DC, I am oftentimes appalled at how we as Black Americans treat one another. Everything bad, or negative that happens to us, is not ALWAYS from the hand of a White person! We, Black America—have become out-of-control. Our attitudes, STINK. Our language is UNFATHOMABLE. Everything that our "forefathers" fought for, everyone younger than 30 care nothing at all about. We know more about the personal business of entertainers, than we do about how to get our children to school on time. We know how to manipulate the system to our own advantage, yet, when things don't go "our" way—it is always someone else' fault!! WHY?? . . . What the hell happened to us?? Sometimes, I am hurt and ashamed. This is not the way it should BE!! . . . WAKE-UP BLACK AMERICA. Prove them wrong!!

A man who called himself "Mark" expressed a similar idea about black people's putatively pathological culture and tried to distance himself from the so-called problem. In the feedback section of the Web site, he explained: "Sadly, one of the things that we as Caribbeans despise surrounds the fact that we're lumped in with Black Americans. In my opinion it would help if the survey differentiated between the two. In general we don't understand their [African Americans'] thought process and don't subscribe to a host of their theories. It's a *[sic]* unwritten rule in the Caribbean community that we stay away from African Americans."

This threadbare narrative regarding black people's pathological culture has been a standard and often quite pat explanation used by academics, pundits, and politicians to explain the reported findings. Harvard sociologist Orlando Patterson is the latest in a long line of august scholars, notably Daniel Patrick Moynihan, who have argued that bad culture produces bad behavior—reasoning that has changed little in well over a century. The culprit is "what sociologists call the 'cool-pose culture' of young black men. . . . For these young men, it is "almost like a drug, hanging out on the street after school, shopping and dressing sharply, sexual conquests, party drugs, hip-hop music and culture."[22]

Although Patterson makes several salient points with regard to the history of oppression and the power of the global marketplace, he too easily falls into the very old trap of concentrating on pathological and destructive behaviors among young blacks in the inner cities while ignoring such behaviors elsewhere and among other demographics. For example, he says nothing about date rape, methamphetamine use, prescription drug abuse, and binge drinking, all of which are problems among whites and in suburbs, small towns, and rural areas. And while he is quick to indict hip-hop culture, he fails to explain that baggy pants, ubiquitous tattoos, and expressive sexuality have been thoroughly adopted by many white youth, from the Outer Banks to Northern California. There is enough pathological culture in America to go around. Poor blacks, very poor whites, and poor Hmong and Laotians, however, seem to be the only subjects for this type of analysis.

One of the most debilitating aspects of this type of analysis is that by raising a simplistic notion of culture as the root cause, one depicts a complex racialized group in homogenizing and essentialist terms and implies that individuals are simply shackled by tradition. Though notions of identity and specific cultural patterns are shared among and between black people in the United States and throughout the diaspora, Irvin Hicks Jr. was correct when he explained, in the readers' feedback forum for the Washington Post, that "we are diverse, complex individuals who are part of a non-homogeneous fabric just like the rest of humanity."

Race, racism, and democracy have always been fluid and flexible constructions, and new formations of race continue to emerge. Whichever way the causal arrow points, it is high time we come up with new understandings of the way that black men who for whatever reason do not graduate from high school are emerging as a specific sociological category, with devastating but increasingly predictable outcomes. The old explanations regarding bad behavior or bad brains do not have enough explanatory purchase to account for the emergence of new formations of race that are classed and gendered and integral to new economies dependent on the prison industrial complex on the one hand and new flows of migratory labor on the other.

Not one commentator for the New York Times, the Washington Post, or the star-studded panel at the Kaiser Family Foundation made the connection that neoliberalism, globalization, and the flow of immigrants to the United States might affect the construction of race in the United States and the life chances for young black men. Nor did anyone offer an explanation that accounts for the way many manufacturing jobs, where black men once had a foothold, have been relocated overseas and replaced by service jobs, often performed by women.

One has to consider that 72 percent of black male high school dropouts are jobless while only 19 percent of Hispanic male dropouts are jobless. Something is going on, and I don't buy the idea that so-called undocumented workers or "Mexicans" work harder. On the other hand, an undocumented worker *is* less likely to say "Fuck you!" walk off the job, and then try to sue the employer for unsafe working conditions.

Three particular studies provide productive ways to interrogate the impact globalization has had on new constructions of race for black people in the United States; together, they provide novel ways of looking at the connections between immigration, neoliberalism, incarceration, and the perilous conditions in which many undereducated black men find themselves today. The first is "Race at Work: Realities of Race and Criminal Record in the NYC Job Market," a study conducted by Devah Pager and Bruce Western. Their team of researchers sent out so-called "testers" to apply for advertised jobs in New York City. "The testers were well-spoken young men, aged 22 to 26," and each was part of a three-man team—one white, one black, and one Latino member per team.[23] The testers had fictitious résumés that represented comparable profiles. Like other such audit studies, Pager and Western's study showed significant differences in "positive responses": white men fared best, then Latinos, and finally black men. The researchers then added a bit of a twist. They sent out white men who disclosed a criminal background. After analyzing the job offers and callbacks in response to this new configuration, the researchers reported that the "white applicant with a felony conviction appears to do just as well, if not better, than his black counterpart with no criminal background."[24] They concluded that "black job applicants are only two-thirds as successful as equally qualified Latinos, and little more than half as successful as equally qualified whites. Indeed, black job seekers fare no better than white men just released from prison."[25]

The second study, by Michael A. Stoll, is titled "Taking Stock of the Employment Opportunities of Less-Educated African American Men." Commissioned by the Congressional Black Caucus Foundation, it sets forth a range of supply- and demand-side explanations for why so many young black men with little education become so-called discouraged workers or find themselves jobless. One of its important findings is that less-educated white and Latino men have been getting jobs in the construction industry, one area in the industrial sector that has experienced growth in the last decade, even as comparably educated black men have not.[26]

The third study was conducted by my friend and colleague Paula McClain. She and her team found that Latino immigrants to North Carolina hold negative and stereotypical views of blacks and feel that they have more in common with whites than they do with blacks. Yet whites there do not reciprocate these feelings toward Latinos and feel that they have more in common with blacks because of shared history and culture.[27]

Triangulating the findings of these studies raises many questions, but one can begin to identify a pattern: there is empirical evidence that racism is thriving and discrimination is real, and this is despite the widespread idea that we are increasingly living in a color-blind society or that luck or pluck can enable anyone to succeed. Although whites, at least in North Carolina, feel that they have more in common with blacks than they do with Latino immigrants, this does not translate into better job prospects for black men in the low-wage job market. Finally, Latino immigrants, it appears, are more likely to identify or find common ground with white people than with black people. Interrogating these findings as they relate to the fault lines of class, ideas of assimilation and belonging, gender, and the wages of whiteness will help us get a better understanding of the new topographies of race in the twenty-first century.

NEOLIBERALISM

Most people will concede that education and taxation, job creation and competition, and the structures of housing and health care opportunity are all undergoing important changes as a result of new flows of immigration. Less obvious, but also important, is the shift in new and old forms of racism, assimilation and acculturation, and constructions of race. The annual influx of seven hundred thousand or more undocumented people from Latin America across the U.S. border to find jobs, start families, and stake their claim to the American Dream has profoundly changed both race relations and the construction of race. But how does one try to explain and unpack these more subtle cultural and sociological shifts, and how do they affect the racial politics of culture and the cultural politics of race?

I find myself cringing at the prospect of agreeing with President Bush, who argues that we need a humane and respectful policy to address the needs of poor and exploited workers who risk everything to come and work in the United States. I am sympathetic to the claim that we did not cross the borders, the borders crossed us, and I am inspired by early La Raza leaders like Rodolfo "Corky" Gonzalez, who organized the Chicano contingent for the 1968 Poor People's Campaign in Washington. I don't trust, however, the neoliberal rational choice theorists who somehow come off as liberal reformers and claim that the market will drive fair wages and efficiently direct the flow of poor and exploited workers to the chicken- and hog-processing plants in North Carolina, the manicured lawns of the Hamptons, and the crop fields of the San Joaquin Valley. Recent immigrants are cast as laborers who simply fill a natural market, keeping prices low, wages down, and the American economy humming along. It seems like a naked play for cheap laborers who are vulnerable, exploited, and simply cogs in the capitalist machine, laborers who do not get workers' compensation, cannot withdraw from Social Security, and do not have access to reasonable health care.

The rhetoric of neoliberalism, to me, is reminiscent of the slavers' portrayals of happy hardworking Negroes who were better off here, enslaved, than free in Africa. I am equally loath to write, speak, or teach about limiting Latino immigration, increasing border security, or cracking down on so-called illegal aliens. The xenophobia and racism inherent in this approach are not an option.

The debate has thus been cast in either-or terms; it seems as though one must support either a neoliberal guest worker program and an eventual bid for citizenship or a racist and xenophobic position that closes the borders. The batten-down-the-hatches approach makes felons out of trustworthy people who are just trying to make an honest living from a dishonest wage, while the guest worker program institutionalizes a second class of noncitizens whose only hope is to go to the end of the line and hope for the day when they might get their bid for citizenship.

RACE IN THE YEAR 2050

Immigration to the United States is a formula for success that has worked for years, but seemingly only for those who have made up the storied "huddled masses." It is worth repeating Emma Lazarus's famous poem that is engraved in the stone base of the Statue of Liberty: "Give me your tired, your poor, / Your huddled masses yearning to breathe free, / The wretched refuse of your teeming shore, / Send these, the homeless, tempest-tost, to me."

For a century, these famous lines served as an unofficial immigration policy. Etched into the mind of many a grade-school pupil, the mantra informs an open-borders policy that emphasizes immigrants' role in making the United States a strong and diverse nation. But if one substitutes "teeming shore" with "teeming borders," or identifies the shore as that of Cuba, Haiti, or the Dominican Republic, the tone and effect of the poem seem to change. When black and brown people come, American racism precludes the same welcoming embrace for the "wretched refuse" who are homeless and tempest-tossed.

By 2050, so-called racialized minorities will be the majority in the United States, and whites will once again be the minority—so goes the rhetoric of everyone from advertisers to demographers. And rhetoric is probably all it is. As with a weather forecast, there is no way to know with certainty what the exact demographic makeup will be in 2050. It is important to note that the same rhetoric and forecasts of certain demographic change were prevalent during Reconstruction after the Civil War: the United States, it was predicted, would soon have no more race problem because black people, deprived of whites' paternal care, would simply die of disease or kill each other.

Nevertheless, a look at countries within the African diaspora suggests that the future will not be what most people are predicting. In a provocative article titled "Are Latinos Becoming 'White' Folk? And What That Still Says about Race in America," Alisse Waterston describes a process that many scholars are familiar with in South Africa, Surinam, Trinidad, Brazil, and indeed Florida, where members of a one-time racialized minority group emerge as "not quite white" and begin to function as "virtually white" or as a buffer race between whites and African peoples, who still suffer the brunt of racism and exploitation at the bottom of the racial and class hierarchy.

Waterston explains that the categories "English oriented" and "Spanish preferred," used by advertising agencies and marketers to split the so-called Latino market, are color- and class-coded euphemisms. Employing Karen Brodkin's notion that an "unholy trinity of corporations, the state, and monopolistic media produces and reproduces patterns and practices of whiteness with dreadful predictability,"[28] Waterston reminds readers that the media, including advertisers, have long played an important role in the construction of race and that these color- and class-inflected monikers might portend the expansion of the borders and boundaries of whiteness.[29]

The result would be a new model minority with class mobility—English-oriented Latinos—who would have access to the wages of whiteness, while the Spanish preferred would emerge as something like a model minority with class immobility. The pattern in Florida, with the whitening of the pre–Mariel boat lift Cubans, will extend its reach from Florida to Texas and California; for that matter, it will extend to any locale where the light and often-white Latino professional class—deemed "English oriented"—assimilates to an expanding and flexible racial category of whiteness. It is a scenario in which ideas about *la familia* merge with family values, a strong work ethic complements the so-called Protestant work ethic, and conservative Catholicism merges with the values of prolife Protestants. More importantly, it is a scenario that leverages the century-long momentum of incorporating Irish, Italian, Jewish, and other racialized minorities into the category of whiteness. The Republican Party, at least, hopes this will result in more voters who favor the likes of Alberto Gonzales and fewer voters who favor the likes of Antonio R. Villaraigosa.

Access to the wages of whiteness is one thing; access to just plain wages is another. The so-called Spanish-preferred Latinos—usually darker, poorer, and more closely tied to their indigeneity—are also playing an interesting role in shifting labor markets. While some pundits employ the oft-cited "jobs no one wants," others color-code their rhetoric by evoking the attractiveness of recent immigrants' strong work ethic to potential employers. In this last iteration, the opposite, but equally racist, dynamics unfold in the same way as they have in the rhetoric about black people's "pathological culture." When nearly everyone from talk radio hosts to roofers to restaurant managers evokes the hard-won and strong work ethic of many recent immigrants, the reference is to Latin Americans, but not to the many hardwork-ing immigrants from Latin America or the Caribbean who are also part of the African diaspora, or to the hardworking African immigrants, or to the many hard-working undocumented workers from Canada, Ireland, or India. The singling out of "Spanish-preferred" mestizos for inclusion in this category increases the unre-markability of whiteness on the one hand and codes black immigrants as lazy or as criminals on the other.

I cannot help but juxtapose this rhetoric with those two hardworking work crews I witnessed on that highway. I think what needs to be addressed is the perception that the so-called Spanish-preferred and often undocumented workers are better workers who will work for less money than their black peers. We need a more so-phisticated and politically responsible analysis that focuses on class and race and gender while exploring how employment opportunities are provided to some while being stripped from others. Employers risk committing a crime by hiring undoc-umented workers because they do not want to risk hiring anyone whom they be-lieve might commit a crime.

NOTES

1. Michael Bloomberg, testimony, Senate Committee on the Judiciary, *Comprehensive Immigration Reform: Examining the Need for a Guest Worker Program*, field hearing, Philadelphia, 109th Cong., 2nd sess., July 5, 2006, http://frwebgate.access.gpo.gov/cgi-bin/getdoc.cgi?dbname=109_senate_hearings&docid=f:30254.pdf.

2. George M. Fredrickson, *Racism: A Short History* (Princeton: Princeton University Press, 2002), 8; Derrick Bell, *Race, Racism, and American Law* (Gaithersburg, MD: Aspen Law and Business, 2000), 9.

3. Brad Knickerbocker, "National Acrimony and a Rise in Hate Crimes," *Christian Science Monitor*, June 3, 2005, www.csmonitor.com/2005/0603/p03s01-ussc.html.

4. U.S. Department of Justice, "Hate Crime Statistics 2007," table 1, www.fbi.gov/ucr/hc2007/table_01.htm.

5. Lanita Jacobs-Huey, "'The Arab Is the New Nigger': African American Comics Confront the Irony and Tragedy of September 11," *Transforming Anthropology* 14, no. 1 (2006): 61.

6. Lee A. Daniels, ed., *The State of Black America* (Chicago: National Urban League Publications, 2006), 19.

7. Michael Bergman, "Revenues for Black-Owned Firms Near $89 Billion, Number of Businesses Up 45 Percent," U.S. Department of Commerce press release, April 18, 2006, www.census.gov/Press-Release/www/releases/archives/business_ownership/006711.html.

8. Joyce A. Martin et al., "Births: Final Data for 2002," *National Vital Statistics Reports* 52, no. 10 (2003): 1.

9. Jay P. Greene and Marcus A. Winters, "Public High School Graduation and College Readiness Rates: 1991–2002," Manhattan Institute for Public Research, Education Working Paper No. 3, 2003, www.manhattan-institute.org/html/ewp_03.htm, 1–36; Christopher Swanson, *Who Graduates? Who Doesn't? A Statistical Portrait of Public High School Graduation, Class of 2001* (Washington, DC: Urban Institute Education Policy Center, 2004), www.urban.org/publications/410934.html; Nicole Stoops, *Educational Attainment in the United States: 2003*, Current Population Reports P20, No. 550 (Washington, DC: U.S. Census Bureau, 2004), www.census.gov/prod/2004pubs/p20-550.pdf, 4.

10. "Black-White Higher Education Equality Index," *Journal of Blacks in Higher Education* 51 (2006): 48.

11. Ibid.

12. Ibid., 49.

13. Erik Eckholm, "Plight Deepens for Black Men, Studies Warn," *New York Times*, March 20, 2006. The studies Eckholm highlighted were Peter Edelman, Harry Holzer, and Paul Offner's *Reconnecting Disadvantaged Young Men* (Washington, DC: Urban Institute Press, 2006); Ronald B. Mincy's *Black Males Left Behind* (Washington, DC: Urban Institute Press, 2006); and Bruce Western's *Punishment and Inequality in America* (New York: Russell Sage Foundation, 2006).

14. V. Dion Haynes, "For the Love of Ballou," *Washington Post*, June 23, 2006, A11, A1.

15. Ibid., A11, A14.

16. Peg Tyre, "The Trouble with Boys; They're Kinetic, Maddening and Failing at School. Now Educators Are Trying New Ways to Help Them Succeed," *Newsweek*, January 30, 2006, 44.

17. "Paths to Success: A Forum on Young African American Men," Kaiser Family Foundation conference, Washington, DC, July 18, 2006; for transcript, see www.kff.org/kaiserpolls/upload/phip071806 trans.pdf.

18. Remarks by Alvin Poussaint at the Kaiser Family Foundation conference "Paths to Success," 33.

19. Ibid, 35.

20. "What Do You Think about the 'Being a Black Man' Project?" *Washington Post*, posted reader comments (June–November 2006), on the paper's "Being a Black Man" series of reports over that year, http://blog.washingtonpost.com/blackmen/2006/05/what_do_you_think_about_the_be.html; for the series Web site, see www.washingtonpost.com/wp-srv/metro/interactives/blackmen/blackmen.html.

21. Richard Herrnstein and Charles Murray, *The Bell Curve: Intelligence and Class Structure in American Life* (New York: Free Press, 1994).

22. Orlando Patterson, "A Poverty of Mind," *New York Times*, March 26, 2006, 13.

23. Devah Pager and Bruce Western, "Race at Work: Realities of Race and Criminal Record in the NYC Job Market," report for the Schomburg Center for Research in Black Culture, December 2005, www.princeton.edu/~pager/race_at_work.pdf, 2.

24. Ibid., 6.

25. Ibid., 12.

26. Michael A. Stoll, "Taking Stock of the Employment Opportunities of Less-Educated African American Men," report for the Congressional Black Caucus Foundation, June 2006, www.cbcfinc.org/pdf/Taking_Stock_Doc.pdf, 5.

27. Paula D. McClain et al., "Racial Distancing in a Southern City: Latino Immigrants' Views of Black Americans," *Journal of Politics* 68, no. 3 (2006): 571–84.

28. Karen Brodkin, *How Jews Became White Folks and What That Says about Race in America* (New Brunswick, NJ: Rutgers University Press, 1998), 177–78.

29. Alisse Waterston, "Are Latinos Becoming 'White' Folk? And What That Still Says about Race in America," *Transforming Anthropology* 14, no. 2 (2006): 132–50.

PART THREE

Insecurity as a Profit Center

8

Normal Insecurities, Healthy Insecurities

Joseph Dumit

There is a cartoon of a doctor talking to a man in an examining room with the caption: "Your blood pressure is off the chart, you're overweight and out of shape, and your cholesterol is god-awful. In short, I find you perfectly normal." The same cartoon also has a different caption: "The good news is that your cholesterol level hasn't gone up. The bad news is that the guidelines have changed." In this essay I want to tell a story of how the health industry works such that both of these captions make sense. They are both funny, and their intersection points to a new kind of health, where to be normal is to have symptoms and risk factors that you should worry about and, at the same time, to not know whether you should be worrying about yet more things. To be normal, therefore, is to be insecure. In fact, to not worry about your health, to not know as much as you can about it, is to be irresponsible. There are even public relations campaigns featuring people who are "the Picture of Health" and warning, "You may look and feel fine, but you need to get the inside story."[1]

Health in America today is defined by this double insecurity: never being sure enough about the future (always being at risk) and never knowing enough about what you could and should be doing. Paradoxically, this insecurity continues to grow despite the equal growth in research about risks, screening, and treatments and a constant growth in the amount of medicine consumed each year—as if the more we know, the more we fear we don't know. This growth in pharmaceutical consumption is actually quite astounding. Put simply, Americans are on drugs. The average American is prescribed and purchases somewhere between nine and thirteen different prescription-only drugs per year. Of course, the range is wide, with many people prescribed few or no drugs each year. Out of a sample of three million individuals in the plans of pharmacy benefits companies and insurance companies such as Express Scripts, 11 percent of Americans, or 40 percent of all those over age fifty, were prescribed cholesterol-lowering drugs in 2003. In 2003, more than 20 percent of women over forty were prescribed antidepressants, and almost 10 percent of boys aged ten to fourteen were prescribed attention-deficit disorder drugs.[2] These numbers explain a significant part of the cost of health care: overall annual health care costs were over $2 trillion by 2003, with prescription drugs accounting for about 10 percent of that, or $203 billion.[3]

Remarkably, the rates of prescription drug use are only projected to keep increasing. The cost of health care has been growing and is expected to continue to grow around 7 percent per year through 2015, drug prescriptions over 8 percent per year, and personal health care spending about 7.5 percent per year. The growth rates for almost all classes of drugs have been in the low double digits for a decade, with prescription rates for kids growing upwards of 30 percent per year. Similarly, both the prevalence (the number of people on each drug) and the intensity (the number of prescriptions for the population) are projected to continue to grow in all drug categories for the foreseeable future. The figures do match the fears, and according to many surveys, Americans are spending more time, energy, attention, and money on health. Health clearly is not simply a cost to the nation to be reduced; it is also a market to be grown.

Explaining this continual growth in drugs, diagnoses, costs, and insecurity can take many forms. One key approach involves following the money and tracing connections between pharmaceutical company profits and disease expansion. The recent books by Marcia Angell, Jerry Avorn, Ray Moynihan, David Healy, and others, and the detailed reporting by the *Seattle Times* in "Suddenly Sick," are each worth mining for how many ways there are to manipulate the pharmaceutical system—from controlling research results, to ghostwriting medical articles allegedly penned by doctors, to influencing guideline committees, to hyping clinical trials, to funding disease awareness campaigns and activist groups in order to drive drug sales.[4] The fact that most biomedical research is underwritten by private industry and therefore most drugs are produced first for profit and second for health means that there is a structural contradiction in medicine requiring vigilant watchdogs. But in this chapter I want to take a different approach. For the past five years I have been conducting fieldwork on pharmaceutical marketing—attending conferences, talking with marketers, researchers, doctors, and patients, and surveying the large literature produced by marketers about their strategies. I have concluded that underlying the continual growth in drugs, diseases, costs, and insecurity is a relatively new definition of ourselves as inherently ill, of health as reduction in risk, and of subjective bodily experience of health as fundamentally insecure. Together these definitions are reinforced and amplified by the pharmaceutical industry, but I think they would still drive the growth in medicines even if the critics were successful in clearing out the abuses.

UNLIMITED HEALTH IMPERATIVES

Health and illness definitions vary historically and culturally. Diseases that today are quite commonly understood and diagnosed depend on clinical work to discover and define the condition and on social work to make the condition culturally visible. Medical anthropologist Robert Hahn highlighted in his 1995 book *Sickness and Healing* how high blood pressure, to be a sickness, requires that its bearers recognize it and want to get rid of it. But where to draw the line between high blood pressure and near-high blood pressure is not clear. Similarly, cancer could be defined as a tumor that caused suffering in a person or as a tumor that might cause such suffering. But Hahn worried about the development of a slippery slope such that almost anything could be called a disease. "We would not want to describe a person as 'sick' from the instant of this [cancerous] cell division, since the disease might never follow or might follow only decades later. With a definition including all first events in causal processes as sicknesses themselves, we would all be sick from birth, for it is likely that causal processes of sickness and aging are present from the outset." In this passage, Hahn makes a normative claim: "We *would not* want to describe a person as 'sick' from the instant of [cancerous] cell division."[5] Since this would be a reductio ad absurdum argument, Hahn thinks it goes without saying that defining everyone as sick from birth does not make sense. He also seems to think that *we* should have some say in what sort of definition of disease we want.

Dr. H. Gilbert Welch, author of the provocatively titled book *Should I Be Tested for Cancer? Maybe Not, and Here's Why,* describes just the sort of absurd progression Hahn feared.[6] Cancer, according to Welch, is variously defined as tumors that kill, tumors that cause symptoms, tumors that will cause symptoms, tumors of any size and sort, and finally, any kind of precancerous cells. The problem, he points out, is that the smaller the tumors and clusters of precancerous cells you look for, the more you find, and the less likely they are to ever cause symptoms. Ironically, the more carefully and frequently you screen for cancer, the more cancers you find, but very rarely has any study found that the benefits of intensive screening for cancers outweigh the costs of the geometrically increasing numbers of people who receive false positive diagnoses of cancer or who are diagnosed with "cancers" and treated for them, even though they do not need to be. Welch's book is a careful walk-through of the morass of often contradictory information and ways of thinking about screening. For purposes of this essay, the ever-increasing sensitivity of screening is producing a country in which everyone is sick from birth.

Many illnesses may also be defined in terms of risks. If I am at a high risk of having a heart attack in the next five years, I may be diagnosed as suffering from a condition defined by this risk and may be put on a treatment to reduce it. By reducing my risk, I become "healthier." But here also is a slippery slope: How much at risk do I have to be to be worried, diagnosed, and treated? Risk, after all, is something I cannot feel; I must be informed about it.

The historian of medicine Georges Canguilhem worried about this. He understood that historically pathology had ultimately been grounded in the suffering experience of the patient: "The patient calls the doctor." But when Canguilhem confronted the notion of risk-defined illnesses, he also was reduced to arguing nonsense. Defining health in 1943 as "being able to fall sick and recover," he asserted that "health is a set of securities and assurances, securities in the present and assurances for the future." But logically, if health is an assurance for the future, we are not actually healthy unless we can be assured that we will never get traumatically ill, so he joked: "But who isn't in the shadow of a traumatism, barring a return to intrauterine existence? If even then!"[7] The idea of assuring the future raises the question "For how long?" Everyone is at a 100 percent risk of dying, and some smaller but finite risk of dying in the next five years. Canguilhem joked about risk before birth (without using the term *risk* or living in a world with prenatal testing) because he found this consequence of infinitely extended risk to be, though logical, absurd.

The slippery, sliding, and expansive notion of illness is present whenever it is defined in terms of a threshold, a numerical measure beyond which a person is ill. Universal screening programs and mass pharmaceutical regimes are regularly appearing in the news, with the line between good use and the absurd increasingly hard to draw. The twenty-first century has already seen recommendations for mandatory cholesterol screening starting at age twenty for all Americans and standard pharmaceutical treatments for the approximately 30 percent of the population expected to be at high risk when tested. Children are subject to screening for obesity and other risk factors for heart disease in similar ways. Each of these screens works by setting a number, a threshold, that when crossed triggers a diagnosis of risk or disease and a recommendation for treatment. Underlying the controversies surrounding mammograms, PSA prostate cancer tests, cholesterol guidelines, and other definitions is the concern whether, in the light of evidence suggesting that a lower threshold might help more people, there could be any reason not to make the test more sensitive.

Once there is a line, in other words, the area just below the line becomes cause for concern. If a doctor puts someone on medication who is 5 percent at risk for an adverse event in the next five years, or who has a LDL cholesterol level of 130, wouldn't it be a safe bet to treat someone who is at 4.9 percent risk or has an LDL of 129? The logic of health as risk reduction makes not treating someone the decision that must be justified, which for doctors is also the decision for which they are legally liable in case an adverse event does happen. With regard to many illnesses, the line just keeps moving. "So there's a lot to be said strategically for identifying people at risk at the earliest possible point," said Dr. Ronald Goldberg, who runs a cardiovascular disease prevention clinic at the University of Miami.[8] Goldberg here sees the same logic identified by Hahn and Canguilhem and runs with it instead of being shocked by it.[9]

INSECURE BORDERS: PREDISEASES

The establishment of new disease categories or states redefines the shift to earlier treatment as the proper treatment of an existing illness. Prediabetes, prehypertension, and metabolic syndrome all exemplify the personal and social reification of risk into new discrete and singular disorders. "'Pre-disease' [is defined as] somewhere between wellness and full-blown disease. A majority of Americans now meet the criteria for at least one of these: they include prediabetes [defined in 2004, with forty million people meeting the criteria]; prehypertension [defined in 2003, with forty-five million people meeting the criteria]; and borderline high cholesterol [defined in 2001, with 104 million people meeting the criteria]."[10] The term *prediseased* is chosen for its effectiveness in psychologically managing people through amplifying the moral valence of self-descriptions. Words and phrases are tested via focus groups and other research techniques for their ability to evoke tension and fear. The term *prehypertensive* apparently works better than *borderline hypertensive* and other terms that merely suggest nearness to a line. "The [National Blood Pressure] committee felt that the term pre-hypertensive would be more of a motivating tool to get people—physicians, clinicians, and patients—to do things."[11] Behavioral science and marketing research are thus employed to manage patients' objective self-fashioning by getting all those involved to redefine the state of patients in the charged form of a disorder that requires immediate response. In this formulation, clinicians and physicians are seen as in need of as much motivation as patients.

The psychiatrist and popular commentator Peter Kramer calls this process in which shadow disorders become newly named diseases "diagnostic creep."[12] But where Kramer and others sense a slippery definitional slope, committees and companies see a challenge to be solved using a combination of test scores, grammar (in a Wittgensteinian sense), and marketing: How far in advance can they market risk?

As if to confirm this strategy of pursuing risk to the earliest possible point, an advertising section on promoting women's health that appeared in *Time* in 2005 contained a section called "Keeping Your Heart Healthy Is a Risky Business." It criticized the classic Framingham Heart Study (which had discovered the high cholesterol link and conceived the concept of risk factors) for not taking a sufficiently long-range perspective. The problem with existing risk scores, the two authors argued, is that they treat risks for heart attacks only over the next ten years.[13]

In place of primary prevention for intermediate-risk women, the advertorial introduced "*Primordial Prevention* . . . identifying women likely to develop a heart condition before any symptoms arise." Symptoms here included cholesterol levels and other biomarkers. The doctors then suggested that women should put this ur-prevention into practice by asking their doctors to "treat them as if they were al-ready 70 years old." One's own future risk is here collapsed into present illness.

Cardiologists have for decades turned this same absurd logical extension into a kind of joke: "So maybe they really should put statin drugs in the water supply as some heart doctors only half-jokingly suggest. The put-it-in-the-water quip in-evitably surfaces, it seems, whenever heart specialists gather to talk pills. It echoes both their confidence in statins' power to lower cholesterol and their frustration that millions miss out."[14] Where Hahn and Canguilhem worry about diagnosis and anxiously joke about its infinite extension, about everyone being deemed ill, car-diologists take universal diagnosis for granted and joke instead about whether every-one should just be forced to take the drugs for the risks that they have.

LOGICS OF INSECURITY:
CLINICAL TRIALS AND PUBLIC HEALTH

While it may be considered common sense today to extend risk treatments to the earliest possible point and screen everyone as often as we can afford, the way we got here needs further study. What Hahn and Canguilhem missed was the conver-gence of three logics of health care management, each of which is quite sensible on its own: those of randomized control trials, public health, and commercial health research.

Randomized control trials (RCTs) are clinical research trials in which large groups of people are randomly divided into two or more groups, with one group given a new intervention or treatment and compared to the others who get the stan-dard treatment or no treatment (often a placebo). One important consequence of the invention of the RCT in the 1950s was to take decision making about new drugs out of individual doctors' hands. The large-scale trial produces "objective" evidence of even small differences in effectiveness between new treatments and older ones. The difference is often so small that a single doctor with a small group of patients would not be able to see it. A finding that a new treatment is 2 percent better than a generic, for instance, might mean that the new drug helped ten people in a hun-dred rather than eight, or that it helped patients on average improve 2 percent more on a scale of symptoms. Either way, doctors would have to accept the results of the trial and prescribe accordingly. While many doctors in the 1950s rebelled against this research by statistics, today's doctors are often "flying blind," to use David Healy's metaphor: "The behavior of clinicians is now progressively less likely to be based on knowledge derived from direct clinical encounters."[15]

Nor can patients tell. When large-scale trials are conducted over many years to find that one drug reduces the rate of recurrence of depression by 1 percent or heart attacks by 2 percent over five years, individual patients must accept that their risk is being reduced. While these clinical trials are one of the greatest advances in modern medicine, and the gold standard for verifying the effectiveness of drugs for conditions, they operate below the level of experience.

The second logic is an older one, but equally commanding: public health. From stopping epidemics to conducting mass vaccinations to putting fluoride in the water supply, public health has been an arm of governmental investigation and enforcement. It has been lauded for its mass action on and mass protection of national populations. The logic of public health is protection through *prevention*, weighing the costs (time, money, discomfort, and health risks) of preventative measures against the value of those measures in increasing the health of the population. This balancing is not easy. Putting fluoride in the water supply to prevent tooth decay is allowed by only some 50 percent of U.S. counties, with ten to twenty counties changing their minds each way each year. Almost all European countries have banned fluoride, and worldwide fewer than thirty-two countries fluoridate their water.[16] The historian of public health Robin Henig, author of *The People's Health*, describes the problem: "The American fluoridation saga captures the struggle in public health to balance benefits to the public against risks to individuals. At what *point* are public health officials justified in intervening on a community-wide basis to protect a group of people who are not all equally at risk and who might not want to be protected? The push and pull of *paternalism versus autonomy* is a constant refrain in the field."[17] Concerns of public health thus raise the problem of mass informed consent. When an intervention is being considered, who should make the decision? Should fluoride in the water supply be put to public vote, or should city councils or mayors or special boards make the decision? There is no simple way to determine how to decide this, and in the United States all of these ways are used in different counties.

Though public health decisions always involve some measure of convincing a public, most are not as easy to implement as pouring a drug into the water supply. Neither do interventions depend on group-biological protection effects in the way that vaccines do (where my getting vaccinated helps protect you). Instead they require convincing people individually that they should take action despite risks of accepting the intervention, and despite the high probability that they will not benefit from it. Many contemporary campaigns to reduce hypertension, heart disease, cancer, and so on, work on the appearance of a model of informed consent, informing people of their risks and options. The paradox of this type of information campaign is that success is measured not by how many people come to *know about* their risk and options but by how many people know about and *actually do something* about it. For public health campaigns, information must be propaganda (in the neutral sense as persuasive communication): it must propel actions.

Together, public health and clinical trials interact to produce a slippery slope. Consider high blood pressure or high cholesterol. Large-scale clinical trials have shown connections between lower levels on these measures and healthier lives. These trials are usually long-term (or pseudo-long-term) prevention studies claiming that if a percentage of the U.S. population took a drug daily for a number of years there would be fewer adverse events in that group. Guidelines committees meet regularly to assess these trials, set rational definitions for "high-risk" and "moderate-risk" individuals, and recommend treatment. This process thus results in the notion of health described earlier by the cartoon: yesterday your risk of a heart attack in the next five years was "normal," but today you hear that a new clinical trial has studied a population that includes you, and now you "know" that if you were taking a particular drug you would have less of a chance of a heart attack. Today you have more risk than you knew about, and now your risk is higher than it *should* be. Your new normal can be achieved by being on the drug. This is what I have called a "dependently normal" state, in which normal (health) is defined via a drug regimen, and in which it is normal (typical) to be on a drug.

Isn't this a good thing, though? Your risk on the drug is lower, or rather the tested population's risk on the drug is lower. Many people in that population would not have had a heart attack in the next five years anyway. As clinical trials are conducted to discover better and better drugs, they need to study larger populations over greater periods of time, often detecting very tiny risk reductions. One way to understand this is by looking at the number needed to treat, or NNT, for the trial. This number is one way of summarizing the absolute value of the drug compared to similar ones. A study with an NNT of 50, for example, means that if fifty people were treated with the drug for five years, one of them would have one less heart attack. The trial cannot say anything about which of the fifty that would be, but it is quite probable that not all of them are equally at risk.

In a fascinating analysis of cholesterol guidelines developed by different countries, researchers assumed that the guidelines could be perfectly implemented: that the cholesterol-reducing statin drugs recommended by each guideline would work as advertised and that they would be taken by those to whom they were prescribed. The researchers found that given the same population to treat, each set of guidelines applied would pick a different percentage of that group to put on statins, and each would prevent a different number of deaths. The most recent U.S. optional guidelines (suggested in 2004) would save the most lives per one hundred thousand overall, but at the cost of treating 25 percent of the population with statins (with an NNT of 198). New Zealand's guidelines, on the other hand, would save somewhat fewer lives but would place less than 10 percent of the population on drugs (with an NNT of 108). The guidelines of each had different combinations of these three numbers. Each drew on different clinical trials and drew different implications from them.[18]

A different sort of guideline has been proposed in the *British Medical Journal*. Drawing on a meta-analysis of existing risk, biomarker, and threshold trial data, the authors have proposed a single multipill that would save lives to such an extent that everyone over fifty-five should be made to take it. Their logic is an extension of public health epidemic response. In a nod to cost but not consent, they suggest that a low-cost version of this polypill, using generic components off patent, would work even if 10 percent of the users were intolerant. "Intolerance" here is a formulation of the literal limit of the body's resistance to too many drugs, manifested in the reaction of throwing them up. Their proposal thus involves calibrating the drug to the maximum number of side effects and cost that the population will bear before rebelling (the NNT of the polypill was estimated to be between 600 and 800). The article concludes with a call to end thresholds altogether by taking them to their natural limit: "It is time to discard the view that risk factors need to be measured. . . . Everyone is at risk."[19] This is a naturalized form of the suggestion to "put statins in the water supply," no longer even a half-joke but a policy proposal.

For our purposes, this research poses the question of not just *where* to draw the line but *how* to draw it. Pharmacoepidemiologists have pointed out that hundreds of possible clinical trials could be done on the relationship between a particular drug and a condition—including different dosages, different combinations of biomarkers, and different populations by age and other characteristics. The researchers in the guidelines article point out that the United States could conduct clinical trials to make their guidelines more efficient, saving the same number of lives but placing far fewer people on statins for life.

A clinical trial designed to *reduce* the amount of medication people take and still save lives sounds like a win/win solution. But actually this kind of trial is remarkably rare, even counterintuitive. If successful, it would take a large number of people out of a risk category, essentially telling them that they had less risk than they thought. The drugs they were taking to gain health would no longer be seen to do so. Reversing the cartoon message, the doctor would tell the patient, "Good news, you haven't changed, but the guidelines have!" As I have talked with doctors as part of my fieldwork, they too have been struck by this oddness. Clinical trials are by and large conducted to test new treatments for healing a disease state or reducing the risk of future disease. These trials are set up so that either they succeed and a new, more intensive treatment regimen is indicated, or they fail and the status quo prevails. Only the trials that backfire and find excessive side effects result in reduced treatment. Doctors are particularly struck by how easy it is to put people on medication because they meet guideline criteria and how difficult it is to get them off. Often no studies are conducted to determine when it would be better or safer to stop giving a medication to a patient, even while there are very few studies of the long-term effectiveness or safety of those medications.[20] The general trend therefore is that trials increase the amount of medication in our collective lives, and the empirical data for U.S. pharmaceutical consumption bear this out.

In the next section we will look at the third logic, clinical trials as big business, to understand how we have come to accept this paradoxical situation: in the twenty-first century, with so much clinical knowledge and so many better treatments, shouldn't it be the case that medicine takes up less of our lives, less time, less attention, less drugs, and less money even? One of the goals of medical research could be its own minimization, so that we would be less worried about medicine, less consumed by prevention, less pharmaceutically inhabited. But this idea is anathema to the core of contemporary medical research.

MAXIMUM SECURITY MEDICINE

Cholesterol Guidelines: A Gift for Merck, Pfizer.
—FORBES, DECEMBER 7, 2004

If the combined logics of mass clinical trials and risk-preventative public health already enable the continual growth of medicine in our lives, the for-profit health research industry, especially that of pharmaceutical companies, is dedicated to ensuring it happens. According to pharmaceutical industry analysts, "Clinical trials are the heart of the pharmaceutical industry,"[21] and conversely, pharmaceutical companies are the main force behind clinical trials. Pharmaceutical companies make money by selling medicines on which they hold a patent and FDA approval to market. The FDA approves a drug on the basis of clinical trial evidence, and this approval allows the patent owner to sell it exclusively until the patent runs out (up to fourteen years but usually less). Pharma companies are therefore constitutionally insecure, continually losing their products and needing to come up with a constant stream, or pipeline, of new drugs to be thoroughly tested through clinical trials.

Current spending on clinical trials exceeds $14 billion per year. According to governmental and nongovernmental studies, in 2004 around fifty thousand clinical trials took place in the United States, involving 850,000 people in industry-funded preapproval testing and another 725,000 in postmarketing (phase 4) trials. In addition, 750,000 more people participated in government-funded trials. While these numbers may seem large, within the health industry they represent a crisis. Four out of every five clinical trials are delayed because of problems in enrolling enough people. "The number of trials has doubled in the past 10 years, forcing companies to seek trial participants in emerging markets outside of the saturated areas in the United States and Western Europe. Emerging markets such as India, China, and Russia offer drug companies a volume of potential subjects, and trials can often be executed at reduced costs."[22]

Economically, the pharmaceutical industry argues that most contemporary clinical trials are too expensive for governments to fund and that the only way to properly fund trials is as *speculative investments*. This argument, for what I call "venture science" after venture capital, has a corollary: since clinical trials are investments, they must be not only carefully and ethically run but also designed to produce a good return on the investment.[23] For a pharmaceutical company, this means that a trial, to be successful, must result in a product that will generate profits covering a number of failed trials as well, either by taking market share from a competitor or by growing the size of the entire market for that drug. "In order to meet aggressive growth projections in a shrinking market, ALL brands must do business like first and best in class—and this means growing the market, attracting new patients."[24]

Since clinical trials define who will benefit from a drug, pharmaceutical companies have explicitly redesigned their clinical research infrastructure to ensure that this market will be large enough to make a profit. Clinical trials that start with a traditional research question may need to be spun too much to make the right point and risk counterattacks by competitors or the medical community. Marketers look at how powerful clinical trials can be in convincing people, organizing them, and enrolling allies, and they ask whether clinical trials can be shaped as "effective marketing tools," to borrow the section title of a brochure on cardiovascular marketing. This is called "evidence-based marketing." In a world where people and institutions want facts, the facts must be produced to order, and marketers are not shy about this: "Before clinical trials ever begin, companies need to think about what they want to say to the market about a product.... With [these] indications in front of you, write the copy for your ideal package insert. What would you like it to say?" The package insert is the description of the drug you get with a prescription. It is what the FDA approves, and it defines what a pharma company is allowed to market. Practically, it defines the size of the market for the drug. The article continues: "This point is counter-intuitive to many companies. Doesn't the science lead the way? Well, yes and no. Without the science there is no product at all. But here's what happens all too often with companies who overemphasize the science at the expense of the messages: they may develop very elegant answers to irrelevant questions.... The result, more often than companies will admit, is a product that is not aligned with market perceptions and needs."[25] On first reading, this passage appears incredibly cynical. The science is secondary to the message. The contradictory designs of clinical science and marketing are an acute problem for pharmaceutical companies, leading to this articulation of a technologically reflexive practice. If there is no profitable market for a drug, it will not matter whether it works or not. Marketers inside pharmaceutical companies have therefore extended the same bioinvestment argument to direct research. By placing science within the ethical context of the market, they construct the oppositional categories of worthy and worthless facts. Marketers are then critically needed to do what science cannot, determine science's value. Therefore companies would be irrational not to learn, for instance, "how leading cardiovascular drug manufacturers design and run clinical trials to help push drug sales, especially after the initial launch."[26] Returning to the paradox of ever-increasing medication, it is clear that pharmaceutical companies *cannot* on good business grounds imagine conducting a clinical trial that resulted in a smaller market, in less medication or less risk. Hence we get Viagra and Rogaine and not malaria pills.

CHRONICALLY ILL, CHRONICALLY WORRIED

Medical observers have noticed that the vast majority of illnesses today are treated as chronic and that being at risk for illness is often treated as being ill and as therefore requiring lifelong treatments, often through lifelong pharmaceutical use: drugs for life. Today, chronic diseases are said to affect 125 million Americans. These are not the chronic illnesses studied by the anthropologists Anselm Strauss, Arthur Kleinman, and others, conditions that are painful and biographically disruptive. What this turn to chronicity represents is a shift in the basic paradigm of health and disease, a *paradigm shift* away from the view of an "inherently healthy" body, which assumes that most people are healthy at their core and that most illnesses are temporary interruptions in their lives, identified by persons as felt suffering. Chronic diseases, like diabetes, cystic fibrosis, and Huntington's, although well known for centuries, were exceptions to the basic paradigm of inherent health. In the 1990s and into the twenty-first century, a very different notion of illness has taken center stage, one in which bodies are *inherently ill*—whether genetically or through lifestyles or traumas. *Health* for the chronically ill is not an existential term (they are never absolute healthy); rather it is a temporal, relative, experiential term (they "feel healthy today").

Diabetes and Huntington's are regularly invoked together today as paradigmatic templates for many conditions. The older notion is not gone, of course; it coexists, and we are quite good at code-switching between both views. But this new notion of illness is one that is now promoted to us in advertisements and in awareness campaigns throughout our daily life. As an index of this paradigm shift, health itself no longer exists as a trend in pharmaceutical reports. It appears only under erasure. In the statement "2004 was in fact a 'healthier' year than 2003," "healthy" is indexed by the five classes of drugs whose consumption is driven by acute conditions. These were all down last year. But *healthy* is in quotes as if it were literally a legacy term. For all other classes there was significant growth in both the percentage of people taking the drugs and the amount of each drug that each person consumed. Increased consumption of a "preventative" or "chronic" drug confounds the analysis of "health." If you find out you have high cholesterol and start taking a statin, are you sicker (because you have an elevated risk) or healthier (because you are reducing that risk)? The distinction between healthy treatment and chronic illness seems to be dissolving.

When talking with a group of marketers about chronic illness and poring over a large flowchart of patient decision points, I was directed to a loop in one corner where repeated prescriptions were encapsulated. "We would love to increase the number of prescriptions a patient takes," said one marketer, "because the profit is the same for one patient taking a drug for four months as it is for four patients taking the drug for one month." This interchangeability of patient numbers and prescription consumption is reflected in the drug trend report of the pharmacy benefits company Express Scripts under the combined figure of "utilization," which is prevalence (the number of people taking the drug) times intensity (how many pills each person takes per prescription). This is an illustration of the fact that marketers consider that "the economic driver in health care has shifted from the physician to the patient. While physicians continue to control episodes of short-term, acute illness, such as hospitalizations, patients increasingly drive the financial and clinical outcomes for chronic diseases through the simple daily act of taking a pill, often over a long period of time. In financial terms, the shift from acute to chronic care medicine means that between 75–80% of a prescription's value is now concentrated in the patient's return to the pharmacy for refills."[27] The economic point of emphasizing this is that the measure of the product's value is the total number of prescriptions taken. The consequence of this formulation is that patients are literally envisioned as points of resistance (rather than consumption) by marketers. Their decisions to stop a prescription for any reason, whether physiological rejection of too many drugs, a desire to stop taking a treatment, or even a sense of their own wellness, are all obstacles to be overcome. "Applying such metrics to a variety of chronic disease states reveals that a marketer's real enemy is less the share lost to competitors than the cumulative effects of patient attrition over time."[28] Note that this means that marketers are directly opposed to your decision not to continue taking a prescription. The business magazine *Forbes* reinforced this battle image against a life of less medication with a cover story entitled "Pharma's New Enemy: Clean Living."

DIRECT-TO-CONSUMER INSECURITY

"The goal of the launch phase is to influence the physician-patient relationship to maximize the number of new prescriptions. Marketers can generate significant product sales by motivating physicians and patients to take action and by influencing their interaction."[29] The direct advertising of prescription-only drugs to consumers is legal in only the United States and New Zealand. The 1997 relaxation of the FDA voluntary ban on direct-to-consumer (DTC) advertising opened the gates to a flood of pharmaceutical advertising. Within a couple of years, they evolved into three standardized formats based on the restrictions given by the FDA: an illness-awareness commercial with no mention of a branded drug, a branded reminder commercial with no disease mentioned, and a full product claim commercial naming the drug and the condition it treats along with its side effects. The reasons for the standardization of each of these formats are more technical than this paper can discuss, but companies were often driven to it through negotiations with FDA officials about what could be safely said to the public and how. DTC quickly became a major presence in print and on television, with pharma companies spending over $2 billion each year. For example, $86 million was spent on DTC for Lipitor alone in 2002, helping to generate sales of $7.9 billion. Among the blockbuster drugs, there is a significant payoff to flooding the airwaves and Web with advertisements.

While it is inherently difficult to make claims about how and how well a particular advertisement works, there is good evidence that DTC is having a significant effect on help-seeking behavior and on perceptions of health, sickness, and drugs. There has still been far too little investigation of consumer incorporation of DTC advice, but a 2002 FDA study found that 92 percent of general practitioners had encountered patients who inquired about advertised drugs and that 59 percent did not find these conversations helpful.[30] More recent studies have found more positive and more negative effects, with DTC influencing the quantity of drugs people ask for and the quantity of drugs they are prescribed. Of particular interest for us here is the fact that DTC ads increase patient anxiety about potential diseases and side effects and increase tension between doctor and patients, including questioning or second-guessing of diagnoses. A majority of the doctors surveyed felt that DTC contributed to patients asking for unnecessary prescriptions and expecting all conditions to have drug treatments.[31] While the FDA continues to debate whether to curtail DTC to prevent inappropriate persuasion or allow it to increase in the name of patient education and the right to information, DTC acts to increase our insecurity about health, illness, and health care.

For pharmaceutical marketers, the point of informing the patient is to motivate action through increasing concern and thereby maximize the number of new prescriptions. When I have talked with marketers, this is their common sense and their job. These marketers work for advertising companies and develop campaigns for drugs. They trust that the FDA is in charge of drug safety and that doctors are in charge of making sure that patients get the drugs they need. Given these gatekeepers, their question is how to get you to add depression, breast cancer, or cholesterol to your lived anxieties, to your personal agenda, enough so that you attend to it, find more information, and talk to your doctor about it. Their problem is how to get their particular facts into your head as facts that you trust.

Most advertising campaigns aim at some sort of bodily insecurity, a facilitated recognition in which you come to see that what you had previously taken for granted or overlooked in yourself is in fact an object of concern. In this manner, your attention to a risk possibility and your self-concern become linked, and you may additionally worry that you missed it before. The archetypal form of this identification is the "ouch test." "Of course, in the world of DTC, it helps to have a product indication in which patients can point to a spot on their bodies and say, 'Ouch!' Prilosec has such luck [connecting heartburn to gastroesophageal reflux disease]. And its DTC creatively makes full use of the fact. Patient self-selection is the point. For a heartburn sufferer, looking at the campaign's ever-present cartoon figures is like looking in the mirror. Does it hurt? Yes. Would you like 24-hour relief with a single pill? Yes!"[32] The grammar of this concise question (Does it hurt?) conceals the interpellation at work. "Patient self-selection" is the retroactive effect of the campaign when it is successful. A person who does not consider herself a patient or even necessarily a sufferer comes to recognize a complaint as illness, and as treatable, and therefore to recognize herself as a patient. She comes to see herself as having been a patient without knowing it. I call this process, when it happens through a scientific fact, "objective self-fashioning" because one's new identity, as suffering from a disease, appears to have been verified as one's real or true identity.

This retroactive effect happens within a subject's body as the ache or complaint is reframed as a symptom. In the following description, by patient compliance expert Dorothy L. Smith, a headache is always already a symptom that the unaware consumer has mistakenly ignored. "DTC ads can make consumers aware that symptoms they have tried to ignore, believing that nothing could be done, are actually the result of a treatable condition. For instance, a person who suffers from frequent headaches may learn from a DTC ad that those may be the symptoms of a migraine and that there is treatment available. Those ads can give us hope. They can help us identify positive steps to take. They can motivate us to talk with the doctor about subjects we find embarrassing."[33] Furthermore, one recognizes that a third-party expert enabled this objective redescription of one's "symptom" as the truth of one's experience. At this point in the DTC process, the target is common sense. First, in an awareness step, I recognize that heartburn is a treatable medical condition and also that I should have known this. As a fact, it should have been part of my taken-for-granted background against which I examine the world. "If we think there is no treatment available for our symptoms, we may decide it's not worth spending the money on an office visit."[34] Then, with what marketers call "personalization," I see that *I* may be suffering from this treatable medical condition. I may be a patient. What I now know is that I am a *possible* patient.

Realto's account of Prilosec (above) notes that it is "lucky" for marketers to have this built-in, auto-identification "ouch" test. There, the problem is only one of medicalizing a portion of experience. The bigger challenge is producing identification with an asymptomatic condition, "*making* patients recognize themselves" despite feeling healthy. Medical sociologists and anthropologists have long used a distinction between *illness* as lived experience framed by lay notions of suffering and *disease* as biomedical knowledge. The aim of risk and symptom personalization is precisely to fuse these understandings of illness and disease together so that one talks in terms of medical facts, risk factors and biomarkers, so that one literally experiences risk facts as symptoms. "Will the same approach work for a cholesterol-lowering medicine? No. But if a way exists to make patients recognize themselves through any DTC communication, therein lies the first lesson in consumer heath care marketing. You can take it to the bank."[35] Even a basic demographic attribute like sex, race, or age can become the basis for risk personalization and marketing. In a commercial for the osteoporosis-prevention drug Fosamax, women are urged to recognize themselves *positively* as healthy, successful, and empowered, and *therefore* as at risk; the woman in the commercial says, "I'm not taking any chances. I'm not putting it off any longer. A quick and painless bone density test can tell if your bones are thinning. . . . If they are, this is the age of Fosamax." Another commercial begins with a scene of many middle-aged people on exercise bikes in a gym, working out but looking tired. The only sound is a ball rolling around and superimposed above them is a spinning set of numbers. Finally the ball is heard dropping into place; the number is 265. The cholesterol roulette is over. The text on the screen: "Like your odds? Get checked for cholesterol. Pfizer."

The aim of personalization is to introduce a medical possibility into a person, the possibility that he or she has symptoms, is at risk, and is a potential patient. These aims are identical to those of the public health agencies when they want to get people into testing and on drugs through stories of unexpected deaths. As with the "picture of health" campaign for cancer, a key approach in these areas is to induce fear through the very fact that the disease is invisible and strikes without warning.

Lipitor's "Surfing" ad exemplifies this approach: a fit, forty-six-year-old woman is shown surfing and enjoying life and is described as a vegetarian. But when she stacks up her surfboard at the end of the day, it falls, taking a row of surfboards with it. This happens as a text message lets us know that her cholesterol is 265. In another commercial, a rich and beautiful woman steps out of a limousine onto a red carpet and trips because her cholesterol is too high. Insecurity is marketed because it makes the connection between attention and intention.

The challenge of thinking through how these ads work dialogically lies in the fact that they aim for a retroactive status change. Rather than showing illness as punctuating ordinary life, they send the message that the everyday conceals illness. As in the doctor-patient cartoon, you do not know your true health until you take a test and compare it to the latest clinical trial results. Your feelings too are suspect. One quiz on a depression awareness Web site asked viewers to rate, "on a scale from 1 to 10, what number best represents the way you've felt over the past week." If you answer less than 7, the quiz results suggests that "you might not feel like yourself." Similarly, on the Prozac.com Web site is a box entitled "Feeling Better Is Not Enough," arguing that your sense of wellness is deceptive and even dangerous in its ability to suggest that you discontinue treatment. Beyond targeting the worried well, DTC in part aims to make us worry because we are well.

SECURING OUR FUTURE

DTC works because it reinforces and amplifies the logics of clinical trials and public health. It gives our insecurities purchase through medical facts. DTC is allowed because the United States is unable to argue against the free market of information or against the understanding that mass health is also a business investment. As I indicated in introducing this topic, I believe that the pharmaceutical industry takes advantage of what it can, every legal loophole, some illegal ones, and many that exist in the twilight zone of the unprecedented. But the out-of-control growth in "health" and treatments, risks and prevention, I do think is cultural, and institutionalized in the United States.

When I present my findings to different audiences, I almost always get asked about two things, patient resistance and complementary and alternative medicine. Both are certainly increasing and getting more creative, but the empirical evidence points to even greater pharmaceutical growth. Aside from the fact that many people take both prescription and alternative medicine, I think that much alternative medicine follows the same logics I have been analyzing. Most strong proponents I have talked with and interviewed spend much time keeping up with the latest results on which medicines and therapies to take. The clinical trials may be far less funded and "objective," but the relation to the evidence is similar—medicines are taken for prevention on the basis of trials. Alternative medicine consumers also report remarkably similar stories of growth and accumulation: more diagnoses, more chronic conditions, and more health-promoting substances consumed each year. They define health as risk reduction, and their subjective bodily experience of health suffers the same pervasive insecurity. If we are going to solve the conundrum of how more research and better drugs might lead to less medicine and less insecurity in our lives, we will need to revise our assumptions about health and risk first.

NOTES

1. Centers for Disease Prevention and Control, "Are You the Picture of Health?" campaign for colorectal cancer screening, www.cdc.gov/screenforlife.

2. Andrew S. Rowland et al., "Prevalence of Medication Treatment for Attention Deficit-Hyperactivity Disorder among Elementary School Children in Johnston County, North Carolina," *American Journal of Public Health* 92 (February 2002): 231–34.

3. National Healthcare Expenditures (NHE) grew 6.1 percent to $2.2 trillion in 2007, or $7,421 per person, and accounted for 16.2 percent of the Gross Domestic Product (GDP). Growth in NHE is expected to remain steady at 6.7 percent in 2007 and to average 6.7 percent a year over the projection period (2006–17). The health share of the GDP is projected to reach 16.3 percent in 2007 and 19.5 percent by 2017. Spending on prescription drugs is projected to grow 6.7 percent in 2007 to $231 billion, remaining at about 10 percent of total. Average growth of 8.2 percent per year for prescription drugs is expected for the entire projection period. Centers for Medicare and Medicaid Services, "NHE Fact Sheet," www.cms.hhs.gov/NationalHealthExpendData/ (accessed February 10, 2009).

4. See Marcia Angell, *The Truth about the Drug Companies: How They Deceive Us and What to Do about It* (New York: Random House, 2005); Jerry Avorn, *Powerful Medicines: The Benefits, Risks and Costs of Prescription Drugs* (New York: Vintage, 2005); Ray Moynihan, *Selling Sickness: How the World's Biggest Pharmaceutical Companies Are Turning Us All into Patients* (New York: Nation Books, 2006); David Healy, *Let Them Eat Prozac: The Unhealthy Relationship between the Pharmaceutical Industry and Depression* (New York: NYU Press, 2006); Susan Kelleher and Duff Wilson, "Suddenly Sick," *Seattle Times,* June 26–30, 2005.

5. Robert Hahn, *Sickness and Healing* (New Haven, CT: Yale University Press, 1995), 31.

6. H. Gilbert Welch, *Should I Be Tested for Cancer? Maybe Not, and Here's Why* (Berkeley: University of California Press, 2006).

7. Georges Canguilhem, *The Normal and the Pathological,* trans. Carolyn R. Fawcett and Robert S. Cohen (New York: Zone Books, 1989), 198–200.

8. Quoted in Stephen Smith, "New Guidelines See Many More at Risk on Blood Pressure," *Boston Globe,* May 15, 2003.

9. One name for this approach to health as risk reduction is "prospective medicine," in which a personalized health plan and "countermeasures" to possible risks need to be employed.

10. Elizabeth Agnvall, "Making Us (Nearly) Sick; A Majority of Americans Are Now Considered to Have at Least One 'Pre-Disease' or 'Borderline' Condition. Is This Any Way to Treat Us?" *Washington Post,* February 10, 2004, F01.

11. Ibid.

12. Peter D. Kramer, *Listening to Prozac: A Psychiatrist Explores Antidepressant Drugs and the Remaking of the Self* (New York: Viking, 1993).

13. Roger S. Blumenthal, "Keeping Your Heart Healthy Is a Risky Business," *Time,* September 12, 2005, Special Advertising Section, Women's Health.

14. D. Q. Healy, "Life-Saving Pill Goes Begging: Cardiologists Puzzled at Underuse of Cholesterol-Busting Drug," *SouthCoast Today,* August 10, 1999.

15. David Healy, *The Creation of Psychopharmacology* (Cambridge, MA: Harvard University Press, 2002), 350.

16. "How Many Nations Fluoridate Their Water?" Fluoride Action Network, www.fluoridealert.org/RFW-nations.htm.

17. Robin Henig, *The People's Health* (Washington, DC: Joseph Henry Press, 1997), 85.

18. D. G. Manuel et al., "Effectiveness and Efficiency of Different Guidelines on Statin Treatment for Preventing Deaths from Coronary Heart Disease: Modelling Study," *British Medical Journal* 332, no. 7555 (2006): 1419.

19. N. Wald and M. Law, "A Strategy to Reduce Cardiovascular Disease by More Than 80%," *British Medical Journal* 326, no. 7404 (2003): 1419.

20. D. F. Klein et al., "Improving Clinical Trials: American Society of Clinical Psychopharmacology Recommendations," *Archives of General Psychiatry* 59 (2002): 272–78.

21. Ernst & Young LLP, "Contract Research: Contracted for Trouble?" *R&D Directions* 12, no. 5 (2006).

22. Ibid.

23. R. M. Califf, "Benefit the Patient, Manage the Risk: A System Goal." *Pharmacoepidemiology and Drug Safety* 13 (2004): 269–76.

24. S. Ramspacher, "Engaging the Untreated: Identifying and Motivating Your Best Prospects," *DTC Perspectives* (2004).

25. R. Daly and M. Kolassa, "Start Earlier, Sell More, Sell Longer," *Pharmaceutical Executive* (March 2004): 30–38.

26. Cutting Edge Information, *Cardiovascular Marketing: Budgets, Staffing and Strategy,* PH59 (Research Triangle Park, NC: Cutting Edge Information, 2004).

27. Windhover Information, "Moving beyond Market Share," *In Vivo: The Business and Medicine Report* 16, no. 3 (2002): 69.

28. Ibid.

29. Jay Bolling, "DTC: A Strategy for Every Stage," *Pharmaceutical Executive* 23, no. 11 (2003): 110.

30. K. J. Aikin, "Direct-to-Consumer Advertising of Prescription Drugs: Physician Survey Preliminary Results," January 13, 2003, www.fda.gov/cder/ddmac/globalsummit2003.

31. Ibid.

32. V. Realto, "Prilosec Spot Hits All the Hot Buttons," *Pharmaceutical Executive* (May 1998), 14–19.

33. Dorothy Smith, "It's Our Health . . . and We Want More Than Advertising," *Pharmaceutical Executive* (July 1998), 23.

34. Ibid.

35. Realto, "Prilosec Spot Hits All the Hot Buttons."

9

Cultivating Insecurity

How Marketers Are Commercializing Childhood

Juliet B. Schor

THE COMMERCIALIZATION OF CHILDHOOD

I write these words in the opening days of a new school year. For adults, this may conjure up nostalgic visions of walking through leaf piles, carefully sharpening a few pencils, and wondering whether one's teacher will be "nice" or "strict." For today's children, the rituals are very different. They will have already gone through the August "back to school" shopping season, now the second-largest buying extravaganza of the year (after the December holiday season). The purchases are no longer no-name basics, according to a *New York Times* article that chronicled the rise of intense fashion awareness among children as young as four.[1] Even if the seven-year-old claiming "I will only wear Seven designer jeans" (which, by the way, are in the $100+ category) is a bit rarified, there's little doubt the *Times* has it right that children today have far more passion, knowledge, and commitment to fashionable apparel and accessories.

The neatly sharpened pencils? They're still there, but they are joined by expensive backpacks, branded lunch boxes, locker decoration kits, and more. Upon entering a big-box office supply store this time of year parents are treated to a "helpful" multipage list of must-have items, grouped by grade, as well as a hefty outlay at the checkout line.

And if almost no one walks to school any longer, at least kids still care about who their teachers are. However, it may matter less, as corporations increasingly influence what happens in schools, including how and what kids will learn. Marketing agencies now produce advertising and branding materials in the guise of curriculum and send them free to teachers. Nutrition curricula are provided by junk food companies; environmental lessons come courtesy of ExxonMobil, nuclear power providers, and timber companies. Kids learn about forensic science from CourtTV. Companies enlist teachers as "brand ambassadors," providing freebies in exchange for pushing products to students. For-profit corporations write, grade, and profit handsomely from the standardized tests that have proliferated in schools around the country.

Cafeterias are full of branded junk foods; athletics programs rely heavily on corporate sponsorships; and some schools have signed on as "Coke" or "Pepsi" only, complete with official events such as "Coke Day" to celebrate the product. All of this has begun to draw sharp scrutiny from parents and child advocates, who wonder what those superintendents have been thinking. With childhood obesity at epidemic rates, and the rise in soft drink consumption identified as a likely major contributor, spending a school day having kids march in a Coca-Cola logo formation no longer seems like such a great idea.

The debate about marketing has developed not only because of food but also because what industry participants call the "children's space" has become one of the most dynamic and fastest-growing areas of advertising and marketing. Children, or persons in the zero-to-twelve age range, are a segment of the consumer market with rapidly growing purchasing power. It is currently estimated that children command over $40 billion in direct purchasing power, which is money children themselves have control over and spend.[2] The leading product category is food and beverages, followed by play items, apparel, movies and sports, and video arcades.[3]

As a result of their growing market power, advertising and marketing to children has risen dramatically in recent years and is now estimated to exceed $15 billion.[4] Food accounts for the lion's share of total expenditures. As markets for many adult products reach saturation, the advertising industry has averted disaster in large part by doing work for drug companies and corporations that target children.

Marketers' interest in children goes well beyond the $40 billion that fills their piggy banks. There's the lure of a consumer for life if kids can get hooked on brands when they're young. And there's an immediate big cash payoff in what industry analysts call the "influence market," that is, children's role in determining parental purchases. Influence ranges from a child's request for a particular brand of cereal to weighing in on the brand of minivan his or her parents should choose. The influence market is estimated by industry analyst James McNeal to be more than $670 billion and growing 20 percent a year.[5] The growth of child influence is enabled by more democratic styles of parenting and children's ease with new technologies, but it is propelled by an increasing volume of direct-to-child ads for food, cars, hotel and restaurant chains, tourist destinations, and consumer electronics. An initial opening of influence identified by marketers has been capitalized on by an intense targeting effort. This triangulation among child, parent, and marketer is altering basic family dynamics in complex and unhealthy ways.

The transformation of family purchasing dynamics has been most consequential in food choices. Children now request not only long-advertised products such as sugared cereals but new items such as entrees, dairy goods, special luncheon items such as Oscar Meyers's "Lunchables," salty snacks, sugared snacks, desserts, and even condiments. (Some famous industry examples in this category include Heinz's green ketchup and Parkay's blue margarine, products geared to kids.) Indeed, marketers have found that children have moved beyond the traditional product request model ("Mommy, I want this" or "Buy me that") to "train" their parents to purchase the items they prefer. Children who have trained their parents exercise more control over total purchases because most parents limit children to a certain number of product requests. These changes have become central to the deterioration of children's diets.

Together these developments represent another dimension in the production of the "insecure American," namely the production of insecure youth, whose identities, self-esteem, and sense of belonging are increasingly tied to their participation in a corporate-driven marketplace. That marketplace tells them that without product X or style Y they are uncool, "less than," not worthy. Childhood, instead of being a time of self-discovery and creativity, becomes a time of marketer-enforced conformity and materialism. Being "in" entails speaking the commercial lingo, being thin, having the right "designer" style, and eating junk food. And increasingly research shows these trends are creating psychic insecurity, as kids who are more immersed in consumer culture are indeed more anxious, depressed, and bored, have lower self-esteem, and are more likely to suffer psychosomatic symptoms such as headache and stomachache.[6] The long-term implications of these developments for individual well-being, a healthy society, and a functioning democracy are ominous.

THE PROLIFERATION OF ADS

Parents are probably most aware of and certainly policy makers have paid most attention to television advertising, but innovation and expansion in the targeting of children are increasingly happening outside the TV box. Advertisers and marketers have opened up new fronts for capturing children's attention and imaginations. Indeed, television advertising represents only a fraction of total marketing expenditure. New advertising areas include the Internet, movies, cultural institutions, schools, playgrounds, social service organizations, and even private homes. These venues are in addition to the ongoing commercialization of public space that is targeted at both adults and children. Examples include corporate naming of stadiums; the growth of advertising in sport; advertising on subways and buses, at the airport, on hospital channels, and in restaurants; and other place-based advertising, such as the illumination of sidewalks with ads. Street advertising is done by "guerrilla teams." Real-life product placement companies enlist volunteers or paid freelancers to use, tout, or otherwise promote a product in everyday life.

The Internet has become a highly commercialized medium that includes very few noncommercial sites for children. A wide range of problematic practices have been discovered on the Internet.[7] A recent study of online food advertising by the Kaiser Family Foundation revealed that 82 percent of the Web sites of the top ninety-six food brands advertised to children on television failed to distinguish between ads and content. This violates a widely accepted basic principle of children's advertising, as well as the guidelines of the Children's Advertising Review Unit, the voluntary industry body that oversees the system of "self-regulation." The survey found widespread advergaming, or corporate creation of branded game environments (e.g., Nabisco's Chips Ahoy Shoot-Out game, M&M's trivia game). Two-thirds of the sites used viral marketing, which encouraged kids to send e-mails about the product to their friends by, for example, rewarding those who send enough e-mails with free toys or codes to unlock higher levels of games. Some sites used branded e-greeting cards. The sites also included sweepstakes and membership in "clubs," which often serve as ways for the company to collect valuable information about the users. They offered the chance to watch the television ads over and over, and half the sites had media tie-ins. Almost 40 percent offered incentives for repeat product purchases.[8]

Movies have become another growth area for advertising, since paid product placements have become ubiquitous in children's films, and since commercials are routinely shown before the coming attractions. Product placement is now a major and highly lucrative aspect of moviemaking, with large numbers of companies paying significant sums not only to be included in movies but, in a growing number of cases, to be written into the scripts. Marketers believe this is a particularly powerful way of getting consumers to buy because it is more naturalistic, less amenable to being "zapped," or screened out by the consumer's "cynical radar," and because it is associated with highly valued celebrities. One extreme example of advertising in movies was *Food Fight*, a feature-length film whose entire story line revolved around a series of junk food brands.

Product placement is also widespread on television, as the example of Coca-Cola on *American Idol* suggests. Indeed, a growing number of companies are moving beyond ordinary product placement to the concept of brand sponsorship, in which a brand "adopts" a television show and becomes closely associated with the programming and the actors. Sensing the "demise of the thirty-second ad spot," the WB Network has taken the lead in pushing this new advertising model, and many in the industry believe it is the wave of the future. Of course, this is in addition to the very pervasive practice of media tie-ins for kids, in which movies or television shows team up with food brands to push specially designed packages and products (Blues Clues macaroni or Spiderman cereal). The major fast food outlets offer a revolving set of toys to kids that are branded with hot new media characters. Cap'n Crunch cereal teamed up with Warner Brothers in 2006, creating a new cereal called "Superman Crunch" to go with the release of the movie. Go-gurt yogurt allied with Disney/Pixar for the movie *Cars,* and Burger King and Warner Brothers did business with *The Ant Bully.* Many Harry Potter fans were disappointed when the relatively commercially uncontaminated wizard teamed up to make magic with Coca-Cola.

In the nonelectronic world, advertising to children is also growing rapidly. Zoos and museums offer corporations the chance to sponsor exhibits and in return give them opportunities to market their brands and products. In the last decade, schools have opened their doors to advertisers in a major way. Examples of in-school advertising include so-called "sponsored educational materials" or ads in the guise of free curricula provided to teachers; Channel One's in-classroom "news" broadcast and daily mandatory viewing of commercials; ads on school hallways, buses, and gymnasium floors; branded product giveaways (such as Phillip Morris's "free" textbook covers); the sale of naming rights for gyms and even schools to corporate sponsors; exclusive soft drink contracts; corporate homework, art, and other contests; and field trip programs that introduce children to particular stores (e.g., a trip to Petco rather than the zoo). Schools have also offered their pupils as participants in market research exercises in return for small sums of money.[9] The latest development is Bus Radio, which began operating in September 2006. It takes the captive audience of children being bused to school and subjects them to radio programming and advertising. Parents have begun to organize against it, but the company anticipates widespread use.

Marketing is also infiltrating social institutions and social dynamics in unprecedented ways. For example, nonprofit organizations such as the Girl Scouts and the Boys and Girls Clubs, as well as churches, are now collaborating with marketers. The Girl Scouts offer a "fashion adventure" badge that consists of a trip to the mall and an introduction to the "Limited Two," a clothing store that targets preteen girls. The national Boys and Girls Clubs are collaborating with market research firms to provide children who will serve as "consultants" and "informants." Ministers and youth service workers who participate in sports leagues are enlisted by footwear and apparel manufacturers to test out products with the children they work with.[10] Finally, marketers themselves entice kids into viral, or word-of-mouth, advertising to their friends, relatives, and acquaintances. This involves finding trendsetting, popular kids and recruiting them to serve as marketing "agents." The children are instructed to market particular products or to extract consumer information from their friends. One company, active among "tween" (i.e., preteen) girls, claims to have organized thousands of slumber parties in "agents'" homes, at which host girls elicit market research from their friends and offer them access to new products.[11] Proctor and Gamble has 240,000 youth involved in Tremor, its word-of-mouth division.[12]

Marketing and advertising have moved out from the bounded world of television, and even the world of media, to virtually all the spaces and places inhabited by children. The nature of ads is also changing, as companies are utilizing many types of communication to convey brand messages to children. This of course complicates efforts to regulate, control, or alter the advertising and marketing, and it increases the areas and types of influence advertising is having on children.

THE CORPORATE PROMOTION OF HARMS

There is little doubt that much of what is being advertised to children is harmful to them. In fact, given the preponderance of junk food in children's advertising plus the fact that companies are also pushing other problematic products, it would not be a stretch to say that *most* advertising to children is for products that have negative effects on their health and well-being. It is a sobering realization for a society that prides itself on caring about its young.

Food marketing is currently at the top of the agenda among those children's advocates who are paying attention to the consumer culture. Food companies are estimated to spend $33 billion a year in direct advertising, with an increasing portion being targeted to children. Current guesstimates of the total directed at children are in the $10 billion range.[13] On the basis of the commonly used estimate that children are exposed to twenty thousand television ads per year, and a benchmark figure of 50 percent as the fraction of ads that are for food products, the average child is exposed to roughly twenty-seven television food ads per day. Seventy percent of expenditures are for convenience foods, candy and snacks, alcoholic beverages, soft drinks, and desserts. Fruits, vegetables, grains, and beans make up only 2.2 percent.[14] Coca-Cola's 2004 advertising for its Coke Classic brand alone was $123.4 million. McDonald's laid out more than half a trillion dollars ($528.8 billion) to advertise its offerings, and an estimated 40 percent of that was targeted at children.[15] McDonald's has responded to the challenge from Eric Schlosser's best-selling book *Fast Food Nation*, Morgan Spurlock's witty but damning film *Super Size Me*, and other revelatory accounts with savvy new campaigns that reposition the chain as cool, youthful, and irreverent. Virtually all children's food advertising is for junk food, and in addition to child-targeted ads, children are heavily exposed to food advertising nominally directed at adults.[16] Nationwide, schools have been reported to receive $750 million a year in marketing dollars from snack and processed food companies.[17]

All this advertising is paying off. One effect is the creation of goodwill. A 1998 study by advertising firm Campbell Mithun Esty found that food items dominate kids' favorite ads. Of the ten most popular ads that year, five were for junk foods (Pepsi, Coke, Snickers, McDonald's, and Hostess) in addition to the perennial favorite—Budweiser.[18]

More importantly, the ads work. Decades of studies also show that food marketing to children is effective in altering what families buy and eat.[19] Years ago, the researcher Marvin Goldberg studied differences between children who saw and did not see television advertising and found that sugared cereals were more likely to be present in the homes of the former.[20] Another research team found that for children aged three to eight, weekly television viewing time is significantly correlated with requests for specified advertised products as well as overall caloric intake.[21] More recently, research by a Stanford pediatrician and his colleagues found that among low-income preschoolers even brief exposure to ads led the children to choose advertised food products more often.[22] A comprehensive analysis by the Institutes of Medicine assessed hundreds of studies and found that, yes indeed, food marketing does affect what children eat.[23]

Recent trends are troubling. Snacking among children has increased markedly over the past two decades, and the fraction of calories that comes from snacks, rather than meals, has risen by 30 percent.[24] Marketing has also boosted sugar consumption, especially through soft drinks. The roughly forty-five grams of added sugar in just one drink is near the total daily recommended limit for added sugar. The fraction of calories consumed outside the home, with their higher fat and sugar content, has also risen markedly, to about a third of the total. By the mid-1990s, fast food constituted 10 percent of kids' daily caloric intake, up from 2 percent twenty years earlier.[25] Kids' diets are bad and getting worse.[26] The marked rise in unhealthy eating is central to understanding what the surgeon general has called an epidemic of obesity among children.[27]

The shift to a diet high in "junk food" also raises the question of habit formation. There is some evidence that sugar, or perhaps even fat and sugar combinations, may be habit forming. Interestingly, the theme of junk foods as druglike has emerged recently in children's advertising—foods create altered states, they are impossible to resist, and they are habit forming.[28] Is junk food, with its cravings, "sugar highs," and subsequent crashes, a precursor to consumption of other addictive substances? Is it a "gateway" substance for tobacco, alcohol, or other illegal drugs? To date, researchers haven't taken up this possibility seriously, but it is overdue for investigation. But whether junk food is ultimately shown to be addictive or not, its consumption has soared. And over the long term, food marketing is likely to be the most harmful commercial influence on children because it will affect such a large fraction of them, with such serious consequences for their health and well-being. But food is not the only questionable product being advertised to kids.

Despite regulations and policies that are supposed to discourage alcohol and tobacco promotion, these products continue to be extensively advertised to children. A 2002 study found that underage youth not only see large numbers of alcohol ads but are *more* likely than adults to see certain ads.[29] The companies are in clear violation of their own voluntary guidelines, which say they will not air ads on programs whose audience is not made up of at least half legal-aged drinkers.[30] Tobacco companies' print advertising to youth reached record levels after the settlement outlawing youth marketing, as they stepped up ads in magazines that are ostensibly targeted at adults but that actually have large numbers of youth readers, such as

Sports Illustrated, Car and Driver, and *Rolling Stone.*[31] Children are also exposed to alcohol, tobacco, and illegal drugs in television programs, films, and music videos. A major content study found that alcohol and tobacco appeared in more than 90 percent of the two hundred most popular films from 1996 and 1997 and that illicit drugs appeared in 22 percent.[32] Estimates are that 75 percent of PG-13 movies contain smoking. In fact, smoking and alcohol use are more prevalent in film and television than they are in the real world. While illegal drugs are not formally "advertised" in the media, there is accumulating evidence of marketing and promotion of performance-enhancing illegal substances such as steroids through athletic coaches. Drug companies are also beginning to advertise prescription drugs to youth. Johnson and Johnson has an extensive marketing campaign for the acne remedy Retin-A Micro, and antianxiety drugs such as Paxil feature in ads that are as appropriate to youth as to adults.

Companies are also using street marketing campaigns, which reach the under-aged. Sky Vodka hired Look-Look, a trends research firm founded by "cool-hunter" DeeDee Gordon, which conceived a campaign to propagate the urban myth that Sky Vodka didn't cause hangovers. Sales among young people rose almost instantly.[33] Other approaches used by alcohol companies include paint wraps on subway cars in metropolitan areas, postering, and T-shirt giveaways. Tobacco companies have also expanded beyond traditional media. In 2001, a group of child advocates and public health organizations requested an investigation into millions of Philip Morris textbook covers distributed in schools, by the same company that has recently started up Bus Radio.

A considerable body of evidence now shows that children and adolescents are more likely to smoke, drink, and use drugs when they are exposed to ads or programming depicting these products. Major longitudinal studies by researchers at the National Bureau of Economic Research show that advertising has a strong positive influence on demand, especially for girls, in contrast to earlier studies based on far cruder data.[34] A study of nearly five thousand students in grades 5 through 8 by James Sargent of Dartmouth Medical School found that the most important variable predicting whether a student would try a first cigarette was the amount of time spent watching Hollywood movies. This was true even after controlling for parental smoking and attitudes, personality traits, self-esteem, and propensity to take risks.[35] Given the high prevalence of tobacco, alcohol, and drug use among American youth (beginning often as early as grade 8) and the use of millions in taxpayer monies for antidrug advertising, the continued tolerance of widespread explicit and implicit advertising to youth for these harmful, addictive substances is remarkable.

These products (junk food, tobacco, alcohol, and drugs) do not exhaust the list of harmful or potentially harmful items marketed to children. There is an extensive literature on violent products, media, and messages that I do not have the space to detail. Other problems are the marketing of unrealistic body images and their connection to eating disorders, the adverse impact of media exposure on academic achievement, the promotion of early and risky sexual activity through highly sexualized products (fashion, music, media), and the continued media prevalence of harmful race and sex stereotypes, as well as messages implying that same-sex orientation is abnormal or undesirable. A 2007 American Psychological Association Task Force found widespread sexualization in the commercial culture and concluded that it is producing a variety of harms, including diminished mental capacity, depression, and lower self-esteem.[36]

Concern about these issues comes in part from the increasing evidence that children are suffering not only from obesity but from mental and emotional disorders such as depression, substance abuse, suicide, attention disorders, mood disorders, behavioral disorders, and eating disorders.[37] Rates of emotional and behavioral problems among children aged four to fifteen soared between 1979 and 1996. Estimates of major depression are as high as 8 percent for adolescents. One large-scale study found that more than one-fifth of all kids in this age group had a "diagnosable mental or addictive disorder with at least minimum impairment."[38] The average level of anxiety among American youth is now equivalent to the rate recorded among children admitted to psychiatric facilities in the 1950s.[39]

Other studies also yield worrisome results. A major national study in 1997 found that one in five parents reported that their children were fearful or anxious, unhappy, sad, depressed, or withdrawn. Two in five reported that their children were impulsive, disobedient, or moody. Nearly 50 percent had at least one of these problems, and record numbers of children have been put on drugs to address them.[40] In 2001, self-reports of physical and emotional health among college freshmen reached their lowest level in sixteen years of surveying.[41] Taken together, these findings are not comforting. In many ways, American children are worse off today than they were ten or twenty years ago. This deterioration suggests that some powerful negative factors may be undermining children's well-being. Is consumer culture one of them?

In recent years, a new literature on materialist values has found that they can be hazardous to health. Among adults and teens, higher materialism is a strong risk factor for developing depression, anxiety, low "life vitality," poor social functioning, psychosomatic medical conditions, risky behaviors (for youth), and psychological disorders.[42] Advertising contributes to the promotion of these values, with its implicit messages about what's important. Ads promise that products will confer social validation (or being "cool,"), happiness, and well-being, and they teach that it is important to be rich. These values are prevalent throughout both advertising and corporate programming. Surveys of children and teens suggest that they are more materialistic than previous generations, that being rich is currently the most popular aspiration of American youth, and that youth have an unprecedented level of brand awareness and passion.[43]

My own research has addressed these issues with children.[44] Using data from a racially and socioeconomically diverse group of three hundred Boston area children aged ten to thirteen, I measured their levels of involvement in consumer culture and exposure to commercial media. The kinds of behaviors and attitudes I looked at were aspirations for wealth; attitudes toward shopping, ads, collecting, and designer labels; the importance of being cool; the intensity of social comparisons of money and goods; and the strength of ongoing desires for products. I asked what effect, if any, high levels of involvement in consumer culture and heavy exposure to commercial media have on children's well-being. I found that media exposure (measured as time spent with television and other media) increases involvement in consumer culture. And consumer involvement in turn leads to a series of problems. Children who are more attuned to the consumer culture suffer higher rates of depression, anxiety, boredom, and psychosomatic complaints such as headaches and stomachaches. They also have lower self-esteem. I used a structural equation model that is designed to illuminate not merely correlations but causal relations. What the results suggest is not that depressed or troubled children are more likely to turn to consumer culture or media. Rather, involvement in the culture is the factor causing depression and anxiety. Conversely, the children who had low media use and low consumer involvement were healthier. They were less likely to be anxious or to suffer from headaches and stomachaches. They felt better about themselves, and in a majority of cases they also had easier relationships with their parents. The interpretation of these results is that the general consumer environment, rather than merely individual harmful products, has become an important part of what is ailing America's children.

DEBATING CHILD-TARGETED ADS:
ARE THEY EXPLOITATIVE OR RESPECTFUL?

Much of the criticism of the commercialization of childhood has focused on the harm that advertised products do. But there is another argument against marketing to kids that motivates many people, particularly child psychologists and other professionals who work with children. Many parents share this concern, which is that advertising to children is inherently flawed because youth are not cognitively or emotionally equipped to deal with these messages. Selling stuff to kids, this view suggests, is a little bit like shooting fish in a barrel. It's just not fair. Most of the literature that has looked at this issue tends to agree. It takes the position of child development theory that children only gradually gain the capacities to understand the world around them, including advertising. Marketers, on the other hand, claim that kids are savvy consumers who deserve ads to tell them about new products, convey information, and fund kids' programming.

The view that ads are inherently unfair and exploitative comes from a series of research studies begun in the 1970s whose aim was to assess what children can understand about ads and how they receive them. The studies ask questions such as: At what age can children discriminate between advertising and programs? When do they understand the purpose of advertising? When are they able to understand the notion of "persuasive intent," that is, the idea that commercials are attempting to persuade viewers to buy products? The critics' argument is that because children cannot adequately understand ads and their purpose, they cannot resist ads' persuasive powers, and therefore the practice of directly targeting children is inherently unfair and exploitative. Many believe that all advertising to children under twelve should be banned on these grounds, regardless of the product being advertised.[45]

On the first question, the age at which children can discriminate between ads and programming, the evidence varies to some extent with research design, but reviews of the literature typically conclude that by age five most but not all children are able to differentiate.[46] At five, children are usually able to describe the differences between ads and programming in very limited terms, noting that ads are shorter, or funnier. Advertising is mainly seen as entertainment or unbiased information. The research also shows that the usual practice for differentiating ads from programs, the insertion of a separator, is not effective as a signaling device for this age group. Similarly, disclaimers and explanations, such as "assembly necessary" or "batteries required," that are designed to prevent unrealistic expectations have also been found to be ineffective with young children.

A second question is whether children can articulate the purpose of ads once they can identify them. At early ages children typically say things like "Ads show you a product" or "They are to sell a product." Deeper understanding of the persuasive intent of ads occurs by about age eight. One study in which children were asked, "What is a commercial?" and "What does a commercial try to get you to do?" found that 53 percent of first graders (ages six to seven), 87 percent of third graders (ages eight to nine), and 99 percent of fifth graders (ages ten to eleven) noted the persuasive dimension of ads.[47] A 1992 study found that only 32 percent of four- to six-year-olds mentioned that ads try to sell products, instead noting that ads are there to entertain or give information.[48]

By eight, children recognize that ads do not always tell the truth, and they have begun to figure out why. The research also finds that, as they age, children become less trusting of ads.[49] In a study of middle-school students, most agreed with statements such as "Advertisers care more about getting you to buy things than what is good for you," and "TV commercials tell only the good things about a product; they don't tell you the bad things."[50] Industry practitioners point to this mistrust as proof that children cannot be influenced. But the available research finds that the presence of skepticism does not affect desire for the advertised product, even among nine- and ten-year-olds. Despite expressing doubts about ads, kids remain vulnerable to their persuasive powers. Although media literacy has been encouraged as a solution to some of the problems raised by children's inability to watch ads critically, at least some research finds that it doesn't really help. In one study of nine- and ten-year-olds, exposure to a media literacy film did not subsequently affect their thoughts while they viewed advertisements because they did not retrieve the consumer knowledge they learned from the film.[51] In recent years, advertisers have studied children's skepticism and tried to use it to their advantage, allying themselves with the skepticism by lampooning advertising, admonishing kids not to trust celebrity endorsers, or imparting a gritty realism to commercials. These tactics are often successful in breaking down children's defenses and fooling them about what is and is not an ad.

Most of the research noted above was done some time ago, when the Federal Trade Commission (FTC) was interested in these questions. Today, the larger shift toward a more proindustry ideology in the country has given more credence to the counterclaims of marketers, who tend to ignore this research. They claim that children are more sophisticated than in the past and are incapable of being fooled by advertising. Industry rarely addresses the ability to withstand ads' persuasive powers. It is a tricky issue for them to negotiate, because to their clients they have to claim that their ads are very powerful, while to parents and the public they have to take the stance that their ads don't have much impact.

Developmental psychologists lean to the view that biological factors rather than social factors or media exposure determine cognitive competence, so they are skeptical of a view that says children today are more cognitively advanced or sophisticated than their counterparts in the 1970s and 1980s. To date, there has been no serious engagement between the two camps on this question. However, it is interesting that in private industry professionals are closer to the developmental psychologists than they admit in public. A 2004 Harris survey of 878 children's marketers found that the age at which marketers believe young people are capable of making "intelligent choices as consumers" is 11.7 years (average response), not far from the 12 years that psychologists identify.[52] The survey also found that the average age at which marketers believe it is "appropriate to begin marketing to children" is 7 years, the age at which children can view advertising critically is 9.1 years, and the age at which children can begin distinguishing between "fantasy and reality in media and advertising" is 9.3 years.

PARENTAL DILEMMAS

The stance of many marketers and many among the public is that if there are problems with kids today, parents are the real culprit. After all, who is letting them watch too much TV, taking them to McDonald's, indulging their every desire, and saying yes when they should say no? Permissive parenting is what really ails our children. While there is truth in this perspective, the reality is more complex. But even if it weren't, do the failures of parents justify the actions of marketers? If parents aren't doing their jobs, perhaps it is even *more* important for companies to be responsible and attentive to children's well-being. The bottom line is that the marketers are pushing harmful products using dubious techniques.

But the stance of the marketers is also hypocritical. Instead of helping parents to be better at setting limits, they have been spending their time trying to figure out how to get around parental opposition. They employ messages designed specially for "Mom," to make her feel she should say yes even when she knows she should say no. This is particularly true for junk food, where marketers make bogus nutritional claims to mothers and use different ads for kids. They use the "guilt" factor, especially with working mothers. They promulgate research such as the influential "Nag Factor Study," which helped companies figure out how to get kids to nag their parents. Other strategies have been an antiadult bias in marketing messages, designed to position the product as cool and in opposition to adults who are out to thwart the child's desire. Marketers have also deliberately gone to parent-free environments, such as schools, to subvert parental authority. The name of the game in children's marketing for more than ten years has been to erode the limits and protections marketers say parents are responsible for upholding.

And so the problem has become more intractable and more complex. The message from the culture to kids is that they have to have these products. That puts parents in the position of constantly having to say no, which undermines good relations. Parents prefer to give their children what they want and especially hate to say no to pleas for food, which, after all, equals love. Indeed, giving gifts, whatever they may be, is a powerful way of expressing love in our culture. And in a consumer culture, where what you have is so important in defining who you are, there is a strong pull on parents to acquiesce. Many of the products are appealing, and who wants to enforce extreme difference from the peer group?

Other pressures are also at work. Families now have to work many more hours to support themselves. Between 1979 and 2000 the average married couple aged twenty-five to fifty-four with children added 388 hours of work to their annual schedule.[53] The number of single-headed households has grown tremendously. These trends have led to kids being home alone more and an enhanced demand for the "convenience" foods being marketed to kids. Among low-income children, the general condition of deprivation—in terms of decent housing and schools—can at least be ameliorated by parents who out of love try to provide some of the many products on offer. Among middle- and upper-middle-class children, parental guilt has been a potent force.

THE POLICY SHORTFALL

In response to the critics, industry has been vigilant about fending off government regulation and control. In cases where industry accepts the need to "protect" children (e.g., alcohol, violence, and other adult content), it has turned to "self-regulation" and voluntary ratings schemes. Typically, these rely on parental oversight. This is consistent with an overarching industry position, which is that the responsibility for protecting children lies mainly with parents, not corporations or the government.

But after years of experience with "self-regulation" of alcohol and tobacco ads and with ratings systems for movies, television, and video games, it is clear that these efforts have not lived up to their ostensible goals of protecting children. Consider the guideline that alcohol advertising should not appear in programming where over 50 percent of the audience is underage. The alcohol companies have repeatedly violated this guideline, with little or no response from the FTC. But even if they were in compliance, the guideline would be ineffective. Underage youth, defined as those aged twelve to twenty, make up just 15 percent of the population. As a result, only about 1 percent of the 14,359 cable and network programs surveyed by Nielsen Media Research are excluded under the 50 percent rule. Furthermore, many youth watch adult programming. In 2001, 89 percent of youth were exposed to alcohol advertising.[54] Clearly, the current guidelines are not a serious attempt to avoid exposing children to alcohol ads.

The media ratings systems are also problematic. In general, the ratings systems are designed to inform parents about violent, sexual, profane, or other "adult" content. In the case of movies, the very existence of these ratings led fairly quickly to increased market demand for higher-rated content (PG-13 and R), which in turn led producers to artificially increase "adult" content in order to obtain coveted PG-13 and R status. This is known in the literature as the "forbidden fruit" syndrome. An example of the perversity of the current system is what happened after 2000 when the FTC exposed the studios' widespread targeting of R-rated movies to children as young as nine. (The FTC, by obtaining confidential marketing strategy documents, found that the studios were using youth in focus groups to help market R movies and so forth.)[55] Embarrassed, industry tightened up, and theaters began requiring parents to accompany kids to R movies. But soon adult content, including a disproportionate rise in smoking, migrated to the PG-13 category, where many films are now equivalent to what R-rated films were before the FTC investigation.[56] More generally, the institution of a rating system has been accompanied by a significant increase in adult content across a variety of metrics. By contrast, the television and video game ratings schemes have had less effect, but that is because adults are far less aware of them.

Failures like these, as well as industry's unwillingness to self-regulate in important areas such as junk food and violent and sexualized products, has led to calls for outright bans on direct advertising to children under twelve.[57] There are precedents for such bans in some Western European countries, such as Sweden, which prohibits television advertising to children under twelve, as does Quebec. Bans have some appeal, but with some exceptions they also have significant drawbacks. The two most obvious are the legal and political feasibility of such regulation. With respect to the former, corporations are claiming First Amendment protection for direct targeting of children.[58] Of course, the courts have a long history of protecting children and have been willing to restrict speech in various areas, but recent decisions (e.g., *Lorrillard v. State of Massachusetts*) are not encouraging. Prohibitions on junk food marketing may be more feasible to enact than comprehensive bans, at least if the case for harm and addictiveness of these foods can be made cogently. However, even if the legal barriers were to be overcome, the political obstacles to enacting regulation would be significant.

There are also logistical and practical questions associated with advertising bans, especially given the size and power of the corporate entities involved. For example, the expansion of advertising beyond television, radio, and print venues to cell phones, computers, and video games, raises the question of what media a ban would apply to. While television has been the major focus of advertising bans and is a relatively easy medium to regulate, even television bans are not without challenges. In Sweden, children are exposed to ads through the growing presence of unregulated satellite television. However, much of the logic of banning ads applies to all types of marketing, including Internet, place-based, and word of mouth. Given that companies are already active in these areas, it will be more difficult to police and enforce generalized bans than it would have been where these practices had not taken root. And, as one word-of-mouth marketer noted recently, "I can't begin to imagine how one can regulate an industry that thrives on its covert nature."[59] However, if bans apply to only some media (e.g., radio and television), the companies can easily shift their expenditures to other outlets, thereby undermining the effectiveness of the ban. The example of the tobacco industry's decision to pull television advertising decades ago shows that companies can continue to market, attract youthful new customers, and thrive without television. Would Big Food have a similar experience?

Bans also raise the possibility of negative unintended consequences. For example, if a ban on advertising to children were to be enacted, it would reduce the financing available for children's programming. If the quantity and quality of their programming declined, children would be likely to watch more adult media. This, in turn, would expose them to other types of inappropriate advertising and content. At the very least, government regulations on advertising need to be coupled with adequate financing mechanisms for quality children's programming.

On the other hand, there is one place where bans are both popular and logistically feasible—schools. Large majorities of parents and even nearly half of all marketers believe that advertising in schools is inappropriate.[60] Schools are bounded environments with workable mechanisms of control, and advertising is a marginal revenue source. This makes the logistics of school bans easier than in other venues. In recent years, a significant number of states, cities, and districts have enacted regulations on soft drink and other junk food marketing in schools. The Seattle School District has gone the furthest, outlawing all forms of advertising as well as the provision of junk food (defined in terms of percentages of added sugar, fat, and salt). This may be a rare wedge issue that has the potential to galvanize children's advocates.

An alternative to ad bans is counteradvertising. This approach is not common in the traditional children's advocacy community, in part because of the long-standing belief among many children's psychologists that advertising is unfair, whatever its message. The counteradvertising strategy is also currently a major thrust of Big Food's response to its critics. For example, the first response of the Bush administration to the obesity crisis was to give millions of taxpayers' dollars to the ad agencies and media corporations that represent Big Food in order to produce ads that touted the benefits of exercise. As the debate has evolved, the companies themselves are committing advertising dollars to nutritional messaging. Recently, McDonald's announced a global ad campaign encouraging children to get the proper "energy balance." These developments have rightly led activists to be cautious about a solution that is premised on more advertising.

But the anodyne messages of Kraft and McDonald's about exercise and "eating right" should not blind us to the possibilities for hard-hitting campaigns that tell the truth about the properties and effects of junk food, or even broader messages that cast doubt on the consumer culture itself. The graphic and powerful antitobacco ads of more than thirty years ago were widely credited for leading the tobacco companies to withdraw from television, and the equally powerful ads of the recent antismoking Truth Campaign are credited with reducing youth smoking. Research has found that industry antismoking campaigns are associated with either no change or an increased likelihood of smoking but that government-sponsored campaigns significantly reduce smoking.[61] The counteradvertising approach comes from theories of culture in a postmodern age. Because media and advertising have become so dominant in the construction of everyday life, especially for youth, some theorists argue that it is only through media and advertising that people can be reached. However, only some counteradvertising is effective. Either messages must be emotionally powerful and hard-hitting enough to pierce the shell of complacency about consumer culture that is characteristic of everyday life, or they must be humorous and undermine the legitimacy of ordinary advertising, as in the genre of "sub-vertising" or "spoof ads" practiced by a countercultural magazine called *Adbusters*.

To date, this strategy has been stymied by the fact that truly powerful anti-ad messaging is difficult to get on the airwaves and almost impossible to sustain. The Truth Campaign was ended quickly. The networks have repeatedly refused to show Adbusters' anticonsumerist ads, in part on the grounds that they will offend their advertisers. Regrettably, there are no First Amendment rights for groups that want to promote an anticonsumerist message. Media outlets are corporate entities that depend on other corporate entities to earn profits, and they have historically resisted messages that jeopardize that relationship.

THE PROBLEM OF CORPORATE POWER AND THE NEW REALITIES OF PUBLIC POLICY

The drawbacks of the standard responses to the problem are ultimately due to the larger economic and political environment in which they are being proposed. Today, the bulk of advertising to children is done by a small number of multi-billion-dollar corporations. In many of the major product categories, the market is dominated by a small number of companies, sometimes only two: in soft drinks Coca-Cola and Pepsico; in toys, Mattel and Hasbro; in fast food, McDonald's and Burger King; in candy, Mars and Hershey; in beer, Anheuser-Busch and Miller. In food there are more than two, but not many—Kraft, Nabisco, General Foods, Pepsico, Unilever, and Nestlé are the major players. Among media companies, rapid consolidation has occurred, and children's media are dominated by Viacom, Disney, Fox, and Time Warner. Indeed, it is estimated that five media corporations now control the majority of U.S. media outlets.[62] The annual revenue streams of these companies are enormous: Viacom, for example, has reported annual revenues exceeding $25 billion, and in 2007 Coca-Cola earned $29 billion. The companies themselves are valued at hundreds of billions of dollars.

Not only do these corporations have enormous economic power, but their political influence has never been greater. They have funneled unprecedented sums of money to political parties and officials. For example, between 1995 and 2002, Phillip Morris gave more than $9 million to the two political parties, with the bulk ($7.8 million) going to the Republicans. Time Warner gave more than $4 million, Disney $3.6 million, and the U.S. Sugar Corporation $2.3 million.[63] For three decades, corporate power and influence have been expanding.

The power wielded by these corporations is evident in many ways, from their ability to eliminate competitors to their ability to mobilize state power in their interest. Consider developments relating to food. In 2005, the expert panel advising the government on revisions to federal nutrition guidelines, a majority of whose members had strong links to industry, proposed guidelines that made no mention of limiting sugar consumption, despite its role in rising obesity. While sugar did eventually appear in the final guidelines after protests by activists, it was buried inside the report under carbohydrates.[64] The sugar industry bullied the World Health Organization into watering down an antiobesity initiative with threats that they would have U.S. funds to the agency withdrawn. In twelve states where they are politically powerful, agriculture and food lobbies have pushed through food disparagement laws that make certain kinds of criticisms of food illegal. Oprah Winfrey was sued by a group of Texas cattlemen under their "veggie libel law" after she did a show on mad cow disease. Biotech giant Monsanto not only has used its clout to have recombinant bovine growth hormone approved by the Food and Drug Administration, even though it is banned in every other industrialized country for its links to cancer and early puberty, but has pressured the U.S. Department of Agriculture to prevent farmers from informing consumers when they do not use the hormone.[65] The companies tout "nutrition education" as the solution to poor diets and obesity but have fiercely resisted government attempts to require labeling on their products.[66]

Recent actions of the FTC also illustrate the growing reach of corporate power. In early 2005, the FTC dismissed a petition by the nonprofit group Commercial Alert to require disclosure of product placements in television. The rationale for the petition was that product placement is a form of advertising, about which consumers have the right to be informed. The FTC's refusal to act violates its long-standing view not only that advertising should not be deceptive but also that ads to children should be clearly marked and identifiable as such. A second example is the failure of the FTC to take action against alcohol companies in the face of evidence that they have failed to comply even with their own voluntary guidelines. Meanwhile, the Federal Communications Commission only belatedly acted on the fact that major networks have routinely been in violation of rules regulating the maximal amount of ad time per hour.

If the earlier arguments about harms are correct, then children's enhanced market clout has earned them a powerful set of enemies. And as childhood becomes more completely commercialized, or more accurately, corporatized, those harms are likely to grow. Indeed, the unchecked growth of corporate power and its fusion with state power have led to a situation in which children's interests and well-being are not being seriously addressed. The foods children eat, the programming they watch, the toys they play with, the curricula they learn in schools, perhaps the name of their school gymnasium (or school), and even the books they read (such as M&Ms or Cheerios counting books) are provided by companies whose commitment to their welfare is minimal or absent. Even corporations whose products are relatively benign are deeply and profoundly entwined through licensing, co-branding, and other financial ties with companies whose products are not. During the Bush administration, children became even more vulnerable. Public policy to protect them, which for decades has been the basis of society's response to problems generated in the market, will not be forthcoming without a dramatic change in the national political scene. This is the new reality that children's advocates must confront.

Corporate and state abdication of responsibility is rationalized on the grounds that responsibility for adverse child outcomes (e.g., obesity, psychological disorders) lies with parents. The corporations' mandate is to make money, the government's is to help them do so. While sometimes corporations act in superficially prosocial ways that might seem to indicate responsibility (e.g., funding exercise programs or positive nutritional messages), they are usually quite open about the fact that they are acting to forestall regulatory action and avoid adverse publicity rather than because they are willing to accept responsibility for the consequences of their actions. However, the industry position relies on an excessively heroic view of parents and their ability to prevail against the corporate giants. Indeed, as I argued above, parents are losing control over their children's environments in profound ways. Further, the emphasis on parental responsibility does not protect the millions of children whose parents are either unable or unwilling to shield them from corporate-induced harms. Does the state not have a responsibility to those children? It acknowledges its role when parents fail to prevent or engage in violence, neglect, and sexual abuse, situations that rarely directly involve a corporate role. The refusal to address corporate-induced harms is inconsistent, and a powerful example of corporate power.

THE POLITICAL LANDSCAPE

The Bush administration and the Republican Party represent corporate interests and have used their control of government to further those interests. But this is not a simple Republican-Democrat divide. While some Democrats have been stalwart advocates of children (Senators Kennedy and Harkin and Representatives Waxman and McKinney have been particularly good on these issues), many are taking money from the corporations who are the problem. The Democratic Leadership Council, which has dominated the Democratic Party since the beginning of the Clinton administration, is as tied to corporate cash and influence as is the Republican Party. The Clinton administration did virtually nothing to prevent corporate-induced harms to children. In a recent speech that addressed how children are affected by media and marketing, Hillary Clinton (a former Wal-Mart board member, incidentally) called for industry-generated guidelines rather than government action, a stance for which she drew praise from an ad industry spokesman.[67] While Democrats may ultimately prove to be allies, this will happen only if the grassroots activism awakened in the 2004 election translates into a substantial shift away from corporate influence within the party.

Industry is spending significant resources to retain control over this discourse. The Center for Consumer Freedom, a group originally funded by Phillip Morris, receives funding from restaurant chains, soft drink companies, and other food corporations. The center has engaged in substantial public relations, advertising, research, and lobbying activity to discredit food industry critics.[68] In January 2005, advertisers formed the Alliance for American Advertising (AAA), whose purpose is to protect companies' rights to advertise to children. The organization, which includes Kellogg, General Mills, and Kraft, has openly challenged the link between obesity and exposure to advertising, a reprise of tobacco strategy.[69] The formation of the AAA should be interpreted as a sign that the critics are making progress, though the current political environment is hardly favorable.

Intriguingly, religious and social conservatives have been allies on some of these issues. James Dobson and Phyllis Schlafly have participated in a number of anti-commercialism efforts. Conservative religious groups have been active against Channel One. The right-wing family values movement has long criticized Hollywood for content (on issues connected to sex and profanity) and is unhappy about negative depictions of parents and about marketers' successes in undermining parental authority. Richard Shelby (R-AL) co-sponsored a children's privacy act with Christopher Dodd. Substantively, there is considerable common ground between the Right and the Left. However, after Bush took office in 2000, the administration consolidated control over these groups, and the space for joint action has narrowed. It remains to be seen whether that space will reopen with the departure of Bush and his team from the national scene. Furthermore, now that the Democrats have retaken the White House and consolidated their gains in Congress, there may be more chance for progress on at least some of these issues.

THE WAY FORWARD: WHAT CAN BE DONE

Where does this leave us? Doing well and right by children requires a direct challenge to the status, legitimacy, and power of the corporations that sell to them. A growing parents' movement has realized this and is challenging what has been called the "hostile takeover of childhood."[70] Quite a few groups now work on the local and national levels, organizing campaigns to ban egregious corporate activities, decommercialize schools in their districts, or influence policy. Some of the groups active in this struggle are the Campaign for Commercial-Free Childhood, Commercial Alert, Dads and Daughters, Parents' Action for Children, and the Center for Science in the Public Interest. Parents are also starting smaller, local groups to raise these issues in their own communities.

Millions of parents are also finding that they can combat corporate predation by decommercializing their own homes. They are shutting off the television, saying no to junk food, and rediscovering the virtues of old-fashioned, less commercial activities for their children. They are finding other families who share their values and coordinating their efforts to influence the larger social and cultural environments. They are linking up over the Internet or through activist groups. They are gaining courage by communicating with each other. And despite the pervasiveness of commercialized childhood, more and more households are realizing there is a better way.

NOTES

1. Ruth LaFerla, "Fashion Aims Young," *New York Times*, August 24, 2006.

2. "Marketing to Children: Trillion-Dollar Kids," *Economist*, November 30, 2006.

3. James McNeal, *The Kids Market: Myths and Realities* (Ithaca, NY: Paramount, 1999), 57.

4. Juliet B. Schor, *Born to Buy: The Commercialized Child and the New Consumer Culture* (New York: Scribner, 2004).

5. See "Marketing to Children"; and McNeal, *Kids Market*. See also Ralph Nader, *Children First! A Parent's Guide to Fighting Corporate Predators* (Washington, DC: Corporate Accountability Research Group, 1996).

6. See Schor, *Born to Buy*, ch. 8; Juliet B. Schor, "Mental Health and Children's Consumer Culture," *Journal of the American Academy of Child and Adolescent Psychiatry* 47 (May 2008): 486–90.

7. Center for Media Education, *Web of Deception: Threats to Children from Online Marketing* (Washington, DC: Center for Media Education, 1996), and *COPPA: The First Year, a Survey of Sites* (Washington, DC: Center for Media Education, 2001).

8. E. Moore, *It's Child's Play: Advergaming and Online Marketing of Food to Children* (Menlo Park, CA: Henry J. Kaiser Family Foundation, 2006).

9. See Schor, *Born to Buy*, ch. 5; Alex Molnar, *What's in a Name? The Corporate Branding of America's Schools. The Fifth Annual Report on Trends in Schoolhouse Commercialism* (Tempe, AZ: Commercialism in Education Research Unit, 2002), www.asu.edu/educ/epsl/CERU/CERU_Annual_Report.htm.

10. See Schor, *Born to Buy*.

11. See ibid.

12. Rob Walker, "The Hidden (in Plain Sight) Persuaders," *New York Times Magazine*, December 5, 2004.

13. Marion Nestle, *Food Politics: How the Food Industry Influences Nutrition and Health* (Berkeley: University of California Press, 2002).

14. See ibid., 22.

15. Ad expenditures from J. M. McGinnis, J. A. Gootman, and V. I. Kraak, eds., *Food Marketing to Children and Youth: Threat or Opportunity?* Institute of Medicine Report (Washington, DC: National Academies Press, 2006), 4–14, table 4–5. The 40 percent figure is from Kelley Brownell and Katherin Battle Horgen, *Food Fight* (New York: McGraw Hill, 2004), 100.

16. Carol Byrd-Bredbenner and Darlene Grasso, "Prime-Time Health: An Analysis of Health Content in Television Commercials Broadcast during Programs Viewed Heavily by Children," *International Electronic Journal of Health Education* 2, no. 4 (1999): 159–69; Juliet B. Schor and Margaret Ford, "From Tastes Great to Cool: Children's Food Marketing and the Rise of the Symbolic," *Journal of Law, Medicine and Ethics* 35, no. 1 (2007): 113–30.

17. Timothy Egan, "In Bid to Improve Nutrition, Schools Expel Soda and Chips," *New York Times*, May 20, 2002, A1.

18. Campbell Mithun Esty, "National Study Reveals Kids' Favorite TV Ads," press release, Minneapolis, June 16, 1998, www.campbellmithun.com/news/archive.html.

19. Marvin E. Goldberg, "A Quasi-Experiment Assessing the Effectiveness of TV Advertising Directed to Children," *Journal of Marketing Research* 27 (1990): 445–54.

20. Gerald Gorn and Marvin E. Goldberg, "Behavioral Evidence of the Effects of Televised Food Messages on Children," *Journal of Consumer Research* 9 (1982): 200–205.

21. T. H. Taras et al., "Television's Influence on Children's Diet and Physical Activity," *Developmental and Behavioral Pediatrics* 10 (1989): 176–80.

22. Dina L. Borzekowski and Thomas N. Robinson, "The 30-Second Effect: An Experiment Revealing the Impact of Television Commercials on Food Preferences of Preschoolers," *Journal of the American Dietary Association* 10, no. 1 (2001): 42–46.

23. McGinnis, Gootman, and Kraak, *Food Marketing to Children.*

24. Lisa Jahns, Anna Maria Siega-Riz, and Barry M. Popkin, "The Increasing Prevalence of Snacking among US Children from 1977 to 1997," *Journal of Pediatrics* 138 (2001): 493–98.

25. Faith McLellan, "Marketing and Advertising: Harmful to Children's Health," *Lancet* 360 (September 28, 2002): 1001.

26. K. A. Muñoz et al., "Food Intakes of US Children and Adolescents Compared with Recommendations," *Pediatrics* 100 (1997): 323–29; K. W. Cullen et al., "Intake of Soft Drinks, Fruit-Flavored Beverages, and Fruits and Vegetables by Children in Grades 4–6," *American Journal of Public Health* 92 (2002): 1475–78.

27. Office of the Surgeon General, *The Surgeon General's Call to Action to Prevent Obesity and Disease* (Washington, DC: Government Printing Office, 2001).

28. See Schor and Ford, "From Tastes Great to Cool."

29. Center on Alcohol Marketing and Youth, *Television: Alcohol's Vast Adland* (Washington, DC: Center on Alcohol Marketing and Youth, 2002).

30. See Schor, *Born to Buy.*

31. Campaign for Tobacco Free Kids, "Tobacco Industry Continues to Market to Kids," August 20, 2003, http://tobaccofreekids.org/research/factsheets/pdf/0156.pdf.

32. Donald Roberts, Lisa Henriksen, and Peter G. Christenson, *Substance Use in Popular Movies and Music* (Washington, DC: Office of National Drug Control Policy, 1999).

33. Patrick Goldstein, "Untangling the Web of Teen Trends," *Los Angeles Times*, November 21, 2000.

34. Henry Saffer and Dave Dhaval, "Alcohol Advertising and Alcohol Consumption by Adolescents" (National Bureau of Economic Research, Working Paper No. 9676, 2003); Henry Saffer and Frank Chaloupka, "Tobacco Advertising: Economic Theory and International Evidence" (National Bureau of Economic Research, Working Paper No. 6958, 1999).

35. James D. Sargent et al., "Effect of Seeing Tobacco Use in Film on Trying Smoking among Adolescents: Cross Sectional Study," *British Medical Journal* 323 (2001): 1–16.

36. American Psychological Association, Task Force on the Sexualization of Girls, *Report of the APA Task Force on the Sexualization of Girls* (Washington, DC: American Psychological Association, 2007), www.apa.org/pi/wto/sexualization.html.

37. Kelly J. Kelleher et al., "Increasing Identification of Psychosocial Problems 1979–1996," *Pediatrics Journal* 105, no. 6 (2000): 1313–21.

38. This was the Methods for the Epidemiology of Child and Adolescent Mental Disorders Study. See Office of the Surgeon General, *Mental Health: A Report of the Surgeon General* (Rockville, MD: Public Health Service, 1999), table 3–1.

39. Jean M. Twenge, "The Age of Anxiety? Birth Cohort Change in Anxiety and Neuroticism, 1952–1993," *Journal of Personality and Social Psychology* 79, no. 6 (2000): 1007–21.

40. Sandra Hofferth, *Healthy Environments, Healthy Children: Children in Families: A Report on the 1997 Panel Study of Income Dynamics* (Ann Arbor: University of Michigan, Institute for Social Research, 1998).

41. Higher Education Research Institute, "College Freshmen More Politically Liberal Than in the Past, UCLA Survey Reveals," press release, January 31, 2002, www.gseis.ucla.edu/heri/pr-display.php?prQry=19.

42. Tim Kasser, *The High Price of Materialism* (Cambridge, MA: MIT Press, 2002).

43. See Schor, *Born to Buy.*

44. See ibid.

45. Tim Kasser and Allen D. Kanner, *Psychology and Consumer Culture: The Struggle for a Good Life in a Materialistic World* (Washington, DC: American Psychological Association, 2004).

46. Deborah Roedder John, "Consumer Socialization of Children: A Retrospective Look at Twenty-Five Years of Research," *Journal of Consumer Research* 26 (1999): 183–213; see Schor, *Born to Buy,* for extensive references.

47. T. S. Robertson and J. Rossiter, "Children and Commercial Persuasion: An Attributional Theory Analysis," *Journal of Consumer Research* 1 (1974): 13–20.

48. Barbara Wilson and A. J. Weiss, "Developmental Differences in Children's Reactions to a Toy-Based Cartoon," *Journal of Broadcasting and Electronic Media* 36 (1992): 371–94.

49. Tamara F. Mangleburg and Terry Bristol, "Socialization and Adolescents' Skepticism toward Advertising," *Journal of Advertising* 27, no. 3 (1998): 11–21.

50. D. M. Bousch, M. Friestad, and G. M. Rose, "Adolescent Skepticism toward TV Advertising and Knowledge of Advertiser Tactics," *Journal of Consumer Research* 21, no. 1 (1994): 165–75.

51. Merrie Brucks, Gary M. Armstrong, and Marvin E. Goldberg, "Children's Use of Cognitive Defenses against Television Advertising: A Cognitive Response Approach," *Journal of Consumer Research* 14 (1988): 471–82.

52. Matthew Grimm, "Research and Insight: Is Marketing to Kids Ethical?" *Brandweek,* April 5, 2004, 44–47.

53. Lawrence Mishel et al., *The State of Working America, 2002/3* (Ithaca, NY: Cornell University Press, 2003), table 1.27, 100.

54. Center on Alcohol Marketing and Youth, *Television.*

55. Federal Trade Commission, *Marketing Violent Entertainment to Children: A Review of Self-Regulation and Industry Practices in the Motion Picture, Music Recording and Electronic Game Industries* (Washington, DC: Federal Trade Commission, 2000), www.ftc.gov/reports/violence/vioreport.pdf.

56. Louise Kennedy, "The Rating Game," *Boston Globe,* June 30, 2002.

57. Susan E. Linn, *Consuming Kids: The Hostile Takeover of Childhood* (New York: New Press, 2004).

58. Sarah Ellison, "Companies Fight for Right to Plug Kids' Food," *Wall Street Journal,* January 26, 2005.

59. Suzanna Vranica, "Getting Buzz Marketers to Fess Up," *Wall Street Journal,* February 9, 2005, B9.

60. On parents, see Schor, *Born to Buy;* on marketers, see Grimm, "Research and Insight."

61. Saffer and Chaloupka, "Tobacco Advertising."

62. Ben Bagdikian, *The Media Monopoly,* 7th ed. (Boston: Beacon Press, 2004).

63. See Schor, *Born to Buy.*

64. OMB Watch, *Industry Influence Weakens USDA Dietary Guidelines* (Washington, DC: OMB Watch), www.ombwatch.org/article/articleprint/2435/-1/235/.

65. Bruce Mohl, "Got Growth Hormone?" *Boston Sunday Globe,* September 28, 2003.

66. For more on the political clout of Big Food, see Nestle, *Food Politics;* Gary Ruskin and Juliet Schor, "Fast Food Nation: Who's to Blame for Childhood Obesity?" *Nation,* August 29, 2005.

67. Teinowitz, "Kaiser Study Documents Childhood Media Saturation," *Ad Age,* March 9, 2005.

68. Greg Sargent, "Berman's Battle," *American Prospect,* January 5, 2005; see also Schor, *Born to Buy.*

69. See Ellison, "Companies Fight."

70. See Linn, *Consuming Kids.*

PART FOUR

The Most Vulnerable

10

Uneasy Street

T. M. Luhrmann

Freedom, equality, and independence are the bold ideas of our culture, and as a society we do more or less well in creating institutions that enact these values. Perhaps we do less well in more settings than many of us would like, but our values nonetheless seep into the bedrock of our characters and culture. They shape the laws we pass, the institutions we create, and our fundamental expectations of how to live a life. Americans expect, for example, that people should be independent of their families and responsible for their own lives. We expect people to work, either outside the family, earning an income, or inside the family, raising children. When people have worked their whole life and come to retire, we support them, through past taxes on their own salaries, so that their children will not have to. When people are past the age of eighteen and unable to work for reasons beyond their control, we support them so that their parents will not have to. We demand that all people should be considered equal, and although we have huge political battles over what counts as equality, rights are written into our laws that presume a fundamental commitment to equality as a good and preferential treatment as a wrong. And we believe in Horatio Alger. We believe that people can make it on their own, and we believe that everyone should be given a chance to try: we call this equal opportunity. There is a peculiarly American narrative of the person down on his luck who against odds struggles back to succeed through hard work and dogged determination.

These values create a specifically American problem for those who suffer from serious mental illness. We offer them housing and we give them an income—niggardly, but money for which they did not work—because we believe that they are unable to work, and they have a right to independence, so it would be unjust and cruel to expect their parents to support them. But because we believe that people ought to work, we offer help reluctantly, and with conditions that humiliate those who seek it. And because we believe in freedom, for the most part we do not insist that people accept our help unless they are so ill they cannot refuse it. As a result, many of those who struggle with schizophrenia and other psychiatric illnesses often see the help that we offer as an acknowledgment of their failure to be competent American citizens who work for a living. When they reject the offer, they fall down through the socioeconomic structure until they hit the bottom. There they live in the socially subterranean world of the street, often soothing their symptoms with drugs or alcohol, in a grim nomadic cycle between hospital, jail, shelter, and supported housing

This is a world I know as well as anyone can who does not live in it. I am an anthropologist, and for much of the last three years, off and on, I have spent afternoons on the street corner and evenings at the shelter. I have hung out in single-room occupancy hotels and drunk coffee at the local coffee shops. Above all I have spent long hours of the afternoon at a drop-in center that has no eligibility requirements, where anyone can go, as long as she is female and wants a warm, safe place to pass some time. There I have met many women who know they need help and who want that help but who experience the search for help as defeat, humiliation, and failure.

Shirley grew up in an inner-city black neighborhood on Chicago's West Side, abandoned by her father, ignored by her mother, and beaten by her grandmother. "It was the old slave culture," she said. "When they came up north they didn't know any better, it was do this, do that, smack." The beatings stopped pretty soon. She was 150 pounds by the time she was fourteen and handy with her fists. She was the youngest child. Her three elder siblings grew into adults who were in and out of jail—drugs, prostitution, even murder. Two of them went to prison and have since died. "Near the end of their lives," she told me, "they were literally both going to court or to jail like it was a regular job." Shirley left in her teens for New York, where she seems to have supported herself mostly through prostitution. She remembers that the going rate was ten dollars. By her twenties she had a regular boyfriend. Jim was thirty years older. He introduced her to day labor, and that was how they made their living, although because it wasn't steady they slept on the street. He also introduced her to vodka, she said, although she had been using drugs and alcohol for years. She began to drink heavily with him, and it was now that she began to hear regularly the sounds that would bother her on and off throughout the years. She had first heard what she called "signals" when she was nine or ten—information about other people carried to her like radio transmissions, so she could hear people talking and even thinking about her from a great distance. But the signals had died down in early adolescence. Now, when she was in her middle twenties, awash in vodka, they were starting up again. She thought of the signals as a kind of supernatural empathy: she would just know about people through the signals, and it felt as if she knew too much, more than they would have wanted. She also began to feel what she called pressure. She would put her hands around her head to show me how she felt the signals pressing in from outside. She worried that it was a kind of covert experiment, governmental agents playing weird mind control games with a poor black woman, a technological Tuskegee. The relationship with Jim ended when she tried to kill him in a drunken rage. She ended up in police custody, but he didn't die and he didn't press charges. Instead, she was hospitalized, for what seems to have been the first time. Now and probably then, she unambiguously meets the psychiatric criteria for a diagnosis of schizophrenia.

Shirley was hospitalized for a week. This was not long enough for a social worker to arrange for the supported housing our mental health system thinks is helpful for persons with schizophrenia: a single room with toilet and shower in a building—often filled with many other such people—supervised by staff who monitor medication and other issues of medical compliance. After discharge Shirley went back to her old neighborhood. If she was given a referral to a community mental health center, she never followed up and never continued the medication she must have been given. She did well for a while. She got her GED and began taking courses at the local community college. She got some kind of job and rented an apartment. But then she started using crack. "I ran into this guy, he was doing drugs and I would do drugs with them. And I could have gone on in school, but I was just knocked out of the box. Then I became homeless because I was into crack and there wasn't anything else to do."

She began to sleep out at the local park. At first she thought it wasn't so bad. She said that if you got tired enough you could sleep anywhere. She'd slept out with Jim, so she knew how to manage, although sleeping out as a lone woman is not the same as sleeping out with a man. Women alone are targets, and single women will sometimes pair up with men whom they know to keep other men, whom they do not know, at bay. Sometimes sex is involved, sometimes not. Margot, for example, a white woman in her fifties with no apparent psychosis but a serious drinking problem, began sleeping out when something went wrong at the shelter where she was staying. She had a disagreement, she called it, with the uptight, paranoid clerk at the front desk one evening, and she was no longer welcome. She had no lover, so she scouted out a couple of guys who were willing to let her sleep by them. They found a place to stay out of the rain and wind in a construction site. Guys would see her and start bothering her, and the guys she slept near would tell them to go away. "You need someone like that," Margot told me. She wasn't intimate with her protectors. She didn't even think of them as friends. A once-homeless man, diagnosed with schizophrenia, in and out of housing, hospitals, and the street, called these kinds of relationships "traveling companions."

You need somebody to watch your back, he told me. You hang out with them. But they are not really friends.

But Shirley didn't have even traveling companions when she slept out in the park back then. The police kept an eye on her—she could tell because of the signals they sent—and she felt pretty safe. She had no mental health care contact. She didn't need it because she felt effective. "It was like every morning I would wake up, I'd go hustle myself a cup of coffee, do my job hunting, come back. I was saying my rosary. There were places I could go to wash up and you know you can even take showers in the park." It is possible that she turned sexual advances to her advantage. She started turning tricks again and using the money for crack.

Despite the crack, she was quite resourceful. When she seems to have been in her thirties—like most women who lead these lives, the chronology is frustratingly vague—she decided to become a carpenter, and she had the wherewithal to get trained and then became an apprentice. She jokes about this—"It was the affirmative action thing, they had to have a black woman"—but it was a remarkable act of will. With the job, she could afford rent. She was no longer prostituting. She had fallen in love, at a distance, with someone on the site who treated her with respect, and she thought she should not sell her body while she felt that way. But she was still doing crack, and the work dried up. She drifted into a shelter, still holding her union card, but no one hired her. She got into trouble at the shelter, and they kicked her out. She ended up back in the park and eventually made her way into another shelter. She liked that shelter because they gave you free meals and you could take a shower there too. She got kicked out of that one too. "I stayed there, but I got barred out of there. This gal, she got brain damage from the way a security guard threw her out one night, and I was there and I said to her, look, you want help finding a lawyer or stuff like that, here I am. So, you know, they pretended I was extremely violent and this and that and that, that was the reasoning behind throwing me out."

At some point, after another hospitalization somewhere, someone offered her a spot in supported housing for which she was eligible because of her psychiatric diagnosis. She agreed to go, but then she got kicked out before she even moved. "I went to Interfaith House. I stayed there about a month. They have this stuff about drinking and staying away from drugs. I can stay away from drugs, but my God, a drink every now and then ain't gonna hurt no one. Anyway, I leave [the alcohol] alone for a while and then Miss Williams, one of the case managers there, she says, well, we can move you, we're going to move you to better housing, because this isn't permanent housing, like you had to be fresh out of a hospital. And I understood and I said, okay, and I figured since she was moving me anyways, I went out and had my beer. So I came back and Miss Williams says, you smell like alcohol, and that was that. She sent me back to the shelter as if it were a punishment."

Then they—a nameless "they," some social worker connected to the shelter she stayed in, that time or maybe later after another bout in the park—offered her housing again. "One of the women insisted that I get housed, I said look, I can sleep in the park, I'll be fine once I get work. She said, Shirley, I insist that you let me look for you. I said okay, I'm going to let you look, but I'm not going to go. That's the thing. I'd always end up getting kicked out and end up back on the street so I said, hell, I may as well go live on the street."

In the 1970s, after the greatest economic expansion this country has ever known, homelessness seemed to appear all at once in American cities. Suddenly there were tramps visibly camping out in the train stations, sleeping in public parks, eating out of trash bins in the airports. Many of them were, surprisingly, women, and many of them seemed to be ill, as if they needed hospitals, not handouts. In New York, the problem seemed particularly acute, although that was mostly a matter of perception—the warmest, easiest place to stay in the city was also the bottleneck through which thousands of middle-class commuters passed twice a day. In 1979 a coalition brought a class action lawsuit against the state of New York on behalf of three destitute men and won. *Callahan v. Carey* established the right of every person to emergency shelter in the richest nation in the world. For a time money flowed into relief and affordable housing. The numbers diminished in Grand Central, the result more of police sweeps than of expanded shelter space, and the sense of public crisis abated.

But homelessness remained. There are now more than thirty-five thousand homeless men, women, and children in New York City alone.[1] Most of us, in the larger metropolitan areas, routinely see people wedged into doorways at night and panhandling during the day. In Chicago, you see homeless men and women huddled against the raw wind outside the Lyric Opera, trying to sell *Streetwise* for a dollar a copy as ticket holders stream by in pearls and fur. Small communities establish themselves under bridges and in tunnels, much as they did in Dickens's day. Sometimes the city sweeps them out. Vagrants look bad to tourists and make the city feel unsafe, although most muggings are done by adolescent boys with guns, not by men who build cardboard barriers against the snow. But when they leave one area, they settle in another where the police will let them be, part of the modern cityscape.

Many people want to blame homelessness on the mental health system. In 1955, half of all psychiatric beds in America held people diagnosed with schizophrenia for months and years at a time. In 1954 chlorpromazine became available, the first of the drugs that promised to cure psychotic symptoms and enable people to live productive lives. Then in 1963 Kennedy created community mental health centers that were to shift long-term psychiatric care from the inpatient hospital to the community. The state hospitals released their patients in a long, slow process called "deinstitutionalization." And as psychiatry shifted from a more psychoanalytic orientation to a more biomedical one, hospitals served less as long-term treatment centers intervening in a patient's unconscious expectations and more as way stations in which a patient might be stabilized on medication and then released. The idea behind community treatment was that the patient would be released to the comprehensive care of a local mental health center, which might coordinate supported housing, outpatient psychiatric care, and vocational training. But the state funds meant to flow to these community mental health centers never fully materialized, and underfunded mental health centers rarely had the money to develop a comprehensive organization. Yet it is a mistake to blame homelessness on deinstitutionalization. The vast majority of those who are homeless are on the street only for a few months.[2] They get there not because of mental illness but because of this economy's harsh combination of a tightening job market and rising cost of living.

Still it is true that the street has become our new long-term psychiatric hospital for people with serious psychotic disorders, the most severe of which is schizophrenia. Although people with mental illness are only a small portion of those who become homeless, they are the ones that remain without housing. At any one time, about a third of those on the street can be diagnosed with serious mental illness.[3] It is slowly becoming clear that many if not most of all Americans who can be diagnosed with schizophrenia become homeless at some point and spend much of their lives cycling between hospitalization, supported housing, jail, and the street, a relentless, nomadic spiral that anthropologist Kim Hopper has dubbed "the institutional circuit."[4]

This is a shocking claim. But that is what the data tell us. In 1998 the *American Journal of Psychiatry* published a study that analyzed the records of all patients treated in the primary hospital cluster in San Diego.[5] One in five clients diagnosed with schizophrenia was homeless at the time of the survey. In 2005 the journal published the results of another study that tracked first-contact patients in ten out of twelve Long Island, New York, hospitals.[6] In this study, one in six patients diagnosed with schizophrenia either had been homeless or would become homeless in the following two years. Both studies undoubtedly underestimate the risk of periodic homelessness for those with schizophrenia or some other psychotic disorder. The San Diego study was a snapshot, a study of one moment in a patient's life across a single year, and even then it excluded two thousand people with those diagnoses in locked psychiatric facilities or in jails. The New York study looked only at the first years of illness, usually the period before the patient's exhausted family reaches the limits of its tolerance and throws the patient out. Meanwhile, recent figures released about the use of state mental health services reveal that of all people making contact with state mental heath services in one year—for any reason, of any age, with any diagnosis—around 10 percent are either homeless or in jail in many states, suggesting that a much higher percentage of those diagnosed with schizophrenia fall into that category.[7] And as the number of inpatient psychiatric beds has declined, from 340 per 100,000 in 1955 to 17 per 100,000 in 2005, our jails have become our largest psychiatric hospitals[8]—an ironic comment, for they often provide little if any psychiatric care.

How did this happen? Certainly part of the answer is that there isn't enough money for people with disability. Money is always a problem for the mental health care system. A recent survey in Chicago concluded that the mental health system had less than a tenth of the supported and assisted housing that it needed for people with serious mental illness, and the need has probably increased since.[9] But a lack of money doesn't explain why Shirley was skeptical about housing. People with schizophrenia end up on the street even when housing is available. In Chicago, the wait for standard low-income housing (Section 8 housing) is currently *seven years*. If a person is willing to be identified by a psychiatrist as eligible for psychiatric housing (usually on the basis of psychotic symptoms), the wait can be as short as *two weeks*. Yet many who are eligible repeatedly refuse offers of such housing, in many cases offered by decent, caring people.

Clinicians are tempted to attribute their refusal to the illness, as if someone like Shirley doesn't understand that she needs housing and psychiatric care. Indeed, an observer might well call Shirley irrational. Although Shirley no longer uses crack or drinks heavily, these days she hears people hissing "bitch" to her as she walks down the street, and she hears their echoing laughter through the radiator pipes in her room. She hears them discussing her in the third person, their voices commenting on her behavior, her clothes, her aspirations. She knows that some of these people wait outside her apartment to taunt and threaten her. Sometimes she doubts that these experiences are rooted in reality, but much of the time they feel real. Nor are these just strange ideas she thinks about. They hurt. She feels the pressure of their thoughts bearing down upon her, and she winces at the sounds.

Yet Shirley is mostly a shrewd navigator of her world. Few people with schizophrenia, or for that matter with any of the other psychotic disorders, are psychotic always and in all areas of their lives. Shirley in fact desperately wanted a place to stay. What went wrong was that she had already failed repeatedly in the system. She thought she would be kicked out again, and she didn't want to deal with yet another failure. That is a story of the grudging way our system makes the offer of help, and the way the offer gets interpreted in the culture of the street.

When Shirley refused housing she was living in what sociologists call a "service ghetto," a neighborhood with a dense concentration of persons with serious mental illness and services set in place to help them. Such neighborhoods are packed with soup kitchens, drop-in centers, medical clinics, apartment buildings with supervisors to monitor and to provide support, programs to rehabilitate you from drugs and alcohol, programs to help you manage your violence and to adjust to life after prison, dozens of well-meaning, often well-run programs and facilities staffed by decent people. They are testimony to the spirit of American philanthropy. Compared to the world of abject poverty George Orwell described in 1933 in *Down and Out in Paris and London,* no one need starve on the American street today. In the neighborhood in which Shirley refused permanent housing, she could eat five free meals a day, pretty good meals at that. It was easy to find free clothes, free shampoo, and free tampax, and not so difficult to find a bed at a shelter. There were dozens of organizations that understood themselves to have as their primary goal leading women like Shirley out of the street and into stable housing.

Yet the very existence of those services creates a conflict that women like Shirley must negotiate. Women like Shirley who live on the street straddle two coexisting social worlds. With their peers and beyond service settings, they live in a world in which police protection is inconsistent and often long in coming. In cities where drug use is common, the police are often busy and not always welcome. Domestic violence is often unreported and physical violence is an everyday interaction. In such a social world, you are better off if you can scare people away. In the inner city, among nomadic pastoralists, even among ranchers and perhaps their descendants, in social settings where police are unreliable and the law is weak, survival may depend upon an ability to overreact, to defend your turf so aggressively at the first hint of trouble that the trouble slinks away. The women know this lesson well. "If you are going to survive," a woman told me, "you have to smack down somebody." The simmering violence of the crack-infiltrated street is considerably exacerbated by this quick readiness to fight, which the sociologist Elijah Anderson called, in the setting of the inner city, the "code of the street."[10] On the street the women flare quickly, and they flare to protect goods or status that a middle-class housed person might quickly cede. As one woman told me, "It's like they say about men going to jail, even if they're innocent, they gotta fight, and if they don't stand up for themselves, the other guys will take advantage and get even rowdier and you can get hurt, so it's better to try to stand up for yourself." She called street dwellers "cowboys."

Yet women like Shirley depend upon the service institutions that feed and sometimes house them day to day and that promise the kind of help through which they will escape the street. That is a world of middle-class morality. It demands that a woman resist the impulse to fire back at someone whom she thinks has insulted her and that she accept that she should be different than she is on the street. Service agencies are filled with rules. You must return your coffee cups by the time the kitchen closes at the drop-in center, and if you don't no one gets coffee the next day. At the shelter you can't smoke in between the scheduled ten-minute smoking periods. You can't use the sink to wash your clothes or to wash your body below your neck. You must shower every night. You can't talk after the lights go out. You can't curse. You can't fight. If you commit any of these infractions, you are thrown out. All the shelters have long lists of rules and regulations. One shelter has all the women recite them before bed. Another posts them up in a long scroll against the wall with the consequences. If you break this rule, you get barred—thrown out—for a day. If you break that one, you get barred for a week. Break that one and you are gone for good.

Shelters are trying to create a safe, clean setting, the opposite of the chaos of the street. That is not easy and it is an understandable goal. Gail had lost a leg to illness around the same time her family threw her out because of drugs and alcohol, and she found herself at the shelter on crutches with a fistful of pills for her circulation. The sheer number of people, she said, was overwhelming. She'd gone from living with two people to living with eighty-five. She found the din unbearable when they came back at the end of the day—fifty people in the backroom changing and chattering, many of them with little portable TVs they'd rented from the shop on the corner, all of them tuned to different channels, thirty-five or more women in the front room arranging thin blue mattresses and tucking in the blankets, lines for the bathroom snaking around the sides. There were lines for the toilets and lines for the sinks, and people showered in ten-minute slots throughout the evening. Lockers surrounded the front room, and women were opening them and clanging them shut, stuffing in their laundry, pulling out the next day's clothes. Beds were only feet apart. In the back, the fifty so-called permanent beds were really thin mattresses resting on milk cartons full of the possessions of the woman who slept on top that didn't fit in the locker. "People stole your stuff every day," Gail said. "You've lost your apartment, lost your job, lost your family, lost everything but your stuff, and people steal your stuff. What's on your person is all you can really count on." Even then people steal. At night when the lights are out, still people move through the space, some because they have jobs that bring them back after lights out, some up for the toilet, some restless and insomniac. Gail had had her heart medication stolen. "My pills are my life to me," she said bitterly, "but to someone else, they're an opportunity to get high." It took her hours of waiting in lines for the doctors at the Salvation Army to get them replaced. Gail wanted a better-policed shelter. She thought the rules were too lax.

So the women must code-switch. They must be tough in the eyes of their peers and dutifully compliant in the eyes of the staff. They themselves recognize the difference between women "of morals and values" and women "of the street." I was sitting at a table in one of the shelters when a woman delivered a speech to me on the bad ways of so many of the women there. "How do you lose all respect for your body?" she said, waving her hands at the backroom where the permanent beds sat close together. "These people, they sleep in the alley, they use drugs." She didn't like the neighborhood, she said, because it was too busy, too noisy, too many panhandlers. "You couldn't walk to the end of the block without someone asking you for a quarter." People can be violent, she continued. They curse. "Walk from the shelter to the lake," she went on, "you'll hear 'motherfucker' twenty-five times." Then there were "good people, moral people," she said. She said that they came to the neighborhood because they were down on their luck and that they were polite and respectful. This, of course, is the kind of distinction that the people who run the shelters, the drop-in center, and the other services promote. Then a woman walked past my speech giver and muttered something insulting, and my interlocutor raised her voice and cursed her out. She got away with it that afternoon. None of the staff heard.

Code-switching is hard. Faced with a conflict, women often defend themselves with toughness in a place of middle-class morality. Then they get thrown out, and they feel humiliated. Angela, for example, was an African American woman in her forties. She'd grown up sexually active since the age of nine, adding drugs and prostitution shortly afterwards. She fled from her mother's house at sixteen, apparently after her mother went after her with an ice pick in a drunken, psychotic rage, and moved in with her boyfriend. Not long afterwards, she gave birth to his baby and he beat her senseless and she fled again, this time back to deposit her baby with her mother and thence into a blur of alcohol, crack, prostitution, and homelessness that seems to have stretched into her late thirties. Like many of the women on the street, her narrative of the years between adolescence and forty is tangled and patchy. By the time I met her she had settled down. She was more or less stably housed, she had a steady boyfriend, and she was even beginning to work. I knew she could be violent. Two years earlier she'd ended up in jail after she tried to strangle her then-boyfriend's new lover in front of the Salvation Army. But she seemed to have calmed down, and everyone liked her. Angela had a big, wide grin. She would come to the drop-in center and lead us all in a game of charades. She helped to collect the coffee mugs before the meal, and she cheerfully swept and cleaned the room before they closed. One afternoon she walked out of the building and asked the front desk clerk for enough money to take the bus to her doctor's appointment. Maybe she said she had a venereal disease; maybe she didn't. In any event, the clerk gave her bus fare. Angela remembers that when she next came into the building the clerk loudly asked for the return of the loan and then just as loudly told "everyone" that she had VD. Angela felt insulted and ashamed, and she cursed the woman out, at top volume. The clerk called the police, and now Angela is no longer allowed inside the building, ever. She can't go to the drop-in center, and she can't use the medical services on another floor.

The comparison between the world of the street and the world of the cowboy has some truth to it. Both are poorly policed. In both people conceive of themselves as tough loners trying to make it in a forbidding land. And both worlds breed the rugged individualism that is so antagonistic to depending on others, to accepting help, the kind of willingness to rely on others that illness demands. Women say that you need to be strong to manage the world of the street. They mean several things by this. They mean that you need to be tough, able to defend yourself on the street and stare down those who want to take advantage of you. They mean also that you need to be able to resist the temptation to be tough, to be able to use the code of "decent people." "Being strong is walking away, you know," another woman told me. "We get into it. Little things a person says can set you off. And it's hard just to stand there. On the street you can walk away from people. When you gotta sleep with them, it's a whole different ball game." So strength also has a moral quality. It is about resisting the urge to snap, to hit, to stand up, to protect your honor, even when it gets insulted. And it means also resisting the lure of the street, its drugs and drink and freedom from demands. Strength also means having the capacity to accept the rules and to change, to resist the temptation to be tough, but also to accept that you have to live in this proper, decent, middle-class world. "When you really seek help you gonna reveal to the people that you're seeking out who you really are," a woman explained over our coffee and donuts. "I had to go to DHS [Department of Human Services] to reveal what was my barriers. I had to talk to these caseworkers and reveal the grimy things I did, and I didn't feel real good. I wanted to fold inside, I wanted to lash out, but I was the author of everything that was done. And I had to be strong and come in here and say, okay, but that was then, I'm trying to be a new person."

It is in this complex, dual-coded system, where a woman knows she must be strong to survive, that our system makes the offer of psychiatric help. We offer people housing and an income if they are disabled. But because our system is eager to make sure that people do not take advantage of so generous an offer, and because we believe strongly that working for a living is good and that handouts are bad, we make it very clear that you must have a disability to get such help. Because such apparent handouts seem so indulgent to our nondisabled citizens, the system that provides the housing is underfunded. There isn't enough housing, so there is little incentive to make the housing easier to get. We insist that people make appointments with caseworkers, who tell them to make appointments with psychiatrists to get the forms filled out that will certify them for housing. When we house people, we often house them conditionally: they can stay for a few weeks, or months, or even a few years, on the condition that they do not break the rules. Such housing offers often expect clients to be in by curfew, to keep their rooms clean, to behave within their walls. They reserve the right to throw clients out if they have drugs on the premises or sometimes even if they come in high from the street. And when that housing is "transitional," often the clients must agree to accept psychiatric care and medication in order to "progress" to long-term housing. If you are hospitalized, often you lose your housing. If you are jailed, you lose your housing. The system sets clients up to fail its requirements.

And in the culture of the street, the offer of help itself is a sign of personal failure. In the culture of the street, "crazy" is about having failed to be strong. To be "crazy" is a sign of absolute failure, for the women will say that the street will drive you crazy, and thus to be crazy is to be stuck in the world you have come to hate, dehumanized and fundamentally other.

Here on the streets, the flagrantly psychotic are always present, and they are what it is to be "crazy." I was talking one afternoon to a woman who clearly had a thought disorder but said something derisive about being "crazy." "Oh, what's that mean?" I asked, and she jerked her thumb over her shoulder to a woman talking volubly and incoherently to someone none of us could see. Such obviously "crazy" women are sometimes disheveled. Sometimes they smell. They get beaten on the street. "Those people," a woman spat, "they don't have self-control. They can't function to like get around. They really are not capable of taking care of themselves, like working, providing for the basic necessities of life, being able to hold an intelligent conversation. There's a lot of people not able to do that." And—speaking now pragmatically—they *are* a problem for those with whom they share their space. When I sat one morning with a group of women at the shelter, one woman—clearly psychotic—complained that the other women were mean to her. "They say rude stuff about me, and then when I try to report it to somebody they say it's all in my head. They say I'm crazy." The shelter director was there at the time, and no one contradicted the woman who complained. Then the director left, and they all lashed out about the woman, who clearly was psychotic. "Now when I first met her, we in the bathroom. I'm just walking through, and I'm singing a song, and she up and says, your momma's a gold digger." "That's how she *acts*," someone else chimed in. "I don't go around here messing with her." "I'm a Christian," another woman added fiercely. "I get along with everybody, every race, every nationality. I do not misjudge nobody for what they are, but when a person constantly says you are messing with them, you are doing something to them, and *you never spoke to them*— if you keep *provoking* me, ain't *nobody* gonna feel sorry for you." When you sleep in two rooms with eighty-five people, the woman who talks out loud to herself when others are sleeping, the woman who is paranoid that other people are stealing and cheating and accusing, is not an object for compassion but an irritant.

No one wants to be crazy. But they know what psychosis is. These women stare it in the face every time they walk down the street, and they fear that the longer they stay on the street, the more likely it is that their minds will crack and they will be one of the demented women on the corner. "She's been on the street too long," women would say to me about someone else, signaling by twirling their fingers or rolling their eyes that the person that they were talking about was crazy. So they associate a psychiatric diagnosis with social death, and they see medication not as the first step on the path to wellness but as the sign of their failure.

Shirley wanted housing so badly, and she found the shelter so difficult, that she was willing to make a risky deal to escape. "The shelter started to feel like Stalag 13. After about a week I ran into this guy who promised me a free room if I'd care for his mom. Oh, my mom needs somebody to take care of her, he said, maybe you'd be interested. And you get up there, you know, and there is no mom to take care of, he's living in an apartment that's literally falling apart, I could smell the mold, and it's like sexual favors and you're so tired and so hungry that you're willing to put up with whatever, so long as you get out of the shelter. You never get enough sleep in the shelter. So I got a chance to sleep."

But she ended up back in the psychiatric hospital. Again she stayed for a week and returned to the shelter. She was so uncomfortable in the shelter that she left again and stayed with a woman who charged her $150 each month for a bed, about as much as she earned from a small job she had managed to land. It was around this time that she began to notice that she was hearing voices again. "Either she had the room bugged or she had people that were listening through the pipes. I swear I could hear people talking about everything I'm doing, right down to when I'm jacking off, I could hear people literally keep track even of that. And something would give me this feeling, like as if I was in constant danger. But it didn't jive—I would meet people in the building, and the people in the building were cool. And I'd hear this voice: 'This one here, that's a super gang-banger, better watch out.' And I'm like, these aren't the normal voices I normally hear, like my own personal inner voice. Where is this coming from?"

She knew that these were symptoms of schizophrenia, but she refused to accept the diagnosis. "I've been in and out of the hospital, you know, having them check me out, checking to see whether it's schizophrenia, checking whether it's this or that. I wanted to get to the core of the problem, I wanted to *know* where this is coming from." She said that even though for most people hearing voices would mean a diagnosis of schizophrenia, it wasn't true in her case—she told me the doctors agreed that "there's nothing wrong with me." She was strong, she wasn't like those hapless women in the drop-in center, talking openly to the air. And she didn't need their drugs, and because they only had drugs to offer her, there was little they could do. She remarked to me that she had spent a lot of time talking to psychiatrists about the hostile voices she heard and that all they had done was to offer medication. When I asked her what kinds of symptoms the psychiatrist thought they were trying to treat, she said, "They don't think. They just offer medication. Here, take the Prozac and shut up."

Shirley is a success story. She's now housed. She's kept the housing for three years, and she intends to stay in it. What got her into it, however, wasn't a change of heart about whether she had schizophrenia, but God. In her late thirties Shirley seems to have made a serious commitment to God. The man she'd fallen in love with at a distance had died of lung cancer, and she began to think of him as still active in her life, as what she called her "cell phone" to God. She told me she'd never thought that God would pay much attention to people like her, but when Dain died, she decided that she had a kind of advocate in heaven and that it was time to take Him seriously. She used to think that she was God's puppet, she said. Now she thought that if she accepted God's importance she could command her own destiny. So she decided she'd better be a decent person. "All the crime and evil that I did—knocking people on the head, stealing, turning dates, stuff like that"—that would have to go.

Crack, she said, was the last to go. But she finally had a debate with God, and she realized that there was too much against it. "First of all, the deterioration to the mind it does. It's not like weed, it doesn't just alter the brain, it actually takes brain cells. So I said, Okay Lord, you win this one." But it was a reluctant concession. She told Him that she wasn't going to buy crack, but if someone offered it to her, she wouldn't refuse. So while she was at the shelter she gave some money to a woman who was going to get crack for both of them (this apparently didn't count as buying). "So I'm sitting there waiting for her to come back, and she must have got distracted as crack-heads do, and it was over an hour, but it was hitting on to the second hour, and this vision of Dain comes into my head and I could see him, he's standing there like this [she put her hands on her hips and smirked], 'So how long you gonna sit there and wait on her, she's not coming back, I'm gonna tell you that right now, she's not com-ing back. How long you gonna sit there and wait on her, you stupid bitch? How long you gonna do this?' That's the day I quit crack. I haven't done it since."

And something changed. There was a shelter that offered housing to people on the condition that they attend a series of weekly meetings. The housing was sup-ported with funding earmarked for people who struggle with psychotic disorder and substance abuse, but they had the good sense not to make that explicit to the clients. When Shirley eventually got housed, she thought that it was because of the vodka and crack. Before she got housed, however, she had to go to the meetings. "All I could hear my Lord saying was, 'Force the issue. Go to the meetings.' " She'd stayed at the shelter before—she'd stayed at most Chicago shelters before—but she hadn't been able to take any of the meetings they required seriously. Now, because of God's in-junctions, she did. "I decided that I was going to, like leave everything in the street. No matter how hard up I was for money, I wasn't going to go out there and turn any dates. I wasn't going to get into selling drugs. I wasn't going to do *anything* like that anymore. I said, for the first time, I'm gonna try and give this system a chance."

She went to meetings for months. She still goes to three a week. She talked about crack and vodka and doing tricks, and she listened to people, and eventually they gave her her own apartment. It's a small apartment in an old hotel, with a tiny kitchen tucked into one corner and a private bath attached to another. It's crowded. There's a double mattress stretched out on the floor, a desk piled with paints and brushes, her bike propped against the wall, and artwork everywhere—large, color oil can-vases, Che Guevara, Malcolm X, small enameled miniatures, icons with black Madonnas. She is a remarkable artist. People don't come up very often to see the work. She told me that I was the second visitor she'd had in three years.

But the success is fragile. She still hears voices. She hears a woman from a con-struction site where she used to work, she hears the president of her building's tenant union and the voice of a woman who used to turn tricks on the corner with her; she hears her bishop and a local priest. They talk to her and they talk about her. Some of them are good voices. Many of them are bad, and in the last few years there have been more bad voices than ever before. In fact, she thinks that she's only heard the bad voices in the past few years, voices that harass her and call her hostile, mean names. They curse her and jeer at her and try to make her feel awful. She sees no psychiatrist, she takes no medication, and she accepts no disability income, because she isn't "crazy." And she is careful not to get too involved in services they offer in the neighborhood. "I can't let myself get too deep into it, otherwise I'll end up like some of these homeless people around here that seem to be forever homeless, and not to be able to take care of business. . . . I guess you could say that being homeless tends to make you mentally ill."

The problem with the American mental health care system is that if we create a safety net for people who are unable to work because they are mentally incompetent, tell them that this is why we help them, and offer them an opportunity to opt out, many people who live in the culture of the street will opt out. They will live on the street, piecing together dangerous and dubious strategies to avoid humiliation, getting hospitalized when their behavior gets out of hand. It does not seem like rocket science to say that living on the street is bad for someone with psychosis and that it may prolong the course and outcome of schizophrenia. There are ways to solve this problem. We could create fewer barriers to care, show more tolerance when people break the rules, and give housing without strings to people who seem to need it most. As awful as it sounds, we probably need more flophouses.

In fact the most promising recent developments borrow their basic approaches from the flophouse: easy access, no questions asked. Programs like New York City's Housing First simply give people housing without treating housing as a return for good behavior, and while minimizing rules and expectations. It is an approach that has been gaining interest in the treatment of substance abuse and dual-diagnosis treatment. (The term *dual diagnosis* refers to people who can be diagnosed with a serious mental illness like schizophrenia and with substance abuse. Shirley is technically a dual-diagnosis client.) In "harm reduction," housing and other services are not offered on the condition that the client give up the addiction or accept psychiatric treatment. The goods are just offered, and the staff slowly and respectfully try to coax the client into a less addictive form of life. These programs still struggle with the basic challenge that they do require a diagnosis. Dual-diagnosis programs, however, allow the client to skirt around the diagnostic demand. Shirley stays in this kind of program, and accepted the housing, only because she thinks that it was offered on the basis of her crack addiction, not because of a psychiatric diagnosis. She is still incensed when people suggest that she may have such a diagnosis, and she swears at them. But she keeps her housing and hopes to stay. There is now decent evidence that just giving people housing is no more expensive than our current system of giving housing for good behavior and hospitalizing people through the emergency room when they become sick enough to need care.

But in our country it is hard to make these programs stick. They are politically unpopular and socially unwelcome. Shirley's neighborhood is gentrifying. I was in one of the new upmarket shops one afternoon when the owner started to explain how awful the supported housing across the street was. That program was one of the few in the area based on harm reduction. It had successfully housed and helped many people who would otherwise have refused to accept a psychiatric diagnosis and psychiatric care and people who would have refused to stop drinking and using drugs. The shop owner was appalled that people could be housed without being forced to accept treatment. He thought the program catered to free riders and lazy louts. His views are very American. Programs like Housing First seem like handouts, as if they aren't fair and aren't right. And because such programs depend on state and federal money, and because governments depend on elected officials, they are vulnerable to such views.

It is worth noting that these problems do not exist, at least in this way and to this extent, in other countries. Homelessness can be found everywhere, and in all societies mental illness seems to exacerbate its risk.[11] But homelessness "means" differently in every country where it is found. In India, the country outside the United States and England that I know best, there is a great deal of homelessness, but in general it is a very different kind of homelessness than described here. People arrive in Bombay with their families and find no place to stay, so they stay on the street in flimsy shacks built out of thatch and fabric. All over India are vast shantytowns rising around the shiny new complexes of the rapidly enriching middle class. But those who struggle with schizophrenia are far less often homeless in the way that they are in this country, where they wander nomadically between living on the street, being jailed or hospitalized, and being housed in supported housing. There are far fewer services. There is no social service safety net. The social world values interdependence more than independence, at least compared to Americans. As a result, families seem to assume that they must care for their ill, and those who are ill more often seem to assume that it is appropriate for their families to care for them. It is not clear that this arrangement is better for the families, but it does seem to be better for those who struggle with the disorder. Recovery from schizophrenia may well be faster and more complete in India than in the United States. The fact that we treat our sickest citizens by hospitalizing them on the street might well be responsible for this contrast.[12]

Even when people with schizophrenia do end up on the street in India, their plight is understood quite differently than in the United States. In Chennai, there is a famous NGO called the Banyan that offers shelter to homeless psychotic women. It describes itself as not only helping to house and treat such women but also reuniting them with families who are frantic that they have been lost, much as Americans worry about losing elder family members who suffer from dementia. "A civilization is defined by how well it takes care of its most wretched," its Web site states. At the Banyan, clients are portrayed as helpless and in desperate need. On their Web site an observer writes: "She is drifting from one street to another, some-times from city to city, searching for the most basic form of meaning—a discovery of who she is as a person, where she came from and where her roots are." The Banyan speaks to its audience by invoking their sense of personal responsibility for others. By contrast, the intense independence our culture cultivates means that we resist offering help and that those who need the help assume that to take it signals de-feat. The Banyan has something right. A society *can* be defined by how well it takes care of its most wretched. That involves—as every anthropologist should know—reaching out to people in ways that do not humiliate them and do not suggest that they debase themselves in accepting the help.

NOTES

1. New York City, Department of Homeless Services, daily census, www.nyc.gov/html/dhs/html/home/home.shtml, accessed March 7, 2006.

2. The discovery that most of those who use homeless shelters do so briefly is usually attributed to Dennis Culhane; see especially his "The Organization and Utilization of the Shelter System in Philadel-phia: Estimating Average Length of Stay and Annual Rate of Turnover," *Journal of Health and Social Pol-icy* 4, no. 4 (1993): 55–78. Obviously, in a different society, with a different economy, the rates of home-lessness would be different. Culhane is also credited with the discovery that the vast majority of the homeless in this society are not mentally ill but down on their economic luck for a wide range of reasons.

3. Rodger Farr, Paul Koegel, and Audrey Burnam, *A Study of Homelessness and Mental Illness in the Skid Row Area of Los Angeles* (Los Angeles: Department of Mental Health, 1986).

4. Kim Hopper et al., "Homelessness, Severe Mental Illness and the Institutional Circuit," *Psychi-atric Services* 48 (1997): 659–65.

5. D. P. Folsom et al., "Prevalence and Risk Factors for Homelessness and Utilization of Mental Health Services among 10,340 Patients with Serious Mental Illness in a Large Public Mental Health System," *American Journal of Psychiatry* 162 (2005): 370–76.

6. D. Herman et al., "Homelessness among Individuals with Psychotic Disorders Hospitalized for the First Time: Findings from the Suffolk County Mental Health Project," *American Journal of Psychi-atry* 155 (1998): 109–13.

7. Substance Abuse and Mental Health Services Administration, "2004 CMHS Uniform Reporting System Output Tables: Illinois," http://download.ncadi.samhsa.gov/ken/pdf/URS_Data04/IL04.pdf.

8. These are figures from a Treatment Advocacy Center report by E. Fuller Torrey et al., *The Short-age of Public Hospital Beds for Mentally Ill Persons*, March 2008, www.treatmentadvocacycenter.org/storage/tac/documents/the_shortage_of_publichospital_beds.pdf; see also Linda Teplin, K. Abram, and G. McClelland, "Prevalence of Psychiatric Disorders among Incarcerated Women: I. Pretrial Jail Detainees," *Archives of General Psychiatry* 53, no. 6 (1996): 505–12.

9. M. Heyrman, pers. comm., March 2006; it was an internal study.

10. Elijah Anderson, *The Code of the Street: Decency, Violence and the Moral Life of the Inner City* (New York: Norton, 1999).

11. Valerie Polakov and Cindy Guillean, eds., *International Perspectives on Homelessness* (London: Greenwood Press, 2001).

12. See the discussion in T. M. Luhrmann, "Social Defeat and the Culture of Chronicity: Or, Why Schizophrenia Does So Well Over There and So Badly Here," *Culture, Medicine and Psychiatry* 31 (June 2007): 135–72.

11

Body and Soul

Profits from Poverty

Brett Williams

During the years I have lived and worked in Washington, D.C., I have grown to know many sick and indebted people. In the 1980s I grew close to an extended family I called the Harpers. I wrote about the Harpers in *Upscaling Downtown* (1988) because their experiences reflected those of many other D.C. residents: they came to Washington after World War II, following kin who helped them find jobs and places to stay. Gentrification twenty years later scattered the Harpers east of the Anacostia River, into the inner D.C. suburbs, and into shelters, hospitals, and the streets. By 2000 almost everyone in the Harper family, except for those who had been small children in 1988, had died: of AIDS, diabetes, stroke, and heart disease.

I followed the efforts of James Harper, who struggled to operate his small flower shop while in the stranglehold of debt. He loved arranging flowers, but he worked so hard that he neglected his health, lost two legs to diabetes, and died, a sad torso, in 2004. I also grew close to his son Kevin, a skilled carpenter with health problems who did time for armed robbery, eventually pawned all his tools, and now lives on the streets. At first I thought father and son were just very unlucky. Now I know that their experiences are more typical than rare.

During the last ten years, I have worked with community ethnographers in the neighborhoods bordering the Anacostia River. A contract with the National Park Service asked us to explore the ways residents felt about national parks that are also precious local green space. Understanding the preciousness of this space has led me to follow the other problems that plague the people I know. In 2007 my friend and collaborator Sue Barnes and I interviewed elderly public housing residents about illnesses that have plagued their families. Here I link conditions that seem separate but that come together in the lives of poor people: debt that leaches wealth from their communities, stresses them, and keeps them on edge; and environmental toxins that are just as predatory, destabilizing, stressful, and hard to understand.

The experience of poverty changes over time and place. But all over the world the poor suffer deadly exposure to poisonous substances so that the rest of us can have corn, or oil, or a baseball stadium with a river view. And to stretch paychecks, survive emergencies, or make ends meet, poor people have taken on debt. The interest they pay on that debt makes other people rich, just as their health problems and shortened lives do. In both cases, the government fails to enact or enforce regulations to rein in greed or protect the people who are vulnerable. While debt and disease, pollution and predatory lending, may seem unrelated to those who do not experience them, they are deeply tangled in many poor people's lives. They are also key lenses for viewing how profits are wrested from poverty and the complicity of public policies in this process. The subprime/foreclosure fiasco of 2008 has at last brought predatory lending to national attention, but it may not have surprised the people who have long labored under its strictures.

This chapter explores these two facets of being poor and grounds them in what I have learned in Washington, D.C. The problems I document are both representative and unique—in many cities, poor people struggle with unhealthy, predatory conditions. But D.C. is both the nation's capital and its last colony: the problems here amount to a social disaster in a city that is supposed to be a shining example of democracy. The lack of democracy in the city makes these problems almost impossible for local residents to solve.

AWASH IN DEBT

Wealthy people grow wealthier by investing in places and projects that have lost value over time. Then, when investors return to those places and projects to flip houses, convert apartments into condominiums, or "revitalize" waterfronts, they realize huge returns. Urban renewal and the displacement of black residents east of the Anacostia River were profitable projects in the 1960s. In the years since, along with the pollution of the river, and the failure of government and business to invest in recreational or health care facilities, schools, or jobs, those neighborhoods have lost value. In the last few years, investors have begun to gentrify these devalued neighborhoods through condominium conversion, speculation and renovation, the construction of luxury housing, and the displacement of the poor from public and private housing. Perhaps preparing the way, most investment until very recently has been in predatory lending.

Poor neighborhoods all over Washington, and especially the neighborhoods along the Anacostia River, teem with pawnshops, check-cashing outlets, rent-toown centers, payday loan shops, and tax brokers offering rapid refunds. These flashy, tawdry, homey-looking shops occupy devalued real estate in poor and gentrifying neighborhoods. Large corporations and finance companies have installed them there instead of retail banking branches because they are much more profitable. Their showy red, white, and blue signs and creative misspellings like QUIK CASH and CASH 2 GO, like faux ATM machines, promise salvation to the cash-strapped. They look like oases in the boarded-up, grim landscapes of many poor neighborhoods. But you must travel a long way to discover where your money goes after you hand it over to a pawnbroker or a check casher.

Pawnshops are the most familiar predatory lenders, but they have grown from mom-and-pop operations to national chains. A pawnshop is filled with people's pawned treasures and broken dreams: gold chains, wedding bands, watches, baseball cards, leather jackets, computers, VCRs, television sets, compact discs, cameras, pianos, guitars, saxophones, power tools, lawnmowers, and deejay equipment. Behind each item on sale is a story of someone desperate for cash to pay a utility bill, buy shoes for a child, or repair a car. Kevin Harper has lost to a pawnshop all of the power tools through which he earned a living as a freelance carpenter/electrician/plumber. Every month, he pays the "fee" on the single treasure the pawnshop holds: old baseball cards gathered from the basement floor of a dead cousin and treasured by Kevin as an inheritance for his little daughter.

A borrower takes a television, for example, to a pawnshop and relinquishes it for $50. He can reclaim it for $55 if he can gather together that amount in a month. (Pawnshops are regulated only by states; this monthly interest can vary from 4 to 25 percent, and the annual percentage rate is of course much higher.) In rare cases the borrower can return in a month, repay the loan and interest, and retrieve the item. More commonly, like Kevin Harper, the debtor returns month after month to pay the interest until the lending period is over or the borrower just gives up, perhaps lacking even the interest due. Then the pawnbroker sells the pawned item for a huge markup.

While pawnshops may appear homey, they are expanding rapidly through franchise operations. I have watched them take over whole shopping centers, swallowing up carryouts, barbershops, and florists like James Harper, who first pointed out to me their piranha-like growth. Cash America and Famous Pawn are national chains, multi-million-dollar operations, and among the fastest-growing stocks on Wall Street.

Another storefront, America's Cash Express, serves customers without bank accounts. Like Famous Pawn, America's Cash Express is headquartered in Texas. It boasts of huge profits, with revenue growth exceeding 20 percent over the past five years.

Checking accounts are increasingly out of reach for poor people: banks have pulled branches out of inner cities, making banking far away and offering limited hours; some banks require a good credit report or a minimum deposit; and some potential customers report feeling unwelcome there. They line up at America's Cash

Express to cash their government and payroll checks, often enduring long waits, intrusive scrutiny, and rejection. Rates vary by the type of check, but America's Cash Express reliably takes a huge chunk of the paycheck for itself. The company has spawned a disgraceful twist on check cashing: the payday loan. To secure a payday loan, you need a bank account and a paycheck or social security check on the way. You write a postdated check for some arbitrary amount, depending on how soon the company can cash it against your check. Borrowers then face the next month already in the hole, short for the cash they need for other bills, so they borrow again and again or simply pay the monthly fee that will keep the postdated check in the hands of the lender, rolling over and over, picking up more fees as it goes.

Payday loan copycats multiply faster than cockroaches, up and down commercial corridors bordering poor neighborhoods. Almost every day I see a new one with a name like Check 2 Cash, Chek 'n Go, or Fast Cash. In the spring, instant tax refund shops join the mix, preying on people who need money fast. At H & R Block, or at one of the many copycat centers, customers can file tax returns and receive cash immediately. These "refund anticipation loans" cost about $100 in fees, plus tax preparation fees averaging $120 and an administrative fee of $130. The twelve million borrowers who take out these loans net H & R Block more than $1 billion in loan fees and another $389 million in other fees, at an effective annual percentage rate of 247 percent.

Borrowing from predatory lenders further impoverishes and disenfranchises the poor. It reflects and exacerbates the harsh inequality in American life, as people who use regular credit cards and pay off the principal each month effectively receive free loans while they rack up perks like airline miles. The disastrous interest rates paid by the poor and the merchants' fees paid to credit card companies subsidize the wealthy and even the shrinking middle class. Those customers the industry calls "convenience users" or sometimes "deadbeats" receive free loans every month and pay off their balances without interest. Interest rates rise with inequality: students and other "revolvers" pay higher interest rates than convenience users, and the poor, through predatory lenders, pay the highest interest rates of all as multitudes of small amounts of cash are sucked out of poor neighborhoods.

Predatory lending works in layered, degrading, and complex ways. The most obvious is the highest interest paid by the poorest citizens. The interest people pay to cash a paycheck, secure a payday loan, file an electronic tax return, rent a couch, or pawn a power tool is hard to discern because the lenders calculate it by the day or the week or the month. For example, low-income car buyers pay two percentage points more for a car loan than those who earn over $30,000; low-income drivers pay an average of $400 more a year on car insurance; and the poor are more likely to buy furniture and appliances through rent-to-own businesses, where a $200 TV set might cost $700 counting interest. People with poor credit also pay higher deposits for utilities and telephones.

Customers often find themselves unable to pay back more than the interest, so that they may owe twice as much as their original loan in as little as three months. People sometimes have to roll over these loans eight, nine, or ten times. It is not unusual to see people caught up in a single loan for eighteen months. They come in, pay off the fees, and just keep rolling over the loan. Or they borrow from one predator to pay another. From the perspective of lenders, however, interest and hefty fees for overdrafts, rollovers, and late payments on predatory loans offer a thin, expansive sink for idle money, with wondrous returns from very little investment in inexpensive real estate, shoddy shops, and minimum-wage labor. But these practices are just the launching pad for layers of profits from poverty and debt.

BUYING AND SELLING DEBT

Since the passage of the 2006 Bankruptcy Act, sponsored by the financial services industry, an aggressive and abusive debt-collection industry has emerged to extract further profits from poor people's debt. Asset Acceptance, for example, specializes in small debts that the industry once charged off as a cost of doing business. But as the sheer numbers of small debts have grown, Asset has acquired a portfolio of debts at a discount of about two cents on a dollar.

Asset Acceptance employs a large staff ranging from attorneys who work on commission through hapless low-wage workers who make maddening daily telephone calls to desperate debtors. Sometimes collection companies pursue debtors years after they have defaulted on small loans and the debtor may not even remember the loan or the credit card involved, although it has accrued interest and late fees all the while. Borrowers often do not know who these companies are—they seem to arrive from another planet with names that mean nothing. Debtors dealing with Asset have no right to examine the original credit card bill or even to know which bank loaned them money because once Asset bundles and buys the debt it becomes an encumbered commodity owned by Asset and owed by the debtor.

If constant, abusive telephone harassment at all hours, calls to neighbors, relatives, employers, and coworkers, threats, and offers to settle at some lower amount do not work, Asset takes borrowers to small claims court. Asset and its competitors have defiled the original purpose of small claims courts, which were set up to help individuals settle minor disputes. These courts offer cheaper filing fees, require less evidence to start a suit, and impose less onerous requirements for protecting defendants' rights. However, poor plaintiffs and defendants are rarely successful there, especially when they face off against a large business and an overloaded court. Companies like Asset file tens of thousands of cases in small claims court each year against poor defendants who may or may not understand the situation, have a lawyer, or even know they are supposed to be in court. Collection agencies, like credit-scoring companies, add layers of profits to the business of selling debt.

SCORING CITIZENSHIP

In the last thirty years, increasingly sophisticated technologies, massive investments in debt, and huge profits from interest have elevated the importance of individual credit reports. Your credit report becomes your identity, your right to be an adult, your right to be a citizen. Most people find it easy to get a starter credit card. But the low limits that poor people receive are quickly reached—just as with payday loans—for car repairs, birthdays, medical bills, routine expenses like school supplies, field trips that low wages cannot cover, or emergencies like death, divorce, foreclosure, or making bail. After that, usurious interest and multiple fees trap poor borrowers in a quagmire of debt. Poor people today are then devalued in part because they have no credit history or "bad credit," which haunts them and excludes them from transactions that middle-class people take for granted, such as paying bills or buying books online, renting cars, buying tickets, and reserving hotel rooms.

The Fair Isaac Corporation produces a FICO credit score for every citizen based on information provided Fair Isaac by three agencies (Equifax, Experion, and Trans-Union) that monitor credit-related activities. We all carry Fair Isaac's computerized credit scores in cyberspace, sometimes with pride, sometimes like Hawthorne's Scarlet Letter. A FICO score may be as high as 850, averaging out at 720. If it is below 620, you are a subprime person, charged the heaviest interest rates if you have access to credit at all. A FICO score is like a thermometer. It may be the most vital of all statistics measuring and evaluating Americans, determining if you can borrow, how much you pay for automobile or life insurance, if you can rent a home, and if you need to pay an extra deposit for a telephone or utility hookup. These emergent identities are a sociologically neglected but crippling form of identity nearly as damaging as stigmatizing racial identities, with which they are entangled.

Employers, landlords, rental agents, car dealers, and insurance providers really treat credit scores not like thermometers, which are most often used for diagnosis and healing, but like permanent inscriptions about what kind of person you are so that they can make decisions about offering you a home, a car, a job or an affordable interest rate. Whether you have become a bad debtor because your life is hard, or your partner has died, or battered or abandoned you, or you've taken in an ill or elderly relative, or your wages are low doesn't matter. This process has become automated and mechanical, far different from going to your local bank manager for a loan.

If you have been a customer of a subprime lender such as Household Finance or Rent a Center, the lender assumes you must be a risk. When you shop for a car and the agent asks for your driver's license, he immediately pulls your credit report. Potential landlords check your score, and so do potential employers. Your car insurance rates vary according to your credit score, regardless of your actual driving record, and although you are required to insure your car.

With bad credit, you are not a full human being anymore. If your lender charges off your account and turns it over to a collection company, you can be ruined. This happens with increasing frequency with medical bills, which some people are likely to triage because they come every month but do not appear as frightening as others. Debtors may feel that they did nothing wrong in getting hurt or sick. Credit reports do not show that you are a good person working for low wages, although they do reveal many other things about your lifestyle. Your credit history becomes your identity, your right to be an adult, your right to be a citizen. With a bad credit history or no credit history, you are dispossessed not only of your resources but of important parts of your self, your goals, and the possibilities for your life. You're stuck in the world of predatory lending, which dominates the streets of poor neighborhoods, reflecting by its presence the absence of productive investment there and linking residents to another world: of Wall Street, financial services, and the production of profits from poverty

STEEPED IN TOXINS

The lack of productive investment in the neighborhoods along the river also means that there are few jobs, theaters, restaurants, recreational facilities, or green spaces. Partly because the natural reprieve it provides is so rare, the Anacostia River is precious to people who live nearby. But the Anacostia is also a tragic place: a political and psychological barrier and a site festering with toxins, reflecting the checkered political and environmental history of the district. While humans have lived along the river for ten thousand years, momentous change occurred in the 1950s under the strangely combined pressures of the Cold War and the civil rights movement.

Washington was supposed to be the capital of the free world, a model of capitalism and democracy. Yet as the city had grown away from the poisoned river, restrictive housing covenants had squashed its black residents in ghettos downtown. Civil rights activism blossomed in the Black Belt, leading both to limited home rule for Washington and to state-sponsored demobilization. In their final years in power the appointed district commissioners and their allies in real estate and media championed a massive urban renewal program that moved black residents across the Anacostia River into titanic developments in hastily patched together street grids. Four superhighways skewered the new neighborhoods, cutting residents off from access to the river while carrying commuters back and forth from Maryland and Virginia. Thus the monumental core was purged of black people, the Anacostia River became a toxic barrier between the eastern and western cities, and the people who suddenly lived east of the river found themselves in a second ghetto with precious few amenities or places to work.

When our research team began working in these neighborhoods in 1999, we did not find the wasteland that was so often evoked for outsiders. We met people who had worked hard to build community and activist groups, plant flowers, cultivate community gardens, develop a whole indigenous musical genre called go-go, and sponsor the only black ice hockey team in North America. They had built these institutions despite the tangled streets, the scant public transportation, the decimation that the war on drugs had brought to town, and official poverty rates as high as 50 percent in neighborhoods adjoining the river.

The residents we talked to were ambivalent about the river. They knew it stigmatized them and set them aside because it was filthy and smelly and because it was inevitably comparable to the gussied-up Potomac River, just as Anacostia Park was a poor reflection of Haines Point across the way. As they looked across it, the river framed the racial inequalities of the city. Yet it was also a precious place: its parklands offered almost the only green space for people to gather for family reunions and birthdays, for children to play, for friends to fish, for couples to court, for individuals to find solitude and solace. Anacostia Park was rich with memories of local civil rights struggles, social gatherings, music-making history, and the life and death of families.

But the people who live along the Anacostia in D.C. live at the bottom of a watershed, an area of land that drains into a body of water. Watersheds, unlike political boundaries, highlight the connections between people, places, and other living things. The Anacostia River is the second most polluted in the nation, and its filthiness reflects the history of urban renewal, suburbanization, overdevelopment, and automobile/commuter patterns. Highways, streets, buildings, and parking lots in the watershed prevent rainwater from soaking into the soil. So the watershed acts like a great chute, sending rainwater into drainpipes or streams mixed with gasoline, oil, battery acid, and antifreeze, or into soil barren of life. The region's overdevelopment also heats the river. Many plants cannot grow in oxygen-poor hot water, but algae go crazy, forming a surface mat that blocks the sun. As the algae eventually die, the bacteria that decompose them use up the rest of the oxygen in the river. Eight sewer overflow openings empty into the Anacostia River. After a heavy rain two or three billion gallons of raw sewage pour into the river. Chemical sediments laced with Roundup from agriculture and lawn management add more poisons. The catfish in the Anacostia River have the highest rates of liver cancer in the United States, and researchers have yet to trace what happens as they move up the food chain.

After a storm, the Anacostia River looks like a landfill on a conveyor belt, choked with plastic water bottles, Styrofoam cups, and lots of other litter that washes from land and streets into feeder streams through the large openings in storm drains. Although two-thirds of the Anacostia drainage area lies in Maryland, poor people who live in Washington, D.C., neighborhoods along the Anacostia suffer the effects of this toxic stew. They also tend to reap the blame because of the visual pollution that is probably the least harmful but the most visible: the garbage. Trash also speaks to the complexities of the watershed, for it comes from far upstream, but to visitors (and politicians, developers, or journalists) it doesn't look that way, and they don't talk about it that way. People living at the bottom of the watershed pay the price for the development enjoyed by others.

The vigilance of varied environmental groups, such as the Seafarers Yacht Club, the Anacostia Garden Club, the Earth Conservation Corps, and the Anacostia Watershed Society, has made the river more attractive in the last few years. The junked cars and islands of tires are gone, and regular cleanups take care of the litter. Although the river is still as toxic as ever, the health of the wildlife is difficult to address because of the complexities and the connections of the watershed. The health of the people has hardly been a concern. Almost alone in his worries, River Terrace health activist George Gurley wrote in a letter of support for a grant proposal for community health care:

> The residents of the River Terrace community have been fighting environmental injustices for several years with little or no results. This area of the city has a long history of environmental injustices dating back from 1972 when the Potomac Electric Power Company (PEPCO) was burning coal and was cited for environmental violations. In 1988, the River Terrace community and several other communities expressed shock and anger when it was learned that potentially deadly hazardous air pollutants were being emitted from the plant as a consequence of PEPCO burning waste fuels. Even today, many unhealthy violations still exist in this area of Benning Road Northeast. Residents are still experiencing frequent malfunctions from the plant causing the discharging of black soot. Many people are still complaining about cancer, chronic bronchitis, shortness of breath and hacking coughs. This community already suffer more than their unfair share of other pollutants in the area. Additional pollutants from garbage and trash in the Transfer Station include odors, dust, airborne bacteria, disease carrying vectors such as mosquitoes, flies, insects, birds, rats, mice, possums, raccoons, and snakes that can cause illnesses on both chronic and acute levels.

But watersheds are so complex that, as with many other instances of environmental racism, Gurley has found it hard to get the attention of people in power or even of environmental justice activists. While many activists have addressed the health of the fish and the ecosystem, fewer have been concerned with the health of the people along the watershed. It is hard to know how living at the bottom of a watershed intersects with other social, political, and environmental factors to make people sick and dead. But connecting the dots is essential for understanding what it is like to be poor in Washington, D.C., where unregulated abandonment and investment, corporate greed and irresponsibility, punitive public policies, *and* the interaction of stress with other ailments mean that poor people literally embody social inequality.

Washington, D.C., has the highest rate of infant mortality and low-birth-weight babies in the nation, but it shares with other American cities the horrific distinc-

tion of infant mortality rates and low-birth-weight babies rivaling the poorest countries in the world. The city, though compared to states, has the highest infant mortality rate in the country at ten per thousand births, and Wards 7 and 8 lead the
city in infant deaths. In 2006 eighty-one babies under the age of one year died. Infant mortality rates often reflect the poor health of the mother as well as an absence of health care facilities. Infant mortality eerily predicts much larger health
problems, and low birth weight may even contribute to such illnesses as hypertension later in life. Poor people all over the country live shortened lives, often cop-
ing with disabling illnesses that afflict them when they are way too young. In Washington, the most common fatal illnesses that are definitively linked to poverty are
hypertension, diabetes, cancer, and HIV/AIDS. Tuberculosis is less common but
shocking in its deadly reemergence, and asthma is also resurgent, although less
likely to be fatal. How closely are these illnesses linked to living at the bottom of
a polluted watershed?

Asthma simultaneously inflames and constricts a person's air passages like a fiery
vise. Asthma kills five thousand sufferers a year, and one in ten D.C. residents suffers
from it. The city is ranked third among the top five most challenging places to live
with asthma (behind Knoxville and Memphis and just ahead of Louisville and
Toledo). Strangely, Washington leads the nation, by far, in what the Centers for Disease Control terms "ill-defined cancers," much like those afflicting the catfish in the
Anacostia River. Despite its recent spread, the causes of asthma are contested: Does
it come from cockroaches, generally poor housekeeping, mold, or something out-
doors? People who live at the bottom of a poisoned watershed are assaulted by air
pollution from the commuter traffic that skewers their neighborhoods and from
the riverside power plant, which spews out fumes filled with particles of nitrogen
oxide, sulfur dioxide, and mercury in particles so small they bypass respiratory defenses and go deep into their lungs, wreaking havoc on the cardiovascular system
and making them more susceptible to flu, pneumonia, asthma, lung cancer, and
heart disease. George Gurley can clearly connect the asthmas and cancers of his
neighborhood to that power plant, but his is a lonely voice.

Diabetes is the only major disease with a rising death rate, with the incidence of
death from diabetes rising 22 percent since 1980. Approximately thirty-six thousand diabetics live in the District of Columbia. My friend James Harper was a hardworking florist who had gone deeply into debt to open his own shop. He had little
time to take care of himself, and when he died in 1999 he had been reduced to a
stump of a man, a torso, as he lost one limb after another to diabetes. His uncle and
two of his first cousins died of strokes.

The neighborhoods east of the Anacostia River starve for grocery stores. People
need healthy food but they get pawnshops instead. The carryouts that serve them
stock what is cheap, popular, hunger-sating, and bad for you: white bread, canned
fruits and vegetables, chips. Many people eat in a hurry on the streets, where the

only legal cooked foods are hot dogs, sausages, and egg rolls. School lunches, sur-
plus commodities, and free food at food banks are most often processed and canned,
stuffed with sugar, salt, and fat. Prison foods are glycemic nightmares, offering up
inexpensive carbohydrates and fats, overcooked vegetables without nutrients, and
thick brown gravy. One out of ten households experiences food insecurity, one out
of three children lives on the edge of hunger, and approximately 175,000 residents
depend on emergency food from food banks, pantries, and soup kitchens. Many
poor people must use food banks to eat, figuring out which ones are open when,
how to get there on the bus or on foot with small children in tow, and how to lug
the groceries home. Every day I see shoppers struggling home on foot or on the bus
with flimsy bags, drooping shoulders, fragile grips, and heavy loads.

Tuberculosis spreads through the air in close quarters when a person with active tuberculosis of the lungs or throat coughs or sneezes, talks or spits. Inhaled,
the bacteria lodge in major organs, often the lungs, and bore holes that turn them
into bloody pulp. A slowly developing chronic infection, tuberculosis can cause incessantly bloody coughing, painful breathing, relentless fever and fatigue, debilitating joint pain, emaciation, and pallor. When undertreated, tuberculosis transforms itself into a superbug, multi-drug-resistant tuberculosis, whose spread is
practically unstoppable even with complicated and expensive second-line drugs.

Washington, D.C., has no infrastructure for diagnosing and treating tuberculosis or understanding its resurgence among the poor. The cramped housing along
the river, a surge in homelessness, and the war on drugs are all implicated. The war
on drugs has sent many young people to prison for nonviolent crimes; and tuberculosis, like HIV/AIDS, festers in prisons, so that patients then take it back into the
community, into crowded homes or shelters where it is easily spread. There is no
follow-up: D.C.'s lone TB clinic sits in the shuttered D.C. General Hospital with a
seventeen-year-old x-ray machine that rarely works. When the machine breaks
down, or the staff runs out of film or chemicals, the office closes. Doctors do not
and cannot supervise these patients or ensure that they follow drug regimens that
might cure them.

Between seventeen thousand and twenty-five thousand D.C. residents are living with HIV, and at least ten thousand people have AIDS. D.C. also has the highest rate of new AIDS cases in the country—twelve times the national average, more
than any other city, including New York, Baltimore, and San Francisco. Blacks are
ten times more likely to die of AIDS than whites. Washington leads American cities
in rates of HIV/AIDS infections, with a thousand new cases reported each year, 75
percent of those among African Americans. Kevin Harper has been living with HIV
for fifteen years, and his first cousin Cedric died of AIDS, wasting away at Howard
University Hospital. Neither man was certain how he contracted the virus, although
Kevin had spent time in prison and both had used some drugs.

The housing crisis in D.C. during the last ten years has made poor people more vulnerable to HIV/AIDS while making it more difficult for them to manage it. These diseases of modern poverty are not particularly profitable. They are diseases of details, where meticulous management of diet, exercise, and medications depends on quality health care in theory but in practice is left to individuals and families. There are almost no health care facilities east of the Anacostia River, and the city offers health insurance only to children and their parents. As in the case of predatory lending, needless suffering from these diseases reflects at least in part unregulated, misplaced investment and noninvestment in poor communities. Extreme cuts in public and affordable housing, as well as the gentrification now oozing east of the Anacostia River, often cost poor, sick people the support systems of kin. Incarceration for nonviolent crimes as well as the difficulties faced by former prisoners in finding work, and the likelihood that they may be homeless, all make them more likely to contract tuberculosis or AIDS. Close living quarters (crowded housing, prisons, and homeless shelters) exacerbate tuberculosis and HIV/AIDS, and residents of those congested places carry the diseases back into poor communities.

I conclude this section with just three of the many health and illness stories that Sue Barnes and I have gathered in public housing along the river. I include these stories to show how complex and mutually reinforcing the illnesses of poverty are, both for individuals and for families, how stressful they are for people who both give and need care, and how hard it is to separate out individual ailments connected to specific causes. They are part of the synergy of living poor.

Ms. Mcleod is fifty-seven years old. Before retiring because of bad health, she worked as a cashier, a chain saw operator, and a lawnmower operator. Her husband died in 1999 after suffering several heart attacks and a stroke. Her father died of a massive heart attack and stroke when he was sixty-two, and her mother died of "every type of cancer" when she was seventy-eight. Her oldest sister suffers from hypertension, "heart trouble," and diabetes; her "baby sister drank herself to death"; one of her sons is dead; her oldest son is diabetic; and her middle boy and daughter experience crippling migraines, which elevate their blood pressure.

Her brother has had AIDS for twenty years but does not take medications or see a doctor. He was in prison for ten years on a drug offense "for drugs they never could prove that he had." She has had two knee replacements, but her knees are still painful and swollen. She suffers from heart palpitations and takes lots of medications. She has high blood pressure, which goes up with headaches, chocolate, and seafood. She can't drink dark sodas, tea, or coffee. A car accident in 1969 damaged the right side of her face beyond repair and left her with headaches. She has had distressing encounters with doctors, whom she feels haven't respected her or listened to her. She speaks at length about the long, long waits to get medical care.

Mr. Washington, a sixty-six-year-old resident of the housing project, has had three heart attacks. He also has respiratory problems and has been intubated six times. His brother was a diabetic, his older brother "died of a heart valve," and his grandmother had problems with her heart too. The "brother next to me died of an overdose." In 1999 he retired from construction work. "I stay by myself. When I feel myself getting sick, I start feeling bad, I get my oxygen backpack on, call an ambulance, and get myself out there. I meet the ambulance outside."

His neighbor Mary Johnson is seventy-six, widowed, and living with her son, who is a schizophrenic diagnosed in 2004. "He would go outside with no clothes on. He couldn't talk. He was breaking up furniture. He ain't got nowhere else to go, so I let him come on back [after he was discharged from St. Elizabeth's]." Her first and second husbands died of cancer, as did her daughter: "She was a workaholic. She wouldn't ask nobody for help, she had to do everything herself. She had surgery on her back—they took out something. I stayed in the hospital with her. She died with a smile on her face." Her other son contracted tuberculosis in jail, where he went for failing to pay child support. Mrs. Johnson suffers from hypertension. She sees a specialist for her hypertension: "Something wasn't right with my blood, the pills. He told me what was wrong but I can't call the name. . . . If I'm feeling all right, I don't go [to see the doctor for a checkup]. I think, 'I'm gonna save the money this month.'" She eats one meal a day—"string beans, chicken, turkey, something like that." She takes the bus with her son when they need medical care. "He goes to his clinic and I go to mine."

EASING POVERTY

This chapter has explored two disastrous consequences of being poor: the deep injustices mired in environmental pollution, which poor people endure so that others can grow wealthy from unregulated industrial, military, and agricultural projects; and the inequities of credit and debt, which make some people very wealthy and others ever poorer. This environmental and economic muck also stigmatizes and delegitimizes those who must wade through it, and the courage and resourcefulness of those who bring class action lawsuits against predatory lenders, polluters, and regulatory agencies is inspiring.

Ironically, this country has laws that could help to defang predatory lenders and polluters. The Community Reinvestment Act (CRA) requires banks to guarantee low-cost banking services to the poor and serve the credit needs of inner-city neighborhoods more imaginatively, working collaboratively with residents to determine their needs and offering appropriate, affordable, and productive credit. But government *could* enforce the CRA instead of undermining it. Cases brought by activists to the Federal Reserve Board almost invariably lose. Government should also extend the CRA to cover fringe banks, insurance companies, mortgage companies, and other quasi-banks. Instituting a national usury cap would help to ensure poor people's access to inexpensive credit.

The 1970s also gave us a host of environmental protection laws and an agency to enforce them. We should end the corporate welfare that subsidizes large companies to come to town even if they despoil the environment, pay poverty wages, and leave if they want without penalty. And we should reinvigorate the Environmental Protection Agency, insisting that it use all its powers to enforce the Clean Water and Clean Air Acts, and grant amnesty to the frustrated eco-whistle-blowers in the agency.

We can no longer stand by as the most vulnerable citizens are sucked into debt because they are poor, drowned by debt because of usurious charges and maddening harassment, and then treated as though they were less than full citizens while, ironically, they subsidize the rest of us by taking in environmental toxins and generating interest. From the district commissioners' construction of a city that worked much better for suburban commuters than urban residents, through Mayor Anthony Williams's harsh neoliberal regime of ethnic cleansing, the city government has failed the poor. Since the institution of limited home rule, Congress has blocked numerous progressive health initiatives: syringe exchange, medical marijuana, publicly funded abortions. However, Congress has let stand the city council's recent law capping interest on payday loans at 28 percent. When states have capped interest on payday loans, the predators leave. It is perhaps a measure of continuing racism and a terrible lack of sympathy for the poor that the residents of the capital could be so sick. Until the District of Columbia becomes a state with community health centers, creative public schooling, affordable housing, a living wage, full employment, civil rights for prisoners, quality public education, universal health care, and public regulation of private investment, this will continue to be a very sick and stressful place, at least for poor people.

12

Useless Suffering

The War on Homeless Drug Addicts

Philippe Bourgois

We're not allowed to just go in to the [county] hospital and try to get help. When I start swelling up with an abscess, I gotta make sure it's fuckin' red enough and infected enough that I got a fever that's wicked enough for them to take me in and give me part of the help that I need.

—SCOTTY

[One month later]
Record of Death
City and County of San Francisco
Name: Scott . . .   Age: 36   Height: 5'7"   Weight: 115
CAUSE OF DEATH *was determined to be:* POLYPHARMACY.
   . . . The body is that of a very slender young Caucasian man. . . .

Diagnoses:

1. CONGESTION AND EDEMA OF LUNGS MODERATE TO SEVERE

2. CONGESTION OF LIVER, SPLEEN AND KIDNEYS, MARKED

3. HEPATOMEGALY . . .

4. SPLENOMEGALY . . .

5. ACUTE PANCREATITIS . . .

6. INTRAVENOUS DRUG ABUSE . . . ACUTE AND CHRONIC

—CHIEF MEDICAL EXAMINER CORONER'S REPORT

When mentally ill men and women flooded onto city streets throughout the United States during the 1960s and 1970s with the closing of state-funded psychiatric facilities, the "able-bodied" homeless were not yet a common sight. Deindustrialization, the gentrification of skid row neighborhoods, the loss of affordable housing, the increased criminalization of the poor (especially ethnic minorities), and the gutting of the welfare safety net since the 1980s turned homelessness into a regular feature of U.S. cityscapes.[1] In November 1994, with the help of a public health needle exchange volunteer, I befriended a group of homeless men and women who lived in a warren of back alleys, abandoned warehouses, and overgrown highway embankments six blocks from my home in San Francisco.[2] They welcomed me into their scene, eager to talk about their lives and teach me about survival on the street. Over the next twelve years, I developed a warm relationship with them and was joined on this project of documenting their daily lives by the photographer and ethnographer Jeff Schonberg.[3] Soon the homeless began introducing us to outsiders as "my professor" or "my photographer doing a book about us."

At any given moment, the core group of homeless that we befriended consisted of some two dozen individuals, of whom fewer than half a dozen were women. In addition to the heroin they injected every day, several times a day, they smoked crack and drank two or more bottles of Cisco Berry brand fortified wine (each one equivalent, according to a denunciation by the U.S. Surgeon General, to five shots of vodka).[4] They usually divided themselves up into four or five encampments that moved frequently to escape the police. All but two of the members of this social network of addicts were over forty years old when we began our fieldwork, and several were pushing fifty. Most of them had begun injecting heroin on a daily basis during the late 1960s or early 1970s. A separate generational cohort of younger heroin, speed, and/or cocaine injectors also exists in most major U.S. cities, but these younger injectors represent a smaller proportion of the street scene, and they maintain themselves in separate social networks.[5] According to national epidemiological statistics, the age and gender profile of our middle-aged social network of homeless drug users is roughly representative of the majority of street-based injectors in the United States during the late 1990s and early 2000s.[6]

Our street scene proved to be remarkably stable despite the precarious income-generating strategies of its members. Most of the homeless survive by engaging in some combination of panhandling, recycling, garbage scavenging ("dumpster diving"), petty theft (primarily the burglary of construction sites), and day labor for local businesses and home owners. They have subordinated everything in their lives—shelter, sustenance, and family—to injecting heroin. Their suffering is eminently visible. They endure the chronic pain and anxiety of hunger, exposure, infectious disease, and social ostracism because of their inability to control their chronic consumption of heroin and other psychoactive drugs. Abscesses, skin rashes, cuts, bruises, broken bones, flus, colds, opiate withdrawal symptoms, and the potential for violent assault are constant features of their lives. But temporary exhilaration is also just around the corner. Virtually every day on at least two or three occasions, and sometimes up to six or seven times, depending upon the success of their income-generating strategies, most homeless heroin injectors are able to flood their bloodstreams and jolt their synapses with instant relief, relaxation, and sometimes a fleeting sense of exhilaration.

To show how the suffering and the destruction of the bodies of homeless addicts in the United States are exacerbated by neoliberal policies and values, I have selected a series of ethnographic descriptions taken from our twelve years of fieldwork notes and interviews. I have edited them to try to reveal how the intimate experience of pain, distress, and interpersonal conflict interfaces with political institutional and social structural forces that ultimately manifest in self-abuse. The homeless are superexploited in a labor market that has no long-term, stable productive use for them. They are pathologized and punished by the social services and related social welfare policies that are supposed to relieve, reform, and discipline them. They are most severely and immediately brutalized by law enforcement in its well-funded mission to protect and control public space and private property. Finally, they maltreat and, for the most part, have been maltreated by their kin since childhood. They continue these patterns of injurious behavior in most of their everyday interpersonal relations on the street despite their extreme dependence on one another. In short, the documentation of the lives of these homeless San Franciscans reveals how America's most vulnerable citizens are affected by the war on drugs, the disappearance of the unionized industrial labor market, and the dismantling of the welfare safety net.

A COMMUNITY OF ADDICTED BODIES

Indigent heroin injectors have an exceptionally intense physical and emotional relationship to their bodies. Their lives are organized around a central physical and psychological imperative to fill their bloodstream with opiates—often supplemented by alcohol, crack, and benzodiazepines. Their topmost physical and emotional priority is to obtain heroin, by any means necessary. This imperative regulates their social relations, gives them a sense of purpose, and allows them to construct moral authority and interpersonal hierarchies. It creates a community of addicted bodies. In fact, they describe themselves with ambivalent pride as "righteous dopefiends."

Ironically, opiate addiction creates order out of what appears at first sight to be chaotic lives that have spiraled out of control. Homeless heroin injectors know exactly what they have to do every morning upon awakening. All of the superimposed problems of homelessness and lifetimes of disruption—often including childhood domestic abuse—become irrelevant. A much more physically overwhelming and immediate pain must be confronted. It erupts at the cellular level every six hours, when body organs run amok and when every single cell screams for the opiate proteins it requires in order to continue operating. Showing up in court, applying for public assistance, meeting family expectations, obtaining shelter, eating nourishing food, finding a job, and seeking medical help for an infection are rendered trivial by the embodied urgency of addiction. Society's opprobrium and personal failure become the least of one's worries. Psychological insecurities, personal confusions, memories of family abandonment, unrequited love, and responsibilities to others fall by the wayside. The craving for heroin takes over.

> Felix looks horrible this morning, his eyes are bloodshot, and he complains of migraines and sweats. "I can't pick up my bones. Been throwing up all night." He has even defecated in his pants.
>
> He gives me money, pleading for me to go buy him a bottle of fortified wine "to wash out my system." Yesterday he fought with the storekeeper and is now forbidden to enter the premises.
>
> He describes how he awoke at 1:00 a.m. and could not urinate in his empty bottle because of "the shakes." He tried to stand up but fell down the embankment because his leg muscles were not responding. He had to crawl back up and spend the rest of the night with heat flashes and a revving heart.
>
> "I thought my heart was going to stop. My knees hurt; my legs are locked; I can't hardly walk; I can't hardly talk; I can't breathe; I can't even think; I feel every nerve in my fingertips, every single one, especially in my knee. I can't stand still. I can't lie down. It sucks. There is nothing enjoyable about this life."
>
> Luckily Hank comes by as Felix is describing his withdrawal symptoms to me and offers to give him a "wet cotton," i.e., the heroin residue from the filter used in a previous injection. (from Philippe's field notes)

One simple act instantly solves all Felix's problems: an injection of heroin. The homeless in the social network we have been following rarely experience the kind of full-blown "dopesickness" that woke Felix up so dramatically at 1:00 a.m. When they are beset by impending crisis they can usually find a friend or acquaintance in their social network to give them an emergency injection of a small amount of heroin to stave off withdrawal symptoms, even if it is only the residue from a pinch of used cotton, such as Hank's gift to Felix. This enables them to get back on their feet and go out and hustle more money for their next injection.

HIGH-TECH U.S. MEDICAL SERVICES

From biomedicine's perspective, injecting the dregs of heroin trapped on a used cotton filter in a filthy homeless encampment with no access to running water is a recipe for ill health. The pragmatic and even moral imperative that compels Felix and Hank to engage in this risky, unsanitary injection-sharing practice to avoid heroin withdrawal symptoms foments the spread of infectious diseases within social networks of street-based addicts. From biomedicine's perspective, homeless injectors appear ignorant, self-destructive, or even pathological. They self-inflict hepatitis, HIV, endocarditis, and abscesses on their bodies in their pursuit of an illegal substance to get high. They are frustrating patients to try to help because they refuse to stay sober after receiving urgent medical services and often return for care a few weeks or months later with newly ravaged bodies. Intensive care units and emergency rooms of county hospitals have been increasingly overwhelmed since the 2000s by the infectious diseases of the homeless. The bodies of the baby boom generation that turned to injection drug use in the early 1970s have entered premature old age. This crisis is exacerbated by the shrinking of the welfare state during these same decades and the entrenchment of neoliberal values of self-help and punitive control. Emergency departments in public hospitals have emerged as one of the few remaining publicly funded sites where the homeless, the addicted, and the mentally ill can seek help during episodes of acute personal crisis.[7]

"FREQUENT FLIERS": HANK AND PETEY

Most of the homeless in our street scene were hospitalized on multiple occasions. Usually they were admitted because of abscesses, but sometimes it was for whole-body infections, liver failure, or cancer. They are disparagingly called "frequent flyers" by the medical staff in county hospital emergency rooms all across the country. This was the case for Hank and Petey, who were "running partners." They coordinated all their income generation and most of their drug consumption, and because they shared everything—money, drugs, needles, companionship, and misery—they passed their infectious diseases back and forth to one another. Both men had hepatitis C and drank heavily in addition to injecting heroin. Both Hank and Petey were visibly sick, but there was no place for them to seek care for their routine ills:

> Shifting his weight from foot to foot to ease the ache, Petey gags and heaves a mouthful of blood into the gutter. His gums have rotted black. He points to the three or four twisted teeth on the bottom half of his mouth. "I need to get these pulled." He thinks this might be why, for the past week, he has been throwing up when he wakes up. I offer to drive him to the homeless clinic, but he refuses to leave his panhandling spot. He is scared of being left dopesick because he thinks his bleeding gums and chronic nausea will not qualify him as "sick enough" to warrant admission into the hospital for medical care.
>
> That night as I drive home, I see Petey, still at his spot, flying his sign. He is standing on one leg, flamingo style, to relieve the ache of his swollen feet. He is wobbling weakly with his eyes closed. (from Jeff's field notes)

Finally Petey's liver shut down, and he qualified unambiguously for hospitalization:

> Hank: "He's laying there in his hammock, not moving around. I figure he's dopesick, so first thing is I give him a shot. I tell him, 'Pick up your blankets and put them behind the wall in case the police come.'
>
> "But he is stumbling, mentally gone, so I took him to the hospital. He collapsed on the bus. When I picked him up, I realized how light he was. I undressed him in

the emergency room on the gurney to put on his hospital gown. He was comatose. I couldn't believe how skinny he is!

"A guy can only take so much. What am I, a black widow? I can't even keep myself fixed anymore. I'm mentally fucked up. I'm physically fucked up. I'm just fucked! I don't even got a blanket. The police came again when I was visiting Petey in the hospital. I'd only had the blanket for two days. Got it at the hospital when I brought Petey in. They've found the spot where I hide my stuff [pointing to a crevice in the freeway retaining wall]. They come every day now." (from Jeff's field notes)

The county hospital deployed the full force of its remarkable technology, and Petey was admitted to the intensive care unit (ICU), where he remained for six weeks at an estimated cost of $6,000 per day:

I go with Hank and Sonny to visit Petey in the ICU. Hank rushes to Petey's side. Petey's legs dangle like twigs from his protruding hipbones. He weighs only ninety-four pounds. Tubes run through his nose and in and out of his neck and chest to various machines. A big blue and white tube goes from down his throat to a machine that suctions his breath.

Hank kneels down and places his cheek next to Petey's, pleading for "Bubba, Bubba, my Bubba" to regain consciousness. Sobbing, he gently strokes Petey's hair to make it flow neatly back over the crown of his skull. His caresses change to a playful tussle, the tips of his fingers intermittently massaging and tangling the hair. "Promise me, Bubba, that you'll hang in there. Keep your promise to me. I love you."

Throughout this, Sonny is holding Hank's shoulders from behind saying, "Look, Petey, Hank loves you and he's holding you; and I love you and Hank; and I'm holding Hank; and Jeff is here too; and he loves you. Everyone's rooting for you. Lord, please protect our Petey."

A pulmonary specialist enters with a resident and an intern, and they use Petey, with his pneumonia and spiking fevers, as a teaching case. The specialist removes the tube from Petey's throat and asks the intern to "reintubate" Petey.

Petey lets out a rasping groan. With a Q-Tip, the nurse gently swabs his lips, tongue, and the inside of his cheeks with Vaseline. She cannot give him water because it might cause the blood clots on his lips, in his mouth, and down his throat to burst. (from Jeff's field notes)

During this same period when Petey was in the ICU, Hank was suffering from a bone disk infection in his lower back. He had sought help several times in the emergency room, but doctors distrust complaints of excruciating back pain by opiate addicts, since the standard treatment is a prescription for opiates. Hank, consequently, was refused admission to the hospital through the emergency room on three or four occasions until finally his bone disk infection spread into his spinal and brain fluid and knocked him unconscious. He was delivered to the hospital by an ambulance driver and was immediately admitted to the ICU.

Both Hank and Petey were resuscitated by the county hospital physicians and placed on high-tech life support. To everyone's surprise they began recovering in the hospital. Unfortunately, their dramatic physical respite—eating three meals a day and bathing regularly—was cut short by the logic of managed care that has been imposed on county hospitals across the country to reduce medical costs for the indigent. In 1997, the federal government passed the Balanced Budget Act to reduce the Medicare budget by $112 billion over the next five years.[8] This initiated a cycle of decreased federal reimbursements for indigent care to local hospitals. By 1999, the San Francisco General Hospital's budget shortfall had risen to $30 million.[9] Hospital administrators conducted cost-benefit audits and a "utilization review" and ordered doctors and nurses to institute aggressive "early release plans" for uninsured, indigent patients. Ironically, neoliberal logics driving U.S. medical care render the conditions of the homeless even more expensive and even more painful, creating a revolving door between the street and the ICU as patients return to the same living conditions that made them sick in the first place. A more physically painful scenario could not have been invented on purpose. It is exacerbated by the high-tech model of emergency treatment that the market forces of a neoliberal health system promote and that inadvertently tortures homeless drug users by attempting to cure them without addressing their social problems.

> Both Petey and Hank are back living under the freeway overpass and Petey is now missing all his clinic and SSI appointments.
>
> I find Petey panhandling at his old spot by the exit ramp of the Jack-in-the-Box drive-thru. The scabs on his face have grown, presumably because the clotting factor of his once again deteriorating liver is weakening. He cannot talk above a rasping whisper because of the scarring in his throat caused by the breathing tubes from his six weeks in the Intensive Care Unit, damaged by having been used as a "teaching case" for medical students.
>
> He is soaked; his brown leather jacket, oily and slick from the rain, is taut against his shrunken, bony frame. I can see the outline of a beer bottle in the side pocket of his jacket.
>
> He is "flying" a cardboard sign: "Will Work for food . . . God Bless." The cardboard is waterlogged and limp. He does not complain of being wet or cold, but his teeth are chattering.
>
> "I don't know what the fuck to do, Jeff. They never told me to return for an appointment. And I can feel my liver going. My liver is going, Jeff! They threw me out of the hospital after two months in a coma. The doctor told the nurse that they needed my bed. 'Since he can walk around he can leave.' They gave me a prescription and told me to move on."
>
> I ask Petey if he has gone back to drinking. "Only beer," he answers. "I stay away from the Cisco." (from Jeff's field notes)

These notes were written at the height of the dot-com boom that made San Francisco one of the richest cities in the United States. The mayor of San Francisco was

celebrating a $102 million surplus even as the county hospital was instituting dra-
conian cuts.[10] Sixteen maintenance workers at the hospital were laid off and one of
the pharmacies was closed. This prompted the hospital to hire four security guards
to control the crowds of impoverished patients now waiting two to four hours in
line to receive their "reduced fee" prescriptions. For the first time in thirty-five years,
a co-payment plan was instituted, forcing uninsured outpatients to share the cost
of their prescriptions. Coincidentally, at the time I was chair of a department at the
medical school that staffs the San Francisco County Hospital:

> The dean and the chief managing services officer of the county hospital present an
> Armageddon scenario for the crisis in the hospital's finances. They are having trou-
> ble retaining doctors and nurses because of burnout and have had to divert 41 per-
> cent of emergency ambulance deliveries due to a shortage of medical staff. There is
> no longer any trash pickup in nonpatient areas. They had an epidemic of antibiotic-
> resistant streptococcus in the ICU and had to shut down cleaning services in the rest
> of the hospital in order to assign all the limited cleaning personnel to the ICU. One of
> the ICU rooms has been closed down, and they are forced now to treat ICU patients
> in postoperative care rooms. An internal census revealed that 22 percent of patients
> sick enough to be admitted to the hospital waited eight hours in the emergency room
> before being assigned to a hospital bed.
>
> Just before his presentation of the "inhumane conditions at San Francisco Gen-
> eral due to federal Medicaid cutbacks," the dean announces that the university is rais-
> ing its mortgage subsidy limit for newly hired clinical and research faculty to $900,000
> on the grounds that "it is a hardship to oblige someone to relocate to San Francisco
> and be forced to buy a $1.5 million three-bedroom home" on the open market. (from
> Philippe's field notes)

Upon his release from the hospital, Hank's health deteriorated even more rapidly
than Petey's. Jeff attempted to broker outpatient services for Hank to prevent his
bone disk infection from spreading once again into his spinal and brain fluid. Jeff
also attempted, in vain, to guide Hank through the bureaucratic maze of applying
for Social Security Disability Insurance (SSDI):

> I arranged to meet Hank at the pharmacy at the county hospital. Petey agrees to come
> with me.
>
> There are a hundred or so people waiting in snake coils of lines to get their pre-
> scriptions because the latest rounds of budget cuts have shut half of the pharmacy
> windows.
>
> Hank looks a wreck and he has only been out of the hospital for a week. He is back
> to fixing heroin every day, and today he is so drunk that he is slurring his words. I am
> struck by the ripeness of his smell.
>
> After about three hours in line, we finally make it to the Plexiglas pharmacy window.
> Hank is handed a piece of paper which outlines his "rights to medication." He does not
> have the $50 co-payment for his prescription—a new requirement—and neither do I.

Hank goes up to the Fourth Floor to find his doctor, the one he likes so much. He returns with his medication that his doctor somehow was able to obtain for free. This doctor has also been thoughtful enough to give Hank a letter about his physical inability to work so that his welfare check can be reinstated. Hank was cut from public assistance while in the hospital for his failure to show up for workfare requirements.

I take Hank to the hospital social worker's office and wait in front of her desk until she is able to talk to us about the status of his Social Security application. It turns out that Hank is missing yet another set of forms that can only be picked up at the Social Security office downtown. We find out that his "reconsideration hearing" for missing his last appointment and having an incomplete dossier is scheduled for the day after tomorrow. (from Jeff's field notes)

Predictably, Hank missed his hearing, and his "incomplete dossier" was rejected. He had to start the whole process of applying for SSDI from the beginning once again.

Hank is crying on the corner because Petey is back to drinking fortified wine. Hank says Petey is throwing up again and insisting that it is due to the hot sauce from the Taco Bell. Hank shoplifted some Maalox for him at the Walgreen's. Petey has not gained any weight. He and Hank are surviving primarily on the sandwiches given to them on their outpatient visits to the hospital—most of which they miss—and the fortified wine they buy on the corner.

Hank missed his appointment again today because he had the opportunity to log six hours of work with Andy, the man who owns a moving van and occasionally hires the homeless for ten dollars an hour. Andy is by far the highest-paying day laborer employer in the homeless scene, and everyone vies for his jobs. Hank is distressed: "It just hurts my back too much. I had to walk off the job. I'm not up to working for Andy anymore."

Their new camp, nicknamed "The Nest," is located on the neighborhood's main artery under the freeway overpass. It is uncannily camouflaged as a heap of dirt and garbage. Hank has gathered branches, twigs, and dried pine needles, piling them together with mud and sand, and has molded this into a circular concave structure that allows their heads to duck below the surface. Less than two feet above our heads the wheels of speeding cars and trucks reverberate against the concrete underside of the overpass.

Jeff takes out a pile of papers from Hank's new batch of SSDI applications and lays them out on the carpet padding lining the bottom of the nest. We give up because it is much too complicated to complete the forms in the candlelight. Jeff displays some photos of Petey taken while he was unconscious in the ICU with breathing tubes down his throat less than a month ago. Hank bursts into tears again. (from Jeff and Philippe's field notes)

Hank and Petey are labeled "nonadherent patients" in the politically correct parlance of medicine. Even the most devoted medical practitioners understandably feel frustrated by the ways indigent drug users repeatedly complicate their already severe medical problems. Further, homeless injectors also frequently abuse the trust of those who try to help them. They pilfer hospital supplies when the orderlies and nurses turn their heads, and they exaggerate their need for opiate painkiller prescriptions. In other words, they are deeply enmeshed in a mutually adversarial cycle of hostile interactions with medical institutions, consistent with the bureaucratic institutional violence to which they have been prey since childhood from school to prison.

During the first five years of our fieldwork, for example, county hospital surgeons were routinely inflicting iatrogenic wounds on the bodies of homeless injectors. When heroin users arrived with infected abscesses, the doctors cut into them with a deep carving-and-scraping procedure that required an overnight stay. Subsequently, this procedure came to an abrupt end when the surgeons discovered in 2001 that most abscesses could be treated more effectively by a simple incision-and-drain outpatient procedure that does not need to be painful when adequate local anesthetic is applied. There is no national standard of care in the United States for treating abscesses. Abscesses are primarily a self-inflicted condition suffered by homeless heroin addicts. Consequently, their treatment is a low-prestige medical procedure that most researchers and clinicians have shunned. Abscesses, however, represent a veritable epidemic of physical suffering among the homeless. In the year 2000, for example, abscesses represented the single biggest admissions category (four thousand cases) at the county hospital.[11]

The hospital's drastic budget cuts and cost overruns, rather than a humanitarian concern with appropriate treatment, provided the decisive impetus for reforming the expensive, disfiguring, and unnecessary surgical procedure for abscesses that had become routine in the 1990s. To the surprise of the surgeons, the new, cheaper outpatient incision-and-drain procedure proved superior.[12] Healing occurred more rapidly, less painfully, and scarring was minimized. Some of the senior surgeons grumbled, however, that the outpatient procedure reduced the opportunities for medical students and interns to learn surgical skills on their rotations through the county hospital.

All of the homeless we followed spoke positively on the whole about the care they received at the county's hospital, but many also told us horror stories during the pre-2001 years of surgeons cutting into them without anesthesia and refusing to prescribe adequate painkillers for aftercare. Sympathetic nurses at the hospital explained to us that these exceptionally abusive clinicians were usually medical students on clinical rotations. They were not prepared to deal with intoxicated patients, and they resented injectors because of their self-inflicted infections. Until the abscess protocol was reformed, Hank responded to the risk of mistreatment in surgery by lancing his own abscesses.

> With his boxer shorts to his knees, Hank juts out his hip and twists into a contrapposto stance to reach the abscess festering in his rear. He explains,
> "First you feel for a pocket and if it be real kind of mushy like this one then you know it's ready.

"Yesterday I was worried that it was an inverted abscess with the pus flowing inside me. So I bled it off a little and left it overnight. Now it's ready."

He slowly inserts a pair of manicure scissors into the center of the abscess, pushing the scissors all the way up to the finger holes of the handle. He leaves the scissors pressed into the tissue for a few seconds, slowly swirling them to loosen the flesh, as pus dribbles out of the gash like a dripping eye. He then pulls the scissors out with slow deliberation, squeezing the open gash between his two thumbs.

After a few seconds of grimacing and squeezing, he grabs a toenail clipper and places it just inside the surface of the abscess, using it to grab at something.

He reassures me,

"There's not much pain and that shit basically ends the abscess. But you gotta get that poison out of your system or it won't heal."

After covering the abscess with ointment and the Sterile Pak bandages given to him by a harm reduction health care activist, he lifts a full syringe of heroin, plunging it almost up to its hilt into the side of the freshly bandaged abscess. Shortly after flushing the heroin he sits down and relaxes his whole body.

No one else in the camp thinks there is anything unusual about this procedure. This is just another day in the encampment; I am the only one who is overwhelmed. (from Jeff's field notes)

Hank's procedure looks horrible and self-mutilating, but at that time he was following an arguably effective logic of self-care in the face of the county hospital's deep carving-and-scraping alternative. Most of the injectors postponed seeking hospital treatment because of the long waits in the emergency room and the hostile triage for admission. This practice sometimes resulted in generalized blood infections that escalated into multiple pathologies throughout their bodies. In Hank's case, postponing treatment may have caused the bone infection to spread to his spinal and brain fluid.

UNHEALTHY LAW ENFORCEMENT

It is easy to criticize the inadequacy of medical care and social services for the poor in a neoliberal society. It is even easier to dismiss the homeless for being self-destructive or even pathological in the self-abuse of their bodies. These critiques, however, distract from another more important structural policy dysfunction that must be emphasized in any discussion of poverty and substance abuse in the United States: the war on drugs. Fear of arrest and eviction is a chronic condition among the homeless. The police and the laws they enforce destabilize the daily lives of all the members of the social network we followed and cause immediate negative health effects even when arrests are not made. The illegality of syringes and drugs forces homeless addicts, driven by the urgency of the physical and emotional craving for heroin, to seek out filthy nooks and crannies to make their injections on the run, hidden from public view. More directly, the police, especially the California Highway Patrol, regularly destroyed the physical shelters of the people we studied. Patrol officers purposefully confiscate the possessions most crucial for everyday survival: dry clothes, blankets, tarps, tents, food, cooking utensils, prescription medicine, and clean syringes. In short, the effects of law enforcement directly contradict the efforts of public health to stem infectious disease and up the ante of violence on the street.

There was another police sweep and Hank looks like absolute hell. His eyes are so puffy that I ask him if he has been in a fight.

"They wiped me out again last week. I went for a drink at the corner and when I returned, there was the CHP [California Highway Patrol]. I'm tempted to get my gun and shoot the next patrol car that I see."

He says that when he asked for his clothes the officer in charge threatened to arrest him. They would not return any of his clothing.

Worse yet, they took the prescription Fentynal [a synthetic opiate painkiller] a doctor at the county hospital had prescribed to relieve the lower back pain caused by the now irreparable decay of his infected bone disk.

"I saw them throw my Fentynal patches in the back of that truck. If I had a gun, I swear on my mother, I woulda shot them cops straight in their goddamn head and there wouldn't have been no proof of arrest.

"They said, 'We're teachin' you a lesson. You're on State Property!' "

Hank is shivering so hard that he is hugging himself across his chest to steady himself. I am not sure if it is his withdrawal symptoms from losing his supply of opiate painkillers or his bone infection revving up again. I urge him to go back to the hospital and offer to take him.

"Why? So they can send me right back out again?"

I suggest calling an ambulance to avoid the three- to five-hour wait for triage in the emergency room.

Instead he asks me for money to buy a bottle of fortified wine.

Max, who has now set up an encampment next to Hank and Petey, comes by. He sees Hank's condition and recognizes immediately that it is withdrawal symptoms. He puts his arm around Hank's shoulder, offering to give him a "taste" of heroin.

We walk through the back alley to the freeway, where they inject. Hank has to borrow Max's used syringe because the police confiscated his entire supply. The shot of heroin revives Hank. I offer to take him to the hospital. He agrees that he needs to see the doctor, but he is embarrassed. "I haven't showered in over thirty days."

Max nods. He has been missing his wound clinic follow-up visits for the abscess on his rear that was so deep and large that it required a skin transfer. He is too embarrassed. "My ass is too skinny." (from Jeff's field notes)

During crisis periods, such as these, when the police increased the tempo of their evictions and search-and-seizure procedures, the homeless began keeping no more than two needles in their possession for fear of being arrested. In California and many other states where syringes are illegal without a prescription, the police have the option when they catch someone with three or more needles of enforcing a discretionary rule whereby they can arrest the injector for the felony of "needle sales" rather than the misdemeanor of possession. In San Francisco, judges usually dismiss charges of needle sales. By the time addicts are processed through the system, however, they have fallen into full-blown withdrawal symptoms. The punishment, consequently, is the severe heroin withdrawal symptoms they suffer in jail while waiting to see the judge for a bogus felony arrest. As one homeless addict explained to us,

> The worst is when you're in jail. Because they don't give a shit if you die. You're in there, curled up in a corner, throwing up and shittin' at the same time.
>
> You get the heebie-jeebies. . . . It's like an anxiety attack. A million ants crawling through your skin and you just want to peel it right off. It's like someone is scraping your bones. . . . You try to sit there and grab your knees and rock.
>
> And in prison there are youngsters there in the cell with you, talkin' shit. "Oh, you dopefiend."

Faced with this risk, the homeless stopped visiting the needle exchange, which was enforcing a one-for-one exchange rule. It is simply not worth it to a homeless injector to spend the time and money to seek out a needle exchange site and obtain only one or two clean needles. As Frank explained when we asked him why he had stopped visiting the needle exchange: "Maybe I ain't got a dollar to catch a bus across town to get to the exchange. It just ain't worth it for a couple of needles, especially if you're feeling sick." They began reusing and sharing their needles more frequently, and their incidence of abscesses increased.

EXPLOITATIVE LABOR MARKETS
IN STRUCTURAL TRANSFORMATION

The negative health effects and the emotional suffering caused by the U.S war on drugs are relatively easy to recognize. More subtle and complicated, and less linear, are the connections between the experience of suffering of street addicts and the less visible, macrohistorical forces of the economy, specifically the long-term restructuring of the U.S. labor market. In 1975, when the homeless in our scene were in their early twenties, the crucial age for integration into the manual labor force, a study commissioned by the City of San Francisco noted that the specific neighborhood we studied was in a "depressed state" and projected a loss of "3,000 jobs by the year 2000."[13] This was part of the long-term deindustrialization of America. For example, between 1962 and 1972, the city of San Francisco lost twelve thousand manufacturing jobs.[14] In other words, the homeless and the families they came from were the obsolete labor force of disappearing industries: dock work, shipbuilding, steel milling, metal smelting, and foundry work.

Economies going through major structural adjustment do not forgive undisciplined, poorly educated workers—especially when they drink and take drugs. As substance abusers without a college education, homeless heroin injectors are at the bottom of San Francisco's hiring queue. The low-wage service industries of the new, postindustrial U.S. economy are supplied from an enormous pool of highly disciplined immigrant laborers who are eager to work for low wages. In California these model workers are primarily undocumented Mexican, Central American, and Chinese immigrants who are fleeing poverty, hunger, and/or violence in their home countries.

The job histories of the homeless we studied reveal how they were structural victims of the changing economy as well as self-destructive in their drug use. The oldest members of our network had actually worked in unionized positions in the old industrial economy—primarily shipyards and steel mills in their early youth. In the late 2000s, however, they find themselves scrambling for day labor jobs in the dilapidated warehouse districts of abandoned factories. They load and unload trucks, or stock merchandise, or sweep in front of corner liquor stores. They strive to develop client-patron relationships with the few still-existing small business owners in order to eke out a few hours of work per day.

Local business owners often choose a particular homeless person to whom they give occasional loans of money and gifts of food. In return, the "lucky addict" checks in every morning to see if work is available. The result is an efficient delivery of the kind of "just-in-time" labor that is celebrated by the neoliberal economy. Employers obtain a cheap, flexible, and desperately dependent source of labor. The downside, of course, is that the business owners have to accommodate the vicissitudes of the lives of the homeless. For example, when Scotty (the man profiled in the epigraph) died, his employer, the manager of a construction supplies depot, was left in the lurch. He had paid Scotty in advance to shovel sandbags. Similarly, Hank walked off a moving job when his decayed lower back disk caused him too much pain.

The savviest business owners calculate the size of their favorite addict's habit and are careful to pay (or loan) only the precise amount of money needed to take the edge off of heroin withdrawal symptoms. Any extra cash might precipitate a binge on crack or alcohol. Ben, for example, the owner of a furniture liquidator warehouse, always paid Al his day's wage in the morning and made sure to remain one day in arrears. In this manner he was guaranteed that Al, driven by heroin withdrawal, would always show up on time for work each morning eager for the $10 he needed to placate his early morning withdrawal symptoms. Ben had to give Al only one more $10 bill at midday along with a pack of cigarettes and a bottle of fortified wine to complete his full day's wage.

> Al has been talking a great deal about wanting to "get clean." So just before sunset I visit him where he works, at the furniture liquidator warehouse, and offer to give him a ride to the treatment center. He is moving furniture back into the warehouse from the sidewalk where they display it in the path of pedestrian traffic.

Al is nervous because the welfare department contacted his employer, Ben, to fill out a form to confirm that he works "part time" for him so that he does not have to participate in the workfare program to receive his check. Ben has refused to sign anything for fear of being taxed, and probably also because he pays Al under minimum wage.

Al curses his boss under his breath, complaining about only getting $20 per day. "It's like I'm a dog on a leash; he knows I'll be sick before morning."

The boss is a burly man in his early fifties with a thick Brooklyn accent. Abruptly, without even saying hello, he asks, "You the guy writing stories about heroin addicts? Huh?"

The next thing I know he is shouting, "Why have they been shooting heroin for so long? At fifty years old it's their responsibility to get out off of this shit. Why should society help? It's their fuckin' problem. No one holds a fuckin' gun to their head and makes them shoot up! Who got them into the drugs? All they gotta do is look into the fuckin' mirror.

"These guys are habitual criminals. They don't need no fuckin' breaks. Leeches, bloodsuckers, and snakes. . . . They'll never change. Anything you give 'em for help they just put right back into their arms. Welfare, SSI, shoot-up, drink-up, what else they want for free?

"Get the fuck outta here! You're part of the fuckin' problem."

Throughout the harangue Al shows no emotion. He continues moving the last of the furniture inside the warehouse. He then sits on the sidewalk waiting for us to finish, as if the argument has nothing to do with him.

Later that evening, back at his encampment, Al feels compelled to apologize to me for his boss's tirade: "I don't understand why he's acting like that. I really don't. I'm sorry. He was just joking." (from Jeff's field notes)

MORALIZING SUFFERING AND ABUSE

Anthropologists and historians have documented psychotropic drug use—usually mediated in formally ritualized and religious contexts—in virtually all cultures throughout the world and throughout history. They distinguish this from the destructive forms of substance abuse that have escalated under urbanization, industrialization, and incorporation into the global market economy.[15] Modern-day homeless substance abusers bear more than their share of human anguish. This may be why they are vulnerable to self-destructive forms of addiction in the first place. In America, drug taking among the disenfranchised has become an especially destructive practice, filling urban streets with social pariahs with ravaged bodies.

In the United States, the land of immigration, opportunity, and economic abundance, popular common sense does not recognize that individual suffering is politically structured. Both the rich and the poor adhere to a puritanically inspired tradition of righteous individualism that defines poverty to be a moral failing of the individual. These judgments are even extended onto the general population of uninsured poor in the United States—more than forty million people in the year 2004.[16] Al's boss Ben, the furniture liquidator, was merely expressing in vituperative language an all-American common sense.

An analysis that allows us to recognize how larger power relations interact with individual failings at the intimate level avoids blaming victims and delegitimizes counterproductive, punitive social policies. At first sight this is difficult to comprehend because the apparently willful self-destruction of homeless heroin injectors confuses even sympathetic advocates for the poor. The lives of homeless injectors are shaped by a total social context of institutions, policies, macrostructural forces, and cultural values that they do not control. In short, the socially structured suffering of the homeless in the social network we studied has been rendered "uselessly" painful by the neoliberal turn in the United States.[17] Recognizing this unnecessary toll of suffering imposed on the lives of America's most vulnerable citizens is especially important at a moment in history when ever-increasing segments of the world's population are being marginalized by global shifts in the economy and by political ideologies intent on dismantling social services in favor of punitive neoliberal policies.

NOTES

Research support was provided by National Institutes of Health (NIH) grant R01DA010164 and the President's Office at the University of Pennsylvania through a Richard Perry University Professorship. Comparative background data were also drawn from NIH-funded grants MH078743, DA017389, and DA021627; California HIV Research Program grant ID06-SF-194; National Endowment for the Humanities grant RA 20229 (through the Institute for Advanced Study in Princeton); and Russell Sage Foundation grant 87-03-04. I thank my ethnographer colleague Jeff Schonberg and my clinical colleague Dan Ciccarone, as well as my office helpers and editors Fernando Montero, Zoe Marquardt, and Nick Iacobelli. Laurie Hart's detailed critiques were most helpful.

1. See Kim Hopper, *Reckoning with Homelessness* (Ithaca, NY: Cornell University Press, 2003), 60–65; Vincent Lyon-Callo, *Inequality, Poverty, and Neoliberal Governance: Activist Ethnography in the Homeless Sheltering Industry* (Peterborough: Broadview Press, 2004); Dale Maharidge, *Journey to Nowhere: The Saga of the New Underclass* (New York: Hyperion, 1996); Anthony Marcus, *Where Have All the Homeless Gone? The Making and Unmaking of a Crisis* (New York: Berghahn Books, 2005); David Snow and Leon Anderson, *Down on Their Luck: A Study of Homeless Street People* (Berkeley: University of California Press, 1993), 17–20, 234–53.

2. Charles Pearson and Philippe Bourgois, "Hope to Die a Dope Fiend," *Cultural Anthropology* 10, no. 4 (1995): 1–7.

3. Philippe Bourgois and Jeff Schonberg, *Righteous Dopefiend* (Berkeley: University of California Press, 2009).

4. Denise McVea, "Wine Punch: The Economics of Selling the 'Wine Fooler' to Dallas' Minority Community," *Dallas Observer*, November 17, 1994, www.dallasobserver.com/1994-11-17/news/wine-punch/1.

5. Philippe Bourgois, Bridget Prince, and Andrew Moss, "Everyday Violence and the Gender of Hepatitis C among Homeless Drug-Injecting Youth in San Francisco," *Human Organization* 63, no. 3 (2004): 253–64.

6. J. M. Gfroerer et al., "Substance Abuse Treatment Need among Older Adults in 2020: The Impact

of the Aging Baby-Boom Cohort," *Drug and Alcohol Dependence* 69, no. 2 (2003): 127–35; Andrew Golub and Bruce D. Johnson, "Variation in Youthful Risks of Progression from Alcohol and Tobacco to Marijuana and to Hard Drugs across Generations," *American Journal of Public Health* 91, no. 2 (2001): 225–32; Judith Hahn et al., "The Aging of the Homeless Population: Fourteen-Year Trends in San Francisco," *Journal of General Internal Medicine* 21, no. 7 (2006): 775–78.

7. D. Dohan, "Managing Indigent Care: A Case Study of a Safety-Net Emergency Department," *Health Services Research* 37, no. 2 (2002): 361–76; R. E. Malone, "Whither the Almshouse: Overutilization and the Role of the Emergency Department," *Journal of Health Politics, Policy and Law* 23, no. 5 (1998): 795–832.

8. Stuart Guterman, *Putting Medicare in Context: How Does the Balanced Budget Act Affect Hospitals?* (Washington, DC: Urban Institute, 2000), www.urban.org/publications/410247.htm.

9. William C. Brady, "Less Care for Sick Poor," *San Francisco Chronicle*, May 5, 1999, A21.

10. Ibid.

11. D. Ciccarone et al., "Soft Tissue Infections among Injection Drug Users: San Francisco, California, 1996–2000," *Morbidity and Mortality Weekly Report* 50, no. 19 (2001): 381–84.

12. Hobart Harris and David Young, "Care of Injection Drug Users with Soft Tissue Infections in San Francisco, California," *Archives of Surgery* 137, no. 11 (2002): 1217–22.

13. Arthur D. Little Inc., Commercial and Industrial Activity in San Francisco: Present Characteristics and Future Trends. Report to San Francisco Department of City Planning (San Francisco: Department of City Planning, 1975).

14. Ibid.

15. Jordan Goodman, Paul Lovejoy, and Andrew Sherratt, eds., *Consuming Habits: Drugs in History and Anthropology* (London: Routledge, 1995); David T. Courtwright, *Forces of Habit: Drugs and the Making of the Modern World* (Cambridge, MA: Harvard University Press, 2001).

16. Gaylene Becker, "Deadly Inequality in the Health Care 'Safety Net': Uninsured Ethnic Minorities' Struggle to Live with Life-Threatening Illnesses," *Medical Anthropology Quarterly* 18, no. 2 (2004): 258–75.

17. Veena Das, "Moral Orientations of Suffering: Legitimation, Power, and Healing," in *Health and Social Change in International Perspective*, ed. L. Chen, A. Kleinman, and N. Ware (Cambridge, MA: Harvard University Press, 1994), 139–67; Emmanuel Levinas, "Useless Suffering," in *The Provocation of Levinas*, ed. R. Bernasconi and D. Wood (London: Routledge and Kegan Paul, 1988), 156–67.

13

Walling Out Immigrants

Peter Kwong

Migration has always been a part of human experience—throughout history, people have moved to places that offered better conditions for survival. In doing so, new immigrant groups have typically had to confront the hostility of the groups that arrived earlier because newcomers are always seen as competitors for resources and jobs. In the United States, immigrant bashing has become a ready-made tool used by politicians to stir up popular support and distract attention from problems that are much more difficult to resolve. And since new immigrants tend to be a small minority without political representation, attacking them is a cost-free political exercise. From the days of the founding of the Republic, the United States has used immigrant bashing against the Catholic Germans, the Irish, the Chinese, other people of color, and "ethnic whites" from Eastern and Southern Europe at the beginning of the twentieth century. The attacks were usually articulated in overt racial and ethnic terms.

Anti-immigrant rage in the United States these days is focused mainly on Mexicans who enter the country illegally. In the current post–civil rights era, instead of being portrayed as inferior and unwanted, they are accused of parasitism on our already limited public social welfare and educational resources.

Congress in 1986 passed the Immigration Reform and Control Act (IRCA) to curb the entry of illegals. The act provided for sanctions against employers who hired illegals "knowingly." In practice the law did not stop the hiring of illegals because few employers could be convicted given the lack of a national identification system. But while the law did nothing to stop employers from hiring illegals, it facilitated employer exploitation of undocumented employees because, under IRCA, illegals cannot report employer abuses against them for fear of deportation. The ineffectiveness of the law has led instead to an increase in illegal immigration and, at the same time, a dramatic upsurge in the number of sweatshops and labor violations all across the country.

With illegal immigration unchecked, the 1990s were years of rising anti-immigrant sentiment. Early milestones came in 1993 when the broken *Golden Venture* steamer, loaded with 286 illegal Chinese migrants, ran aground just a few miles from downtown Manhattan, and when the first World Trade Center was bombed in 1994. The U.S. Congress, pandering to rising anti-immigrant sentiment, passed a series of harsh anti-immigrant bills that expanded the criminalization of the undocumented. Even liberal Democrats began to vie among themselves to introduce tough measures against illegal immigration, some of which went so far as to target the rights of legal immigrants. Once these mean-spirited bills were passed and President Clinton signed them into law, many politicians returned to their home districts to present them to their voters as "achievements" of their campaigns.

Needless to say, the new laws have not slowed down the influx of illegal immigrants. Ten years later, House Republicans, anticipating a turbulent 2006 midterm election, returned to the hot-button illegal immigration issue. After 9/11 the immigration issue gained a new edge from the urgent "national security" priority to fix the borders in order to prevent "terrorists" from entering among the illegals. At the end of 2005, the Republican House majority pushed through HR 4437, which, if passed by the Senate, would have turned all illegal immigrants into felons subject to deportation. It would also have criminalized all those who aided them, including welfare organizations and church workers. It was a very nasty piece of racial political pandering to vigilante armed citizen groups like the Minutemen, who patrol the U.S.-Mexico border although they lack legal authority to stop illegals from crossing it.

The congressional move, however, stirred up a "sleeping giant." The Latino community, no longer willing to allow the least fortunate in its ranks to be used as a political tool, mobilized millions of protesters on the streets of all major U.S. cities to protest the congressional bill. To show that the initial success of their grassroots mobilization effort was no fluke, Latino community leaders called on all immigrants to boycott work on May Day of 2006. Upward of 1.5 million people participated in daylong walkouts, strikes, and protests all across the nation. In Chicago an estimated seven hundred thousand took part in the May Day "day without immigrants" action, with one-third of the city's students refusing to attend schools. Similarly large turnouts in other major cities exposed to the world the dirty little secret of the affluent society in the United States—its dependence on cheap immigrant labor.

The scale of these demonstrations shocked the Washington establishment. Republicans, following Karl Rove's electoral strategy, had hoped to attract a larger number of Latino voters and use their vote to gain advantage over the Democrats as the party with a permanent majority. Now they were caught between the needs of angry white voters in their base and their hope to peel Hispanic votes away from the Democrats. In response to the demonstrations, they decided to back off and introduced more subtle versions of the immigration bill in the Senate. Moderate Republicans with the backing of George W. Bush called for guest worker programs and some avenue for those illegal workers who were already in the country to legalize their status. But by then many members of Congress had lost interest in pursuing this complicated and divisive issue any further. They opted to take the easy route: to provide funds for border patrols and the building of more barriers along the U.S.-Mexican border. This included funds for Boeing—expected to reach $8 billion by 2011—to build a "virtual fence": 1,800 towers, each ninety-eight feet tall, jam-packed with radar, cameras, and communication gear networked to body-detecting sensors on the ground, pilotless drones flying overhead, and remote command and control centers.[1]

These measures are popular because many Americans still believe that the country would be overrun by illegals if nothing were done to control the borders. Many also assume that the United States lets immigrants enter only out of simple generosity rather than in response to employers' need for cheap labor. This mind-set was on full display in the 2007 national debate on immigration. The initiative this time came from George W. Bush, who wanted passage of an immigration reform bill as one of the few legacies that he could claim for himself during all his years in office. Democrats, newly in control of Congress, are mindful of the growing political power of the country's Latino voters. They agreed with the president to cobble together a new "comprehensive immigration bill." The proposed "grand bargain" was devised by a small bipartisan group of Senate leaders with little public debate and discussion. The main provisions were a path to permanent residency or citizenship for approximately twelve million illegals already in the country, after they paid a fine and served a few years on probation; a merit-based point system based on skills and education that would eliminate many of the family unity provisions of the past in deciding whether to give people permanent residency; a temporary guest worker program that would allow people to come to the United States to work on short-term visas, which could be renewed only twice; and the deployment of a high-tech verification system to ensure that workers were in the country legally.

The main Democratic sponsor of the bill, Senator Ted Kennedy (D-MA), said the bill's purpose was to "uphold the humanity and dignity of those who come here seeking a better life." George Bush agreed and praised the proposed law for honoring "the great American tradition of the melting pot" as well as maintaining "the great American tradition of welcoming those who share our values and our love of freedom." But critics viewed it as a piece of legislation designed to appeal mainly to the business community by ensuring a legal, easy, and disposable supply of cheap immigrant labor for service, agricultural, and high-tech industries.

This hodgepodge "grand bargain" faced opposition from all sides. Many Hispanic and Asian Americans objected to what they saw as a racist merit-based point system, which abolished their right to unite with members of their families; labor rights groups opposed the guest worker program, which they expected to further undermine the already stagnant wages of nonimmigrant workers; and most importantly conservatives condemned the legalization program for illegals as an "amnesty bill." Conservative anti-immigrant forces stirred up a huge grassroots mobilization to oppose what they considered an "amnesty bill that rewards the criminals." After protracted maneuvering, a coalition of Republican and Democratic senators killed the bill before it even had the chance to reach the floor for a vote.

MASS MIGRATION AND NEOLIBERAL POLICIES

Immigration laws are typically used as legal tools for shaping the flow of immigrants allowed into a country. In the case of the United States, these laws have always been used to give shape to what Americans think their country should be as a nation. In the Cold War they kept out Nazis and communists and allowed those who had already immigrated to reunify their families on American soil. Judging by the failure of the last two attempts to fashion an immigration bill, Americans are now too divided to agree upon a national vision for citizenship and immigration. In this globalized world, especially in the aftermath of the Cold War, people criss-cross national borders in response to much larger social and economic factors beyond the control of national policies and independent of American wishes. Some employers want to increase the permissible quota of high-tech workers, while others want to facilitate access to cheap, disposable labor. Immigration policies are, to some degree, like King Canute ordering the tide to stop.

In the vacuum created by the collapse of communism as neoliberal ideology took hold, the world started marching to the drumbeat of an intensified market economy while singing the anthem of free trade. In the decade of Francis Fukuyama's *The End of History* and Thomas Friedman's *The Lexus and the Olive Tree*, the unimpeded flow of capital, goods, and services promised universal peace and economic well-being for generations to come, or so we were told. Advanced Western nations have used the International Monetary Fund, the World Trade Organization, the World Bank, and other "international institutions" to set economic norms for Third World nations, who are told to reduce their tariffs, import restrictions, and monetary controls once put in place to protect their sovereignty and promote competitive advantages. They are told to allow multinationals the right to take over banks, public utilities, and industries and to exploit natural resources without restrictions in order to promote all-around economic growth. In today's "global economy," capitalist market ideology has diffused around the globe more thoroughly than any time in the past, drawing more zones of the world and a growing portion of the population directly into capitalist social relations. The result is increasingly uneven development and ever-greater social disruption worldwide. Yet there is an incompleteness to globalization: even as tariffs have been lowered and trade and investment barriers lifted around the world, national borders remain closed to the movement of people.

Mexico offers a good example of this distorted process of globalization. During the NAFTA negotiations, for instance, Mexican president Carlos Salinas was so anxious to have the free trade bill passed that immigration was left unaddressed. On the other hand, the inclusion of a freedom-of-movement provision would have proved a "poison pill" that would have killed any chance of U.S. congressional approval of the trilateral treaty. Then, once the bill was signed into law, Mexico had to devalue its currency. This caused a huge loss of purchasing power for Mexicans. Mexico also had to end subsidies to farmers, while at the same time opening its agricultural markets and exposing them to foreign competition. Heavily subsidized U.S. corn flooded the Mexican market and decimated Mexican corn production. Even though jobs were created in the country's north as American companies in search of cheap labor moved their production to Mexico along the U.S. border, the economy of the southern rural areas was devastated. As a result, increasing numbers of Mexicans were forced to flee north into the United States for survival.

Ironically, then, the surge in Mexican immigration to the United States, including illegal immigration, has been caused by the United States' own neoliberal globalization policies. These policies have had the same effects elsewhere around the world. Thousands migrate each day, voting with their feet: they move across national borders to get jobs, legally if possible, seeking political asylum if they can, and illegally if they must. This movement of human bodies is so pervasive that migration is no longer limited to those from the poor nations of the South moving to the North; people are moving from east to west, from the relatively developed to the more developed nations. As of 2000, according to estimates by the International Migration Organization, there were 150 million international migrants. People that migrated little in the past, from places like Senegal, Nigeria, and the Mayan regions of the Americas, are now trekking in the hundreds of thousands to live and work overseas. Countries that have never before received large numbers of immigrants, such as Italy, Japan, South Korea, and Spain, are today the destinations for millions of migrant workers. No wonder some scholars have called this the "Age of Migration."

DEMAND FOR IMMIGRANT LABOR

However, all too often discussion focuses simply on the "supply side" of immigration. It is one thing for people to want to migrate to a country; if there are no jobs for them there, what is the point? In the end, the "demand side" is the decisive factor in enabling migration.

The driving force behind the current surge of globalization, and hence human migration, is the corporate drive to cut labor costs and maximize profit. In addition to moving production overseas, to wherever the labor is cheaper and less organized, businesses also subcontract work to smaller domestic production sites whose operations remain more flexible because they employ unregulated labor. The cited rationale for this restructuring is cost cutting, but its much more important objective is a readjustment in the balance of power between labor and business communities established since the New Deal. The destruction of the powerful labor movement that was able to make significant gains in collective bargaining, higher wages, health and retirement benefits, unemployment compensation, and other social welfare safety nets is the chief objective of this new business order in the United States. The best way to achieve it is by hiring the least organized and most vulnerable labor available—new immigrants or, even better, undocumented aliens who have no protection at all. Mexican, Central American, Caribbean, and Chinese illegal workers are among us to fulfill this demand.

Reports collected about the experiences of undocumented Chinese workers in New York provide an intimate view of the insecurities they suffer. On June 6, 1993, a Honduran-registered steamer named the *Golden Venture* rammed aground just outside New York Harbor. The ship carried 286 illegal immigrants, most of whom were rural farmers from Fujian Province in southern coastal China. This was the first time the problem of Chinese illegal immigrants came to public attention, though they had arrived in the United States and other advanced industrial countries as laborers soon after Deng Xiaoping's liberalization program in China in the late 1970s. What is unusual about this traffic is that the migrants arrived via sophisticated international smuggling networks charging exorbitant fees that had to be paid off through years of work after arrival.

The current price of a clandestine trip to New York from Wenzhou or Fuzhou, where most of the Chinese illegals are from, ranges from $33,000 to $50,000. Individuals who intend to make it have to raise $1,500 to pay a "snakehead" (human smuggler) in China. The rest is to be paid upon arrival in the United States, usually by the relatives already in the country. If the relatives make the payment, the new arrival pays them back, normally within three to five years at a 3 percent interest rate.

In the last twenty years, so many people have been coming that their relatives can no longer help because they are already burdened with debts of others who came earlier. In these cases, the new arrivals are forced to borrow from loan sharks or the snakeheads themselves, at a 30 percent interest rate. New immigrants, without the knowledge of English, can get only menial jobs, often earning less than $1,000 a month. That is just enough to pay the interest portion of the loan, not counting money needed for survival. But the debts must be paid, lest the snakeheads hire "enforcers" to beat the money out of the debtors. One favorite tactic for convincing the victim's relatives to come up with quick cash is to threaten them with the victim's imminent execution. In some cases, the snakeheads simply make the debtors their virtual slaves. During the day, the victims work at restaurants affiliated with organized crime. At night, after they are brought back to prisonlike dorms, they hand over all the money and are locked up until the next day. These immigrants, in virtual indentured servitude, are forced to accept practically any job just to keep up with their debt payments.

With the flood of desperate undocumented aliens willing to work, Chinese employers are in a position to depress labor conditions to the utmost. Chinatown wages, already low by American standards before the arrival of the Fuzhounese, have declined even further. Testifying in 1995 at a Senate hearing for antisweatshop legislation, Mrs. Tang, once a schoolteacher in Guangdong Province who had immigrated ten years ago to Brooklyn, recalled that in the early 1980s she had worked eight hours a day and earned $40 to $50 a day. Today, with competition from the Fuzhounese, she slaves twelve hours a day to make a paltry $30.

In her case, she has to work almost twice as long to make the same amount of money. It is common for workers to work seven days a week, twelve hours a day, at an average hourly wage of $3.75. Competition from the illegals is forcing documented Chinese workers to settle for less if they want to maintain steady employment. Thus the employers have effectively erased the distinctions between legal and illegal immigrant workers. They all line up outside the factory long before the doors open to be the first ones to begin work. At night, they refuse to quit even after ten, just to get a few more pieces done for a few more dollars. Some of the seamstresses on sewing machines are known not to drink anything during the day lest they interrupt their work, calculated by piece rate, by going to the bathroom. One Cantonese garment lady has testified to a congressional committee that Fuzhounese illegals work until two in the morning, sleep in the factory, and start again right after sunrise. If they are not able to complete a given order, they ask their children to come in to help.

The undocumented have given their employers the leverage to force workers to accept many obviously illegal labor practices. Home work, thought to have disappeared in America fifty years ago, is a common phenomenon in Chinatown, as is child labor. The most egregious practice at both unionized and nonunionized Chinese garment factories in New York is withholding workers' wages. Previously, the normal withholding period was three weeks; now anything under five weeks is considered good. Of course, there is never a guarantee; after the employment starts, the employer can claim cash flow problems or manufacturers' nonpayment to postpone his own wage payments. After a few weeks, the workers are faced with the difficult decision of whether to hope against hope and work for another week or quit and cut their losses.

After several years of working like machines, at the rate of eighty-four hours a week, some workers begin to develop physical ailments. Restaurant workers complain of pinched nerves, back and shoulder pains, swollen feet, stomach cramps, and insomnia. Kitchen help can be temporarily blinded by the sudden rush of steam to the eyes from pots or dishwashers. Some even develop battle fatigue syndrome and are unable to move at all.

Seamstresses complain of sore arms, headaches, dizzy spells, and heart palpitations. Bronchial asthma is common, caused by exposure to the chemicals used in treating fabrics. The worst problems develop from working with polyester, whose shredded fibers, if inhaled over a long period of time in the dry, unswept conditions of most workplaces, can cause nosebleeds and asthma. Problems like repetitive stress syndrome can be avoided by taking regular breaks and by working shorter hours. As for back and shoulder aches, a change in the construction of the chairs workers sit in could minimize their problems. Of course, none of this will ever happen.

The illegal Chinese workers have also been used for union busting. In 1994, the owners of the Silver Palace Restaurant—one of Chinatown's largest restaurants, which was unionized in 1980—locked out all their union workers, claiming that their wages were too high. The owners saw that it made no sense to pay union wages when there was such a large supply of cheap labor to be had. The locked-out union workers picketed the restaurant for more than seven months. "If the owners win this one," the leader of the picketing workers stressed, "employers all over Chinatown could impose any kind of conditions they want on the working people, no matter whether they are legal or undocumented. We are then nothing but slaves."

The issue is no longer just the treatment of illegals. In Chinatown, where employers use illegals to depress wages for all legal workers, they have transformed the problem into a class struggle between labor and management. Though most Americans see the Fuzhounese as an aberration—an isolated ethnic phenomenon at the fringes of society—in the past ten years undocumented Fuzhounese have deeply penetrated the garment, construction, and restaurant trades all over New York City. Non-Chinese-owned small electronics factories and vegetable farms in New Jersey, construction companies specializing in pricy loft renovation in the fashionable Manhattan neighborhood of SoHo, and Long Island farms alike use Chinese employment agencies to find Chinese labor contractors who will take care of the selection, transportation, payment, and management of their workers.

Moreover, Chinese illegal immigrants are not the only group paying high fees for their passage to enter this country. This contract labor phenomenon has spread to other immigrant groups as well. Mexicans are paying $5,000, Poles $8,000, and people from the Indian subcontinent up to $28,000 for their passage. Thai women were discovered in Elmonte, California, working and living in a locked and fenced-in factory because they could not repay their transportation fee. They were routinely abused and told that, if they escaped, their captors would "go to their homes in Thailand to burn their houses down."

INSECURITY AND EXPLOITATION

The presence of these immigrants in the workforce enables employers to cut wages for domestic workers. At the same time, immigrants are presented as the "model" for domestic American workers. Their work ethic and spirit of self-reliance—demanding no "handouts" and no benefits—are used as justification to cut retirement and health care benefits. No matter that these immigrants are forced to work long hours, receive less than minimum wage, and are given no benefits and job security. Some labor under nineteenth-century sweatshop conditions, where child labor and home work, long thought to have been banished from American labor practices for good, have reemerged as the new standard of the immigrant workplace.

In effect, the employers have created a subclass of workers without having to worry about the consequence. The legal "protection" for this pattern of behavior is in the "employer sanctions" provision of the Immigration Reform and Control Act of 1986. The act focuses on employers' "knowingly" hiring illegals as a violation of the immigration law, rather than on their exploitation of a cheap and docile illegal labor force as a violation of the U.S. labor law. It has shown to be totally ineffective in deterring employers because it is difficult to prove that an employer is "knowingly" hiring an illegal when there is no foolproof national identification system. But even if an employer is guilty no one finds out because the illegal he or she has hired will not report the violation. Before the 1986 act was passed, it was not illegal for an employer to hire an illegal; most instead followed the "don't ask, don't tell" policy. But since the passage of the Employer Sanction Act, employers must inquire about the legal status of their workers in order to protect themselves. After checking, if an employer still hires an illegal, he has leverage over him. He can now offer to pay less because the illegal is not likely to complain, lest he risk being fired or even reported to immigration authorities. Now the employer is in a position to get away with all types of labor violations. Moreover, the illegal is unwilling to change jobs and risk new problems with new employers.

What is worse is that the American government is forcing the undocumented to live under constant fear and extreme exploitation when there is no distinction between law enforcement and immigration enforcement. The principal federal agency responsible for enforcing the Employer Sanction Act is the Department of Labor. Employers must complete I-9 forms for each person hired, regardless of his or her citizenship status. The department's agents have the responsibility to investigate employees' work permits and legal status during workplace inspection in order to determine whether employers have violated the employer sanctions provision.

But in 1992, the Labor Department and the INS, to ensure "more efficient use of resources, reduce duplication of effort, and delineate respective responsibilities," signed a "Memorandum of Understanding" that commits the two agencies to share and exchange information in their respective investigations. Thus if during an inspection the Labor Department inspector finds irregularities in a company's I-9 forms, the agency is required to alert the immigration authorities. Such reporting often results in the deportation of the undocumented workers found in the inspected workplace.

Immigration officials generally refuse to acknowledge the labor-law implications of their actions, insisting on pursuing deportation proceedings against workers involved in labor disputes. So if an employer is found guilty of withholding back wages by the Labor Department or the National Labor Relations Board, the victimized employee, if an illegal, is not able to collect on the judgment—instead, he risks being deported. This arrangement also makes labor organizing very difficult.

Even though this kind of treatment of illegal laborers is part and parcel of the overall attack on American working people, few understand it that way, mainly because people see American workers as a category distinct from immigrant labor. American workers and their leaders have historically been wary of newcomers. Native workers, often working through labor unions, have built institutional shells around their jobs to exclude immigrant competitors. Even progressive labor leaders see immigrants, like racial minorities, as serious obstacles to organizing the working class because they see immigrants as lacking in class consciousness and willing to conspire with employers; they consider them unfit to be organized. The constant presence of immigrants has ensured the perpetuation of such xenophobic anti-immigrant sentiments, which have served only to further accentuate divisions within the working class. One might say that the business and corporate community has used immigrants to blackmail the entire working class.

Further, some small-scale employers hire illegals because they cannot get locals to take poorly compensated jobs and cannot pay more for labor because their profit margins are too narrow. Small family-owned farms, for example, are trying to remain competitive with cheaper fruit and vegetable imports from offshore locations that benefit from low labor costs in a U.S. economic environment that favors large-scale, highly capitalized agribusinesses with subsidies and tax breaks. Many families in the United States who depend on illegal child care workers do so because they struggle to find affordable child care in a country that devalues such work and refuses to provide government assistance for early childhood programs. In an increasingly insecure economy oriented toward supporting corporate profit, small farmers, small businesses, and working families depend on illegals to perform poorly compensated, undesirable jobs.

Many current union leaders now appreciate that the revival of their union membership depends on the inclusion of immigrant laborers, including illegals. Their efforts in this respect are complicated by the fear that pushing their employers too forcefully will lead to companies' relocation overseas. The need to join forces with illegals may thus be particularly important for jobs that cannot be relocated, in such sectors of the economy as construction, the hospitality industry, agriculture, and child care. Unfortunately, both unions and employers have identified the guest worker program as a way to meet the desires of both parties, not by giving immigrant workers more rights, but by creating a class of marginalized temporary workers.

THE PROBLEM WITH THE GUEST WORKER PROGRAM

The current proposal for a guest worker program originated with President Bush when he first took office and was partly urged on him by Mexican president Vincente Fox. The rationale behind it was to "match willing foreign workers with willing American employers." By issuing them temporary worker cards, the United States would "allow them to travel back and forth between their home and the United States without fear of being denied re-entry into our country." President Bush emphasized at the time that this was "not amnesty, placing undocumented workers on the automatic path of citizenship." The legal status granted by this program would last three years and be renewable, but it would have an end.[2] Even without provisions for a legalization process or any offer of amnesty to the millions who were already here, the proposal encountered significant opposition within the Republican Party. But the entire issue became moot as American national attention turned to the Middle East in the aftermath of the 9/11 attacks.

Bush and the Senate revived the guest worker proposal again during the 2006 and 2007 immigration reform debate. Their proposals would have legalized illegal immigrants but did not adequately address their rights as workers. Unfortunately, a number of union and immigrant advocacy groups supported this program, saying it would lead to a more "realistic" approach to the immigration issue. The problem with such calls for pragmatism and "realistic" solutions is that they concede the terms of the debate to the business sector, which is interested only in profit margins.

Guest worker policies have seduced politicians in many countries, but they are full of contradictions. Wherever these programs have been tried, they have never turned out to be temporary in practice because employers become addicted to the advantages of employing cheap labor while guest workers inevitably end up putting down roots—marrying, having children, joining churches—in short, becoming part of the fabric of local community. The policies act as a disincentive for investment in labor-saving technologies because they prop up declining industries with low productivity and low wages—as is the case with garment manufacturing in the United States at the moment. In the end, they harm productivity and the growth of the economy as a whole.[3] Above all, immigrant workers are never easily disposable. Germany, which imported "guest workers" from Italy, Yugoslavia, Turkey, and North Africa starting in the 1960s, was not able to get rid of them when the economy slowed down. Guest workers are not machines. They are people, with social ties, families, and children, and their extended "visits" have been the cause of persistent, ugly racial and ethnic strife. The second- and third-generation off-spring of Turkish guest workers, born and raised in Germany, have yet to gain legal status and social acceptance, but they have no desire to return to Turkey—a country where they did not grow up. Immigrant specialists Philip Martin and Michael Teitelbaum, who have studied guest worker programs in other nations, have come to a simple conclusion: there is nothing more permanent than temporary workers.

The United States had its own "guest worker" Bracero Program, instituted in 1942, to bring a stable supply of farm laborers into the country from Mexico to cover wartime shortages of agricultural workers. The program actually accelerated the flow of illegal immigrants across the border and contributed to the hostility of the white population toward Mexican immigrants, including those with proper documentation. This ugly xenophobia led the INS in the 1950s to deport three million undocumented and documented Mexican immigrants, as well as U.S. citizens of Mexican descent, through a campaign known as "Operation Wetback." It was a campaign of fear and gross violations of human rights, with INS agents declaring war on anyone who "looked Mexican"—stopping them in the street, asking them for identification, and interrogating them without due process. Longtime residents of the United States and their American-born children were often deported along with the illegals, leaving deep scars in the collective memory of Chicanos.

A major effect of the Bracero Program was a de facto apartheid labor system that separated special-status Mexican workers from American workers and allowed farmers and employers to violate labor laws—sometimes even to have workers deported before they got paid. The Labor Department official in charge of the program when it ended, Lee G. Williams, called it "legalized slavery." This is certainly not a historical experience that ought to be repeated.

An earlier guest worker program was tried with the Chinese after the Civil War, when American employers, threatened by the emergence of the labor movement, looked for alternative sources of cheap and docile labor. The result was the organized importation of contract laborers from China, first to build the railroads and then as the chief workforce to develop the American West, particularly its agriculture and mining. At the urging of the business community, the American government signed the Burlingame Treaty with the Chinese government in 1868 to encourage large-scale migration of Chinese to this country. At the same time, the treaty specified that the Chinese would not be granted the right of citizenship. It was America's first attempt to introduce a "guest worker program." The Chinese workers were welcomed to the United States but were not given the legal status that would allow them to enjoy equal rights and labor protection; nor were they given the right to remain in the country after their usefulness as cheap labor expired. They were imported by employers to undermine American labor standards and, most specifically, to demobilize the nascent American labor movement. White labor, unfortunately, did not view them as part of America's working class. Instead of including them in the organizing effort, it denounced them as "unfair competition" and "aliens" that should be excluded. The ensuing efforts to exclude and expel Chinese laborers who were already in the country sapped the energy and the moral authority of the American labor movement. This tragic history of Chinese exclusion, though more than a century old, left wounds that have yet to heal.

The exclusion of the Chinese showed that employers counted on American workers' racial hatred as a tool to subvert their class consciousness and vitality. Bush's new temporary work program replays this dangerous script. The civil rights of all Mexican Americans, Chinese Americans, and others could easily come under attack if just one segment among them—the alien "guest workers"—were to be subject to superexploitation and deportation.

LABOR RIGHTS AND PROTECTION CENTRAL TO IMMIGRANT DEMAND

The worst problem with the guest worker program is that employers are supporting it now as an easy way to legally exploit immigrants without having to take responsibility for treating immigrant workers as permanent employees. It is a plan to create a subclass of disposable people. But what is to guarantee that the employers will continue to hire the legal guest workers if they can get even better deals with the illegals, who will still be arriving? If the employers offer jobs, a new wave of illegal immigration will surely ensue. The compromise made by labor leaders and immigrant advocates may thus be self-defeating. By focusing only on the legal right to work without insisting that labor rights be guaranteed, it would neither improve the life of immigrant workers nor stop illegal immigration.

Still, instead of concentrating on immigrants' labor rights, liberals and immigrant advocacy organizations make amnesty—legal status for the undocumented—their primary objective. During the 2007 immigration debate, major proimmigrant groups like the National Council of La Raza and National Immigration Forum took the position that, while the proposed bill had many flaws, its central provision for the legalization of twelve million illegals was enough reason to support the compromised bill. According to executive director Frank Sharrey of the National Immigration Forum, the stakes for "immigrant workers" and their families were high. If this bill were to fail, they would have to wait many years for legalization. They wanted to support this "grand bargain" even though it would have eliminated the family unity provision in immigration law secured in the struggles of the 1960s, and even though the bill also provided for a subclass of guest workers.

These organizations were willing to sacrifice the interests of future immigrants for the benefit of those illegals already here. This is short-sighted. It is like the decision of a failing union to protect the benefits of those members with seniority by agreeing to sell out the interests of younger and future members of the labor force. The justification is the same: this is the best deal we can get. But this kind of compromise fragments the American labor force into legal, illegal, and guest worker categories for employers to divide and conquer.

All workers can work together, including illegal immigrants. They too do not want to be exploited. If labor laws existed and were enforced without regard to the legal status of workers, workers would gladly report abuses. If the focus was on labor laws and their enforcement, rather than on the deportation of undocumented immigrants, exploitation would be curbed and American labor standards would be maintained. The current Employers Sanction Act does not do that. The Labor Department acts only if an employer "knowingly" hires illegals. This is difficult to prove, and very few employers have been convicted under this offense since the existence of the law. Instead, the Employers Sanction Act has actually silenced exploited workers and may even encourage employers to commit more abuses.

One effective way to discourage employers from exploiting immigrants would in fact be to get rid of the Employers Sanction Act. Labor laws should be enforced independently of the victim's immigration status. The separation of immigration and labor enforcement would go a long way to improve the lot of all American workers. There are those who argue that if illegal immigrants were given equal labor rights, more illegal immigrants would come. They do not understand that if employers had to abide by American labor standards, they would no longer have the incentive to seek out employees with illegal status, whom they now exploit at will.

TIME OF GREAT OPPORTUNITY

American workers are experiencing a one-two punch from globalization: losing jobs because of both outsourcing and the influx of immigrants. They need to fight back against a neoliberal political establishment that favors large corporations at the expense of workers, small businesses, and small farms.

Internationally, people are already fighting back. Beginning in the 1980s, many countries liberalized their economies, which led to a polarization of wealth, violence, and political instability. Almost every country in Latin America, with the exception of Cuba, implemented neoliberal policies for decades. As governments ceded sovereignty to the multinationals, U.S. banks, and the International Monetary Fund, these policies, instead of generating more wealth for all, only brought more poverty and misery. The resulting mass protests and the weakening of military regimes eventually opened up new political space. In country after country, voters have been choosing to elect leftist candidates to lead them out of the neoliberal trap. Voters in three of the most economically developed countries—Argentina, Brazil, and Chile—have done so. Among the poorer nations, Peru is going the way of Venezuela and Bolivia, which have done so as well.

Here in the United States the same thing could happen. Popular resistance has emerged here against globalization from many quarters, including from among immigrants. In 2006, we saw that Latino American activists have built a powerful civil rights movement for immigrants. Its scale and impact, judging by their current organizing potential and the degree of political consciousness, could match the African American movement of the 1960s. If its leaders can expand the scope of the struggle beyond winning immigration status for illegals to encompass the key issues in the economic arena—their labor rights and their right to economic equality—they could achieve the one goal that escaped the African American movements of the mid-twentieth century. In the past immigrants were not expected to play a significant role in the transformation of American society. However, today's immigrants are the direct product of globalization. This situates them in a strategic position to challenge our neoliberal policies in shifting the nation's balance of power away from the tyranny of the multinational corporations.

NOTES

1. Spencer S. Hsu and Dana Hedgpeth, "Bush's 'Virtual Fence' Faces Trouble, Delays," *Washington Post*, September 26, 2007, A4. The pilot version of the fence was having problems distinguishing people from animals and operating in rainy weather.

2. White House Office of the Press Secretary, "President Bush Proposes New Temporary Worker Program: Remarks by the President on Immigration Policy," January 7, 2004, www.whitehouse.gov/news/releases/2004/01/20040107-3.html.

3. Philip Martin and Michael Teitelbaum, "The Mirage of Mexican Guest Workers," *Foreign Affairs* 6 (2001): 117.

PART FIVE

Insecurity and Terror

14

Compounding Insecurity

What the Neocon Core Reveals about America Today

Janine R. Wedel

Since 2002, much debate in America has focused on the decision to go to war in Iraq and the course of the occupation. The "neoconservatives"—working to pursue their goal of remaking the world in their image of America—have won mainstream media recognition as never before. Names such as Richard Perle, Paul Wolfowitz, and Douglas Feith—chief architects of the war—have easily rolled off the tongues of television commentators. And although there is considerable awareness of the influence of these figures in shaping the Bush administration's policies toward Iraq and the Middle East, how and why their views prevailed in taking the United States to war has not been satisfactorily explained. It is like knowing that a particular drug has a specific result but not knowing how and why it works and not having the tools to analyze the mechanisms that produce the result.

This chapter attempts to illuminate these mechanisms by charting a social network phenomenon I call "flex nets."[1] The appearance of this phenomenon signals transformations taking place in governing and society that bear crucially on the accountability of decision makers to the public in a democracy. This chapter is primarily concerned with the United States, although I note global changes that have given rise to flex nets in the wider world. In America, the reconfiguring of the balance between state and private interests, combined with a hollowing out of the regulatory and monitoring functions of the state, has created new opportunities for coordinated groups of players, or flex nets, to take over public policy agendas in pursuit of their own interests. Examining the modus operandi of such groups provides a lens through which to explore the environments in which they operate. This chapter highlights the workings of a particular flex net, drawn from the ranks of the neoconservatives who pushed for the U.S. invasion of Iraq, to show how it mirrors the changing American system while playing on its limits and thereby revealing emerging rules of the influence game.

Flex nets are among the most effective means of wielding influence. They draw for membership on a limited circle of players who interact with each other in multiple roles, both inside and outside government. They resurface in different incarnations and configurations to achieve their goals over time, be they ideological, political, or financial. The cutting-edge modus operandi of flex nets perplexes prevailing thinking about corruption and conflict of interest and confounds conventional means of holding players to account. Flex nets pool the positions of their members, many of whom assume overlapping and shifting roles in government, business, and nongovernmental organizations. Their members are adept at relaxing both governments' rules of accountability and businesses' codes of competition, thereby challenging the principles of both democracy and capitalism. Flex nets conflate state and private interests. Through their activities, their members embody the merging of state and private power and help the two to reinforce each other.

Flex nets are noted for their dexterity in positioning and repositioning themselves amid a changing environment. They fill a niche that evolved in the more networked ecosystem of the late twentieth and early twenty-first centuries. Several reorganizing forces converged to create the conditions under which flex nets would thrive, among them the diffusion of authority spurred by several decades of government outsourcing and deregulation as neoliberalism took hold and was widely promulgated; the end of the Cold War—that is, of relations dominated by two competing alliances; and the advent of ever more complex information technologies.

The first force, the neoliberal reorganization of government, occurred within countries, often under pressure from international financial institutions such as the International Monetary Fund (IMF) and the World Bank. Beginning in the early 1980s, the policies of governing administrations promoted outsourcing, privatization, deregulation, and free trade. As these prescriptions were being advanced around the world by the international financial institutions, the communist governments of Eastern Europe collapsed.

The end of the Cold War became the second driving force in the reconfiguring world. No longer did two great behemoths locked in decades-long conflict dictate the fates of Third World nations and regional conflicts. As the system of bipolar authority vanished, many boundaries broadly became less distinct, more permeable, and harder to regulate. Self-organizing networks and entities surged. New playing fields without rules and referees—or sham ones—offered profitable targets for corporations, consultants, activists, and nongovernmental organizations (NGOs), as well as organized crime and terrorist groups, which, of course, thrive on ambiguous borders.

A third restructuring force was spurred by the innovation of increasingly complex information technologies. Both the development and use of these technologies favor flat networks over hierarchy, flexible maneuvering over bureaucratic process. Such networks can respond quickly to unpredictable events, be they sociopolitical, technological, or climatic. (The Internet, for example, enables vast and indiscriminate contact.) Sprawling business activities, surging multinational movement of goods and services, and the development of world markets—characteristics of "globalization"—are intertwined with these restructuring forces. These forces—the neoliberal reorganization of government, the end of the Cold War, and ever more complex technologies—unleashed developments that advantage the use of networks to cut across bureaucracies and boundaries.

My exposure to the power of social networks—and their ability to reshape institutions—began some twenty-five years ago in a different context. As a social anthropologist in communist Eastern Europe in the 1980s, I witnessed firsthand how people organized themselves for survival and charted the networks that they used in and outside the formal bureaucracy and economy to get things done. An environment of scarcity and distrust of the state encouraged "dirty togetherness," a Polish sociologist's reference to cliquishness and close-knit networks of family, friends, and other trusted associates who help each other out through under-the-table transactions.[2] Being "dirtily" together implies mutual complicity in such dealings. As communism collapsed at decade's end, a dirtier togetherness took hold among the well-placed and savvy few who mobilized their social networks, now not merely to survive, but to thrive. In Poland, Russia, and Ukraine, I charted the workings of close-knit circles that morphed into "clans," "oligarchs," and "financial industrial groups" as they rose to fill leadership vacuums and to seize large chunks of state-owned wealth at fire-sale prices.

When I returned to the United States in the late 1990s, it too, had been changing, though much more gradually. My Eastern European experiential lens provided a fresh perspective. I noticed patterns in governing, policy making, and the overlapping networks of those engaged in the process in Washington that I had seen in the formerly communist countries, ostensibly on their way to something much better. My curiosity was piqued by a certain group that, in its mode of operating and considerable influence, bore striking similarity to the Eastern European circles that I had observed. I refer to the now-legendary neoconservative or "Neocon" core—a group of a dozen or so long-connected players whose strategizing and influencing helped thrust the United States into war in Iraq.

Recently, the most visible individuals in the group have been Paul Wolfowitz, deputy secretary of defense in the first term of George W. Bush and later head of the World Bank; I. Lewis "Scooter" Libby, the former chief of staff to Vice President Dick Cheney, who was indicted in October 2005 (on charges including obstruction of justice and perjury in the Valerie Plame CIA "outing" case); Richard Perle, Defense Policy Board chairman and member during part of George W. Bush's first term; and Douglas Feith, undersecretary of defense until August 2005.

For several decades, members of the Neocon core have pursued their foreign policy ideals, first primarily to bring down the Soviet Union and later to transform the Middle East—and the world—according to their own vision. The thinking of neoconservatives appears to have been significantly shaped by their experience of World War II and the age of American preeminence that followed. The heroic fight against fascism contributed to their sense that constant vigilance is necessary to avert the next Nazi-type threat and that it is America's right—even duty—to export organized violence in the service of U.S. interests. And the achievement of victory over fascism far from U.S. soil, without the trauma of war at home, contributed to their sense that America can triumph in war abroad without endangering security at home. The post–World War II experience of American dominance, buoyed by notions of progress and democracy, further honed the neoconservative view that America can, and should, refashion the world.[3]

Since the end of the Cold War in particular, the Neocon core has embarked on a concerted effort to reconfigure the Middle East and depose Saddam Hussein. In 1998 core members Paul Wolfowitz and Elliot Abrams, an operative in the arms-for-hostages Iran-Contra affair who has served the George W. Bush administration as deputy assistant to the president and deputy national security adviser for global democracy strategy, were among the signatories of a letter to President Clinton calling for the removal of Saddam Hussein. Donald Rumsfeld, secretary of defense under George W. Bush, also signed the letter.[4] While President Clinton sought regime change in Iraq, mostly through sanctions imposed by the United Nations, neoconservatives considered sanctions ineffective. It was after 9/11, in a George W. Bush presidency, that the group saw an opportunity to advance its vision for toppling Hussein. The core positioned its members to emerge as key American decision makers with broad influence in Middle Eastern affairs. Core members were so intimately involved in advocating, executing, and justifying the war from so many complementary and interconnected positions (as detailed below) that it is difficult to imagine the decision to invade Iraq or the administration's agenda vis-à-vis the region independently of the group.

In addition to its goals for Iraq, the Neocon core also has had designs on Iran and has been pressing for American intervention there. Its stated aim in Iran was—and is—"regime change." Again, neoconservatives favor military action, not sanctions, as the means of achieving this goal.

I wish to make clear at the outset that this is not a polemic against Neocon philosophy or an accusation of conspiracy. Like most members of social networks, members of the Neocon core are not necessarily conscious of their own patterns of activity. They see themselves as friends and associates who have worked together over the years to further their careers and promote their vision of America's role in the world. But at the moment they are the most prominent identifiable flex net in the United States, and understanding how such a group operates is critical to grasping the implications of new trends in government and their potential for weakening American democracy.

ROLES OF A NEOCON CORE PLAYER

To study the operations of these players and how they help drive policy formation and implementation, I have chosen two primary foci: (1) the players' roles, activities, and sponsors; and (2) their social networks, organizations, and modus operandi. In the service of group goals, members shift roles and sponsors, form networks that tie them to each other and to myriad organizations, and empower ambiguous might-be-state, might-be-private entities.

Members of the Neocon core excel at a game I call "representational juggling." Take, for example, Richard Perle, a well-known figure who some of America's top investigative reporters and inspectors general of government agencies have tried to prove is corrupt, yet who eludes prosecution precisely because he is a master of these skills. A former assistant secretary of defense under President Ronald Reagan, Perle surfaces at the center of a head-spinning array of business, consulting, quasi-governmental, and advocacy roles and ideological initiatives, consistently courting and yet skirting charges of conflict of interest. He played a significant role in taking the United States to war in Iraq, through, for instance, his efforts to organize the gathering and dissemination of "information"—both inside and outside government—demonstrating that Iraq had weapons of mass destruction, and his sponsorship and promotion of Ahmed Chalabi, the Iraqi-born businessman, exile, and founder of the Iraqi National Congress bent on the overthrow of Saddam Hussein. (Perle introduced Chalabi to the Neocon core, and Chalabi served as a key broker and representative for the core in the Middle East.) Perle also worked for U.S. military intervention in Iran—all while being involved in defense-related business and consulting ventures and earning lots of money. In one 2004 deal alone, Perle pocketed $2.5 million for his role in a merger.[5]

Perle avoided congressional confirmation hearings by eschewing a full-fledged position in the first term of George W. Bush. He instead accepted chairmanship of the Defense Policy Board, a Pentagon advisory body with a mixed state-private character that provides its members access to classified information and secret intelligence reports. During the run-up to the Iraq war, Perle used the board as a policy platform from which to call for the overthrow of Saddam Hussein—a cause for which he had long been working. At the same time, Perle also represented a company, the telecommunications firm Global Crossing Ltd., in its dealings with the U.S. government (as he does not deny) and for which he was investigated by the Pentagon.[6] According to the *Los Angeles Times*, he allegedly also offered defense-related clients sensitive information that he had through his position on the board.[7] And he angled for investment funds from a Saudi national who was endeavoring to influence U.S. policy toward Iraq, according to the investigative reporter Seymour Hersh.[8]

In these examples, one role (chairman of the board) enhanced Perle's usefulness in other roles (advocate, consultant) and hence Perle's financial and influence opportunities. Perle is larger than any of his roles—an institution unto himself—and has no necessarily fixed address. Although his influence may be aided by a particular role, it is not defined by or confined to any one of them. The Pentagon investigated some of his consultancy activities, but Perle wriggled his way out of trouble. His model—the government advisor, business consultant, and policy advocate all wrapped up in one contemporaneous figure—is a relatively recent appearance. It was not common in the day when fewer nongovernmental and hybrid bodies were involved in governing, when they generally held less sway, and when it was clearer where organizations began and ended.

The new breed of players can lead with one role and leave others in the shadows, publicize one role and marginalize another. For instance, Perle promoted a tanker deal in a coauthored *Wall Street Journal* op-ed piece from which he stood to profit, billing himself simply as a resident fellow at the American Enterprise Institute (AEI).[9] An uninformed reader would not know that Perle had any financial interest in the deal or that he was both lobbying and advising the government as a (supposedly) impartial expert. Presenting his activities under the guise of his role as a resident fellow at the AEI gave Perle the appearance of a disinterested public intellectual and neutral observer, at least to an uninformed audience. In this case, Perle cloaked his interests, which were ostensibly motivated by one role (lobbying for a policy that would make him money) under the persona of another (pundit and fellow at AEI).

Perle's repertoire of roles—which can be kept separate, merged, combined, and interplayed to reinforce each other—yields him not only flexibility but deniability. The ability to attribute activities under one role (Perle, promoting the tanker deal to further his business interests) to those under another (disinterested analyst) enables a player to plausibly deny responsibility.

Operating above and beyond institutions as well as within them, actors like Perle skirt, obfuscate, and play on the boundaries of state and private. This is not to say that they erase the boundaries altogether. In fact, the players often need the distinction: they use the spheres of state and private selectively for what each can enable and mitigate the constraints of one sphere by switching to another. While tapping into the state sphere for specific resources, privileges, and the trappings of state authority, they cannot operate effectively if they are fully accountable to it. They thus also operate in the private sphere, which additionally avails them of profits and opportunities that the state cannot realize, even when the state is the sole source (for instance, of classified information or government contracts).

In the process of crossing and even collapsing the boundaries of state and private (as well as legal and illegal, national and global, top-down and bottom-up, macro and micro, and so on), these players obfuscate the old clear-cut frameworks that have dominated public thinking. The ambiguity that swirls around them is not just a by-product of their activities; their influence is enhanced by it. Their ability to skirt accountability in one rubric by claiming that they were operating within another—and to benefit from the dust cloud of ambiguity and deniability that trails them—confounds traditional means of accountability.

The new breed of players is highly skilled. They dazzle both governments and electorates because they serve a need; they connect a confusing, fragmented world. But there is a downside to a world run by such players. They are increasingly removed from the input of voters and the oversight of governments.

While not inherently unethical, these players are often inherently unaccountable—subject to no greater oversight than their own consciences. But the reorganizing world has yet to recognize the phenomenon of such players, let alone come up with a comprehensive system to monitor their activities.

A SNAPSHOT OF NEOCON CORE NETWORKS

Although Richard Perle is often in the news as an individual, he could not be where he is if not for the flex net to which he belongs—a close-knit dozen or so neoconservatives. Members of the Neocon core have been interlinked for as long as three decades through government, think tank, business, and advocacy roles, as well as family ties. Although membership in the group is dynamic and all members are not equally important at all times, its members have included Richard Perle, Paul Wolfowitz, Douglas Feith, I. Lewis "Scooter" Libby, Elliot Abrams, Michael Ledeen, Frank Gaffney, James Woolsey, and David Wurmser. Flex nets are not strictly bounded. A number of associates who have facilitated the group's agenda at times, in conjunction with group members, also can be identified. In recent years these have included such luminaries as William Kristol and Reuel Marc Gerecht, who have been public spokespeople for the neoconservatives' agenda for Iraq.

Members of the Neocon core have long interacted with each other in multiple roles both inside and outside government to achieve their agenda—notably a long-established strategy for American foreign policy. The group has a history of some thirty years in which they have bypassed standard government procedures, regulations, and bodies dating from before the arms-for-hostages Iran-Contra affair. In that period this core has demonstrated its distrust of American intelligence agency findings; its capacity to bend, if not break, regulations set by government; and its reliance on personal relationships with trusted (by them) brokers of questionable loyalties who manage vital aspects of relationships between nations.

A running example of the relationships among Richard Perle, Paul Wolfowitz, and Douglas Feith over several decades illustrates many of the features of flexians and flex nets and betokens their success. Armed with a conviction that the mission is a higher good than the government's rules (in this case those pertaining to intelligence and classified materials), they operate through personalized relations to accomplish the mission, breaking official rules to do so. Not only do they help each other secure public positions central to their private missions, but they bail each other out when caught, a practice that embodies the intertwined, self-protecting, and self-propelling nature of the network and the players' commitment to each other and their cause.

What at first glance might look like serendipitous opportunities in career development, shared interests, and friends aiding one another soon evolved into dynamic pursuit of joint goals. It is not just a matter of loyal friends helping their friends get good jobs; here the shared mission supersedes other concerns. In 1973, as a senior staff member of the Senate Armed Services Committee, Perle helped Wolfowitz, then an assistant professor at Yale, find employment in the Arms Control and Disarmament Agency (ACDA). Five years later, Wolfowitz was investigated for passing a classified document to an Israeli government official through a go-between, according to Stephen Green, a retired journalist who has written for two decades about Israeli espionage in the United States and has been interviewed by the FBI in recent years about long-ago activities of these and other members of the Neocon core.[10] (An inquiry was launched and dropped, and Wolfowitz continued to work at the ACDA until 1980.)

Also in 1978, while working as an aide to Senator Henry "Scoop" Jackson on the Senate Armed Services Committee, Perle was caught in a security breach by CIA director Stansfield Turner, who urged that Jackson fire him. Perle received a reprimand but was kept on staff, according to a report in the *Washington Post* by Sidney Blumenthal.[11] In another instance, according to investigative reporter Seymour Hersh, Perle was questioned by the FBI after a wiretap picked him up talking with an Israeli Embassy official about classified information (which he said he had obtained from a National Security Council [NSC] staff member).[12]

In 1982, Perle, as an assistant secretary for international security policy in President Reagan's Defense Department, hired and later promoted Feith after he had been fired from his post as a Middle East analyst at the NSC. Feith had been fired, Green found, because he was the subject of an FBI inquiry into whether he had supplied classified material to an Israeli official.[13]

After leaving the Pentagon in 1987, Perle became a highly paid consultant for a lobbying firm, International Advisers, Inc., that Feith established in 1989. By serving as a consultant only, Perle—who had supervised U.S. military assistance to Turkey while at the Department of Defense—was able to bypass federal regulations prohibiting anyone from representing a foreign government right after leaving American government employment.[14]

The mutual assistance among these three men has continued into the new millennium. In 2001, Perle and Wolfowitz championed Feith for the position of undersecretary for policy in the Pentagon. In that post, Feith in turn selected Perle as chairman of the Defense Policy Board. (Perle resigned as chairman in March 2003 amid allegations of conflict of interest and from the board altogether a year later.)

For a quarter-century, in fact, members of the Neocon core have been under frequent investigation for alleged misuse of classified information. Stephen Green, who has been interviewed multiple times on the issue by the FBI, told me: "I was asked extraordinarily detailed questions about Paul Wolfowitz, Richard Perle, Douglas Feith, Michael Ledeen," and other members of the core group.[15] Ledeen is a Neocon core member long associated with those three.

These players—and others of the core—would repeat this pattern in many venues. Their practices would echo—and reverberate—into the new millennium. Distrust and disrespect for government intelligence findings and expertise, creation of "intelligence" to compete with or supplant that of government, and disregard for the usage rules of classified documents of the intelligence community would be perennial themes of the Neocon core. The core's propensity to work concertedly to achieve their goals over time—even to the point of skirting regulations that might keep them from doing so while still appearing to uphold the letter of the law—lies at the heart of their effectiveness in virtually privatizing foreign policy in key instances.

Perle, Wolfowitz, and Feith are an excellent example of the behavior of a flex net and how its members' mutual assistance multiplies the group's effectiveness. What may have been at first serendipitous opportunities in career development, shared interests, and friends helping one another evolved into dynamic pursuit of joint goals. Each one of these players owes much of his mark to the group—even the peripatetic Perle, who stands out for the sheer number of balls he manages to keep in the air.

As evidenced by the mutual aid round-robin in these examples, none of these players could have continued to secure such important positions and wielded such influence merely as individuals on their own. Moreover, Perle, Wolfowitz, and Feith are but a microcosm of the larger Neocon group of roughly a dozen or so players, all of whom are intertwined with other members many times over, just like these three. The division of labor and pooling of resources that characterize a flex net are crucial to its effectiveness. Empowered by longtime trust and shared goals, a flex net serves at once as a protective nest and a springboard from which to launch initiatives.

MODUS OPERANDI OF THE NEOCON CORE

For these horizontal relations to have significance, they would have to influence policy while undermining democratic processes. Over the past decade and a half in particular, the Neocon core has embarked on that course in part by creating and empowering alternative structures, both within and outside government, to realize its policy aims. The core's success in achieving those aims is tied to its ability to do what flex nets do—to reconfigure existing structures and create alternative authorities. In the 1990s the Neocon core worked largely through lobbying organizations that it set up and empowered. Post-9/11 insecurity and a presidency favorably disposed toward parts of the neoconservatives' agenda enabled the core to activate, in practical terms, its longtime goal of toppling Saddam Hussein. The core set out to meld relevant government units and processes to its purposes and also exerted influence through quasi-government entities and might-be-official, might-not-be-official dealings.

Setting Up Organizations

To further its agenda in the Middle East, members of the Neocon core founded a host of ideological and think-tank-styled organizations, primarily in the 1990s, which, as one observer put it, "act as a vast echo chamber for each other and for the media." Members of the group were prime movers in a series of organizations of influence, including the Jewish Institute for National Security Affairs, the Project for the New American Century, the Committee for the Liberation of Iraq, the U.S. Committee for a Free Lebanon, and the AEI and created all but one of these (the long-established AEI). In addition to their many other roles vis-à-vis each other in and around government and business, as well as social life, members of the core connect with each other through leadership in these entities. They support the core's activities in, among others, drafting policy directives, raising money, and lobbying presidents, members of Congress, and other policy makers.

Reorganizing Government for Policy Results

Encouraged by a malleable political environment after 9/11, Neocon core members set out to overthrow Saddam Hussein. They exerted influence, at least in part, by bypassing or altering standard government units and workings, such as intelligence-gathering and decision processes, and supplanting them with their own. They marginalized officials who were not part of their group and operated through cross-agency cliques that enabled them to limit information and activities to their associates.[16]

The key centers of decision making with regard to national security and Iraq were the Pentagon and the office of Vice President Dick Cheney, according to numerous accounts by previously well-placed officials. For instance, Lawrence B. Wilkerson, who served as chief of staff to Secretary of State Colin Powell from 2002 to 2005, speaks of a covert "cabal" led by Vice President Cheney and Secretary of Defense Donald Rumsfeld. Wilkerson characterizes its "insular and secret workings" as "efficient and swift—not unlike the decision-making one would associate more with a dictatorship than a democracy."[17]

Neocon core members played pivotal roles in both the vice president's office and the Pentagon. In the latter, Paul Wolfowitz, deputy secretary of defense, and Douglas

Feith, undersecretary of defense for policy, influenced and justified the decision to go to war, aided by alternative structures that they set up and controlled. They established their own duplicative governmental entities that sometimes served to bypass or override the input of otherwise relevant entities and processes. Two secretive units in the Pentagon that dealt with policy and intelligence after 9/11—the Counterterrorism Evaluation Group and the Office of Special Plans—were created under Feith. The units were staffed in part by people whom Richard Perle helped to recruit from Neocon-associated organizations, especially the AEI. One alternative hub of decision making in the Pentagon set up and run by the Neocon core was characterized by the vice chairman of the Senate Select Committee on Intelligence as an illegal "private intelligence" operation.[18]

As in the Pentagon, in the vice president's office Neocon core members exerted great influence. "Scooter" Libby, who had worked with Paul Wolfowitz in the Reagan administration, was a principal player. He served simultaneously as Vice President Cheney's chief of staff and his national security adviser,[19] and he ran an informal national security operation. Wilkerson observed the process from his perch as Powell's chief of staff. He reports that Cheney's office operated an "alternate national security staff" that undercut the actual NSC.[20] Wilkerson contends that "many of the most crucial decisions from 2001 to 2005 were not made within the traditional NSC process."[21] A substantial role of a vice president's office in national security policy, let alone such a huge one as that of Cheney's shop, is regarded by a number of scholars as unprecedented in U.S. history.[22]

When Scooter Libby resigned after being indicted in October 2005, David Addington, a loyal Cheney ally, replaced him as Cheney's chief of staff. In his previous position as Cheney's counsel, Addington had drafted opinions supporting the use of what human rights professionals considered torture techniques on terrorism suspects and helped create the military tribunals at Guantánamo Bay.[23]

Working through Might-Be-Official, Might-Not-Be-Official, Structures and Activities

Paradoxical to conventional theories of representative government, the effectiveness of a flex net's efforts, even when some of its members are in an administration that is "in power," depends partly on having key members outside formal government. A major reason for this is that being on the outside enables members to work through might-be-official, might-not-be-official structures and to engage in ambiguous activities, as illustrated by Richard Perle's overlapping roles, described earlier.

The Neocon core member Michael Ledeen provides another example of this ambiguous status. He served as a consultant to Feith's Office of Special Plans in the Pentagon, according to Stephen Green, while holding the "Freedom Chair" at the AEI (with which many members of the Neocon core are or have been affiliated) and has engaged in might-be-state, might-be private policy initiatives vis-à-vis

Iran.[24] (Although Ledeen was, for a time, barred from working in government as a result of his criminal offenses arising from his involvement in the Iran-Contra affair, he is among the Neocon core members who were brought back in the administration of George W. Bush.) Ledeen brokered and participated in secret meetings with Manucher Ghorbanifar, the discredited expatriate Iranian who had served as an intermediary between the government of Iran and the United States and Israel during Iran-Contra. These meetings, which took place in Rome in 2001 and Paris in 2003, were found by the Senate Intelligence Committee to have been authorized by Deputy Defense Secretary Wolfowitz, among others.[25] Also participating in the meetings was Lawrence A. Franklin, the Pentagon employee who worked in the office of Undersecretary of Defense for Policy Feith and has been convicted of passing classified documents about Iran to Israel via the American Israel Public Action Committee, the pro-Israeli lobbying group.[26] Ledeen continues his long-standing and steadfast agitation for U.S. intervention to effect regime change in Iran.[27] Being outside full-fledged government roles has afforded Ledeen and Perle more flexibility than they could have as government officials—and hence deniability and more potential influence.

Merging State and Private Power

The Neocon core exemplifies the melding of state and private power integral to the modus operandi of a flex net. This melding of powers can be seen not only in individual players, such as Richard Perle, but in the might-be-state, might-be private dealings of the core; the coordinated positioning of its members variously in government, quasi-government, and nongovernmental organizations; the involvement of Neocon private citizens in secretive government units run by Neocon officials; and the network-based decision-making apparatus of the group.

A SHAPE-SHIFTING SYSTEM

What does the modus operandi of flex nets reveal about the systems in which they operate? On a world scale, several restructuring forces—the neoliberal reorganization of government, the end of the Cold War, and the innovation of ever more complex information technologies—converged to create conditions favorable to flex nets, as noted earlier. Because this chapter focuses on the operations of a flex net in the United States, I concentrate on how these forces have played out within the U.S. government.

The impact of the first two reorganizing forces is unmistakable in Eastern Europe and the former Soviet Union. When the command structure of a centrally planned state that has owned virtually all the property, companies, and wealth breaks down and no authoritarian stand-in is put in its place, a network-based mode of governing and business develops to loosely replace it. Further, after 1989 and 1991, the states of Central and Eastern Europe and the former Soviet Union began, respectively, privatizing their national resources—with the help especially of U.S. and UK models, sponsors, and consultants. The introduction of the new policies, combined with the unraveling of state control, presented ideal conditions for long-standing informal groups, schooled in circumventing the overbearing communist state through "dirty togetherness," to move in and both substitute for and transfigure official structures. Flex nets and other groups that position their members at the state-private nexus were at the forefront of this activity.

Governing by network is obviously much more intense in states moving away from communism than in stable democracies such as the United States. But another version of "privatization" appears to have tipped the balance toward the private sector in America. Of the three restructuring forces specified here, the effects of the first one—the neoliberal reorganization of government—are the most palpable.

The contracting out of government services and functions, which has a sixty-year history, gained momentum with the neoliberal push a quarter of a century ago (exemplified in Ronald Reagan's "small government" and Margaret Thatcher's "deregulation"). Increasing bipartisan support for the accelerated outsourcing of government services today combines with a proliferation of entities involved in governing, diminution of monitoring and regulation, and movement of policy making legitimacy to the private sector.

Several facts illustrate the trend. By the time the United States launched its current campaign in Iraq (the most privatized war in U.S. history), two-thirds of those doing work for the federal government in any capacity were *not* on its payroll but instead received their paychecks from consulting firms or other companies.[28]

Not only are services subject to appropriation; so are government functions, information, and legitimacy. The role of contractors may be especially visible in military, nation-building, and homeland security activities. But their involvement is by no means limited to these areas. Contractors are developing government budgets and policies; coaching executives of government agencies; interrogating prisoners; managing the space program; and managing other contractors. For example, contractors

- *Perform most information technology (IT) work:* According to the market research firm INPUT in Chantilly, Virginia, contractors were doing upwards of three-quarters of the federal government's information technology work even before the current drive to contract out.[29] IT is, of course, a crucial component of contemporary military operations.
- *Control crucial databases:* In the largest contract awarded to date by the Department of Homeland Security, Accenture LLP was granted up to $10 billion to supervise and enlarge a mammoth U.S. government project to track citizens of foreign countries as they enter and exit the United States. As the

undersecretary for border and transportation security at the Department of Homeland Security, Asa Hutchinson, told the *Washington Post*, "I don't think you could overstate the impact of this responsibility, in terms of the security of our nation."[30]

- *Carry out military and occupying operations:* To a greater extent than ever before in America since the Revolutionary War, private military contractors are doing government work, as evidenced by U.S. operations in Iraq and Afghanistan. As of January 12, 2006, at least 302 private contractors had been killed in Iraq, of whom at least 117 were Americans.[31] Yet these "private" hires are not counted in U.S. casualty figures.

- *Draft official documents:* Web sites of contractors working for the Defense Department have been known to post announcements of job openings for analysts for functions such as preparing the Defense budget. One contractor boasted of having written the army field manuals on contractors on the battlefield.[32]

- *Choose other contractors:* The Pentagon has employed contractors to advise it on employing other service providers.[33]

While private companies are acquiring government functions, government oversight over them is diminishing. The number of government contracts and contractors is rising (driven in part by the increase in demand for military, nation-building, and homeland security services after 9/11), but the number of civil servants available to oversee them is falling,[34] thus decreasing the government's capacity to monitor the process. In 2002 Comptroller General David M. Walker remarked that he was "not confident that agencies have the ability to effectively manage cost, quality and performance in contracts."[35] The list of "high-risk" activities includes large procurement operations such as those of the Departments of Defense and Energy and NASA.[36]

Just who is "minding the store" is not clear. For example, in April 2002, *before* the U.S. invasion of Iraq, the army reported to Congress that its best guess was that it directly or indirectly employed between 124,000 and 605,000 service contract workers—a discrepancy of half a million workers.[37]

And just as government information and authority have been fragmented through the contracting out of its functions, institutions such as the Foreign Service and other well-established modes of representation have weakened, while the use of special envoys and quasi-official consultative bodies has proliferated. State-private bodies and boards such as Vice President Dick Cheney's Energy Task Force and former First Lady Hillary Rodham Clinton's Health Task Force have proliferated. According to the Congressional Research Service, "quasi government" organizations—"federally related entities that possess legal characteristics of both the governmental and private sectors"—"have grown in number, size, and importance in recent decades."[38]

The ambiguous not-quite-state, not-quite-private organizations that are appearing under American auspices are reminiscent of the unaccountable parts of governments that I observed in transitional Eastern Europe. For instance, after toppling Saddam Hussein, the United States established a transitional government in Iraq—the Coalition Provisional Authority (CPA)—that, until its dissolution in June 2004, vested itself with supreme executive, legislative, and judicial authority over Iraq. The CPA was created and funded as a division of the U.S. Department of Defense. Its U.S.-appointed head, L. Paul Bremer, a temporary viceroy, reported directly to the U.S. defense secretary. Yet the U.S. Justice Department ruled in 2004, in response to a case brought by former employees of a U.S. contractor in Iraq, that the CPA was beyond the purview of U.S. authority. In response to the same charges, a federal judge likewise ruled, in the words of the *Washington Post,* "that it was improper to bring the charges up in U.S. court because the [Coalition Provisional] authority was not a U.S. entity."[39] These rulings render the CPA very similar to the indistinct state-private bodies of transitional Eastern Europe.

As I learned there, state-private entities with ambiguous status can serve as vehicles through which private interests direct state resources and functions. Such entities can enlarge the unaccountable use of state power and resources and even spawn other taxpayer-supported entities. As such bodies proliferate (sometimes under the guise of "privatization"), an unaccountable state sphere expands.[40]

In the United States as well, it is misleading to think that the growth of a "shadow government" shrinks government.[41] Rather, as spending increases for private contracts and state-private entities, government risks becoming less accountable while creating more opportunities for players to pursue their private interests. Flex nets are primed to take advantage of such a fragmented system: a resilient network that can cut through bureaucracy, connect entities doing government work, and streamline decision making can seem an attractive antidote to sluggish governing.

Flex nets also thrive amid intensified executive power. They are poised to work closely with executive authorities, and they try to avoid legislative and judicial branches of government that may interfere with their activities. The trend in the United States toward executive power provides yet another favorable condition for flex nets.

BEYOND ACCOUNTABILITY

While post-9/11 insecurity enabled the Neocon core to achieve its goal of toppling Saddam Hussein, the modus operandi of such a group and what it portends for the system in which it operates can only increase the sense of insecurity that besets Americans today. That is because the workings of the group and the system it reveals take the country into uncharted territory.

Flex nets represent a different animal from the "kitchen cabinets" and the revolving-door syndrome that have defined political influence in the past. These phenomena have by no means disappeared and may even have become more prevalent. For example, the ranks of those who circulate through the revolving door have probably swelled because of accelerated outsourcing of government, accompanied by lack of oversight. But there is great potential for them to be joined by flex nets whose members may employ the revolving door when it suits themselves and their group but also go beyond it.

Although flex nets call to mind the notions of conflict of interest and corruption, they are a living example of why those labels no longer suffice. These familiar terms are too rigid and static to convey the complex interactions of the members of flex nets. The conventional definition of corruption—the abuse of public office for private gain—depends on the existence of a clear state (or public)-private divide and fixed roles. It cannot account for the peripatetic members of flex nets, all the while working in concert with their group. It is out of sync with the ways in which these players exert their influence while eluding checks and balances. Such players are not inherently unethical or corrupt, but their modus operandi renders them inherently unaccountable to the public. As a Washington observer sympathetic to the neoconservatives' aims told me, "There is no conflict of interest, because they define the interest."

The current system of accountability is ill equipped to monitor flex nets, let alone hold them to account. A key problem is that auditing practices tend to break things down into parts. But the potential influence and "corruption" of members of flex nets are based on a network that crosses defined organizational boundaries. To audit flex nets effectively, it is crucial to consider all the components collectively and how they interact. Only then can one begin to identify the multiple masters that their members may serve, the agendas that might motivate their actions, and the influence they are capable of wielding.

By controlling policy agendas through their not-quite-state, not-quite-private activities, while making new rules in pursuit of their own interests, the Neocon core has demonstrated the potential of flex nets to concentrate and perhaps even expand unaccountable state power—and with it, insecurity in America. The group has demonstrated the potential of flex nets to short-circuit the rules of accountability and to undermine democratic institutions. In short, it has demonstrated the potential of flex nets to undercut the national interest.

NOTES

1. I used the term *flex groups* for the same concept in a *Washington Post* article ("Flex Power: A Capital Way to Gain Clout, Inside and Out," December 12, 2004, B04; the electronic version, at www.washingtonpost.com, is titled "Flex Power: An Influential Band of Policy Brothers"). For a detailed analysis of these groups and the conditions that gave rise to them, see Janine R. Wedel, *Shadow Elite:*

How the World's New Power Brokers Undermine Democracy, Government, and the Free Market (New York: Basic Books, 2009).

2. Adam Podgorecki, "Polish Society: A Sociological Analysis," *Praxis International* 7 (April 1987): 57–78.

3. For the history of the neoconservative movement and thought, see Alan M. Wald, *The New York Intellectuals: The Rise and Decline of the Anti-Stalinist Left From the 1930s to the 1980s* (Chapel Hill: University of North Carolina Press, 1987); Gary Dorrien, *The Neoconservative Mind: Politics, Culture and the War of Ideology* (Philadelphia: Temple University Press, 1993); Sidney Blumenthal, *The Rise of the Counter-establishment: From Conservative Ideology to Political Power* (New York: Times Books, 1986), esp. 122–65; Alan Weisman, *Prince of Darkness: Richard Perle* (New York: Union Square Press, 2007), esp. 11–44; and James Mann, *Rise of the Vulcans: The History of Bush's War Cabinet* (New York: Viking, 2004), esp. 21–36 and 90–94.

4. Project for the New American Century, "Letter to the Honorable William J. Clinton," January 26, 1998, www.newamericancentury.org/iraqclintonletter.htm.

5. Jerry Knight, "Merger Delivers Princely Profit for Digital Net Insiders," *Washington Post*, October 18, 2004, E01.

6. See, for example, Stephen Labaton, "Pentagon Adviser Is Also Advising Global Crossing," *New York Times*, March 21, 2003; and Ken Silverstein and Chuck Neubauer, "Consulting and Policy Overlap," *Los Angeles Times*, May 7, 2003, 1.

7. In one instance, following a Defense Policy Board briefing on post-Saddam Iraq, Perle advised clients of Goldman Sachs on investment activities in postwar Iraq (Silverstein and Neubauer, "Consulting and Policy Overlap," 1).

8. Seymour M. Hersh, "Lunch with the Chairman," *New Yorker*, March 17, 2003.

9. Thomas Donnelly and Richard Perle, "Gas Stations in the Sky," *Wall Street Journal*, August 14, 2003. The article did not mention that the deal would have been worth $20 billion to Boeing and would have cost the Pentagon millions more than buying the tankers outright. Additionally, Perle did not disclose his own financial ties to Boeing, notably the company's $20 million share in Trireme Partners, an investment capital firm where Perle is a principal (David Hilzenrath, "Perle Article Didn't Disclose Boeing Tie," *Washington Post*, December 5, 2003, E01). Boeing is the largest investor in Trireme. William D. Hartung, "The Booming Defense Business," *Los Angeles Times*, December 10, 2003, www.commondreams.org/view03/1210-03.htm, B15.

10. Stephen Green, interview, August 30, 2004.

11. Sidney Blumenthal, "Richard Perle, Disarmed but Undeterred," *Washington Post*, November 23, 1987, B1.

12. Seymour Hersh, "Kissinger and Nixon in the White House," *Atlantic Monthly*, May 1982, www.theatlantic.com/issues/82may/hershwh2.htm.

13. Stephen Green, interview, August 30, 2004.

14. See, for example, Jack Shafer, "Richard Perle Libel Watch, Week 4: He's Just Too Busy Resigning to Sue This Week!" *Slate*, April 2, 2003, http://slate.msn.com/id/2081053/.

15. Stephen Green, interview, August 30, 2004.

16. Jim Lobe, "Ex-Pentagon Aide Hits 'Deceit' and 'Subversion' on Iraq Analysis," IPS, August 5, 2003, http://ins.onlinedemocracy.ca/index.php?name=News&file=article&sid=1219.

17. Lawrence B. Wilkerson, "The Whitehouse Cabal," *Los Angeles Times*, October 25, 2005, B11.

18. According to a report by the Senate Select Committee on Intelligence, "When the analytical judgments of the intelligence community did not conform to the more conclusive and dire administration views of Iraqi links to al-Qaeda . . . policymakers within the Pentagon denigrated the intelligence community's analysis and sought to trump it by circumventing the CIA and briefing their own analysis directly to the White House." The Senate report also notes that in a communication sent to Wolfowitz and

Secretary of State Donald Rumsfeld regarding a CIA report that failed to establish a convincing connection between Iraq and al Qaeda, Feith's people recommended that the "CIA's interpretation ought to be ignored." Senator Rockefeller, vice chairman of the Intelligence Committee, said in a news conference that Feith's "private intelligence" operation was "not lawful." Senate Select Committee on Intelligence, "Report on the U.S. Intelligence Community's Prewar Intelligence Assessments on Iraq," July 7, 2004, 457, section containing the "additional views" of Senators John Rockefeller, Carl Levin, and Richard Durbin.

19. John Prados, "The Pros from Dover," *Bulletin of the Atomic Scientists* 60 (January–February 2004): 44–51.

20. Wilkerson reported this in an interview by Steve Inskeep on National Public Radio, November 3, 2005, quoted in "Former Powell Aide Links Cheney's Office to Abuse Directives," *International Herald Tribune,* November 3, 2005.

21. Lawrence B. Wilkerson, "The Whitehouse Cabal," *Los Angeles Times,* October 25, 2005, B11.

22. See, for instance, Prados, "Pros from Dover."

23. See, for example, Ryan Lizza, "White House Watch Chief of Gaffe," *New Republic Online,* November 14, 2005, www.tnr.com/doc.mhtml?i=20051114&s=lizza111405.

24. Stephen Green, "Serving Two Flags: Neo-Cons, Israel and the Bush Administration," Counterpunch, February 28/29, 2004, www.ifamericansknew.org/us_ints/nc-green.html, 5.

25. Laura Rozen, "Investigation Update: Three Days in Rome," *Mother Jones,* June 20, 2008. See also Senate Select Committee on Intelligence, *Report on Intelligence Activities Relating to Iraq Conducted by the Policy Counterterrorism Evaluation Group and the Office of Special Plans within the Office of the Under Secretary of Defense for Policy,* June 2008, http://intelligence.senate.gov/080605/phase2b.pdf.

26. See, for example, Jerry Markon, "Pentagon Analyst Given 12½ Years in Secrets Case," *Washington Post,* January 21, 2006, A1.

27. See, for example, Michael A. Ledeen, "Do the Right Thing: Let's Avoid Making a Catastrophe Out of an Embarrassment," *National Review Online,* January 18, 2006, www.aei.org/include/pub_print.asp?pubID=23696.

28. By 2002 some two-thirds of the federal labor force worked indirectly for government—in "off-budget" jobs created by contracts and grants, as opposed to "on-budget" jobs made up of civil servants, uniformed military personnel, and postal service workers. Calculated from data compiled by Paul Light, "Fact Sheet on the New True Size of Government," September 5, 2003, Center for Public Service, Brookings Institution, www.brookings.edu/articles/2003/0905politics_light.aspx.

29. Noted in *Government Executive* and cited in Dan Guttman, "The Shadow Pentagon: Private Contractors Play a Huge Role in Basic Government Work—Mostly Out of Public View," September 29, 2004, Center for Public Integrity, http://projects.publicintegrity.org/pns/report.aspx?aid=386.

30. Anitha Reddy and Sara Kehaulani Goo, "Database on U.S. Visitors Set for Huge Expansion: Reston Firm's Contract Worth Up to $10 Billion," *Washington Post,* June 2, 2004, E01, www.washingtonpost.com/wp-dyn/articles/A7961-2004Jun1.html.

31. See Iraq Coalition Casualty Count, "Iraq Coalition Casualties: Contractors—A Partial List," http://icasualties.org/oif/Contractors.aspx.

32. Guttman, "Shadow Pentagon."

33. Larry Makinson, "Outsourcing the Pentagon: Who Benefits from the Politics and Economics of National Security?" Center for Public Integrity, September 29, 2004, updated March 31, 2006, http://projects.publicintegrity.org/pns/report.aspx?aid=385.

34. Paul Light, *The True Size of Government* (Washington, DC: Brookings Institution Press, 1999), 207–9.

35. Comptroller General David Walker, "Remarks at the George Washington University Law School Symposium on the Future of Competitive Sourcing," September 15, 2003, transcript on file with the *Public Contract Law Journal.*

36. Government Accountability Office, *High Risk Series: An Update*, GAO-05-207 (Washington, DC: Government Accountability Office, 2005), www.gao.gov/new.items/d05207.pdf.

37. Reported in Guttman, "Shadow Pentagon."

38. See Ronald C. Moe and Kevin R. Kosar, "The Quasi Government: Hybrid Organizations with Both Government and Private Sector Legal Characteristics," updated May 18, 2005, Congressional Research Service, https://www.policyarchive.org/bitstream/handle/10207/1034/RL30533_20050518.pdf?sequence=3, Summary.

39. Dana Hedgpeth, "Judge Clears Contractor of Fraud in Iraq," *Washington Post*, February 9, 2007, D1.

40. See Janine R. Wedel, "Blurring the State-Private Divide: Flex Organisations and the Decline of Accountability," in *Globalisation, Poverty and Conflict: A Critical "Development" Reader*, ed. Max Spoor (Dordrecht: Kluwer Academic Publishers, 2004), 221–29.

41. This phenomenon was described as early as 1976. See Daniel Guttman and Barry Willner, *The Shadow Government* (New York: Pantheon Books, 1979).

15

Deploying Law as a Weapon in America's War on Terror

Susan F. Hirsch

Five weeks after the attacks of September 11, 2001, in a federal courthouse in lower Manhattan, I watched as a judge sentenced four men convicted of crimes related to the 1998 bombings of two U.S. embassies in East Africa. For me the legal proceeding was a milestone along a painful journey that began when I survived the embassy bombing in Dar es Salaam, Tanzania, only to find that my husband, Abdulrahman Abdallah, had been killed. He had waited outside the embassy while I entered to run an errand. Simultaneous blasts in Dar es Salaam and Nairobi killed over two hundred people that day and injured thousands. Most of the casualties were Africans, although the bombings, which killed twelve U.S. government employees, represented a major attack on American interests abroad. Soon after the bombings, U.S. federal prosecutors launched a huge international investigation that resulted in indictments of over twenty individuals, including Osama bin Laden, and the trial of four suspected al Qaeda operatives in Manhattan in the first six months of 2001. I followed the investigation and attended much of the trial. At a time when media attention had yet to focus on al Qaeda terrorism, the embassy bombings trial promised an explanation of what had happened and who was responsible as well as public recognition for my loss. My training as a legal anthropologist made me sensitive to the power dynamics of the trial. I was especially concerned that the U.S. government's desire to avenge the deaths of its own might stand in the way of a fair trial for the defendants. The prosecutors' avid push for the death penalty was, for me, a worrisome manifestation of the capacity of those harmed to seek vengeance. It was important to me that justice, not vengeance, be the trial's ultimate accomplishment. Although the trial had failed to answer many of my questions about the reasons behind the al Qaeda attacks, it had succeeded in publicizing the crime, recognizing victims' losses, determining guilt, and punishing appropriately, while, for the most part, keeping the government's power in check and treating the defendants humanely. In short, it had achieved something I could call justice. Although symbols are an anthropologist's stock in trade, no expert training was required to recognize the profound symbolism of the sentencing of four convicted embassy bombers just blocks from the 9/11 ground zero, in a nation still gripped by fear and anger. The proceedings epitomized a sober legal response to the destructive violence of terrorism and, as such, symbolized American law's capacity for justice.

In the weeks after the sentencing, I waited for criminal investigations of 9/11 to begin and then watched as the U.S. government responded to the attacks by ramping up a "war on terror." That war began with conventional warfare—the bombing and invasion of Afghanistan—with the goal of killing al Qaeda members. Killing the enemy, controlling enemy territory, and forcing a surrender (i.e., winning) are standard goals of war. At the same time the government pursued other counterterrorism strategies, such as gathering intelligence about al Qaeda, increasing security at borders and sensitive targets, and impeding the flow of al Qaeda funds and information. Using law to investigate terror plots and prosecute suspects has always been an important counterterrorism strategy. Citing law's importance in fighting terrorism, the Bush administration presided over the creation of new laws and the transformation of existing ones with the goal of empowering law enforcement and the Justice Department to work against al Qaeda and other threats. Early protests against the drive to strengthen police and prosecutorial powers at the expense of preserving civil liberties were dismissed by Bush administration officials who insisted that such emergency powers were justified during a state of war, which, as they pointed out repeatedly, the U.S. Congress had authorized. As the war expanded beyond Afghanistan and extended indefinitely, and the temporary measures appeared to have become permanent, criticism mounted against violations of civil rights and liberties both in the United States and abroad. The Bush administration's defense of warrantless wiretapping and other data collection techniques, presidential signing orders that reserved the executive branch's right to ignore certain laws, and procedures of investigation and detention that violated domestic and international standards led to a showdown over the limits of presidential powers in the middle of Bush's second term. This struggle over the fundamental problem of protecting both individual liberty and governmental authority while also preserving the checks-and-balances system of democratic governance will lead to further battles in courts and the media. In the meantime, I direct attention to a related question: What are the effects on law of the U.S. government's approach to the war on terror?

I attempt to answer this question by analyzing the various uses of law as a weapon in America's response to terror attacks. Examples demonstrate that, through the powerful metaphor of the "war on terror," law—a legitimate tool of counterterrorism—

became subsumed into the logic of war and was deployed to serve the ends of war rather than the ends of justice typically associated with law and legal processes. In the next two sections, "Legal Tools to Legal Weapons" and "Deploying Law against Enemies," I explore the conceptual underpinnings of law's role in fighting terrorism under the Bush administration. The transformation of law into a weapon results in part from the power of the metaphor of the war on terror. For instance, standard criminal justice tools, such as investigation and prosecution, were honed to carry out the aggressive tactics of the war and wielded in new ways consistent with the aims of conventional war. These deployments of law as a weapon incorporate violence and the threat of violence.

Deploying law as a weapon draws attention to a relationship between law and violence that is usually hidden. Legal scholars depict law as the opposite of violence or the means of controlling it. As an oft-mentioned example, law in the form of a criminal prosecution substitutes retributive justice for the violent revenge that a harmed victim, in the heat of anger and hurt, might want desperately to pursue. Yet defining law as the opposite of violence misconstrues a more complex connection. Law operates effectively because the force of the state (i.e., police and army) lurks always behind it and stands (sometimes visibly) at the ready. In the war on terror, the principles that hold that force in check have repeatedly been questioned, altered, and ignored, thus allowing government bodies to move easily and with too little rationale to the use of law as a weapon. In addition to the confusion that results, using law as a weapon has the problematic outcome of recasting law as a response to terrorism that more closely resembles revenge than justice, by virtue of its evident violence. It is hard to argue against the claim that vengeance motivates the use of certain tactics in the war on terror, such as secret, incommunicado detention and harsh interrogation methods, including torture. These brutal and punishing experiences render suspects "socially dead." By *social death* I mean the condition that results when individuals are intentionally denied access to social networks and relationships that recognize their humanity, especially their right to exist as humans. The Bush administration's insistence on the legality of the dehumanizing practices used on terror suspects is further evidence of the failure to recognize a crucial line between law and violence.

Drawing on examples of law used as a weapon, and to render terror suspects socially dead, I argue that the deployment of law in the war on terror has undermined legality, specifically the law's assumed role as a mechanism for countering, not promulgating, violence. The ensuing crisis over legality has eroded the efficacy of the American legal system, including as a counterterrorism measure. Equally important, the use of law as a weapon has diminished American law's symbolic value in the United States and abroad. As I describe in the later section "Prosecutions as Weapons," terror prosecutions held after 9/11 squandered law's symbolic potential. In comparison to the embassy bombings sentencing, which appropriately symbolized a just response to terrorism, the trials of the Lackawanna Six and Zacharias Moussaoui were lost opportunities, in effect show trials where the government's zealous exercise of power overwhelmed any possibility of symbolizing justice. Those failed efforts, combined with the Bush administration's strong resistance to open trials for most suspects in custody, confirm the rise of injustice as a key symbol of America's war on terror.

Some of the most trenchant criticisms of the injustice of the war on terror come from abroad—not, as I argue in the section "Exporting America's War on Terror," from America's "enemies" but from those nations that have long admired American democracy and justice and refuse to endorse unlawful provisions of the war on terror. Perhaps they realize that unjust responses to terrorism make nations and individuals less secure, not more. I conclude by offering several observations to defend the argument that, in addition to undermining legality and distorting law's legitimate counterterrorism functions, the deployment of law as a weapon in the war on terror has made America and Americans less secure.

LEGAL TOOLS TO LEGAL WEAPONS

Even prior to the 9/11 attacks, American responses to terrorism included strategies and tactics ranging from conducting missile strikes on al Qaeda camps to freezing bank accounts of suspected terrorist sympathizers. After 9/11 government actions expanded further to include, as described in the February 2003 "National Strategy for Combating Terrorism," every "instrument of national power—diplomatic, economic, law enforcement, financial, information, intelligence, and military."[1] Accordingly, the tactics of the war on terror (to the extent that we have knowledge of them) are quite diverse and include assassinations, infiltration of groups, mechanisms to interrupt the flow of funds, domestic surveillance, increased security at borders and public buildings, bombing of suspected hideouts, arrests, interrogations, and prosecutions of terror suspects. America's war on terror draws on the tools of law and law enforcement. Investigators' dogged efforts to track down suspects, foil plots in the making, and bring to justice those suspected of attempting, promoting, or accomplishing violence are crucial to preventing and punishing terrorist acts both domestically and abroad. In an attempt to lend coherence to the war effort, the 2003 National Strategy articulated the government's ultimate goals as the "4Ds": Defeat terrorist organizations; Deny sponsorship, support, and sanctuary to terrorists; Diminish the conditions that terrorists seek to exploit; and Defend the United States, its citizens, and interests. As described below, the deployment of legal tools to achieve these goals underpins my argument that, in the transition from the post-9/11 combat in Afghanistan to a broader war on terror fought on a variety of fronts, the force of conventional warfare remained at the heart of the campaign and shaped the tools used: legal tools became weapons.

As a metaphor, the "war on terror" draws on the power of conventional warfare and of previous metaphorical wars (e.g., the wars on drugs and communism) and shares with them a commitment to a forceful campaign against a formidable opponent. The words of war come easily to the tongues of many government officials: we will kill the enemy; we will win the war on terror; we will never admit defeat. Waging war on terror implies that the United States will wield the weapons of war to vanquish the enemy and, as described in the National Strategy, will achieve the "total domain awareness" that would preclude future enemy attacks. In his popular book on political rhetoric, George Lakoff illuminates the powerful consequences of launching a metaphorical war. For instance, any war, even a metaphorical one, requires an enemy.[2] As Lakoff points out, though, the realities of metaphorical wars differ from those of conventional wars, as is the case for the U.S. war on terror, which lacks the enemy camp and opposing national government characteristic of conventional war. Such disjunctures around the metaphor lead to inappropriate and awkward conceptualizations of parties, tactics, objectives, and goals. For example, the United States is leading the war on terror, yet who is the enemy? Terror? Terrorism? Terrorists? Answering this question has proved difficult for the Bush administration, which has named the enemy variously as al Qaeda, evil, radical Muslims, people who hate freedom, and Islamofascists.

The war on terror metaphor also ensures that the logic of conventional war will underlie the deployment of weapons against terrorism. The war metaphor assumes, for instance, that a more powerful weapon should always be substituted for one that is weaker or potentially ineffective. Used in the same "campaign" as more overtly violent weapons, such as assassinations and bombings, some legal tools can appear weak, and the war on terror metaphor easily justifies bolstering their capacity. Bush administration officials have repeatedly claimed that the available legal tools are not sufficient to fight this serious war and have called for more powerful measures. With this rationale, they have strengthened laws so as to mount more aggressive investigations and prosecutions. The two acts titled "United and Strengthening America by Providing Appropriate Tools Required to Intercept and Obstruct Terrorism"—the USA-Patriot Acts I and II, for short—empowered law enforcement by authorizing more robust legal tools for investigating terror suspects (such as secret or "sneak and peek" searches), for detaining terror suspects or anyone associated with them, and for gathering information about potential terror plots through the sanctioning of data dragnets, information sharing among government agencies, and limited judicial oversight of data collection procedures. The lack of due process and judicial oversight has made government demands for information from individuals and institutions harder to resist. Before the passage of these laws, such heavy-handed domain control was more characteristic of military intelligence collection during wartime than lawful domestic investigation.

Critics charged that the government gained too much power with the lightning-quick adoption of Patriot Act I. The central concerns were that changes to the law risked violating civil liberties. They decried the fear and oppression experienced by people deemed a suspect population, especially immigrants, Muslims, and Arabs, and condemned the reliance on racial and religious profiling. The strengthening of legal tools has made it more difficult for suspects to consult with attorneys, to obtain information about the charges against them, and to defend themselves. The formerly innocent acts of walking around a Manhattan skyscraper or taking a picture of a bridge in California or contributing to a religious charity or buying a truckload of cell phones for resale can lead to arrest or detention, depending, in some instances, on a person's identity. Other criticisms focus on the government's newly acquired authority to monitor open religious and political meetings.

When the first Patriot Act was proposed, I shared the general concern that its provisions violated some important civil liberties. I not only worried for the individuals whose lives would be unjustly disrupted but also wondered about the debilitating effects of these powerful legal tactics (especially their lack of attention to due process) on the values of individual liberty underlying the American judicial system. As the Patriot Act's effects began to emerge in 2002, my concern became more self-centered. At the time I was a fellow at the Library of Congress, writing a book on my experience of the embassy bombings and the subsequent trial. In my research I explored many terrorism-related topics using the library's vast resources, including a computer provided to me as a fellow. On occasion, I wondered whether the government monitored the library's computer users—did too many searches for "terrorism" or the names of notorious terror suspects trigger attention in some Washington office? My concern heightened when it became clear that government surveillance increasingly relied on strong-arm and secretive tactics, such as forcing librarians to provide officials with evidence encountered in their jobs and denying them the right to contest such requests, to inform targeted clients, or even to consult superiors or attorneys. One day at the library, while following up on testimony about ballistics from the embassy bombings trial, I found myself searching site after site with information about explosives of all types. I felt a chill as I realized that anyone perusing these sites could arouse suspicion. As I thought about it, other aspects of my life—taken together and out of context—could similarly position me as worthy of investigation: I had copies of the al Qaeda handbook and many of bin Laden's messages in my files; I made frequent calls to areas in Europe and East Africa where al Qaeda cells still operated; I had wired money to Muslim individuals and organizations in Kenya at a time when several Islamic charities had been shut down on suspicion of supporting terrorism; I had spoken out against the U.S. government's handling of terrorism and other political issues. Although my status as a researcher and as someone with family ties to East Africa could certainly account for my actions, I occasionally felt fear and vulnerability at the thought of coming under investigation. My status as a well-educated, Caucasian, American citizen would no doubt protect me, yet this experience showed me that no one was immune from fearing law's new power.

Others, of course, suffered more than fear of these laws. The hundreds of primarily Muslim men apprehended in the United States in the months after 9/11 experienced firsthand the anguish of investigation and detention, although few were ever formally charged with crimes. These sweeps disrupted everyday routines and financial support in many families and created anxiety, especially for those who were not told the whereabouts of a detained loved one. The use of tactics to prolong detention when no criminal charges could be brought, such as holding individuals on immigration violations or as material witnesses, was coercive and punitive, as well as legally questionable. It would be several more years before a lawsuit brought by Rachel Meeropol of the Center for Constitutional Rights and by a student in the anthropology department where I had long taught would win recognition that the government had violated the rights of these individuals.[3] Those early uses of Patriot Act provisions exposed law's tendencies toward violence, violation, and vengeance.

Much later in my fellowship, in October of 2003, the Library of Congress hosted a panel presentation on the topic "Freedom or Security? Civil Liberties and the War on Terror." By then criticism of Patriot Act provisions was widespread. During the question-and-answer period, an audience member asked James Comey, then assistant attorney general, why captured terror suspects were being sent to an uncertain future at Guantánamo Bay instead of facing prosecution in the criminal justice system. In responding Comey first referred to his own service as a prosecutor in New York's Southern District, the site of the embassy bombings case as well as several other high-profile terror trials prior to 9/11, and then to the danger posed by those captured in Afghanistan and the likelihood that many held sensitive information about terror plots. Questioning the ability of law enforcement to obtain such information through standard interrogation, he quipped, "At Guantánamo, they have better tools in their toolbox. As a prosecutor, my pliers aren't that good." His remark generated a murmured chuckling from the audience. At that point, we had yet to learn about the brutal interrogation techniques used at Abu Ghraib and other U.S.-run prisons, and the allegations that torture was integral to U.S. intelligence gathering in the war on terror had not yet been exposed.

I raised my hand to ask Comey why he was willing to abandon open prosecution as a tool in the war on terror and how he could justify subjecting suspects to interrogation techniques unacceptable in the U.S. criminal justice system. He did not call on me, and my curiosity remains. As prosecutors he and his colleagues had relied extensively on the criminal justice system to investigate and prosecute terror suspects and had taken pride in their successes, notably the embassy bombings case. Moreover, after 9/11, they had gained access to tools that were more powerful than any they had previously wielded. Yet this top government official believed he needed even more aggressive measures, including ones that abandoned recognized legal principles and processes. More disturbing to me than Comey's cynicism about the legal prosecution of suspects was his casual attitude toward exposing them to harsh interrogations or even torture. Throughout the discussion Comey refused to acknowledge that Bush administration tactics in the war on terror were contributing to the erosion of legality, although he broke with the administration not long after.

DEPLOYING LAW AGAINST ENEMIES

The influence of conventional war on the war on terror results not only from the power of "war" as a metaphor but also from the reality that the war on terror began with a bona fide conventional war, albeit undeclared. Treating enemies as killable, as lacking the right to life or recognition as humans, is a routine military strategy when the primary aim—as in the U.S. attacks on Afghanistan after 9/11— is to kill enough of the enemy to disrupt their ability to engage in further aggression. In a context where the frontier justice slogan "Wanted: Dead or Alive" applied, key leaders of al Qaeda and the Taliban, as well as their many followers, were targeted for killing. At least initially, calls were widespread for Osama bin Laden's battlefield execution. When one of the early bombing raids resulted in the death of Mohamed Atef, a bin Laden deputy who had been indicted as an architect of the East African embassy bombings, I felt frustration rather than satisfaction, relief, or closure. I yearned to see bin Laden, Atef, and others brought to justice for their alleged roles in planning and financing the embassy bombings as well as other crimes. Yet my own preference for confronting live terror suspects in a domestic or international justice system was drowned out amid the calls to obliterate the enemy, and the latter view permeated the war on terror long after active combat in Afghanistan had abated.

As the broader war on terror ramped up, new tactics in the treatment of terror suspects emerged, and at their core lay a profound disregard for the humanity of those suspected of terrorist involvement. For instance, in November 2002, Hellfire, a predator missile drone launched by either the U.S. military or the CIA, blew up a car traveling in a remote area of Yemen. Killed in the explosion was its target: Ali al-Harithi, a leading al Qaeda figure thought to have masterminded the attack on the USS Cole battleship two years before. The officials who sent the missile screaming across the desert knew that assassinating an individual off the battlefield could be interpreted as a violation of both international and domestic law. The legality of the act became even more complicated when officials realized that also killed in the attack was Kamal Derwish, an American citizen, wanted in the United States on suspicion of recruiting young men from Lackawanna, New York, for al Qaeda training. Although the U.S. government has never confirmed or denied involvement in

Derwish's death, the incident sparked a brief public debate about whether assassination was an appropriate weapon in the expanding war on terror. Even before 9/11, suspected terrorists in Sudan, Afghanistan, and elsewhere were targeted for elimination by the U.S. government. Yet prior to the missile strike in Yemen, none of these efforts had killed an American and thereby prompted the questions about citizenship, due process, and assassination as a tactic in the war on terror that were raised around the Derwish incident. With 9/11 still so fresh and so convincing a justification for all manner of violent incidents, including the deaths through direct bombings of the war in Afghanistan, Derwish's fate hardly troubled a public that generally continued to accept the U.S. government's assertions that defeating the terrorist enemy required harsh measures. But quietly the Bush administration scuttled plans for several other assassinations.

Assassinating an enemy in the manner described above requires a fundamental disregard for due process and the abandonment of certain legal instruments and principles. Accordingly, it represents a cynical perspective on law and also on the possibility of legal justice for some offenders. Almost as troubling as assassination is the resort to tactics that fall short of killing enemies but instead render them "socially dead." The epitome of that condition is secret, incommunicado detention. In such situations the identities of those being held are kept secret, and they, their families, and their advocates are unable to achieve recognition of their claims to rights as detainees, thus rendering them socially dead. Much more than a denial of due process, incommunicado detention refuses to recognize the very humanity of those held by terminating their connections to a social world in which they would be regarded as human. Initially, those individuals held in Guantánamo Bay experienced social death as I have defined it. Officials refused to disclose or confirm the identities of the Guantánamo detainees, who were not permitted any contact with other individuals, including legal counsel. Their conditions of detention, and those of Jose Padilla, Yassir Hamdi, and others known and unknown, have the primary intention and effect of rendering these individuals socially dead and, in my view, dehumanized. In one of the first exposés of conditions at Guantánamo Bay, David Rose expresses aptly the connection between the denial of legal rights to detainees and their social death, although he does not use that phrase: "Consigning prisoners to the legal black hole of Guantánamo reflected a broader sense of their dehumanization, an inferior status that made them undeserving of a normal enemy's privileges; a status that was not based on evidence of what they had done, but who they were."[4]

Although initially denied any access to counsel, detainees at Guantánamo and other facilities eventually acquired military and civilian advocates, some of whom opposed their designation as enemy combatants and their treatment. The Bush administration justified incommunicado and secret detention at Guantánamo Bay and elsewhere (e.g., on prison ships roaming international waters) with the assertion that neither nation-state laws nor international conventions applied. Even as legal challenges filed on behalf of the detainees began to result in findings against the position that enemy combatants deserve neither the rights of soldiers nor the rights of criminal suspects, the Bush administration did an end-run around the law by continuing to insist that the president, as commander in chief, holds ultimate power to determine the disposition of an enemy combatant. Invocation of the war metaphor bolsters this perspective on enemies and results in denying law's relevance.

The growing evidence that the Bush administration's position on Guantánamo detainees would not stand up to legal scrutiny spawned other tactics of social death, such as holding suspects in undisclosed locations or "black sites" and turning them over to other governments for questioning and incarceration through the process known as extraordinary rendition. For example, the whereabouts of Khalid Sheikh Mohamed, an al Qaeda leader who had allegedly planned numerous attacks on United States interests, including the 9/11 attacks, remained unknown from the time of his capture in Pakistan in 2003 until he was brought to Guantánamo Bay in November 2006 as one of fourteen "high-value detainees." The social death of terror suspects such as Khalid Sheikh Mohamed not only violates their individual rights but also robs victims and the public of the right to justice in its sense of establishing who was responsible for crimes of terror, what they did, and why they might have participated, as revealed through a fair process where those accused can defend themselves. My experience at the embassy bombings trial led me to believe that these aspects of justice can be enormously valuable for a recovering victim. Yet it is unlikely that embassy bombings suspects captured in recent years will be brought to trial in U.S. federal court. For instance, Ahmed Khalfan Ghailani, whose alleged actions in planning the Tanzania bombing went well beyond those of men now serving life terms for their roles, was arrested in Pakistan in 2004. Despite a 1998 indictment against him for participating in the embassy bombings, the United States made a public request for his extradition, and he "disappeared" until November 2006, when he showed up in Guantánamo. Another alleged high-level member of the East Africa cell responsible for the embassy bombings was Souleyman Abdallah Salim Hemed, alias Chuck Norris. Hemed was kidnapped in Somalia in 2003, possibly by Kenyan government officials who took credit or by Somali warlords financed by the CIA, who were rumored to have made the "snatch." According to media accounts, Hemed was subsequently released to American officials, although no government agency will acknowledge that he was ever in U.S. custody. Hemed's whereabouts remain unknown.

Social death also describes the status of an individual subjected to torture. By definition, a torture victim is denied recognition as a human deserving of rights. In situations of torture the request for humane treatment is explicitly denied, thus confirming an individual's social death. Torture also enacts both vengeance and violent dehumanization on its subjects. Given these qualities, the defense of torture as lawful and appropriate in some circumstances, as the Bush administration has argued at times, undermines the distinction between law and violence that government is supposed to protect and thereby erodes legality. The government has been willing to take this risk despite evidence that the resort to torture, or even highly coercive interrogation techniques that (arguably) fall short of torture, is ineffective as a counterterrorism strategy. Torture rarely produces reliable information; it creates a backlash of aggression among outraged populations; it risks exposing U.S. personnel to similar treatment; and it dehumanizes and damages its victims.[5] Torture also damages those who practice it. Torturers suffer psychic wounds both from dehumanizing others and, in some instances, from recognizing the illegality and immorality of their actions. Moreover, torture damages the public that endorses it. A potent symbol, torture conveys the absolute power of those who practice it and their willingness to embrace injustice. Torture's ascendance as a symbol of the U.S. war on terror and its eclipse of other symbols of justice are among the crowning failures of the American response to terrorism. This is the case despite the insistence by President George W. Bush—in contradiction to considerable evidence—that "the United States does not torture."

I can surmise (on the basis of accounts of others similarly detained) that violations of the rights of Khalid Sheik Mohamed, Ahmed Khalfan Ghailani, and other "high-value" detainees while in custody contribute to the U.S. government insistence on trying them through military commissions rather than in open criminal court. Thus the social deaths of these individuals make it impossible to learn more about the roles they played or to see them brought to trial in conventional justice proceedings, as well as anyone they might implicate. Although a detailed critique of the Military Commissions Act is beyond the scope of this chapter, it bears mentioning that these newly created tribunals have garnered criticism for prosecutorial reliance on secret evidence and for the limits placed on due process, access to counsel for defendants, and access to the proceeding for victims and the public. Beyond my interests as an individual terror victim, I have argued that the public benefits from holding perpetrators responsible through open trials.[6]

As shown in the previous sections, when efforts to increase law's power as a weapon in the war on terror have breached the limits of law, U.S. authorities have obfuscated their use of these tactics in some instances and defended their prerogative to determine the legality of war tactics, including torture, in others. Insistence on the legality of deploying tactics that result in social death provides evidence that the Bush administration understands its own power as including the power to define the social world and to render some individuals no longer humans in that world. "Commander-in-chief logic," which asserts the president's right to use any and all methods in the defense of the United States during wartime, has been invoked repeatedly to defend social death and other legally specious tactics, even though prior invocations of those powers saw them limited to short, well-defined periods. Under the direction of the president and vice president, a clutch of bright and zealous legal advisors—including David Addington, John Yoo, and Jay Bybee—provided the rationale, a bizarre twist of the legal theory of "the unitary executive." Whether these efforts to seize power over key legal functions involved conscious exploitation of Americans' post-9/11 fear remains unclear. But they resulted in frightening deployments of law. Challenges to executive branch policy have increased steadily, including through the courts, where some have already found support. But in the long run the effects on law's symbolic power could prove to be profoundly debilitating for the American legal system. For one, the criminal terror trial as a site for achieving justice against terrorism is no longer a prevalent or especially impressive symbol in the United States.

PROSECUTIONS AS WEAPONS

Prosecutors across the globe have pursued individuals suspected of conspiracy, the provision of material support to terrorists, perjury, and treason. They have been especially aggressive, and probably most successful, in their attempts to use prosecution or threats of prosecution to stop the flow of funds to suspected terrorist organizations. Indicting a suspect provides victims and the public with information about the crime and serves to warn potential violators. Public trials of terror suspects are often the only site for revealing information that perpetrators and even their targets (e.g., the U.S. government) have tried hard to conceal. Thus a trial is the moment for exposure welcomed by victims, who also, in that context, gain public recognition for their suffering. At a trial a government can show its ability to bring violence under control through law. Trials of suspected terrorists can fulfill one interpretation of the promise made by the Bush administration to bring terrorists to justice. From my perspective the embassy bombings trial served as a symbol of that possibility. Although since 9/11 many suspects have been held for questioning, brought before grand juries, and threatened with serious charges, only a handful of indictments and prosecutions have gone forward in the United States, and the symbolism of those trials contrasts with the justice of terror trials in earlier years.

The Bush administration thought it had the perfect example of bringing terrorists to justice when, in the early fall of 2002, a prosecutor, acting on orders from the Justice Department, announced on national television the arrests of six men from Lackawanna, New York, on charges relating to terrorism. Accused of providing material support to a terrorist organization, the six were depicted by prosecutors as a sleeper cell of American terrorists who had traveled for al Qaeda training in Afghanistan in the spring of 2001 and returned to America to commit unspecified violence. Coming just a year after 9/11, it was a startling revelation that played well on newscasts that, as a defense attorney noted, "scared the pants off the American people." Bush administration officials received daily briefings on the Lackawanna case and mentioned it repeatedly to justify the need for tough provisions against internal terrorist threats.

According to their lawyers, the Lackawanna Six faced enormous pressure to plead guilty, which two did early on. They admitted to traveling to Pakistan and being taken to a training camp in Afghanistan, where they encountered Kamal Derwish, who had allegedly recruited them for the travel. But as their stories emerged, the earlier vivid image of a terrifying "sleeper cell" in Lackawanna faded. Mukhtar al Bakri, a twenty-three-year-old arrested while on his honeymoon in Bahrain, said he had "felt as if a shovel hit his head" when he realized that the group he had joined and traveled with to Pakistan would move on together to Afghanistan, where they would meet Osama bin Laden. Terrified, one of the six faked a broken ankle and begged to be sent home. Most of the men left early. When contacted by the FBI after they returned to the United States, none mentioned that they had traveled to Afghanistan while away. Were they wannabes or true believers or dupes or small-time thugs or big-time terrorists or terrified at what they had seen? If Kamal Derwish had been captured in Yemen (rather than assassinated) and brought to a public trial (rather than into the incommunicado detention that would more likely have awaited him), he might have clarified what he had told the group about their mission. His fate must have weighed on the Lackawanna Six as they contemplated whether holding out for trial might lead them to a sentence far worse than ten years in federal prison. Not surprisingly, they admitted some of the charges, and each was sentenced to a hefty prison term. Family members and defense attorneys continue to express fury at what they believe was a highly coercive process.[7]

Prosecutors have come to rely on tactics developed in prior terror prosecutions to push terror suspects toward confessions and guilty pleas. "Overcharging" confronts suspects with indictments for a wide range of crimes, any that might plausibly be charged and some that carry long sentences. Essentially, prosecutors throw the book at suspects, and the number and seriousness of offenses make proving one's innocence so daunting a task that defense attorneys counsel plea bargaining. The tactic advantages the prosecution in the process of pleading down to lesser charges. When prosecutors have only weak evidence, an initial slate of stunning charges still makes an impressive threat, even if most charges are eventually scaled back and whittled down and the final plea is to lesser crimes, such as perjury or issuing false statements, crimes that result from participating in the criminal process itself. By then, prosecutors hope that media attention has turned elsewhere. Other terror cases highlight a second questionable tactic: the extensive use of conspiracy charges. Writing from his perspective as a defense attorney for one of those accused of conspiracy and other crimes relating to the 1993 World Trade Center bombing, Robert Precht expressed concern that "even minor players in a terrorism plot can easily find themselves charged in a conspiracy indictment and facing death."[8] The risk of assuming guilt by association is a strong tendency in conspiracy cases, where it is hard to determine whether a person was a full-fledged conspirator, a business associate, a former conspirator, or merely a friend or co-religionist. The secretive nature of conspiracies compounds the problem of establishing whether any individual is "in" or "out." Moreover, proving a conspiracy often relies on former members of the conspiracy with murky connections to illegal activities and plea agreements with prosecutors in the balance. The case against one of the embassy bombers relied on the testimony of several former al Qaeda operatives who had been working with the U.S. government for years in an effort to reduce the charges that they faced. In peacetime, overcharging combined with a reliance on conspiracy charges would be called prosecutorial railroading, which is not uncommon. In the post-9/11 war on terror prosecutorial weapons are stronger. Their increased power stems not only from their efficacy in producing convictions but also, and perhaps more importantly, from the complementary symbols they produce: overcharging channels anger at dangerous terrorists and justifies harsh punitive measures, while charges of conspiracy keep members of the public on guard against being swept up in activities that might have the appearance of supporting terrorism. These operate all the more effectively because they are deployed alongside other more overtly violent weapons of war.

The Bush administration must have hoped that the Lackawanna case would symbolize the government's ability to bring terrorists to justice. But ultimately they stood in the awkward position of having thrown the book at offenders less frightening and perhaps less culpable than initially alleged. Nonetheless, the case was invoked to applaud Patriot Act provisions that had supposedly facilitated finding and charging the suspects. At a news conference in upstate New York, President Bush combined lobbying for renewal of the Patriot Act with recognition of those who had worked on the case. In a congratulatory gesture, the president asked, "We got a couple of them overseas, isn't that right?" The FBI regional head was forced to agree, even though the government had never previously admitted responsibility for Kamal Derwish's death by assassination in Yemen. Bush realized his gaffe and tried to joke, "Maybe I'm not supposed to say anything." Did the law enforcement officers who laughed with him at his blunder note its irony? Bush had come to New York to embrace legal justice but could not help acknowledging that it operated simultaneously with much harsher actions. The president's endorsement of killing as a form of justice is hardly surprising. Killing the enemy was the goal from the first salvos of the conventional war on terror and gained new vigor with the full-blown military campaign in Iraq. Similarly unremarkable was President Bush's later statement that the killing of insurgent leader Abu Musab al-Zarqawi by U.S. special operations forces "delivered justice to the most wanted terrorist in Iraq."

In the case of Zacharias Moussaoui, the only person to stand trial in the United States for crimes related to the attacks of 9/11, prosecutors sought justice through another form of killing: the death penalty. Conspiracy was among the charges against

Moussaoui, and his case was touted as an important symbol of the U.S. government's commitment to bringing al Qaeda operatives to justice. The success of high-profile symbols depends on the clarity of their message, and the many ambiguities surrounding the Moussaoui case made it an ultimately unsatisfying symbol. For one, Moussaoui pleaded guilty against the advice of his attorneys. That plea, and his many contradictory outbursts in court, cast doubt on his veracity, his sanity, and—if he was sane—his judgment. The behavior of prosecutors also created doubts, as they repeatedly blocked Moussaoui's access to witnesses and information by citing national security concerns. Information leaked inappropriately to prosecution witnesses was a grave procedural breach that almost derailed the trial. Many observers questioned the trial's fairness and the government's wisdom in directing so much effort toward prosecuting someone who might have *wanted* to play a direct role in the attacks but most likely did not. At his worst, though, spewing invective against America, Moussaoui himself symbolized perfectly the heartless enemy that Americans were encouraged to hate and fear.

Prosecutors set out to kill that enemy by asking for the death penalty despite the arguably indirect nature of Moussaoui's involvement in the 9/11 attacks. This decision not only heightened the potential symbolic payoff of the trial—and raised the stakes for Moussaoui and his lawyers—but also shaped the entire proceeding. Once Moussaoui pled guilty, all attention turned to the two-part sentencing phase, where jurors assessed, first, if Moussaoui was responsible for the offenses charged against him, and second, whether he deserved to die. Testimony by carefully selected 9/11 victims figured largely, as jurors would weigh their experiences of pain, loss, and grief against mitigating factors presented by the defense. Political scientist Austin Sarat has argued eloquently that prosecutors' use of victims' stories of harm in a capital trial's sentencing phase undermines the state's goal of retributive justice by bringing the specter of revenge into the proceedings.[9] Victims who testify are assumed to support the prosecution's call for the death penalty, and their stories are thus used to achieve the state's ends, which may well be their own. As one 9/11 family member noted outside court, "Moussaoui's the only person charged with 9/11. Someone has to pay." In their courtroom statements, victims were precluded from overtly calling for vengeance, but their raw sentiments were apparent. Prosecutors repeatedly insisted to the jury that justice for Moussaoui demanded the harshest punishment.

My own experience as a death penalty opponent participating as a victim in a capital terror trial leads me to conclude that, in the embassy bombings case and in the Moussaoui case, prosecutors' tactics, especially their use of victims' stories of pain, can be construed as vengeful. In part, the slippage from retribution to revenge results from prosecutors' zealous pursuit of the death penalty, which is encouraged, monitored, and rewarded (with promotions) by Justice Department officials. The pressure to get convictions and harsh punishment can lead the government to make cynical use of victims. In writing about the embassy bombings trial, I argue that prosecutors abandoned victims, like myself, who opposed capital punishment or otherwise failed to fit their notions of a "good" victim.[10] Moreover, they used victims for an implicit goal never articulated directly. Prosecutors never admitted that in terror cases the most important "victim" is the nation, not the harmed individuals whose tears and voices of pain are relied on for emotional effect. This second cynical use offers additional evidence that prosecutors' connection to the state—their role in representing that particular victim in capital terror cases—transforms their efforts from retribution into revenge.

In both the Moussaoui case and the embassy bombings case, jurors could not agree to impose the death penalty, and the judges issued life sentences without parole. In the Moussaoui case, one juror repeatedly (albeit anonymously) voted against death, yet no one expressed his or her reservations in the jury room or afterwards. Perhaps the reasons given by embassy bombings jurors offer insight. One juror said that, as a Jewish American, he believed that people like himself would face further violence from al Qaeda if one of their own was executed. His vote against the death penalty can perhaps be interpreted as an effort to break the cycle of revenge killings between the United States and al Qaeda. A handful of jurors agreed that executing the convicted embassy bombers would make them martyrs, although it was unclear whether this was, for any of them, a reason to do so or not. At least some jurors understood the death penalty as a weapon in an ongoing war and sought to avoid the clear message its application would send.

Despite my criticisms of post-9/11 terror prosecutions, my experience leads me to embrace public noncapital trials as important counterterrorism measures and responses to terrorist acts. Trials provide information about the nature of terrorism and, in the Moussaoui case, the extent of the U.S. government's efforts against it prior to 9/11. Trials also offer the recognition that victims desire. If pursued appropriately, a trial can bring a perpetrator to justice and thus constitute an important symbolic response to terrorism. The continued violence of the war on terror, including law used violently, undermines the retributive function of trials that is so crucial to their role as symbols of justice. Given the spectacle and outcome of the Moussaoui case, and the treatment of detainees and other suspects rendered socially dead, more high-level terror trials are unlikely.

Social death—so contrary to legal norms and ethical standards—is an inherently unstable status; the power required to effect it is not easily sustainable over time. Pressure on the U.S. government led first to the release of information about the identities of the Guantánamo prisoners and then to the repatriation of many deemed innocent to their home countries. Former detainees who have spoken publicly about their experiences are poignant symbols of unlawful and unjust treatment. The socially dead brought back to life tell terrible tales about the beyond. The U.S. government must fear that in the court of international public opinion the former socially dead are winning their cases and further publicizing the U.S. reputation for injustice. In proceedings at Guantánamo Bay, any prisoner who tries to mention details about his experience of torture is silenced and the record is censored—yet another symbol of the quality of justice available through that controversial forum.

EXPORTING AMERICA'S WAR ON TERROR

Thus far, this essay has focused on domestic laws and trials. Yet the U.S.-led war on terror is a global initiative, as U.S. military, CIA, FBI, and other personnel operate internationally. Moreover, the U.S. government has worked hard to enlist the support of other nations in its campaign against terror and has succeeded in convincing many to sign international counterterrorism agreements and to strengthen their own domestic legal provisions. In more than a few instances, attempts by U.S. officials to "export" tactics in the war on terror to other nations, especially those that wield law as a weapon, have created sharp resistance. Many of the same criticisms lodged against U.S. legal policies domestically, as described in previous sections, have emerged in those nations that have adopted tactics resembling the Patriot Acts, sometimes in response to pressure from the United States. Although U.S. efforts have encountered widespread opposition, the account below focuses on Kenya, where I have long conducted anthropological research and where the U.S. commitment to civil and human rights was, for many years, a beacon of hope to those working to replace a dictatorial regime with multiparty democracy. But that was in the 1990s, when America exported "democracy and good governance," not the tactics of a war on terror that, as charged by a bipartisan panel, constitute exporting fear.[11]

Kenya and the United States have an intertwined history of experiences with terrorism and the war on terror. Prior to the embassy bombings in 1998, the U.S. government had been working with East African authorities to track al Qaeda cell members operating in the region, whom they suspected might be planning an attack. The Nairobi area, the coastal city of Mombasa, and Kenya's border with Somalia were all treated as hiding places for terrorists. After the embassy bombings, the FBI launched its largest-ever foreign investigation, with a special focus on East Africa. U.S. and Kenyan investigators collaborated closely and arrested two of the suspects, who eventually stood trial in the United States. Joint investigations gained new vigor in 2002 following almost simultaneous attacks on a Kenyan hotel and an Israeli jet taking off nearby. Over the next few years, various agencies of the U.S. government worked closely with Kenyan counterparts to mount a wide range of counterterrorism initiatives. For example, Kenyan police have traveled to the United States for training; the U.S. military has used Kenya's ports and airfields for counterterrorism exercises; and FBI agents have trained and carried out investigations with Kenya's

U.S.-funded antiterrorism squad. U.S. officials and consultants have developed modifications of the Kenyan criminal justice and judicial systems and urged their adoption. Relatedly, U.S. diplomats have pressured the Kenyan government to sign several international counterterrorism conventions.

In an essay in *Foreign Affairs,* political scientist Joel Barkan describes the ramifications of the U.S.-led war on terror as pursued in Kenya.[12] On the one hand, Kenya has benefited from receiving considerable funds and new security capabilities; these have leant some legitimacy and strength to its new liberal government, which took power in 2003 after decades of dictatorial rule. On the other hand, participating in the war on terror has, according to Barkan, created a major domestic crisis. Asked by the United States to play a key role in the war on terror in the region, Kenya, with its fragile leadership, history of ethnic conflict, and enormous economic and security problems, has struggled to meet the demands made by the United States and other politically powerful donor nations. It has faced great difficulties in attempting to balance the need for internal security with the desire to maintain and build a democratic and open society that contrasts with the years of one-party rule. With the postindependence history of a terribly repressive regime in mind, many civil society organizations have expressed concern over proposed changes in laws, which would, in their view, negate recently gained civil liberties protections.

Kenyan Muslims, a minority community concentrated at Kenya's coast, have watched as the initial war on terror that was supported by Islamic leaders and many other Kenyan groups morphed into a war that terrorized Muslims. They complained of being subjected to arbitrary arrest and of fearing the extraordinary renditions publicized in local media. In investigating incidents, Kenyan authorities—often working with the FBI or CIA—detained family members of alleged terrorists, held suspects incommunicado, entered mosques to make arrests, employed harsh interrogation techniques, and scuttled any protests. Feelings of anger, frustration, and humiliation—especially in the Muslim community—received little response. The Kenyan state, along with the U.S. government, has long held that Muslim terrorists operate in East Africa. From their perspective Muslim leaders have insisted that terrorists from outside Kenya have cruelly used their communities. Those leaders, who initially pledged to work against terrorism with the Kenyan government and the FBI, witnessed the detrimental effects on Muslim people and charged that the turmoil had created dangerous sympathizers willing to use violence.

Tensions over the Kenyan government's approach to the war on terror culminated in reactions to the Suppression of Terrorism Bill introduced in the Kenyan parliament in April of 2003. News accounts alleged that the bill had been drafted by the United Kingdom and the United States, which strongly urged the six-month-old Kenyan government to pass it. The bill, which resembled the U.S.A. Patriot Act, provided strict penalties for terrorist activity and for supporting terrorism and was criticized from many sectors of Kenyan society. Critics believed that it violated individual rights in several ways. For instance, provisions would weaken safeguards for suspects to have attorneys present during questioning and would allow indefinite detention without charges for suspects believed to threaten national security. Ironically, the latter would strengthen a provision under which some of the new Kenyan political leaders had been jailed by the former dictatorial regime. Critics also alleged that passage of the Suppression of Terrorism Bill could set religious and ethnic minorities against one another. A demonstration against the bill was broken up by police, as was a subsequent demonstration against police brutality. The Kenyan government experienced enormous pressure from the United States to adopt the bill. In response Kenyan lawyers and human rights advocates joined Muslim activists in forcing several redrafts. Since its initial introduction, the bill was rejected five times by the Kenyan parliament.[13]

Kenyan Muslims have taken great exception to the Suppression of Terrorism Bill. Leaders expressed particular concern about a provision, since eliminated, that would have made it an offense to dress or otherwise present oneself in a manner that arouses suspicion of support for terrorism. Although the provision left vague the type of appearance that might constitute evidence of terrorist sympathies, Muslims feared that the skull caps and robes they routinely wear might render them uniformly suspect. Their concern stemmed in part from the fear that without an appropriate definition of who is being targeted as a terrorist and which means are legitimate for fighting terror authorities (and even some powerful citizens) would use this mechanism to suppress opposition, intimidate opponents, discriminate on the basis of religion and ethnicity, and settle old accounts with enemies.

American critics of the Patriot Act share many of the concerns expressed by Kenyans. Yet it bears noting that Kenyan opposition is shaped by the quite recent experience of living under repressive laws, including ones used repeatedly to violate individual rights and limit civil liberties and political opposition. Kenyans' refusal to revert to a strong-arm legal system offers a lesson for those in the United States who would trade rights and liberties for the "security" promised by tough terror laws. The Kenyan position might also reflect the population's familiarity with the unlawful tactics of the war on terror. The U.S. military's decision to locate a new base for regional counterterrorism in nearby Djibouti reorganized the Horn of Africa region for security and counterterrorism purposes and positioned Kenya to play host to counterterrorism operations by the U.S. military and other agencies. Critics within Kenya and representatives of human rights organizations have decried tactics used by U.S. personnel operating in Somalia and on Kenya's border with Somalia, such as funding bounty hunters and "snatch" operations (e.g., the one described earlier that resulted in the rendition of "Chuck Norris") and arming Somali warlords and their militias against an Islamist movement called the Islamic Court Union. These actions, and related efforts to support Ethiopia as a regional power, have destabilized not only the Somali state but the entire area. The evident lawless behavior of U.S. personnel and the involvement of their own government have frustrated Kenyans, who must look elsewhere for effective solutions to the threat of terrorist violence in their region and for symbols of justice.

The Bush administration has repeatedly pointed to the absence since September 11, 2001, of terrorist attacks in the United States as evidence of the war on terror's success in making America more secure. Critics contend that many of the war on terror's violent and unjust tactics, including those used in Iraq, where the continued U.S. occupation has been justified by administration officials as crucial to winning the war on terror, have swelled the ranks of those willing to fight against U.S. interests and thus increased American insecurity. Verifying either of these positions is beyond the scope of this essay; however, bombings in Spain, England, India, Indonesia, and elsewhere outside the United States confirm that violent attacks are a global reality and justify the fear that many of us feel. I end with several observations about my own sense of insecurity, which stems not only from my fear of violence but also from my concern over law's role in the war on terror.

My sense of insecurity derives partly from my inability to trust the post-9/11 U.S. legal system. Deployments of law in the war on terror make no pretence of holding law's capacity for vengeance and violent dehumanization in check. Under the Bush administration, those under suspicion of acts related to terrorism could not predict how they might be treated, including whether their civil rights or their very humanity might be violated or law ignored entirely. The combination of an eagerness to use law as a weapon against terrorism and a readiness to refashion it or abandon it in the pursuit of more aggressive tactics, despite their illegality, conveyed the Bush administration's profound cynicism about law's efficacy as a retributive response in the war on terror. As a survivor of a terrorist attack, I take exception to the apparent disregard for law, to which some victims of terror along with the public, turn for justice and for just responses to acts of terror. The effects on the legal system of using law as weapon, of sanctioning social death, of treating law with cynicism and disdain will take a long time to undo in the United States, if that project becomes viable. The reality of a debilitated legal system does not bode well for the Bush administration's own plan to fight terrorism. The National Strategy's long-range projection of the war on terror asserts that, once the short-run goals of stopping the international operation of terrorist webs are achieved, terrorism will be confined within nation-states and can be addressed as criminal activities by national legal systems. The war on terror has yet to achieve this imagined scenario, but if and when it does, domestic law will be crucial to preventing and punishing terrorist acts. My concern that the legal system will lack effective tools and legitimacy to meet that future challenge fuels my sense of insecurity.

My sense of insecurity arises also from the failed reputation of American justice abroad. The violence threatened and unleashed by al Qaeda operatives and by the many other groups who have followed their lead is substantial and devastating. Averting future attacks will take concerted, collaborative effort at the international level, including just applications of criminal law and creative solutions that address the root of the conflicts that lead some adherents to violence. One of the consequences of the loss of international respect for U.S. justice as a symbol and for the American legal system as a just and effective response to terrorism is that the nation is no longer a credible participant in international deliberations over responding to terrorism. With attention given primarily to "winning" the war in Iraq and dominating the global war on terror, the United States has shown only limited interest in international mechanisms that might address terrorism through legal, quasi-legal, or other nonmilitary means (e.g., various United Nations bodies, truth commissions, or the International Criminal Court). Even as the U.S. government has turned away from a seat at the international table where such processes are developed, its tarnished image makes it unwelcome. The lack of U.S. participation makes me profoundly insecure.

I suppose my sense of insecurity stems also from the demise of the criminal terror trial as a symbol of the American response to terrorism. The future of that symbol remains uncertain, although the move by President Obama to close the Guantánamo Bay detention camp opens the possibility that high-level terror suspects might face prosecutions in civilian courts rather than military commissions. Initial proceedings of the commissions fail to inspire confidence that justice will be done. In his arraignment before the commission in early June of 2008, high-value detainee Khalid Sheik Mohamed said the following of the commissions: "It's an inquisition. It's not a trial. After torturing they transfer us to inquisition-land in Guantánamo." It galls me to agree with the alleged mastermind of so much violence. When I wish for other victims that they might experience the intense emotion of the sentencing of those who have harmed them in a recognizable legal proceeding, it is not the failure to achieve "closure" that I mourn. Rather, I wish for them, and for the public, the sense of satisfaction—perhaps it can be called security—that comes from seeing justice done.

NOTES

1. "National Strategy for Combating Terrorism," February 2003, www.whitehouse.gov/news/releases/2003/02/counter_terrorism/counter_terrorism_strategy.pdf.

2. George Lakoff, *Don't Think of an Elephant! Know Your Values and Frame the Debate* (White River Junction, VT: Chelsea Green, 2004).

3. Barbara Olshansky, Michael Ratner, and Rachel Meeropol, *America's Disappeared: Secret Imprisonment, Detainees, and the "War on Terror"* (New York: Seven Stories Press, 2004).

4. David Rose, *Guantanamo: The War on Human Rights* (New York: New Press, 2004).

5. Thomas Lue, "Torture and Coercive Interrogations," in *Protecting Liberty in an Age of Terror,* ed. P. B. Heymann and J. N. Kayyem (Cambridge, MA: MIT Press, 2005), 149–78.

6. Josh White and Joby Warrick, "Detainee Is Charged with Capital Murder in Embassy Bombing," *Washington Post,* April 1, 2008.

7. Dina Temple-Raston, *The Jihad Next Door: The Lackawanna Six and Rough Justice in the Age of Terror* (New York: HarperCollins, 2007).

8. Robert E. Precht, *Defending Mohammad: Justice on Trial* (Ithaca, NY: Cornell University Press, 2003).

9. Austin Sarat, *When the State Kills: Capital Punishment and the American Condition* (Princeton, NJ: Princeton University Press, 2001).

10. Susan F. Hirsch, *In the Moment of Greatest Calamity: Terrorism, Grief, and a Victim's Quest for Justice* (Princeton, NJ: Princeton University Press, 2006).

11. Richard Armitage and Joseph Nye, *CSIS Commission on Smart Power: A Smarter, More Secure America* (Washington, DC: Center for Strategic and International Studies, 2007), 70.

12. Joel D. Barkan, "Kenya after Moi," *Foreign Affairs* 83, no. 1 (2004): 87–100.

13. Wanjiru Kamau, *Exporting the US Patriot Act: Kenya and the War on Terrorism* (Washington, DC: African Studies Association, 2005).

PART SIX

Insecurities of Body and Spirit

16

Death and Dying in Anxious America

Nancy Scheper-Hughes

Claude Lévi-Strauss predicted that once anthropologists ran out of "exotics" to study they would be forced back on their own societies to study the margins of human life—the domains of the homeless, the mad, the exile, and the refugee, to be sure, but also the changing dimensions of birth and death.[1] In this chapter I will reflect on the "cultures" of death and dying in anxious America today, the place of death in our social imaginary, and the impact of biotechnology, bioethics, and bio-markets on the meanings of death and dying for ourselves and for those we love. While social policy specialists measure and monitor the quality of life in American cities, there is no attempt to measure the "quality of death," an endeavor that is perhaps overdue.

Although Americans spend more money on "end-of-life" care and on medically deferring death than any other industrialized nation, we are more anxious and less trustful of the institutions and professionals charged with the care of the aged, mortally sick and dying. This insecurity is fueled by a sense of a loss of control over the dying process. Americans worry about where and how they will live out their final days, about who will pay for their own, or their loved ones', end-of-life care,[2] about the quality of medical and nursing care they will receive, and about age-based inequities and exclusions from life-prolonging or life-enhancing technologies, such as organ transplants. Conversely, Americans worry about who will have the right to order or to decline extreme medical measures when these might serve only to prolong suffering and grief.

WHY NOT LIVE FOREVER?
TRANSPLANT AS TRANSCENDENCE

Driven by the cult of medical perfectibility, death in America has been transformed into a treatable condition, one that can be endlessly postponed. As aging, morbidity, and death are increasingly viewed as "technological failures" rather than as inevitable human trajectories, older patients grasp for technological straws, and their physicians often collude with them. So, for example, patients over seventy constitute the fastest-growing and most impatient segment of those waiting for renal transplants. And rather than wait for a deceased donor organ, older Americans are asking for a "spare" kidney from an adult child or grown grandchild in last-ditch and desperate bids to prolong life at any cost. Those lacking children can look to others who might owe them honor and respect. An elderly Catholic priest in a midwestern city had no scruples about taking a kidney from one of his parishioners, a working-class father of three young children. The priest had publicized his need in the diocesan newspaper and several parishioners responded. "Father Sylvester" (a pseudonym) chose the young policeman and former marine because he seemed "fit" and because the priest had given First Communion to the man's seven-year-old daughter. There was a bond there, he told my research assistant.[3] When asked if he had any qualms about soliciting the kidney, Father Sylvester replied: "No, no debate there at all. As soon as I saw what was coming, I sent that ad in right away. I told my doctor that I don't care about the risk. I just want to be done with dialysis. Besides, it is a very low-risk operation." When asked about the risk to the donor, he replied: "Yes, I did hear later that there might be more risk to the donor than the recipient. With the donor they have to go in through the back. It's pretty severe. But I figured that the doctors would turn him down if he wasn't healthy. That's why they give them a physical exam. I thought about this and I asked myself, 'Does this make me selfish? I'm seventy-six, he's only thirty-eight. But he can live a normal life, and me too. And the Lord has more for me to do.' "

In the early years of kidney transplants, surgeons hesitated to borrow life and vitality from the bodies of the young and the healthy to rescue the old and mortally ill. In the 1970s, when live donor transplants were permitted only among genetically related family members, statistics compiled by the kidney transplant registry show that mothers were the primary living related organ donors (to their children), followed by fathers to children, and siblings to each other. Less than 1 percent of living organ donations were from children to parents. Today that has changed. As of November 2007, 15,377 Americans over age sixty-five were wait-listed for a transplant organ.[4] A hospital in Pennsylvania was criticized for transplanting a kidney into a ninety-year-old patient.[5] Of the 2,390 kidneys transplanted to patients over sixty-five that year, 646 were from living donors, overwhelmingly adult children of the recipients. Children in their thirties, forties, and fifties were giving kidneys to parents in their sixties, seventies, and eighties.[6]

"What if it was *your* ninety-year-old father who needed a new kidney?" Art Matas, the head of kidney transplant at University of Minnesota, challenged me in response to an essay I had written, "The Tyranny of the Gift," dealing with increasing pressures on kin to serve as organ donors.[7] "I would be very reluctant," Matas said, "to discourage any patient of mine from looking for a transplant that could help them regardless of their age." And he was not alone in that view. The University of California–San Francisco medical anthropologist Sharon Kaufman observed a physician saying to a seventy-one-year-old woman with kidney failure, "Getting you a *live* donor kidney would be a great thing." Another physician counseled a seventy-seven-year-old man with heart disease: "Realistically, you will have to have someone donate you a kidney if you ever want to get one."[8] In other words, since it is unlikely that such patients at their advanced age would be able to get a scarce organ from a deceased donor through the UNOS (United Network of Organ Sharing) waiting list, the only solution is to ask a younger and healthier living person to organ-share. The success of these nontraditional transplants is measured in terms of the longevity of the graft from a live donor—its "half-life"[9]—as compared to that of grafts from deceased donors. Never mind the differential life of the kidney had it remained in the body of its living donor.

If, on the one hand, Americans behave as if they expect to live forever, on the other they worry about who will have the right to order or to decline extreme medical measures. Will one's own death be about intimate feelings and relationships, or will it be reduced to a duel between one's failing body and biomedical technologies?

THE DANCE AGAINST DEATH

In his sweeping cultural history of death, Philippe Ariès described the epistemic changes in normative representations of death.[10] Premodern death as "familiar" or "tame," ordinary and expected, part of everyday life, was replaced in the nineteenth century by "invisible" death, death "banished" from polite society and denied. Although Ariès' grand narrative has been debunked as a romantic myth, *something* did happen between the Civil War and the early twentieth century, when death in America was gradually expelled from the home, where, at least among the bourgeoisie, "the parlor" had been reserved for the formal "last viewing" and wake. By the beginning of the new century death and dying were exiled to hospitals, nursing homes, funeral parlors, and crematoria. By 1910 a feature article in the popular *Ladies Home Journal* advised modern American housewives that the parlor was passé; the heavy drapes were to be pulled back, and fresh air and sunlight allowed to pour into the room that would now become the "living room" rather than the dying room.[11] As death was professionalized and removed from the home, new anxieties arose.

Americans began to worry about end-of-life decisions made by medical staff in emergency rooms, intensive care units, and even hospices. How dead is dead? Frederick Wiseman captured the doubts and insecurities of doctors, nurses, dying patients, and their family members in his unflinching documentary *Near Death*,[12] which treats late twentieth-century dilemmas around the management of medically mediated and therefore often excruciatingly slow and agonizing decline and death. Even when it is clear that little more can be done, doctors often refuse to steer their dying patients away from futile death-prolonging efforts. "In this day and age," one doctor says on camera, "we are extremely reluctant to say, 'We really can't do anything for that.'" Where once the family doctor was called into the home to pronounce the moment of death, even hospice doctors are hamstrung by legalistic anxieties. In what can only be labeled an absurdist moment filmed by Wiseman, a nervous hospice doctor tries to coax (legal) consent from a barely conscious dying patient to the termination of his futile and painful life support. In the name of patient "autonomy," a new American fetish, the dying are asked to give consent to their death, an impossible, even cruel, demand for most people.

Physicians fear the recriminations of angry family members of the dying, and well they might. New patients' rights organizations formed by family members of dying comatose patients post Web site blogs on how to detect subliminal signs of awareness in persistent vegetative state (PVS) patients.[13] The family activists refer to PVS patients as "the slow to recover" or "the silent ones" and reject the more common term, *vegetative state*, as a slanderous anachronism expressing a "fatalistic" attitude toward a medical condition they believe to be treatable, even though it has not yet been "conquered" by the expected biotechnological breakthroughs.

Finally, Americans today face not only uncertainties about "when death ends" but also an additional insecurity regarding death: Will the dead bodies of loved ones, altruistically donated to organs and tissue banks or to medical schools through willed body programs, end up sold for parts to biotech industries or to the advertising, pharmaceutical, and cosmetic industries? Is cremation a safe option, or has it become an invitation to "vulture capitalism" (as Berkeley graduate student Jeff Schoenberg described my report on the bio-piracy of the dead by corrupt funeral homes and organs rackets operating in New York City in 2005)?[14]

My argument is straightforward. When death is seen as a technological failure, albeit one that occurs with alarming regularity, the dead body, as the evidence of that failure, is a vulnerable and embarrassing object to be disposed of as quickly (and invisibly) as possible. If *everything must* be done to "make live" the persistent vegetating patient,[15] then *anything* can be done to the "failed patient," that is, the deceased. In the late modern, post-human era, the boundaries between living and dead have shifted beyond recognition, and the value of "life" itself—even the minimalist "bare" life of the PVS patient—has banished death to the margins, exposing the dead body to the threat of the new body brokers, disarticulation specialists, and "resurrection men," poised to procure these "things," these devalued objects, for commercialized and profitable recycling.

Insecurities are compounded by personal and political inertia. While Americans express fears about ending their days "artificially maintained by 'life-support' machines, they avoid having conversations with family members to secure their end of life wishes; even fewer sign advanced directives." While Americans fear being "warehoused" in so-called nursing homes ("If this is a 'nursing' home," my dad once said, "where are all the nurses?"), they often "choose" that fate rather than move in with willing adult children and grandchildren lest they be a "burden" to them. And while Americans now fear what could possibly happen to their "remains" in a world where human body parts have become salable commodities and feature in high-profile cases of criminal corruption in hospital morgues, tissue banks, funeral industries, and willed body programs,[16] they resist increased government surveillance of these for-profit institutions as incursions of socialized medicine.

VULTURE CAPITALISM—COOKE'S BONES

Wherever the corpse is, there the vultures will gather.
—MATTHEW 24:28

I think it is good and proper that in 1976 we should celebrate what is best in the American past. But we should remember that our history, like that of all nations, is sometimes fine and sometimes foul. The important thing is to know which is which.
—ALISTAIR COOKE'S 1974 ADDRESS BEFORE THE U.S. HOUSE OF REPRESENTATIVES

Just after Christmas, 2005, Susan Cooke Kittredge, a middle-aged Episcopal priest, mother of five, and pastor of a little white wooden church in rural Vermont, the "Old Meeting House," received a phone call that changed her life. It was from a detective with the Brooklyn Attorney General's Office who wanted to know if Reverend Kittredge had heard anything about a police investigation of corruption at several New York City funeral homes, including the one that had handled the body of her father.

Susan's father, Alistair Cooke, a radio and later television broadcaster, was one of the most insightful interpreters of American society since Alexis de Tocqueville. Cooke diagnosed the strengths and weaknesses of the difficult nation he had adopted as his second home. Through wartime and peacetime, he dissected U.S. political events from the Kennedy assassinations and the Vietnam War to the terrorist attack of 9/11, commented with wisdom and discretion on political figures and celebrities, and took note of the changing moral character of the American people. In an interview celebrating the three-thousandth edition of his BBC radio program *Letter from America*, he nailed the bimodal personality of the nation: "In America the race is on between its decadence and its vitality, and it has lots of both."[17] If Americans owned one book on the history of their country it was likely to be *Alistair Cooke's America*, resting heavily atop a glass coffee table. Whether they read it and contemplated the "fair and the foul" of that history is uncertain, but at the announcement of his death at home in Manhattan on March 30, 2004, Americans grieved as much as the British for the end of an era (the twentieth century) and of a personable and intimate sort of radio and TV journalism, born of a vast knowledge, keen intelligence, discretion, and, above all, civility, the likes of which would not be seen or heard from again. But a final installment of Cooke's life in America was fiendishly in the making.

"No," Susan Cooke Kittredge replied to the detective, she had heard nothing about the grisly traffic in body parts stolen from several hundred dead bodies by a ring of body brokers posing as undertakers and tissue bank operators. One of the several New York City funeral parlors that police were investigating was the same "New York Mortuary Services Inc." that Susan had found online and had chosen because it was conveniently located and inexpensive. At ninety-five and mortally ill with lung cancer, Alistair Cooke had known that his final act was near and had requested a modest, unceremonious disposal of his remains through cremation. When Susan had asked just where this was to take place, her father had shrugged his shoulders and said, with a smile, "Surprise me!"

The funeral company responded immediately to Susan's call and sent a van to pick up the body from Cooke's elegant home on Fifth Avenue. Two days later Kittredge received the ashes. Peeking into the container, she noticed that they looked different from human ashes she had seen before: these were a powdery substance rather than splinters of bone, and somehow a piece of metal had gotten mixed into the packet. When the director of the funeral parlor failed to return her calls, she put the matter aside. Why dwell on it? She had fulfilled her duty and had to resign herself to her loss.

Now, more than a year later, Kittredge learned that police were busy tracing the activities of rogue morticians in Brooklyn who had distributed her father's and several hundred other victims' body parts to a dozen shady tissue and bone "processing plants" in the New York area. Cooke's bones had been cut out of his body and then sold for more than $7,000 after they had fallen into the hands of the owner of a New Jersey company called Biomedical Tissue Services or BTS.[18] The detective cleared his throat to ask if, by any chance, her late father was *the* Alistair Cooke of *Masterpiece Theatre*. Yes, he was, she replied sadly.

The detective described the investigation's gruesome job of opening and verifying the contents of coffins and discovering bodies missing skin, bone, tendons, solid organs, and other body parts. Plumber's pipes had been used to replace bones that were removed; sawdust filled empty abdominal cavities. Grave robbing was just the half of it. The other half was malignant fraud and deception. Cooke's name had been intentionally misspelled, his social security number was bogus, the next of kin who supposedly gave consent was made up. Worse, her father's age had been reduced by ten years, and his morbid condition, lung cancer that had metastasized to his bones, had been expunged from his record. The documents filled out by BTS listed the "donor" as an eighty-five-year-old man who had died of a heart attack. Metastasized cancer would have rendered his bones and tissues ineligible and unsafe for medical use. In the parlance of the body trade, Cooke's bones had been "disarticulated," divided, fragmented, and some portion of them pulverized so that they could be sold and used in various orthopedic procedures, transplants, and oral surgeries, possibly endangering the lives of the recipients.

Behind the scheme was BTS's owner, a former Fifth Avenue "celebrity" dentist and author of a book on dental implants (made from pulverized human bone), Michael Mastromarino. After being temporarily stripped of his medical license in 2001 following malpractice complaints linked to his addiction to the painkiller Demerol, Mastromarino had teamed up with Joseph Nicelli, a New York City funeral director who also freelanced as an "on call" embalmer for several New York funeral homes. Together they founded BTS, a tissue bank, in 2002.

Although New York State is one of the few states to regulate tissue banking, there is no national registry of tissue banks and no national tracking of human tissues bought, sold, packaged, and distributed (sometimes in FedEx packets) throughout the United States, not to mention internationally. Throughout most of its recent history, the U.S. tissue industry has been self-regulated by a professional organization, the American Association of Tissue Banks (AATB). Beauticians, manicurists, and cosmetologists are licensed throughout the United States, but just about anyone can ship a human body, whole or in disarticulated parts, in private refrigerated trucks. As in any other organic industry, freshness counts. An FDA official once told me that it was "easier to ship a crate of human heads than a crate of chickens across state borders in the United States."

Mastromarino's partner, Nicelli, a resident of working-class Staten Island, had multiple interests in real estate, poultry, corpse transport, and funeral homes. Together, their modus operandi was to visit local funeral parlors and offer $1,000 for each new corpse to which they were granted quick and easy access for the purpose of human strip mining. "There is not much difference between cutting up a chicken [chickens again!] and cutting up a human corpse," a key informant told Annie Chennie during her research on body brokers in the United States. After removing the loot—salable tissues and bones—Mastromarino and his sidekick would leave the funeral director to handle the "reconstructive work" necessary to make the body "presentable" for the family and the funeral. Cremation made the task much easier, and bodies marked for cremation were particularly vulnerable to body theft. The stolen body parts were then sold to various biotech firms, including Regeneration Technologies, Inc. (RTI), a large, innovative firm in Alachua, Florida, that processes human tissues, including bone, cartilage, tendon, ligament, and cardiovascular tissue, for use as surgical implants to repair bone and other tissue defects, fractures, urinary incontinence, and heart valve disorders and to do musculoskeletal and periodontal reconstruction. RTI distributes its products nationally and globally.

. . .

They have pierced my hands and my feet, they have numbered all my bones.
—PSALM 22

These and other revelations made Reverend Kittredge sick at heart. Her professionally disciplined sense of charity made her more mindful of the threat that her father's cancer-ridden bones posed to surgical patients than about her own sense of loss and betrayal. In her first sermon to her congregation following the revelations, Reverend Cooke expressed empathy for the recipients of her father's (and other donors') diseased tissues, who must now be at war with their own bodies, thinking, "How do I get this [bad stuff] out of me?" As a priest she was comfortable with death, and in her work with bereaved parishioners she tried to have them see the corpse as an evacuated object. The "essence" of the person was gone, she counseled, having moved on to a new spiritual plane of experience. "I tell them that the person has gone to God," though where that was exactly she could not say. Now Kittredge's own faith was sorely challenged by the cruel fate that had befallen the body of her father. The cruelest revelation was that her father's legs had been sawed off by the Brooklyn body brokers of BTS.

In a moving and searing editorial in the *New York Times,* Kittredge blamed our alienation from death for creating the circumstances exploited by body vultures. Our societal values put us at odds with death, made us want to shun death, to run away from it; "We place death in a box, and we are able to grieve and to heal so long as it is nailed firmly shut."[19] Body theft would not be possible if relatives and loved ones of the dying stayed close to the body, sat vigil with it, and supervised preparations for burial or cremation. While rationally in control of the situation by day, at night she was haunted by an apparition of her father standing silently before her, in life a large, dignified, and imposing figure, now "truncated" from the waist down. At last she understood what "haunting" meant; for try as she might, she could not dismiss the ghostly visitor. How could she put his body aside when it had gone missing and all she had left were its silent recriminations? She told her congregation: "For the last three weeks I have lived with my father's cadaver pressed against my cheek. It has all been about the body, that still, empty vessel. It's hard to get beyond the body when the body is the story."[20]

The months slipped by, and on Easter Sunday, April 26, 2006, Kittredge was forced to reflect and speak on the Resurrection, a professional task that now struck her as a cruel irony, even as "a sick joke." She structured her homily around the "fear and trembling" that Mary Magdalene, Mary the mother of James, and Salome, bearing spices to anoint Jesus' body, experienced on finding an empty tomb. The beloved body "was gone, vanished, stolen perhaps."[21] You can imagine, she told the congregation, "where I am going with this." Unlike the female apostles, however, who were reassured by an angel that the body they were seeking was safe, since Jesus had risen from the dead, Susan had to face the reality of a body that had actually been stolen and to which "terrible things were done, some parts sold for a lot of money, other parts thrown in the trash." Kittredge discovered that the deceased body was not as easily detached from the "person" as she had believed; the dead body seemed to have a life of its own.[22] More than a semimagical residue, more than a symbolic representation of the person who once was, her father's corpse was a tangible, palpable material object, a real presence recognized only after "it" had disappeared and then returned in its spectral form.[23] Her only consolation was the hope that some good might come out of the tragedy, "that what happened to my father will serve as a wake-up call for Americans—at least for those who are still able to sleep."[24]

. . .

I shall have more to say when I am dead.

—EDWIN ARLINGTON ROBINSON, *THE THREE TAVERNS: JOHN BROWN*

In September 2006, the Organs Watch "hot line" was ringing off the hook in Berkeley, California, but I was away at Harvard trying to write. I had been meaning to quietly euthanize the Organs Watch project, but reporters from the BBC, CBC, SBC, and Fox News wanted interviews. They had just discovered that some twenty-five British hospitals had purchased bone tissue from BTS in New Jersey and from RTI in Florida. At least forty British patients had received bone grafts and dental implants from human remains now known to have been stolen in the United States.

The least one could say was that Alistair Cooke's bones had found their way home. But unlike the bottled brain of Ishi, the famous "last wild Indian" of Northern California, which had been sent as a specimen to the Smithsonian Institution by the anthropologist Alfred Kroeber in 1916 but then had been repatriated to Native Californians and buried in a secret glade near the top of Mount Lassen, California, Cooke's bones will never be sorted out. There will be no prayers, no apologies, no forgiveness such as occurred following the repatriation of Ishi's remains—just the sadness of Susan Cooke Kittredge in a continuing saga of pain and displacement.[25] When a body goes missing, she says, it strikes terror into the survivors and plunges them, no matter how secular, how rational, no matter how reconciled with the

ORGANS WATCH

Organs Watch was founded by Nancy Scheper-Hughes and Lawrence Cohen in November 1999 with the support of the Open Society Institute (OSI) as an independent, University of California, Berkeley–affiliated research and documentation project concerned with monitoring the illicit global traffic in human bodies, dead and alive, whole and in parts; global justice and fairness in organs procurement and distribution; and medical human rights violations related to the use of vulnerable people and social groups, including prisoners, the mentally deficient, political and economic refugees, and children, as organ and tissue donors.

The specific goals of Organs Watch are:

- To conduct original, exploratory, multisided, ethnographic research on the social cultural, economic, political, and medical context of transplant tourism and illegal trafficking in vulnerable people to serve as paid international kidney donors

- To document flagrant violations of existing laws and of international transplant norms and regulations and guiding principles for transplant medicine

- To investigate serious allegations of medical human rights violations in the procurement and use of human organs

- To publish and make available reports, monographs, scholarly papers, newsletters, documentary films, media interviews, etc., on the medical, social, economic, and psychological consequences of the global commerce in human bodies and body parts

- To work with national and international entities such as the World Health Organization, the UN Office on Human Trafficking, the European Economic Community, the European Parliament, the U.S. Congress, the Food and Drug Administration, and transplant organizations on reviewing organ and transplant legislation, revising existing codes and regulations, and participating in congressional hearings and parliamentary inquests on organs trafficking and transplant tourism

- To assist and collaborate with other researchers and with journalists and human rights professionals concerned with investigating and reporting on the global trade in tissues and organs

- To train postgraduate and postdoctoral students and scholars and to help them set up research projects in areas of the world where organ and tissue trafficking and transplant tourism are growing

- To sponsor guest speakers, international conferences, and colloquia on human trafficking, global medical ethics, and questions bearing on the ownership and use of the human body

FIGURE 16.1. Whose organ? Gift or commodity? A kidney held by a transplant surgeon is the logo of Organs Watch. Photograph by Organs Watch/Viviane Moos.

original death, into a second death and a second mourning process worse than the first. And the haunting continues, made worse by the latest revelation. Not only her father's legs but his arms and his pelvis were taken by the body brokers. Now that her father's remains have been reduced to pure spirit, Kittredge *will* finally be able to sleep again.

One solution, proposed by Kittredge, that I want to entertain in this chapter is that Americans reassert our authority over and familiarity with death as part of rather than outside everyday experience. We might follow the example of the women's movement's struggle to recapture womanly authority and control over birth, a struggle that resulted in the reestablishment of nurse-midwifery, birthing centers, and birthing rooms. While recent efforts to recapture familiar death, a death at home or in a simulated homelike experience, through the hospice movement and the palliative care movement are certainly moves in the right direction, neither has made sufficient inroads into everyday life in America. One hopes that what happened to Alistair Cooke, that beloved paragon of civility and human decency, might serve as a warning, his last cautionary message to America.

Below I explore the "culture of fear" around the "space of death" in an insecure America today through a discussion of a recent political controversy, ethnographic juxtaposition, and a painful personal vignette.[26]

THE DUTY TO SURVIVE

Dead bodies have another great advantage as symbols: they don't talk much on their own[, so] words can be put in their mouths.

—KATHERINE VERDERY, THE POLITICAL LIVES OF DEAD BODIES (1999)

The tragic tug-of-war over Theresa ("Terri") Marie Schiavo's right to live (sort of) versus her right to die with dignity turned into an unseemly circus in which neither side looked very pretty (Dr. Strangelove vs. Dr. Death) or behaved very well. Now that Terri's body has ended its prolonged struggle to die, we can reflect on some of the painful ironies and paradoxes of that tortured death in particular and of death, more generally, in America today.

Terri's entrapment in a liminal state, neither quite dead nor yet quite alive, her living-in-death, if you will, was the result of a mortal chemical imbalance brought on by self-starvation, through a liquid diet of NutriPeptide shakes and as many as fifteen glasses of artificially sweetened ice tea a day, and exacerbated by bulimia. After the young woman collapsed on the floor of her home in 1990 and was rushed to a hospital, her lab tests indicated an electrolyte imbalance with low levels of potassium in her blood, consistent with the diagnosis of a severe eating disorder. One could conclude—as did the Swiss psychoanalyst Ludwig Binswanger in his treatment of the "inevitable" death of another famous anorectic, Ellen West[27]—that Terri

Schiavo had "chosen" death over living in a body that continually defeated her heroic efforts to be slim and beautiful. Schiavo's regime of fasting and purging was well established in the early years of her marriage to Michael Schiavo and contributed to the amenorrhea and infertility for which she sought medical intervention. However, her underlying and lethal condition of body hatred remained hidden and undiagnosed.

In the complicated legal maneuvers over the abdominal feeding tubes that maintained the inert body of Schiavo, entombed and lying in state in a kind of permanent twilight sleep, both sides argued on behalf of the young woman's wishes. Would Theresa herself, if she were able, choose life support, or would she choose the right to die? Her husband, Michael, claimed that Terri had once told him before her fatal illness that she would never want to be kept alive on a machine without any hope of recovery. Her parents just as firmly insisted that their daughter was a devout Catholic who would never violate her church's moral stand against euthanasia by refusing nutrition and hydration, an act that would also put her precious soul in peril.

But here's the rub. Michael Schiavo had no supporting evidence about his wife's end-of-life wishes. Meanwhile, his motives were questioned by the court-appointed guardian *ad litem* for Terri. Terri's husband had aggressively pursued a malpractice suit against the doctors who had treated Terri for infertility but had never diagnosed her underlying eating disorder. Moreover, the media implicated the presence of a new girlfriend that made Terri's lingering existence an inconvenience, if not an outright impediment, to Michael's current life.

On the other hand, Terri's parents invoked Catholic teachings on end-of-life care selectively. While the church is adamantly opposed to euthanasia, Catholic theologians and moral philosophers do not insist on extreme measures to stave off death. To the contrary, church authorities, including several popes, have argued against the use of "extraordinary means" to delay death as a sin against faith in God's Providence. Pope Pius XII, a staunch theological conservative, stated: "Normally one is held to use only ordinary means—according to the circumstances of persons, places, times and culture—that is to say, means that do not involve any grave burden for oneself or another. A stricter obligation would be too burdensome for most people and would render the attainment of the higher, more important good too difficult. Life, health, all temporal activities are in fact subordinated to spiritual ends."[28]

Catholic teachings on medical futility have had little bearing on the nation's bioethicists, who have so fetishized "patient choice" that dying patients are subjected to deathbed visits by doctors trying to elicit comatose patients' "consent" to the termination of extraordinary but life-prolonging measures.[29] Have we completely lost our senses? The radical shift from classical medical ethics to a consumer-oriented ethics based on a pragmatic utilitarianism, shorn of any social (let alone spiritual) content, has all but obliterated long-standing medical virtues of compassion, beneficence, care, and guardianship of the mortally ill and dying. These have been replaced by a single, "supersized" value, patient autonomy. But invoking the "choices" of an unconscious, dying person is either a cruel ruse or a perverse political ploy.

How did death become so alien, so unthinkable, that it must be beaten back with extreme "treatments" resembling punishments? In the Schiavo case there was a cruel irony in the hospital staff's force-feeding of a woman who in life had had a tortured relationship to food. Would Schiavo's "culture of life" advocates have demanded that she be force-fed when she was fully alive, alert and conscious, and risking her life through bulimia? The "disability community" in the United States was divided. One faction drew analogies between the removal of Schiavo's "life support" and the medicalized exterminations of the disabled by Nazi doctors.[30] Another faction of the disability rights movement defended the individual's right to die with dignity.

Another irony: former Senate majority leader Bill Frist, a transplant surgeon, intervened to save Schiavo's life. Meanwhile, Frist had shepherded bills through the U.S. Senate that would allow "financial incentives" to encourage resistant family members to accede to the diagnosis of brain death so the organs of their loved ones might be retrieved for use in transplant surgeries. True, PVS, Terri Schiavo's condition, is not the same as brain death. But in both instances family members and even some ICU staff feel that the patient is not yet "dead enough," whether to proceed with organ harvesting (in the case of brain death) or to remove life support machines (in the case of PVS).[31] Just as Terri Schiavo's parents used videotape clips to demonstrate their daughter's "responsiveness," medical critics of brain death, such as the pediatric neurologist Alan Shewmon, use videotapes of brain-dead patients to demonstrate evidence of vestigial biological life.[32] Shewmon has even advised the Vatican to reconsider its "uncritical" acceptance of brain death as a simple and singular condition.

So who can we trust to decide when the person is dead? Americans are still adjusting to shifting definitions of "life" and "death" under the impact of advanced medical science and biotechnology. It all began with an arrogant young doctor from Cape Town, South Africa, who dared to use an almost but not quite dead person (as then legally defined) as an organ donor for the world's first heart transplant in 1967. Critics accused the surgeon of medical homicide. Christiaan Barnard replied belligerently, "The patient is dead when the doctor says he's dead."[33] Barnard got his way, but the controversy required redefining death to avoid criminal charges against organ harvesters and transplant surgeons.

In the year following Barnard's first heart transplants, the dean of Harvard Medical School appointed a committee to examine and establish brain death as a new category of death for the express purpose of organ procurement from bodies that were still, under existing legal codes, alive. In 1968 the Harvard Ad Hoc Committee, made up of ten medical specialists, a lawyer, a historian, and a theologian, produced a report published in the *Journal of the American Medical Association* entitled "A Definition of Irreversible Coma."[34] Following a description of diagnostic procedures to be used in declaring "brain death," the report cited "The Prolongation of Life," an address given in 1957 by Pope Pius XII to an International Congress of Anesthesiologists, in which the pope declared that the determination of the precise moment of death was not in the competence of the church to decide but was instead a task for the physician. Moreover, Pius XII said that it was not obligatory for the physician to continue to use extraordinary measures in obviously hopeless cases.[35] Thus, from the outset, the medical reinvention of death (as brain death) for the express purpose of organ harvesting for transplantation escaped the acrimonious debates on abortion, euthanasia, and stem cell research in which Roman Catholic and evangelical Protestant theologians have played such a decisive role. Nonetheless, PVS and brain death are confusing to the general public. Perhaps the contentious question of when the patient is truly dead, when death *really* occurs, went underground only to surface later in the impassioned arguments on behalf of the right to (some sort of vestigial or nominal) life for PVS patients.

Cultural anthropologists have long understood death as a social process based on cultural judgment rather than as a single, definitive event, like the splitting of an atom or the exact moment of human conception. Death occurs gradually and in stages as the organs—heart, lungs, brain, skin, nails, hair, et cetera—die sequentially and over a period of hours, days, or weeks, during which the person-in-the-body may or may not be viewed as still present. Thus the famous Irish wake was so long and rollicking an affair in County Kerry up through the mid-twentieth century because, as my friend Morisheen explained it to me in 1975, "We don't like to put the person into the grave too soon, as the soul could still be hovering about the body."

Prior to the spread of medical technologies and medical professionals, the ability and the right to declare a person dead belonged to families and to communities and relied on "common sense" and intuitive perception. Pierre Bourdieu recorded the words of an old Algerian peasant woman who explained what it meant to be sick and die before doctors became a permanent feature of village life: "In the old days, folk didn't know what illness was. They went to bed and they just died. It's only nowadays that we're learning words like liver, lung . . . intestines, stomach . . . and I don't know what!"[36]

In other words, people died what was once called a "natural" death, a common and commonsense phrase that has all but disappeared from our vocabulary. Americans today behave more like Evans-Pritchard's classical description of the Azande people of East Africa who attributed all sickness and death to human malevolence.[37] For the Azande, as for the highland tribes of New Guinea and some Australian "aboriginals," there was no "natural" death, only death by sorcery, by bone pointing, by evil spells and incantations.[38] Who was responsible for the death was the main preoccupation of the grieving and aggrieved relatives. Similarly, for many Americans, no death escapes suspicion that more might have been done to prevent it, that malpractice might be involved, the American version of sorcery. Even in our medical schools death seems to be presented and taught as if it were a kind of medical error, though one that occurs with alarming frequency.

FRIENDLY DEATH

Sing a song at a wake; shed a tear when a baby is born.
—IRISH PROVERB

In rural County Kerry, Ireland, where I conducted my first ethnographic research in 1974–75 in the little mountain village of Cloghane ("Ballybran"), villagers still called on the priest, Father Leahy, not on the local country doctor, Dr. Healy, when one of the old ones approached death. "Why call a doctor to the bedside of a dying person? Sure, the doctor'd be useless at a time like that!" I was told. So the priest would be summoned to hear the confession, administer last rites, and perhaps wait around a bit to declare that another soul, God bless it, had left the earth. But more likely it would be left to the "wise woman" next door or down the road—the woman skilled in the arts of catching babies and coaxing and coaching the dying along ("It's all right to go now, Micky, we're all here beside you. You'll be fine. We'll give you a grand send-off, one to do you proud")—to declare and publicize another death in the parish. "Do you have clean sheets and some warm soapy water?" she would ask, as she tied on her apron to get down to the business of preparing the body for the wake. There was little mystery to death, though villagers still entertained each other with the occasional ghost story about olden days when one or another old one had been buried alive, or would have been if they hadn't sat bolt upright in their coffin! But the stories were told in fun, even while they brought to the surface a subconscious universal nightmare.

It took Father Leahy a few weeks of prodding from me to finally dig up the old parish death registry that had served as the official death record through the midtwentieth century. All deaths, dates, and presumed causes of death were recorded in neat columns of an ordinary ledger book, the same kind used by local shopkeepers to keep track of credits and debits. When I remarked to the young curate that the causes of death listed seemed a bit strange—"the evil," "inwardly disease," "the wind," "the sadness"—he laughed, saying that the doctor was never bothered to weigh in on this matter. The priest often signed the death certificate, and it was left to the parish gravedigger—"Poor man, not all there, if you know what I mean"—to assign the cause of death by drawing on local folk categories.

I was not in the village of Cloghane with a mind to study death or death rituals, but during the year of my stay thirty-eight old ones passed away in this aging and dying community of shepherds, fishermen, and dairy farmers. Thus death was on the mind of older villagers, and they often spoke about it and about their horror of dying in a hospital or in an old folks' home over the mountain pass in Dingle, something that was just beginning to replace a predictable death and wake at home and among kin. The unattached elderly bachelors and spinsters, widows and widowers were particularly fearful that when their time came they might be rushed off to Dingle Hospital to "finish up" so that their more distant kin could be spared the bother of a home wake. But wake or no wake, they could all still be assured of being carried, ceremonially, back over the mountain pass to lie in state overnight in the little stone church of St. Brendan. This practice and the home wake persist to this day in the village of Cloghane despite so many other radical changes around the management of birth, courtship, sexuality, and religious devotions. When our old friend the village schoolmaster, Aidan Mulcahy, died suddenly in October 2006, we were consoled by the news that he was properly waked for two days in his lovely wooden bungalow on the Cappagh strand of Brandon Bay and visited by family and friends from near and very far.[39]

The familiarity with death—friendly death, as it were—was accompanied by careful preparations for it among village elders. More than once I was asked to open a wardrobe or to take a peek behind a door where a special dress or a new suit of clothes was hung, ready and waiting for the last "dress-up." The old widow woman Bridget McCarthy, my next door neighbor and best friend during the year of fieldwork in Cloghane, was something of a trickster, and on showing me her funeral dress she held it up pressed to her chest with her face suddenly frozen into a death mask held so long that I was forced to shake her—"Bridge! Bridge! Are you all right?" "Yerra, I was just showing ye how peaceful I'll look," she said with a wicked laugh.

So at ease with death were these good Catholic country people that even youngsters in the local secondary school were conscious of the "hour of our death," about which they prayed before the start of every school day. I sometimes volunteered to teach in the village school so that I could assign essays or conduct little exercises that would help me understand young people's views and understandings on a broad array of topics. One day I assigned a "Values Hierarchy Scale" in an attempt to gauge what adolescents saw as most important to them. The simple scale consisted of a list of presumably universal key values—health, love, friendship, respect, wealth, knowledge and learning, and so on—that they were to list in order of importance to them. "Mrs. Hughes," a few in the class objected. "This test is no good. It leaves out the most important thing." "And what is that?" I asked. "The happy death," said one as the others nodded their heads. "What good is riches, and knowledge and respect, if you don't die well?" And the youngsters went on to instruct me in exactly what that meant.

A happy death in Cloghane was a death attended by family and friends and blessed by the priest who administered the last sacraments. A good death was slow and gradual, and not too sudden, for the person would need some time to put things in order, to alert friends and relatives ("Death is coming—I see him on the way from Cork already"), and to gather them around for the days or last hours. A good death was one experienced awake and aware, and in familiar surroundings, be it home or bog, or mountain, or farm. The defining moment of the "good death"—sometimes called the happy death—was the lively party held around the body of the deceased, who might be laid out on the kitchen table if the bed was not available or suitable. Before the Catholic Church was tamed and made more respectable by generations of contact with dour Protestant landlords, a wake meant lots of good drink, singing, step dancing, pranks and jokes, and outside the house games of strength, wrestling, with perhaps even a few punches thrown, alongside a little shy courting among the singles. And why not include the deceased in the fun? "Give our Johnnie a sup of Paddy's [a taste of Irish whiskey]," someone was sure to say. And a shot glass of good whiskey would be put in the dead man's hand. And so villagers prayed for a good death and would curse an enemy by wishing him "a death without a priest" or "a death among strangers."

Alongside the more exotic causes of death listed in the Cloghane registry were the more banal notations "old age" and "natural death"—in other words, intuitive death, unmarked death, expected death, the hour of "our" death, the death after having lived a long and productive life. But what, you might ask, had "really" precipitated the final end of their lives (that is, in biomedical and technical terms)? Since much of my ethnographic research took place among the oldest old ones in Cloghane, I am able to tell you:

1. They died of untreated infections because of poor hygiene, especially from fireplace soot and earth under fingernails and embedded in the wrinkled skin of hands and fingers that were carried into their mouths.
2. They died of respiratory ailments and especially of pneumonia, which some in the village still called "the old man's friend" ("an easy death," it was said).
3. Some died of gradual but severe malnutrition, slow starvation, dehydration, from forgetting to eat enough, from a "naturally" diminished appetite. ("Wisha, I can't be bothered to eat any more," they would say, or they would complain that the dinner, no matter how lovingly prepared, "taste like dirt in me mouth." "Leave me be. I've no more need of all that.")

Now, I worried a great deal about how little this old villager or another was eating, and I would try to tempt them during my frequent visits with sweets and other treats I often had packed in the big bag I carried along with my notebooks and tape recorder. I sometimes passed the word along to a distant relative that old Maggie or Tom or Mary, living alone, was not eating well. And I would be told, "But that's because they don't want to eat, because it's their time coming to a close." I was a bit alarmed at the time, thinking it a callous way to ignore, or misrecognize, an unmet need. But many years later, after closely following the decline and eventual deaths of my very old parents and those around them, I could see the wisdom in that observation.

Many old people lose their sense of smell and taste, and with it any desire to eat. My mom, always a finicky eater who had enjoyed watching others eat the wonderful hearty Eastern European dumplings, stews, and soups she produced and barely touched herself, refused to eat at all during the last year of her life. To forestall the nursing home's threat of feeding tubes, I begged her to eat but found, to my horror, that she would only swallow spoonfuls of her meals, whatever was on the menu, if they were heavily dusted with sugar or mixed with vanilla ice cream. She had simply lost her "taste" for anything except "sweet."

In Cloghane no one thought that it was obligatory to force-feed, to inject, or to otherwise cram nutritional supplements, electrolyte solutions, or pills down the tired throats of the old ones. They simply "let nature take its course." Here, for example, is a telling description of "the good death" from a rather long footnote in my book *Saints, Scholars, and Schizophrenics*:

> According to tradition in West Kerry, the "old ones" are expected to sense the approach of death, which was often personified as in the saying, "Death hasn't left Cork on its way to meet me yet!" or "He has struck me. I feel his blow in my heart." Many an older villager would tell with great satisfaction of the moment his old mother or father took to bed and sent for the priest with the words, "Today is my dying day" or "Sure, I won't last the night." A more discreet way of signaling that death was near was to ask for the final meal, what the old ones called the Lon na Bais. "Auntie" Anne explained it as follows: "One morning, about two weeks after I had returned from America, my father called me to his bedside and he asked me to bring him a large bowl of tea and two thick slices of fresh baked bread. 'Father,' says I, 'you must be mistaken. Our people haven't used bowls for more than a century. You must mean a large cup of tea.' 'It's a bowl I want,' he replied. I offered him some cognac to ease the pain, but he stopped me saying, 'No, my daughter, I have no more use for that—I had plenty enough when I was a boy. But today I am going to see my God.' So I did bring him the tea and the toast and I laid it next to his bed, but he never touched any of it. He just sat up in bed, smiling at it, anxiously waiting. He died that night. . . .Wasn't that a beautiful death? It was what the old folks called the Lon na Bais, the death meal."[40]

Now, to be sure, a great many of those thirty-eight villagers who died a "natural death" in Cloghane during that year (1974–75) might well have lived several months more or perhaps even another year or two if they had been hospitalized and treated with antibiotics, nutritional supplements, and, when that failed, tube feedings. But that would have robbed villagers of what they valued most—the chance to play a role in their own deaths, to set accounts straight, to have a crack, play a joke, and so on.

When I first returned to the village in 1980 and Bridget was, as it turned out, just a year away from dying, she screwed up her skinny face and yelled "boo" at my seven-year-old daughter Sarah, who was startled until Bridget teased her: "Aren't I the old witch now?" Then she asked me if I had remembered to bring a little sweet wine for her, as of course I had, mindful of how much she enjoyed a glass of Sanderman Port. As we sat side by side on her lumpy bed, Bridget extracted the cork with a penknife. Then, eschewing glasses—"I haven't washed a dish in quite a while," she warned me—we passed the bottle back and forth, taking swigs like two winos having a great old time. But when I pressed on her some dates and nuts and cheese that I had also brought, the old woman tossed them away with the flick of her wrist. "Not hungry," she said, though I could see that there was no fire in her old-fashioned cookstove and though the cottage seemed bare of anything except a package of dry cream crackers, which my old friend did finally take down and seemed to enjoy with her port.

ARS MORIENDI

I am reminded here of the late Ivan Illich's profound critique of modernity and all of its healing, educating, communicating, transporting, "developing" institutions. In his writings as well as in the way he lived and died, Illich bore witness to the power of modern institutions to create needs faster than they could be satisfied and to generate rapacious desires capable of consuming the earth and all that is in it. Above all, Illich resisted the lure of the market and what an unrestrained pursuit of health and of life itself, as the ultimate commodity, would bring. He wrote outrageous and scholarly texts, like *De-schooling Society, Medical Nemesis,* and *Tools for Conviviality,* in which he questioned the pride and accomplishments of the technological and the medical sciences and called for a return to vernacular practices of living, learning, moving, healing, loving, and dying.[41] The "ethos of non-satiety" was, Illich warned, at the root of physical depredation, social polarization, and psychological passivity. Instead of "medical management," Illich emphasized the healing virtues of friendship and conviviality, of modest desires and self-limitation. Ivan was a prophet and like all prophets was at various times and places sent packing. I cannot remember another *New York Times* obituary (December 4, 2002) in which the deceased was roundly criticized for his views rather than honored! However, Lionel Tiger's mean-spirited obituary of Clifford Geertz published in the *Wall Street Journal* (November 7, 2006) comes close.

Illich argued against the spirit of the times, against the commodification of knowledge and the "pursuit" of health that turn both into fetishes of consumption. What was celebrated as "progress" was often, in Illich's view, a new addiction to desires refashioned as "needs," based on insatiability and envy. Just a few months before he died Illich wrote: "Yes, we suffer pain, we become ill, we die. But we also hope, laugh, celebrate; we know the joy of caring for one another; often we are healed and we recover by many means. We do not have to pursue the flattening-out of human experience. I invite all to shift their gaze, their thoughts, from worrying about health care to cultivating the art of living. And, today with equal importance, the art of suffering, the art of dying."[42]

Ivan lived what he wrote. During his final decade, Illich suffered from a large, "unsightly" growth on the side of his face—cancer, one would think, but for the fact that he had lived with it for such a long time. Ivan did not seek to treat it or even have it diagnosed. He was living, and now he was dying, by the book, *his* book, *Medical Nemesis*. When asked by his friend Mayor Jerry Brown, of Oakland, why he voluntarily suffered, Ivan replied: "*Nudum Christum nudum sequere*" (I follow the naked Christ).[43] During his last visit to the Bay Area as a guest of the mayor, Illich was a sight to behold, speaking to overflow crowds both at the University of California and in downtown Oakland. He was unapologetic about his odd appearance, and many people moved, with discomfort, from the right to the left side of the auditorium to avoid having to gaze at the tumor that by now had consumed half his face. Added to the cognitive dissonance was the sight of Ivan's chipped, broken, and missing teeth. "So what?—I am an old man," he seemed to be conveying. "This is what old looks like. If I don't mind, why do you?" After the initial shock wore off, the audience accommodated and rose to give him standing ovations. Illich died a few months later, on December 2, 2002, in Bremen, Germany, untreated by medicine and no doubt unshriven by his church, while resting on the living room couch of his companion, the medical historian and anthropologist Barbara Duden.

In contrast to the "good death" of Auntie Ann's beloved "Da" in County Kerry, or the stubborn death of Ivan Illich, raging to the end against the machine, is the way my own dear parents died, which I will always grieve.

DEATH AND DYING IN HAPPY VALLEY:
ZONES OF SOCIAL ABANDONMENT

Several years ago I stepped outside "Happy Valley" Nursing Care Center near Baltimore, Maryland, to take several deep breaths before returning inside to face what was left of (and left to) my impossibly dear and now impossibly frail parents, both in their nineties. Because I lived three thousand miles away from my parents in New York City and because my older brother who lived in Baltimore spent a good part of each year traveling, the once unthinkable idea of a nursing home crept up on us after all else failed. My parents refused to move when moving close to one of us was still an option. But as my eighty-five-year-old mother's strength and fiercely independent spirit was gradually but relentlessly sapped by Alzheimer's, and as my then ninety-three-year-old father's mobility was hampered by a broken hip and by Parkinson's disease, we tried at first to hire home care workers. Eventually, when my parents' condition deteriorated further, they went to live in a small, pleasant-looking nursing home in Baltimore (close to my brother), where they soon became almost completely physically dependent, immobile, and incontinent, but only Dad, then ninety-five, was painfully conscious of his reduced condition and circumstances.

Mom was maintained in the end (against her and my wishes) by a plastic sack of brown liquid suspended from a movable pole and dripped by tubing into her abdomen. By this time she had lost language and communicated by gentle and lady-like howls. When not thrashing about, she seemed resigned, but with the hopeless, open-eyed, and desperate stare of a hooked rainbow trout. Whenever Mom saw me, and when, ignoring the nurse's rules, I would release her from her final hook and line and wheel her into the sunny courtyard, she would smile and be attentive to the birds overhead and to the bright pink azaleas that were always one of her favorite flowers. She would hold the blossoms in her hand and try to speak.

Just as I steeled myself to return inside the nursing home, high-pitched sirens announced the arrival of emergency ambulance and fire engines. The engines were killed in front of the entrance, and several young men, dressed in white and in blue, jumped from their trucks, carrying a stretcher, an oxygen tank, and other heavy-duty medical equipment. I was frozen with fear, less of my dear parents' timely deaths than of their untimely medical rescue. But it was another birdlike fragile creature who was carted away under an oxygen tent as she clawed at the plastic tent flaps like a startled tabby cat. Her body was handled efficiently, even gracefully, by the boys in white, who nonetheless eased their work by making sport of the absurd drama of rescue into which a resistant Ms. Kelly had been recruited.

My dad saw through the sham of benevolence in the nursing home poster welcoming new residents to Happy Valley's "circle of care" and informing patients of their rights. He often made sport of the poster to show that he was still on top of things, but his jokes were tinged with the double-edged humor of the prisoner on death row.

The nursing home staff needed, no less than myself, to duck away out of sight as often as possible, for a smoke, a snack, or a breath of air. Nursing home staff in America are paid even less than child day care workers, so their survival tactics are understandable if nonetheless unacceptable.[44] The direct result of undervaluing those paid to care for our old loved ones is the minimum-wage, Kentucky Fry "care" that they dispense. Depersonalization is the product of cheaply commoditized caregiving. Staff drop the personal names of residents and often address them as "you" instead of "Mr. Scheper." They take little or no account of expressed wishes, so that sooner or later any requests based on personal preferences—to turn up or down the heat, to open or close the window, to bring a cold drink, to lower the TV volume or change a channel—are quickly and effectively extinguished. Passivity sets in. When staff roll the inmate's body from one side to the other to clean it or to clean the sheets (body and sheets are equated), or wheel the resident into a corner so that the floor can be more easily mopped, when they do little to suppress expressions of disgust at urine, feces, or phlegm "out of place"—on clothing, under the nails, on wheelchairs, in wastepaper baskets—the person trapped inside the failing body also comes to see him- or herself as "dirty," "vile," "disgusting," as an object or non-person. A posthumously published essay by Jules Henry documenting the attack on the individual's dwindling stock of personal and psychological "capital" by nursing home administrators and staff rings as true today as when it was first written.[45] American nursing homes fit Joao Biehl's concept of urban zones of abandonment, which he describes so eloquently with respect to a charitable institution called Vita (life) that is anything but pro-vita.[46]

The "institutional destruction of personhood," as Jules Henry called it, is aided and abetted by the material circumstances of the home. Although individualized laundry baskets were supplied for each resident, the nursing aides refused to take any responsibility for lost or mismatched clothing, even when each piece was carefully and painstakingly labeled, including every sock. Several times I arrived for a visit as late as 11:00 a.m. to find my father in bed and under his sheets, completely nude, because, he explained, he had "no clothing" to wear, although my brother and I had supplied him, like a kid at camp, with eight of everything, a change of clothes for every day of the week plus one extra, just in case. Arguing with the staff was, of course, counterproductive and could easily backfire into passive hostility toward the complainant's family member.

When all personal objects—toothbrush, comb, glasses, towels, dentures, hearing aid, pens and pencils—continue to disappear no matter how many times they have been replaced, inmates (if they know what is good for them) finally accept the situation and adapt in other ways, following the logic of the prisoner, the kidnap victim, the debt peon, the peasant, the abused and neglected child—that is, the oppositional tactics that James C. Scott referred to as the weapons of the weak.[47] In response to the inexplicable disappearances of the few personal objects they own, the residents are compelled to use other objects, which are more available, for purposes for which they were certainly never intended. The plastic wastepaper basket becomes the urinal, the urinal becomes a washbasin, the water glass turns into a spittoon, the despised and humiliating adult diaper is used defiantly as a table napkin tucked under the chin, and so forth. But predictably these creative responses and subterfuges against the institutional violence and indifference of the nursing home are treated as symptoms of the patient's mental confusion and incompetence. Meanwhile, everything in the structure and nature of the institution invites the resident to lose hope, to surrender to the institutional regime, to accept his or her dehumanized and depersonalized status as inevitable.

Where are the forces of human liberation in all this? Why is no "human rights watch" keeping a watchful eye on "the small wars and invisible genocides" enacted by degree in normative for-profit institutions of violence such as these nursing home chains? Chains, indeed. So how can I write this so personal reflection without screaming? But I *am* screaming—most of all at myself for failing to react beyond carefully worded letters of complaint and the patient restocking of personal belongings and frequent bicoastal flights and unannounced visits. Despite my anger and my love, I was unable to do the only thing that could have reversed this mad pseudotherapeutic system—to run down the halls of Happy Valley Nursing Home, pull out the tubes, detach the liquid bags, knock over the Porta-Potties, and pick up my ancient loved ones and carry them away with me, on my shoulders, no matter what the cost to my liberty and that of my husband and then three teenage children.

My point in revisiting this painful personal experience is not simply to indict a business that indicts itself by its own profit-generating motives. Nor do I want to lay all the blame on the nursing home aides, who were paid less than fry chefs at the local McDonalds to care for our parents. My point is to ask what kind of civilization, what kind of people we have become when we—social critics and "militant anthropologists" among us—can succumb to a lethal passivity in the face of malignant institutional practices masquerading as caregiving.

What social, political, and cultural forces have contributed to this sorry state of affairs? As I have tried to indicate thus far, the defamiliarization and estrangement from death and dying, the loss of vernacular roles and competencies, the hidden injuries of apartheid-like work structures, remnants of a slave-owning society, that assign the underclasses to the work of caring for the very old and the very young, the political tolerance of for-profit institutions of caring for the aged, and the fear of government regulation of private institutions all play a role. The consuming demands of hyperprofessionalization and the overvaluing of professional labor—whether of lawyers, professors, or business consultants—that "requires" an ill-paid supporting staff of caregivers together create a master-slave dialectic that fosters passive aggression among the caregivers.

In the fall of 1997 my dad was rushed to the local hospital in Baltimore County for perhaps his sixth rescue from pneumonia. I was notified by a nurse at the hospital who refused to answer my questions about how severe the attack was this time and whether I should fly out immediately that morning or teach my undergraduate class and take a red-eye special that night. She explained that she was not empowered to give me any advice that I might then hold against the hospital if she were wrong. I replied that I was asking her, as one human being to another, whether, if she were me, she would drop everything and come immediately or whether she would delay the trip till evening. "I can't tell you," she said firmly. My older brother, an academic like me, was present at the hospital but simply had no idea how severe my Dad's state was. I tried to have him imitate the sound of our dad's breathing, but to no avail.

So I taught my class, like the hyper-responsible professional I considered myself. It was a good class, and I went home, satisfied, to pack my small overnight bag and grab a flight that brought me into Baltimore by 5:00 the next morning. My older brother George, as we had agreed, was waiting for me as I stepped off the plane so that we could drive out to the hospital and he could apprise me beforehand on Dad's condition. I hugged him briefly and pulled him by the arm: "Come on, George, let's get a move on, I'm dying to see Dad."

"Wait a minute," George said, "Let's sit down for a minute."

"Are you crazy?" I said. " Let's go!" and I rushed on ahead of him toward the exit.

"Nancy, listen to me. Dad died an hour ago. I was with him. We said the Hail Mary together. I told him that you were on your way."

I stopped dead in my tracks. "*What! What! What! What are you saying?*" I asked. Then I let out a howl, more like a bellow, ripped from the pit of my stomach. The "whats" were replaced by the self-recriminating "whys": "*Why? Why? Why* did I have to teach that stupid class? What did that matter?" Only later, much later, could I console myself in recalling that I had been saying goodbye to my ancient father, who was almost ninety-six when he died, for the last decade, since at every visit we always knew that it could be the last. But still, why hadn't I been close enough to realize that the end was imminent this time?

After the funeral and my return to Berkeley and to my undergraduate class in critical medical anthropology, I told my students this story. They were adamant in saying that I had done the right thing, that my father would be proud to know that his daughter was a good teacher who cared about her students. "No," I insisted. "No. The good teacher would have left a note saying that she was sorry to have to miss a class but she had to attend to a pressing family matter."

Several months later, in the late spring of 1998, my mom passed away, taking her bloody nursing home feeding tubes, hook, line, and sinker, with her. The news came via a phone call to me in South Africa, where I was doing what anthropologists do, fieldwork, in this case in a large new squatter camp in the Western Cape. On that same day I had organized a festive meeting of local *sangomas,* who greeted me in all their ritual finery. They were miffed that I was an hour late, for I had been delayed by receiving the call and then trying to compose myself. But when they heard that I had just received word of my mother's death, these Xhosa-speaking strangers with faces painted white with black and red dots really became angry and they chided me, like a misbehaving child, for coming to the meeting at all under the circumstances. After conferring among themselves, they said that the afternoon would now be spent in dancing and celebrating the life and death of my first-generation Czech mother, Anka Znojemska.

My faithful brother told me that Mom's final moments were peaceful. I rushed back from Cape Town in time for her funeral mass and was relieved to learn that at least in death her bodily dignity was restored. The young working-class funeral director in Queens, New York (who had attended to my father's remains a year earlier), supervised the transport of her tiny body from Baltimore to Queens, New York City, for a simple funeral. A true craftsman, Vinnie executed his tasks with great care and concern for my mother's dignity. He dressed Mom in a becoming blue silk dress, her favorite color and fabric, cut and brushed her still-dark chestnut brown hair into a classic 1920s "Flapper Girl" wave, and dusted her prominent cheekbones with a red blush. Her anxious face was finally relaxed in death, and her personhood, like that of my father, was restored in death by the careful ministrations of a small, family-owned funeral parlor in Woodhaven.

It is good to know that decency can still be found in some of those businesses. But it is a deadly commentary on late modern America that the bodies we love are often given greater honor in death than in the final years of their long, gentle, and beautifully ordinary lives.

I have tried to show through these ethnographic vignettes, cultural morality tales, and personal illustrations some sources of the alarm, anxiety, and insecurity that Americans experience regarding death and dying in the "life at any cost" era. But the life and death of Ivan Illich, and of the "old ones" of the village of Cloghane, Ireland, from the 1970s to this day, show that death does not have to lose its human face in a muddled and mistaken insistence on a "duty to survive." Advanced biotechnologies need not lead to the bio-piracy described in the sad tale of Alistair Cooke's unseemly end. And nursing homes do not have to be zones of social neglect and abandonment, as they were for my own dear parents in their last years. Death and dying can be, if not exactly "tamed," reclaimed and even greeted with wisdom, patience, grace, and humor. As my Dad reassured me on one occasion when he almost died of pneumonia: "Gawd, Nancy, I thought that it was curtains this time for sure!" And as we savored the realization that he had stolen a few more days, months, actually an entire year as it turned out, I was quick to reply: "Yeah, Dad, but you *still* have to die *one* of these days." To which he replied, "Do I *really?*" And we both laughed.

NOTES

I wish to thank the editors for suggesting that I write an essay on this topic and Arthur Kleinman for his salty comments following the "What's Wrong with America" conference hosted at MIT in May 2006. Susan Cooke Kittredge generously shared her thoughts and sermons with me. My Berkeley colleague Charles Briggs read a draft of this paper and cautioned me against my "fatalistic" attitude toward death and certain "Luddite" sentiments toward the promises of advanced biomedicine and biotechnology. Aihwa Ong challenged me to defend my anthropological interest in dead bodies, the supposed province of archaeologists, not social cultural anthropologists like ourselves. Gail Kligman has continued to inspire me with her own research and writings on death rites and (human) rights. Parts of the section on the desecration of Alistair Cooke's dead body were previously published as "Alistair Cooke's Bones: A Morality Tale," *Anthropology Today* 22 (December 2006): 3–8.

1. Claude Levi-Strauss, pers. comm., Berkeley, California, fall 1984.

2. Total health care costs in the United States now exceed $1 trillion, 14 percent of the Gross Domestic Product. Of this expenditure a disproportionate share is spent on the care of elderly patients in the weeks and days preceding their deaths. Medical care at the end of life consumes about 12 percent of the total health care budget and 27 percent of the Medicare budget.

3. Interview by Ken McKinley, September 10, 2007, transcript.

4. United Network for Organ Sharing, data reports, national data, waiting list, organ by age, www.unos.org/, accessed November 2007.

5. "More Elderly Having Transplants," *USA Today,* February 4, 2008.

6. United Network for Organ Sharing, data reports, national data, donor, all donors by donor type, living donors by donor age, www.unos.org/, accessed November 2007.

7. Nancy Scheper-Hughes, "The Tyranny of the Gift: Sacrificial Violence in Living Donor Transplants," *American Journal of Transplant* 7 (2007): 1–5.

8. Sharon Kaufman, A. Russ, and J. Shim, "Aged Bodies and Kinship Matters," *American Ethnologist* 33, no. 1 (2006): 82.

9. *Half-life* is the term used to calculate the life expectancy of functioning organs graft at one-year intervals after transplant.

10. Philippe Aries, *Western Attitudes toward Death: From the Middle Ages to the Present* (Baltimore, MD: Johns Hopkins University Press, 1974).

11. See Stanley Burns's collection of nineteenth- and early twentieth-century "post mortem photographs" illustrating the formal presentation of the newly dead laid out in the family parlor as compared to their display in commercial funeral parlors in his book *Sleeping Beauty: Memorial Photography in America* (Santa Fe, NM: Twelvetrees Press, 1990).

12. *Near Death,* dir. Frederick Wiseman (Exit Films, 1989).

13. See, e.g., the Headway Homes Web site, http://headwayhomes.blogharbor.com/blog/.

14. Nancy Scheper-Hughes, "Biopiracy and the Global Quest for Organs," *NACLA Report on the Americas* 39 (March–April 2006): 14–21.

15. See Sharon Kaufman, *And a Time to Die: How American Hospitals Shape the End of Life* (New York: Scribner, 2005).

16. See Annie Cheney, *Body Brokers: Inside America's Underground Trade in Human Remains* (New York: Broadway Books, 2006); Nancy Scheper-Hughes and Loïc Wacquant, eds., *Commodifying Bodies* (Thousand Oaks, CA: Sage Publications, 2005); Lesley Sharp, *Bodies, Commodities, and Biotechnologies* (New York: Columbia University Press, 2006).

17. Quoted in "Radio Legend Cooke Dies Aged 95," BBC News, March 30, 2004, http://news.bbc.co.uk/2/hi/entertainment/3581465.stm.

18. Alec Russell, "Alistair Cooke's Bones Stolen by Transplant Gang," *Daily Telegraph,* December 23, 2005.

19. Susan Cooke Kittredge, "Black Shrouds and Black Markets," *New York Times,* March 5, 2006.

20. Quoted in "Radio Legend Cooke."

21. Susan Cooke Kittredge, "Found and Lost," homily delivered on January 8, 2006, Old Meeting House, East Montpelier Center, VT.

22. Susan Cooke Kittredge, "Because . . . ," homily delivered on Easter Sunday, April 16, 2006, Old Meeting House, East Montpelier Center, VT.

23. The liveliness of dead bodies is, of course, a key theme of anthropological importance, from Frazer's *The Golden Bough* and Malinowski's *Magic, Science and Religion* to Katherine Verdery's *The Political Life of Dead Bodies* and Gail Kligman's *Weddings of the Dead.* Further, not only the religiously devout but secular humanists and Marxists have contributed to the privileged place of the dead body in the cultural and political life of societies, as the recent history of Lenin's tomb, Eva Peron's missing body, and the repatriation of the body of Ernesto "Che" Guevara to Santa Clara, Cuba, illustrate.

24. Kittredge, "Because . . ."

25. Nancy Scheper-Hughes, "Ishi's Brain, Ishi's Ashes: Anthropology of Genocide," *Anthropology Today* 17, no. 1 (2001): 12–18.

26. The quoted phrases are a play on the title of Michael Taussig's paper "Culture of Terror—Space of Death: Roger Casement's Putumayo Report and the Explanation of Torture," *Comparative Studies in Society and History* 26 (July 1984): 467–97, which depicts the horrors of the nineteenth-century colonization of the Putumayo region of Colombia, when torture was used to extract hard labor from local Indians drafted onto local rubber plantations.

27. See Ludwig Binswanger's famous existential psychoanalysis, "The Case of Ellen West" [1944–45], in *Existence: A New Dimension in Psychiatry and Psychology,* ed. Rollo May (New York: Simon and Schuster, 1958), 237–364. West was a young Central European bourgeois Jewish woman, imbued from her early childhood with a visceral disregard for and hatred of her own material flesh so strong that the only possible solution, according to Binswanger, to the problem of West's embodied existence was suicide, first through foiled attempts at self-starvation and then, successfully, by poison.

28. Quoted in National Catholic Bioethics Center's guidelines on end-of-life care in *A Catholic Guide to End-of-Life Decisions,* pamphlet (Philadelphia, National Catholic Bioethics Center, 1997), 3.

29. In another scene from Frederick Wiseman's documentary *Near Death,* a half-dozen young doctors gather around the bed of an old woman, a stroke victim who cannot speak and can communicate only by the faintest movements. They discuss the possibility of removing her breathing tube and the machine to which it is connected. Does she understand what the consequences of this may be? Is she prepared for the worst? Is she worried about the way her death may affect her devoted husband? The woman attempts to answer this barrage of questions by weakly signaling yes or no, but she is soon exhausted. She indicates that she would like the conversation to stop.

30. See the discussions at the Web site of Not Dead Yet, www.notdeadyet.org/docs/about.html.

31. On brain death and organ harvesting, see Margaret Lock, *Twice Dead: Organ Transplants and the Reinvention of Death* (Berkeley: University of California Press, 2002); on PVS and the removal of life support, see Kaufman, *And a Time to Die.*

32. Alan Shewmon, "Commentary on Pope John Paul II's Address to the 18th International Congress of the Transplantation Society, August 29, 2000," unpublished manuscript. Shewmon's tapes, shown and discussed at the Third International Symposium on Coma and Brain Death in Havana, Cuba, in 2001 included those of a young boy, declared brain dead but taken home by his religious parents who refused to accept the diagnosis and who arranged for round-the-clock care, including artificial respiration and feeding tubes. The boy has persisted in what can only be described as a reptilian state similar to PVS for thirteen years. One observer described the boy as a decapitated frog. Shewmon does not contest the diagnosis of brain death—the boy was, he maintains, brainless and decapitated—but he hypothesizes that the boy's living-in-death is possible through the compensatory evolutionary capabilities of the reticular function, located in the base of the reptilian brain stem. The reaction of the medical audience in Cuba to these video clips was sharp and angry. To the majority, the maintenance of a dead child with autonomic nerve responses—similar to the reflexes of a chicken without a head—in the name of saving human life was simply an abomination, biotechnology gone haywire. Shewmon's conclusion seemed to support the need for establishing a more rigid diagnosis of brain death that would effectively diminish the number of organs available for transplant. Ironically, the organizer of the symposium, Dr. Calixto Machado, an orthodox Cuban Marxist, was forced into sounding like a traditional Latin American Catholic, claiming the existence of a soul-like force that integrates the organs of the body and breathes a life spirit, when he argued that the brain dead did not evidence any of this soul-force.

33. Dr. Jose de Nobrega, protégé of Barnard, interview, Cape Town, 1997. This bit of transplant folklore also appears in Christiaan Barnard's autobiography, written with the assistance of Curtis Bill Pepper, *One Life* (New York: Macmillan, 1969).

34. "A Definition of Irreversible Coma: Report of the Ad Hoc Committee of the Harvard Medical School to Examine the Definition of Brain Death," *JAMA* 205, no. 6 (1968): 337–40.

35. Pope Pius XII, "The Prolongation of Life," *The Pope Speaks* 4 (Spring 1958): 398.

36. Pierre Bourdieu, *Outline of a Theory of Practice* (Cambridge: Cambridge University Press, 1977), 166.

37. E. E. Evans Pritchard, *Witchcraft, Oracles, and Magic among the Azande* (New York: Oxford University Press, 1937).

38. Shirley Lindenbaum, *Kuru Sorcery: Disease and Danger in the New Guinea Highlands* (Palo Alto, CA: Mayfield, 1979); G. W. Milton, "Self-Willed Death or the Bone-Pointing Syndrome," *Lancet* 23 (June 1973): 1435–36.

39. The following message came to us from Aidan's wife Sheila Mulcahy by e-mail: "My beloved husband, Aidan, and your friend, died suddenly on Friday, 6th October. We had just attended the official opening of the new [village] Secondary School which has replaced the one we founded in 1961. . . . It was a very happy occasion. When all was over . . . Aidan was not looking well. He allowed me to drive him to the doctor's surgery. . . . The lady doctor examined Aidan and thought there was no cause for alarm. . . . All this time Aidan was lying on the couch chatting to the doctor and complaining only of discomfort, not pain. I left his side to tell our daughter in the waiting room what had been decided. I had barely gone through the door when the doctor called out. . . . We rushed in to find Aidan keeling over on his side. It was all over instantly. The doctor tried very hard to resuscitate him, as did the ambulance men who arrived soon after, but it was hopeless. By that evening we had him back here in the house in his coffin and kept him here at home for the following two days."

40. Nancy Scheper-Hughes, *Saints, Scholars, and Schizophrenics: Mental Illness in Rural Ireland*, updated and expanded ed. (Berkeley: University of California Press, 2001), 358 n.

41. The relevant books by Ivan Illich include *Deschooling Society* (New York: Harper and Row, 1971); *Tools for Conviviality* (New York: Harper and Row, 1973); *Medical Nemesis: The Expropriation of Health* (New York: Pantheon Books, 1976); and *Toward a History of Needs* (New York: Pantheon Books, 1978).

42. Quoted in Jerry Brown, "Ivan Illich," contribution to "Remembering Ivan Illich: Reflections on a Seminal Cultural Critic/Intellectual Gadfly," by Carl Mitcham et al., *Whole Earth*, Spring 2003, http://wtp.org/.

43. Ibid.

44. When my home institution, the University of California, Berkeley, was pressured by protesting students (of which I was one) in 1969 to open and financially support day care for students (and later for faculty and staff as well), the administration decided on a pay scale for the day care teachers, who were originally classified under a preexisting category, "animal lab attendants" for the Division of Life Sciences at Cal.

45. Jules Henry, *On Sham, Vulnerability and Other Forms of Self-Destruction* (New York: Random House, 1973).

46. Joao Biehl, *Vita: Life in a Zone of Social Abandonment* (Berkeley: University of California Press, 2005).

47. James C. Scott, *Weapons of the Weak: Everyday Forms of Peasant Resistance* (New Haven, CT: Yale University Press, 1985).

17

Get Religion

Susan Harding

Do words sometimes betray you, leaving you a stranger in your own land?
—BREGJE VAN EEKELEN ET AL., *SHOCK AND AWE: WAR ON WORDS*

Language is a kind of informal plebiscite: when we adopt a new kind of word or alter the usage of an old one, we're casting a voice vote for a particular point of view.
—GEOFFREY NUNBERG, *TALKING RIGHT*

GetReligion is a blog managed by two evangelical Christian journalists. They gather "ghosts," "religious images that are hidden in news stories," to educate other journalists about the religious backstories that they miss as they report the daily news. The GetReligion bloggers are theologically conservative biblical inerrantists, and they speak modern journalist discourse with perfect pitch, but from a point of view that is different from and in ways opposed to that of their secular counterparts.[1]

In this same sense, white, theologically and socially conservative Protestants have been "getting" secular culture for several decades: not as the GetReligion bloggers say they want their colleagues to "get religion," by recognizing religious dimensions in daily news stories, but as the bloggers are "getting" secular journalism, by taking up the language of their cultural others and speaking it from an alien point of view. "Getting" as in improvisation, appropriation, poaching, channeling, ventriloquism, repetition with a difference, culture jamming—as in what I will call here "revoicing."

In the 1980s and 1990s, the Reverend Jerry Falwell built the first modern fundamentalist revoicing empire.[2] The church ministries, media and political organizations, and educational institutions he built were, in effect, a hive of cultural workshops in which both fundamentalist and secular ideas, images, narratives, and practices were smelted, refashioned, melded, packaged, and distributed.

The Falwellians converted the demon-friendly haunted house of Halloween into Scaremare, an ensemble of creepy encounters with sin, dying, death, and the saving grace of Jesus Christ. They took up the secular beauty contest and turned it into a "pageant" that emphasized Christian virtues more than physical appearance. They published *Fundamentalist Journal*, a glossy news and opinion magazine that staged its world-consuming rhetorics on coffee tables across the country (figures 17.1 and 17.2).

Falwell's Bible college, Lynchburg Baptist College, morphed into a liberal arts college, Liberty Baptist College, and then into a university, Liberty University. The Museum of Earth and Life History on its campus occupied in meticulous detail the cultural space of a museum of natural history but coded the displays of man and beast with the assumptions of creation science, not evolution. Liberty Godparent Homes appropriated, literally, the space of a former home for unwed mothers and converted it into a staging ground for prolife save-a-baby narratives that in turn revoiced feminist story lines in born-again Christian terms.

Parallel world-consuming industries emerged during those years all over the country in theological conservative Protestant churches, ministries, parachurch organizations, and religious businesses. The end of the twentieth century was a period of cultural morphing among born-again Christians that left nothing untouched, not even the Bible.

BibleZines are Christian Bibles published in the form of glossy magazines with chatty sidebars, quizzes, and calendars interpenetrating Bible text on every page. *Revolve*, the New Testament for teenage girls (figure 17.3), came out first, in 2003, followed shortly by *Real* for urban (which means here multiethnic, edgy, and guy-centered) teens and *Refuel* for teenage boys. Tweens, adults, and baby boomers have since been targeted as well with their own BibleZines: *Blossom, Magnify, Explore, Becoming, Align, Divine Health, NT:Sport,* and *Redefine*.

These are revoicing practices. They redirect, recode, and re-version. At the same time, they occupy, colonize, and deeply disturb the worlds of their cultural others. Revoicing requires intimate, inside knowledge of the discourses of one's political and cultural others. It is work done from within their discourses, work that creates unprecedented points of view within the discourses and ventriloquizes and redirects them to other, sometimes entirely opposite, ends.

Christianity emerged out of several centuries of appropriating and revoicing Jewish stories and texts. Its expansion has always relied on both individual conversion and cultural revoicing practices. American Protestant evangelicals, unlike their mainline counterparts, have continuously evolved their revoicing techniques and practices, and in moments of public activism they deploy them with great force and skill to advance their causes.

FIGURE 17.1. Front cover of *Fundamentalist Journal,* a publication from the early 1980s that revoiced images from secular futurology and business culture. *Fundamentalist Journal* (June 1984).

THE LIBERTY WORD STUDY SERIES

Influence.

*Jerry Falwell, Chancellor of Liberty Baptist College,
speaks out on an issue of critical concern.*

"To educate is not simply to impart facts and figures, but to influence
a life. Even a machine can disperse information. Influence is that indefin-
able impact of one person upon another — that force which shapes the
thinking processes and sharpens decision-making skills. Each
of us is the product of combined influences. Our parents,
family members, friends and acquaintances serve to
mold us in myriad ways.

"During our college years we are especially
pliable as we are confronted with the challenge of
new ideas. A college bears the enormous responsibility of exerting the right kind of influence. At
Liberty, we take this responsibility with utmost
seriousness. Our faculty is consummately prepared to
communicate knowledge — to give essential instruc-
tion. But they're also committed to leading by Godly
example. That is the influence that really counts. We
must produce young men and women who are not only
authorities in their field, but individuals of true
Christian character.

"Something else: we make sure the
Liberty student body is influenced by
today's pacesetters. By bringing to our
campus world leaders, we stimulate and
inspire the pacesetters of tomorrow.
Influence. It is synonymous with
Liberty."

LIBERTY
BAPTIST COLLEGE

Write or call for more information:
LIBERTY BAPTIST COLLEGE, Lynchburg, VA 24506

800-446-5000

Financial Aid information available on request.
Applicants for admission are considered
without regard to sex, race, national
origin, or handicap.

FIGURE 17.2. Back cover of *Fundamentalist Journal* (June 1983).

FIGURE 17.3. Front cover of *Revolve: The Complete New Testament* (Nashville, TN: Thomas Nelson, 2006). Cover design by Four 5 One Design, Dublin, Ireland.

THE RELIGIOUS RIGHT GETS LIBERALISM

BibleZines show how sophisticated—glossy, hip, and slick—theologically conservative Christians have become in revoicing "the world" (in this case, teen magazines, urban youth culture, niche marketing, etc.) in their own cultural terms. As activists, voters, and lobbyists, Christians who are socially as well as theologically conservative have also transformed the American political landscape. Their ability to revoice and dominate the basic language of politics became dramatically apparent in the presidential elections of 2000 and 2004. During the years leading up to those elections, Religious Right leaders, as well as Republican politicians and pundits, became increasingly adept at rethinking and respeaking their liberal opponents' terms, at reinflecting and redirecting them into their own terms. They did not just reify and criticize their cultural and political adversaries; they metabolized them. They went deep inside hitherto secular and liberal institutions and practices, not to be assimilated, but to assimilate, consume, digest, and convert both the partisan and the cultural politics they encountered to their ends.

The linguist Geoffrey Nunberg argued in his 2006 book, *Talking Right,* that the Right had "captured" the language of the nation's everyday political discussion. "When we talk about politics nowadays—by 'we' I mean progressives and liberals as well as conservatives and people in the center—we can't help using language that embodies the worldview of the right." The Right wove into "the fabric of American political discourse . . . a collection of overlapping stories about the currents of contemporary American life—stories that illustrate declining patriotism and moral standards, the out-of-touch media and the self-righteous liberal elite, the feminization of public life, minorities demanding special privileges and unwilling to assimilate to American culture and language, growing crime and lenient judges, ludicrous restrictions on permissible speech, disrespect for religious faith, a swollen government that intrudes officiously in private life, and arching over all of them, an America divided into two nations by differences in values, culture, and lifestyle."[3]

Religious Right preachers were pioneers in revoicing the language of liberalism. They trained their church people how to do likewise, and they created and revamped a network of day schools, colleges, and universities to train growing generations of students in the skills of challenging, confronting, and converting the world, its politics as well as its culture, to their terms. They revoiced liberal ideas, tropes, and story lines about citizenship, government, America, democracy, freedom, liberty, class, family, civil rights, social justice, the Constitution, and peace. In doing so, they provided much of the intellectual ammunition that displaced liberal "reality-based" versions of social policy, political economics, and geopolitics with conservative "faith-based" ones.

Religious Right preachers are masters of insecurity. Fundamentalist preachers routinely produce and manipulate personal insecurity in lost and wayward souls to convince them to accept Jesus as the path to "eternal security." In their crusade to "save America," Religious Right preachers have further produced a profound sense of moral insecurity among their faithful. The aggressive reentry of the Religious Right into public life, its considerable political influence and electoral successes, and its hold on everyday political language have, in turn, made many other Americans, especially those targeted by Religious Right rhetorics, politically and culturally insecure. One distinct advantage Religious Right activists have over their secular critics and rivals is that, while Religious Right activists have no inhibitions about revoicing secular idioms, most of their secular critics and rivals cannot, or will not, revoice conservative religious idioms.

GETTING THE RELIGIOUS RIGHT

So who is revoicing the Religious Right? Are other voices, images, and practices emerging that take up, appropriate, redirect, reaccent, and recode socially and politically conservative Christianity? Revoicing requires intimate knowledge of the language and practices of one's political and cultural others, so the question becomes, Who knows best the language and practices of fundamentalism and the Religious Right? Who is in the best position to revoice them in contexts that pluralize points of view within those discourses? The obvious answer is, other Christians, some of them liberal, lapsed, or ethnic Christians but most of them theologically conservative evangelical Christians who, one way or another, beg to differ with the Religious Right.

"Getting" the Religious Right in the sense of explaining, criticizing, or mocking it has a long history among secular and liberal religious outsiders. "Getting" the Religious Right in the sense of insider revoicing from a critical point of view also has precedent (see, for example, the *Door,* a gentle satire magazine, and "Landover Baptist Church," an outrageous Web parody of fundamentalist superchurches like Jerry Falwell's). However, insider revoicing really took off after the 2000 and 2004 presidential elections in which the Religious Right played a starring role. Suddenly, it seemed, what was being said under the rubric of "evangelical" or "faithful Christian" became less predictable, more diverse, less monologic, and more complex.

Neil Young took up the evangelical God of all creation and converted him from the moral politics of the Religious Right to social liberalism in his song "When God Made Me." The United Church of Christ's 2004 "bouncer ad" portrayed with ominous, apocalyptic overtones two beefy bouncers at a church door turning away a gay male couple, two blacks, and a disabled man, then reclaimed Jesus with images of diverse UCC congregations while scrolling, "Jesus didn't turn people away. Neither do we." The evangelical blogosphere brimmed with new sites that implicitly, and sometimes explicitly, challenged fundamentalism and the Religious Right ("The OOZE," "Open Source Theology," "ginkworld," "rural praxis," "Church Marketing Sucks").

A loose, tacit, and growing coalition of voices, left, right, and center, has turned "social justice" into a mainstream white evangelical issue, even putting it on a par theologically with "personal salvation." The evangelical Left (Jim Wallis, Ron Sider, Tony Campolo) rose from the undead, and politically ambiguous evangelical figures (Rick Warren, Richard Cizik, Gregory Boyd, Brian McLaren, Bono) came into focus, sometimes with surprising force. There were news stories about antiwar protests at evangelical colleges, gay evangelical Bible study groups, green evangelical initiatives, and alliances between evangelicals and ACT UP.

In part, we are simply seeing that the category "evangelical," in spite of its recent identification with the Religious Right, was always more diverse. Many evangelicals never identified with the Religious Right, and an increasing number have become disillusioned with it. But more is going on of preexisting and growing political and cultural diversity than meets the eye. As ever, evangelicals are revoicing worldly practices and liberal idioms, but now too they are revoicing the Religious Right and effectively vying for control over the definition of the public face of evangelicalism. Here are some glimpses of three efforts from the Bush years to remake public evangelicalism: gay evangelicals, green evangelicals, and the emerging church.

GAY EVANGELICALS

Google "gay" plus any Christian denomination, network of churches, or style of worship, no matter how conservative, and you will churn up support groups and organizations for gays, lesbians, bisexuals, and transgendered people: Evangelicals Concerned; the Gay Christian Network; the National Gay Pentecostal Alliance; Rainbow Baptists; Other Sheep ("a multicultural mission for sexual minorities"); the Metropolitan Community Churches and other gay evangelical churches; and the Christ Evangelical Bible Institute (training "disenfranchised Christians," including sexual minorities, for the ministry). The gay evangelicals who have formed these and dozens of other organizations are recoding their theologically conservative religious idioms so that they embrace rather than reject homosexuality and gay rights.

Soulforce, one of the organizations founded by gay evangelical Christians, applies "the principles of Gandhi and King to the struggle for justice for sexual minorities," thus revoicing the civil rights movement as well as theologically conservative Christianity. Established in the late 1990s, Soulforce organizes yearly rallies, vigils, and protest marches at the annual meetings of both mainline and evangelical denominations and parachurch organizations (most notably James Dobson's Focus on the Family), and public rallies and vigils at the trials of gay clergy and of clergy, gay and straight, who have married or ordained gay church members. It has established chapters in many cities and states to carry out local actions.

In 2006, Jacob Reitan and other Soulforce activists launched a series of "equality rides" that took busloads of gay evangelical young adults on two-month trips around the country visiting major Bible colleges and socially conservative religious universities to witness to students and to protest school policies that ban gays and lesbians or confine them to a life in the closet (figure 17.4). The blending of the language and practices of the civil rights movement and white evangelicalism in the

FIGURE 17.4. Soulforce Equality Riders, 2006

"equality ride" was at times awkwardly conscious, but the rides, which were repeated in 2007, effectively disrupted the taken-for-granted equation of evangelical Christianity and heterosexuality on many Christian campuses.

Soulforce activists, including the Equality Riders, have not found ways to violate socially conservative Christian civility with the same force with which the civil rights movement confronted southern civility: that is, in ways that demand an escalating response; that are visceral, visible, and won't go away; and that embody and enact gays' place and their right to remain in the churches that deny them. When gay evangelicals come out, they usually leave their socially conservative churches, but what if they refused to accept their church's view of them as sinners and did not leave? What if they returned to the churches that rejected them, or went to other churches that reject homosexuals, and claimed a place in the pews?

In 2002, Mel White and Gary Nixon, the founders of Soulforce, moved to Lynchburg, Virginia, and bought a house across the street from the Reverend Jerry Falwell's Thomas Road Baptist Church.[4] Together, as a couple, they started attending Sunday morning and Wednesday evening services. Whenever Falwell said something against gays, gay sexuality, gay rights, gay relationships, or gay marriage, Mel and Gary stood up to witness to their dissent from what Falwell was preaching. Among Falwell's congregation (it includes several thousand Liberty University students) are men and women who are, were, or have wondered if they are gay, as well as parents, siblings, children, cousins, aunts, and uncles of gay men and lesbians. What if one or two or three of them started talking sympathetically about what Mel and Gary were doing? What if one day one of them stood up when Mel and Gary stood up? What if other Soulforce activists made similar commitments to attend weekly services at churches in their areas preaching against homosexuality? What if socially conservative Christians could not so comfortably count on going to sexuality-segregated churches and instead had to encounter the reality of homosexuals worshiping the same God they do?[5]

Revoicings are potent because they work inside a discourse, opening it up, creating new, sometimes illegitimate and subversive, points of view, rearranging the lines between the said and the unsaid, and complicating the realms of the possible. They alter both speaker and spoken. Given that many theologically conservative evangelicals reject gay sexuality as a sin and that for them "gay evangelical" is an oxymoron, the mere existence of gay evangelicals is an act of radical revoicing.

GREEN EVANGELICALS

Al Gore's mainstream film *An Inconvenient Truth* may be seen as an instance of secular environmental apocalypticism, but some reviewers and viewers caught its distinctly evangelical form and tone.[6] Specifically, in *An Inconvenient Truth,* Al Gore, who attended divinity school and is a lifelong practicing Baptist, preached an "American jeremiad," a Protestant political sermon that laments "that a people has fallen into sinful ways and face ruin unless they swiftly reform."[7] Doom is imminent but conditional, not inevitable. It can be reversed by human action, but time is short.

A jeremiad is, invariably, a message people do not want to hear, so the life of the preacher/prophet is a hard one. "I've been trying to tell this story for a long time. And I feel as if I've failed to get the message across." Over the years Al Gore took his message to many high places, and he suffered trials and tribulations. "So-called skeptics," among them presidents and his fellow senators, ignored and scoffed at him. When his son was at death's door, he asked himself, "How should I spend this time on earth?" When his sister died from lung cancer after a life of smoking cigarettes, he realized "that there can be a day [a day of reckoning] when you wish you had connected the dots more quickly." The 2000 presidential election debacle "was a hard blow. It brought into focus the mission I had been pursuing all these years." He saw that others carrying the message suffered as well: "I've seen scientists who were persecuted, ridiculed, deprived of jobs, income, simply because the facts they'd discovered led them to an unconventional truth that they insisted on telling." He believes we can turn things around. Redemption is possible. Our world, the planet Earth, the future of civilization is at stake. "I believe this is a moral issue. It is your time to seize this issue. It is our time to rise again and secure our future."[8]

Is this just another incursion of religious rhetoric into the secular arena? I don't think so. According to Sacvan Bercovitch, the jeremiad has played a significant role throughout the development of modern American political culture. "Its function was to create a climate of anxiety that helped release the restless 'progressivist' energies" that motivate collective social and political projects.[9] The jeremiad continues to do such work, but lately it has done so mostly on behalf of right-wing and fundamentalist Christian projects. Al Gore's was the first efficacious opposition to those Religious Right jeremiads, the first to oppose them not merely through naysaying and critique but through performance, performance that takes up the voice, the narrative, and the rhetorical forms currently dominated by the Religious Right and turns them to other ends.

Al Gore's movie performed a powerful alternative conditional apocalyptic to the ones articulated by the *Left Behind* series, dominion theology, and end-timers such as the Christian Four Wheelers who read Micah 4:2 ("Come let us go up on the mountains") as an invitation to tear up the mountainsides with all-terrain vehicles because "global environmental annihilation is a divine requirement for Christ's return."[10] And it works as an alternative precisely because of its aggressively religious and specifically Christian Protestant undertows.

Neither Al Gore nor the gay evangelicals speak from a position of evangelical orthodoxy; hence they are in no position to revoice orthodoxy per se. The Evangelical Environmental Network, on the other hand, is "a biblically orthodox Christian environmental organization" that has been interpreting, and revoicing, the inerrant Bible on behalf of "creation care" since 1993. Nearly five hundred evangelical leaders signed its Evangelical Declaration on Creation Care in 1994. In 2002, an Evangelical Environmental Network public advertising campaign in national newspapers, magazines, and television asked, "What Would Jesus Drive?" (figure 17.5).

The campaign, full of eye- and ear-catching ironies, deftly redirected and reinscribed biblical orthodoxy about creation as it appropriated and resignified a classic nineteenth-century image of Jesus as well as the morally conservative teen-oriented inflection of "What would Jesus do?" (abstinence from sex, etc.), which was itself a recoding of the question coined in the 1920s, when it carried connotations of good works and abstinence from drinking.

More recently, the National Association of Evangelicals, under the leadership of its vice president Richard Cizik, took up the cause of creation care and in 2005 enlisted eighty-six mainstream evangelical leaders to sign a statement on global climate change. These and a number of other initiatives and organizations distinguished themselves explicitly and, by their use of Bible-based language, implicitly from (their caricature of) liberals and environmentalism at the same time that they forcefully argued essentially the same case for global warming. The simultaneous appropriation and distancing from—the revoicing of—Religious Right single-issue politics by some green evangelicals are at times blatant: Cizik and the Evangelical Environmental Network co-founder Jim Ball attended the 2005 March for Life in Washington, D.C., carrying a banner that read "Stop Mercury Poisoning of the Unborn."

Religious Right leaders, not surprisingly, have attacked Al Gore's movie, but they

What Would Jesus Drive?

T o some, the question might seem amusing. But we take it seriously. As our Savior and Lord Jesus Christ teaches us, "Love your neighbor as yourself." *(Mk 12:30-31)*

Of all the choices we make as consumers, the cars we drive have the single biggest impact on all of God's creation.

Car pollution causes illness and death, and most afflicts the elderly, poor, sick and young. It also contributes to global warming, putting millions at risk from drought, flood, hunger and homelessness.

Transportation is now a moral choice and an issue for Christian reflection. It's about more than engineering—it's about ethics. About obedience. About loving our neighbor.

So what *would* Jesus drive?

We call upon America's automobile industry to manufacture more fuel-efficient vehicles. And we call upon Christians to drive them.

Because it's about more than vehicles— it's about values.

Rev. Clive Calver, Ph.D. President, World Relief	**Rev. David H. Englehard, Ph.D.** General Secretary, Christian Reformed Church in North America	**Rev. Steve Hayner, Ph.D.** Past President, InterVarsity Christian Fellowship
Rev. Richard Cizik Vice President for Governmental Affairs, National Association of Evangelicals	**Millard Fuller** Founder & President, Habitat for Humanity International	**Rev. Roberta Hestenes, Ph.D.** International Minister, World Vision
Loren Cunningham Founder, Youth with a Mission President, University of the Nations	**Rev. Vernon Grounds, Ph.D.** Chancellor, Denver Seminary	**Rev. Richard Mouw, Ph.D.** President, Fuller Theological Seminary
		Rev. Ron Sider, Ph.D. President, Evangelicals for Social Action

Sponsored By THE EVANGELICAL ENVIRONMENTAL NETWORK

10 East Lancaster Ave., Wynnewood, PA 19096   **www.WhatWouldJesusDrive.org**

Partial list of signatories. Affiliations listed for identification only.

FIGURE 17.5. "What Would Jesus Drive?" Evangelical Environmental Network Ad Campaign, November 2002.

have also tried to vilify Cizik and the Evangelical Climate Initiative. James Dobson, head of Focus on the Family, accused Climate Initiative spokesman Cizik of "dividing evangelicals," urged his radio listeners not to let environmental "doomsday theories" distract them from abortion and same-sex marriage, and joined other Religious Right leaders in calling for Cizik's ouster from the National Association of Evangelicals.[11] However, such appeals only served to isolate the Religious Right from its larger, more diverse, evangelical constituency. Green evangelicalism, like social justice, is being powerfully proof-texted and is passing muster as Bible-based orthodoxy. It is spreading within theologically conservative churches, even though—and perhaps partly because—it is opposed by the Religious Right and is fast becoming evangelical common sense.

An Emerging Church

In 2004, Dan Kimball moved his booming young adult group from Santa Cruz Bible Church into the building of First Presbyterian Church, a languishing, moderately conservative, evangelical church, and relabeled it Vintage Faith Church. Kimball and his Vintage Faith team converted the small old brick church with wooden pews, stained glass, and raised chancel into a swinging, pop culture-friendly, revoicing machine.

Kimball, who once played in a rockabilly band, favors that look—dyed and gelled hair combed to a peak, Doc Marten shoes, Levis with wide cuffs, white T-shirt, and a short black jacket. He, his co-pastors, church people, and the church cut and paste rockabilly, punk, alternative rock, computer graphics, graffiti and collage art, hip coffeehouse décor and accessories, and "sensory materials" drawn from a vast palette of artistic, subcultural, and religious genres. Their practice is not one of imitation so much as citation; you can hear, see, feel, quotation marks around their appropriations. Vintage Faith is a self-consciously postmodern church.

Dan Kimball is one of the leading spokesmen for an increasingly conscious but unorganized international fellowship of churches known as the "emerging church movement." Most emerging churches, like Kimball's, have evangelical roots but have left many of their cultural as well as institutional trappings behind. Some remain theologically conservative, while others are opening up a terrain for discussion around the role of women in the church and homosexuality. What unites them is their embrace of popular youth culture, technology, and art, their quest for "authentic" worship practices, and a disdain for "organized religion" and Religious Right politicking.

Kimball is the author of *The Emerging Church* and *Emerging Worship*, which together present a good deal of the thinking behind the emerging church movement and its practices.[12] In contrast to those who would argue that America is, or should be, a Christian nation, Kimball says we are leaving the modern era and entering a post-Christian era and a postmodern world (figure 17.6).

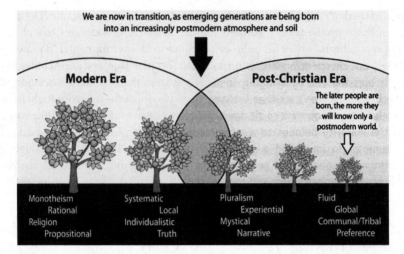

FIGURE 17.6. Emerging church leader Dan Kimball charts the generational shift in America. Dan Kimball, *Rethinking Church for Emerging Generations,* Youth Specialties Youth Workers Convention, 2002.

The bubbles designating eras recall the way time periods were portrayed in old-fashioned premillennial dispensationalist charts, at the same time that the chart appropriates and customizes distinctions between modern and postmodern culture that have their origins in secular cultural theory. In the postmodern context, churches do not "have missions," they are "missions," minority voices in a larger culture that is tone-deaf to the message of Christ, not out of hostility so much as ignorance. "Pre-Christians," a shrinking population, have some acquaintance with Christianity and may be reached through more conventional evangelical outreaches. "Post-Christians," who are growing rapidly in number, have little or no knowledge of Christianity and must be reached on their own terms. Emerging church bywords are narrative (not truth); organic and interactive (not linear and top-down) worship; collaboration and interconnection (not hierarchy); multicentered (not pastor centered); creativity; diversity; small groups; participation; eclectic blends; and the arts.

Kimball is an articulate analyst and critic of contemporary evangelical ministry practices. He posted on his blog a long critical history of pews, "What Are These Strange Things Called 'Pews'?" and another more expansive critique, "Pews, Pulpits, Pastors, Preaching and Other Things That Can Get in the Way of the Church 'Being' the Church." His 2007 book, *They Like Jesus but Not the Church,* was based on interviews with many non-Christian teens and young adults, as well as with young Christians who were disaffected from "the church," "organized religion," and, especially, fundamentalism and the Religious Right.[13] In the fall of 2006, Kimball delivered a series of messages on "the clash of cultures" that addressed what he found to be common perceptions (the church has a political agenda; is judgmental; oppresses women; is homophobic). In the spring of 2007, he delivered another series on the metaphors Jesus used to talk about himself in the New Testament, which he called "the Tao of Jesus."

As I sat through the stylish, edgy, cool, broad-minded worship services at Vintage Faith, I found myself listening and looking for telltale signs of underlying fundamentalist faith. It took me months to find them, and most of them came from Kimball's books, not Vintage Faith church services. Kimball holds the fundamentals of the faith regarding the death, burial, and resurrection of Christ, Creation, and the Second Coming. He thinks that God (the Bible) does not want women to be pastors and does not want anyone, including gays, to have sex outside heterosexual marriage.

When I discerned Kimball's theology, my first reaction was to see his church's look, sound, language, and practice as a surface covering up its depth, its true nature, its essence. I thought: Vintage Faith Church is fundamentalism (or conservative evangelicalism) in postmodern drag. It looks like something else, but it's really just the latest round of cultural appropriations by evangelicals designed to recruit teens and young adults to Christianity.

Old-fashioned religion is in some ways under construction at Vintage Faith, but the campy, citational style also puts it at risk. Kimball willfully, dramatically, and repeatedly downplays his orthodoxy. He's pared it down, muted and domesticated it, placed it in the background, hidden it in a closet. He has rendered public displays of fundamentalism inappropriate and unacceptable and has abolished any sign of the Religious Right. *Judgmental* and *fundamentalism* are bad words in his vocabulary. He does not affiliate with any particular kind of Christianity, denominational or otherwise, and does not even like to call himself a Christian, preferring "follower of Jesus." He often talks about "the church" and "organized religion" as if they were foreign cultures. Nothing about his self-presentation scans as "evangelical," and he appears most at home, even when he is uncomfortable, in the nether regions of pop culture—the Sopranos, *The Da Vinci Code,* rock concerts, new modes of spiritual expression, YouTube videos about Jesus, blogs galore, cafés and music clubs.

It is as if Kimball had gobbled up the Religious Right, fundamentalism, and the larger evangelical culture along with a good deal of popular "postmodern" culture and made something else, something in between, something both/and and neither/nor. Like androgyny and transsexuality, Kimball and his church do not fit binary conceptions. They rattle the cages of religious essentialism all around, right and left, secular and fundamentalist, popular and academic, theoretical and practical. They are practicing, and preaching, a kind of culture jamming—transforming a cultural practice from the inside by pirating existing media and using them to comment upon and disrupt dominant messages. Are they jamming pop culture? Or fundamentalism? Or both?

AN AGONISTIC PLURALISM

These and other evangelical revoicings of fundamentalism and the Religious Right will not make them go away, but they do, paradoxically, promise a somewhat more securely secular public arena.

A narrowly defined secular arena in which public life is defined as off limits to all but banal forms of religious speech depends on everyone playing by a tacit set of rules that restricts politically potent religious speech. Labeling someone who breaks the rules a "religious extremist" works to police the boundaries some of the time but not all of the time. If only one religious party breaks the taboos restricting religious speech, everyone else is at a disadvantage, for that party has access to discursive resources, powerful ones, that their opponents disavow. If, on top of that, the extremists become adept at absorbing and digesting their opponents' narrative and rhetorical resources and run amok and unopposed through the body politic, a code red situation develops in terms of secular insecurity.

Extremist religious rhetorics must be actively opposed, and that opposition must include insider revoicings that are immersed in the rhetorical forms and perform them with a difference. Reason, explanation, critique, counterargument, alternative "framings," resistance, oppositional politics, parody, blasphemy, vilification, and attack are not enough. The political, cultural, and linguistic territory of movements such as the Religious Right must be occupied, colonized, and relandscaped from internal and contrary points of view. As insider revoicings of fundamentalism and the Religious Right gain density, intensity, passion, complexity, diversity, historical depth, and charisma, the result will not be the end of secularity any more than it would be the reinstallation of a narrow secularity that relies on everyone playing by the rules of areligious reason. It will be instead a more "robust secularity" in which access to all kinds of rhetorical and narrative resources, including religious and other "visceral registers," is widely distributed.[14]

NOTES

Many thanks to Catherine Besteman, Hugh Gusterson, Sarah Bracke, Chris Connery, Bregje van Eck-elen, Francis FitzGerald, Donna Haraway, Gail Hershatter, Helene Moglen, Kathleen Stewart, students in Anthropology 208 and 155 at the University of California, Santa Cruz, and interlocutors at the University of Texas, Austin, Cultural Studies and Anthropology Seminar. The chapter's epigraphs are from Bregje van Eekelen, Jennifer González, Bettina Stötzer, and Anna Tsing, introduction to *Shock and Awe: War on Words*, ed. Bregje van Eekelen, Jennifer González, Bettina Stötzer, and Anna Tsing (Santa Cruz, CA: New Pacific Press, 2007), and Geoffrey Nunberg, *Talking Right: How Conservatives Turned Liber-*

alism into a Tax-Raising, Latte-Drinking, Sushi-Eating, Volvo-Driving, New York Times-Reading, Body-Piercing, Hollywood-Loving, Left-Wing Freak Show (New York: Public Affairs, 2007).

1. See Terry Mattingly, "What We Do, Why We Do It," February 1, 2004, www.getreligion.org/?p=3.

2. Theologically conservative and orthodox Protestants are all called, and most call themselves, "evangelicals," including independent Baptists such as Falwell's church people (who until the late 1990s were called, and called themselves, fundamentalists) and Pentecostal and charismatic Christians. In this essay, I use the term *fundamentalist* to refer to evangelicals formerly known as fundamentalists and to evangelicals who are socially as well as theologically conservative and actively identify with and participate in Religious Right politics. See Susan Harding, *The Book of Jerry Falwell* (Princeton, NJ: Princeton University Press, 2000).

3. Nunberg, *Talking Right*, 5, 15, 35.

4. During the 1980s Mel White ghostwrote dozens of books and speeches for evangelical Christian leaders, including Jerry Falwell, Jim and Tammy Faye Bakker, Pat Robertson, Billy Graham, Ollie North, Frances Schaeffer, E. V. Hill, W. A. Criswell, and James Kennedy.

5. It was in the context of insider protests such as this, combined with outward pressures (blacks picketed and attempted to enter his church several times in the 1960s), that Falwell discreetly ceased his support of racial segregation and opposition to racial integration in the early 1970s. Mel White is well aware of this backstory as the ghostwriter of Falwell's autobiography, *Strength for the Journey* (New York: Simon and Schuster, 1987).

6. Some film review titles: "Al Gore, Preacher Man" (*Christianity Today*, April 31, 2006); "Born-Again" (*Guardian*, May 31, 2006); "Al Gore's Apocalyptic Environmentalism" (*San Francisco Chronicle*, June 14, 2006).

7. James Morone, *Hellfire Nation: The Politics of Sin in American History* (New Haven, CT: Yale University Press, 2004), 14.

8. Quotes are from Davis Guggenheim, dir., *An Inconvenient Truth* (Paramount Studios, 2006).

9. Sacvan Bercovitch, *The American Jeremiad* (Madison: University of Wisconsin Press, 1978), 23.

10. Stephenie Hendricks, *Divine Destruction: Dominion Theology and American Environmental Policy* (Hoboken, NJ: Melville House, 2005), 22–23.

11. Steve Thorngate, "False Stewardship," *Sojourners*, August 2006, 7.

12. Dan Kimball, *The Emerging Church: Vintage Christianity for New Generations* (Grand Rapids, MI: Zondervan, 2003), and *Emerging Worship: Creating Worship Gatherings for New Generations* (Grand Rapids, MI: Zondervan, 2004).

13. Dan Kimball, "What Are These Strange Things Called 'Pews'?" March 10, 2006, www.dankimball.com/vintage_faith/2006/03/what_are_these_.html, "Pews, Pulpits, Pastors, Preaching, and Other Things That Get in the Way of the Church 'Being' the Church," October 10, 2006, www.dankimball.com/vintage_faith/2006/10/pews_pulpits_pa.html, and *They Like Jesus but Not the Church: Insights from Emerging Generations* (Grand Rapids, MI: Zondervan, 2007).

14. William Connolly, *Why I Am Not a Secularist* (Minneapolis: University of Minnesota Press, 2000). See also his "Refashioning the Secular," in *What's Left of Theory*, ed. Judith Butler, John Guillory, and Kendall Thomas (New York: Routledge, 2000), 157–91, and "Pluralism and Faith," in *Political Theologies: Public Religions in a Post-secular World*, ed. Hent de Vries and Lawrence E. Sullivan (New York: Fordham University Press, 2006), 278–97; Chantal Mouffe, "Religion, Liberal Democracy, and Citizenship," in de Vries and Sullivan, *Political Theologies*, 318–26.

CONTRIBUTORS

LEE D. BAKER is a historian of anthropology and author of *From Savage to Negro: Anthropology and the Construction of Race*. His forthcoming book is *Anthropology and the Racial Politics of Culture*. He is currently Dean of Academic Affairs for Trinity College of Arts and Sciences at Duke University.

CATHERINE BESTEMAN is Professor of Anthropology at Colby College. Her previous books include *Transforming Cape Town* (2008), *Why America's Top Pundits Are Wrong* (coedited with Hugh Gusterson, 2005), *Violence* (ed., 2002), *Unraveling Somalia* (1999) and *The Struggle for Land in Southern Somalia* (co-edited with Lee V Cassenelli, 1996). She is currently working on a book about Somali Bantu refugees in Maine.

PHILIPPE BOURGOIS is the Richard Perry University Professor of Anthropology and Family Medicine and Community Practice, at the University of Pennsylvania. He is the author of over one hundred articles on drugs, violence, ethnic conflict, and urban poverty, as well as several books, including *In Search of Respect: Selling Crack in El Barrio* (1995), winner of both the C. Wright Mills and the Margaret Mead Awards. He has just completed the book *Righteous Dopefiend* with Jeff Schonberg.

JANE L. COLLINS is Evjue Bascom Professor of Rural Sociology and Gender & Women's Studies at the University of Wisconsin. She has written widely on low-wage work, including *Threads: Gender, Labor and Power in the Global Apparel Industry,* and has a forthcoming book on intersections between the low-wage labor market and welfare reform in the United States.

JOSEPH DUMIT is Director of Science & Technology Studies, and Associate Professor of Anthropology at the University of California, Davis. He works on the anthropology of neuroscience, pharmaceutical culture, and medical anthropology. He is the author of *Picturing Personhood: Brain Scans and Biomedical Identity* (2003) and co-editor of *Biomedicine as Culture* (2007), *Cyborgs and Citadels* (1998), and *Cyborg Babies* (1998).

DAVID GRAEBER is a Reader in Social Anthropology at Goldsmiths, University of London. Trained in Chicago, he is author of several books, including *Toward an Anthropological Theory of Value, Lost People: Magic and the Legacy of Slavery in Madagascar, Possibilities*, and a forthcoming ethnography of direct action.

HUGH GUSTERSON is Professor of Anthropology and Sociology at George Mason University. He is the author of *Nuclear Rites: A Weapons Laboratory at the End of the Cold War* (1996) and *People of the Bomb: Portraits of America's Nuclear Complex* (2004). He is also co-editor (with Catherine Besteman) of *Why America's Top Pundits Are Wrong* (2005) and (with three political scientists) of *Cultures of Insecurity* (1999). He has a monthly column for the *Bulletin of Atomic Scientists*, and has also written for *the Los Angeles Times*, the *Boston Globe*, the *San Francisco Chronicle, Foreign Policy, New Scientist*, and *Tikkun*.

SUSAN HARDING is Professor of Anthropology at the University of California, Santa Cruz. She is the author of *The Book of Jerry Falwell: Fundamentalist Language and Politics* (2000) and *Remaking Ibieca: Rural Life in Aragon under Franco* (1984). She also co-edited *Statemaking and Social Movements* (1984) and *Histories of the Future* (2005). She is currently writing a book on secularity and new evangelicalisms in America. She is also collaborating on a radio and web project about gleaning in the Salinas Valley and on *Anthropology Now*, a new magazine that publicizes anthropological knowledge.

SUSAN F. HIRSCH is Associate Professor in the Institute for Conflict Analysis and Resolution (ICAR) at George Mason University. Her book *In the Moment of Greatest Calamity: Terrorism, Grief, and a Victim's Quest for Justice* (2007) received the 2007 Herbert Jacob Book Prize awarded by the Law and Society Association. She has also published *Contested States: Law, Hegemony, and Resistance* (co-edited with Mindie Lazarus-Black, 1994) and *Pronouncing and Persevering: Gender and the Discourses of Disputing in an African Islamic Court* (1998). Her work focuses on Islamic law in the post-9/11 era, the politics of capital punishment and victims' rights, debates over the war on terror, and new forms of global justice.

PETER KWONG is a Professor of Sociology at the Graduate Center of the City University of New York and a writer on modern Chinese politics. His books include *Chinese America:The Untold Story of One of America's Oldest New Communities* (2005), *The New Chinatown* (1987), *Forbidden Workers: Illegal Chinese Immigrants and American Labor* (1998), and *Chinatown, N.Y.: Labor and Politics, 1930–1950* (1979). Kwong is also a documentary filmmaker producing award-winning programs for PBS and HBO.

ROGER N. LANCASTER is Professor of Anthropology and Director of the Cultural Studies PhD Program at George Mason University. His books include *Life Is Hard: Machismo, Danger, and the Intimacy of Power in Nicaragua* (1992), which won the C. Wright Mills Award and the Ruth Benedict Prize, and *The Trouble with Nature: Sex in Science and Popular Culture* (2003). He is currently completing a book tentatively titled *Sex Panic: How Fear Undermines Democracy in America*.

SETHA M. LOW is Professor of Psychology, Anthropology, Geography and Women's Studies and Director of the Public Space Research Group at the Graduate Center of the City University of New York. She is currently serving as President of the American Anthropological Association, completing an ethnographic study of co-op residents and private governance in New York City, and working on a book, *Spatializing Culture: An Anthropological Theory of Space and Place.* Her publications include *The Politics of Public Space* (with N. Smith, 2006), *Rethinking Urban Parks: Public Space and Cultural Diversity* (with S. Scheld and D. Taplin, 2005), *Behind the Gates: Life, Security and the Pursuit of Happiness in Fortress America* (2003), and *On the Plaza: Public Space and Culture* (2000).

T. M. LUHRMANN is Professor of Anthropology at Stanford University. Her work focuses on the way people interpret their experience and, in particular, on the way people understand sensory or imaginative phenomena without an obvious material cause. Previous books include *Persuasions of the Witch's Craft, The Good Parsi,* and *Of Two Minds: An Anthropologist Looks at American Psychiatry.*

CATHERINE LUTZ is a Professor in the Department of Anthropology and the Watson Institute for International Studies at Brown University. She is the author of *Carjacked: Americans and Their Automobiles* (with A. Fernandez Carol, in press), *Breaking Ranks* (with M. Gutmann, in press), *The Bases of Empire* (ed., 2009), *Local Democracy under Siege* (with D. Holland et al., 2007), *Homefront: A Military City and the American Twentieth Century* (2001), *Reading National Geographic* (with J. Collins, 1993), and *Unnatural Emotions* (1988). Lutz is recipient of the Leeds Prize, the Victor Turner Prize for Ethnographic Writing, and the Delmos Jones and Jagna Sharff Memorial Prize for the Critical Study of North America. She has conducted some of her research in conjunction with activist organizations, including a domestic violence shelter, Cultural Survival, and the American Friends Service Committee.

NANCY SCHEPER-HUGHES is The Chancellor's Professor of Medical Anthropology at the University of California, Berkeley, where she directs the doctoral program in Critical Studies in Medicine, Science and Technology. Her research focuses on violence, suffering, and premature death on the margins of the late modern world. Her early work focused on madness, culture, and power (see *Saints, Scholars and Schizophrenics: Mental Illness in Rural Ireland,* new updated edition, 2000 and *Psychiatry Inside Out,* edited with Anne M. Lovell). *Death without Weeping: The Violence of Everyday Life in Brazil* was the recipient of several awards, including the J. I. Staley Prize and the Wellcome Medal (Royal Anthropological Institute). She is the editor of *Child Survival* and co-editor (with Carolyn Sargent) of *Small Wars: The Cultural Politics of Childhood.* She is the co-editor (with Philippe Bourgois) of *Violence in War and Peace.* For the last decade she has been involved in a multisited ethnographic and human rights–oriented study of the global traffic in humans, dead and alive, to serve the needs of international transplant. She is the co-editor (with Loic Wacquant) of *Commodifying Bodies,* and her next book, *A World Cut in Two: The Global Traffic in Organs,* is forthcoming. She serves as an advisor to the World Health Organization on global transplantation and is a member of the Asian Task Force to Combat Human Trafficking for Organs. She is the founding Director of Organs Watch, a documentation and medical human rights project.

JULIET B. SCHOR is Professor of Sociology, Boston College, and author of *The Overworked American* (1992), *The Overspent American* (1997), *Born to Buy* (2004), and *Consumerism and Its Discontents* (forthcoming 2009). She was formerly Associate Professor of Economics at Harvard University. She has published in a wide variety of academic journals, including the *Economic Journal,* the *Review of Economics and Statistics, Ecological Economics,* and the *Journal of Industrial Ecology.* She is the recipient of the 2006 Leontief Prize for Advancing the Frontier of Economic Thought. She is a co-founder and serves as board co-chair of the Center for a New American Dream (www.newdream.org), an organization devoted to making U.S. lifestyles ecologically and socially sustainable. Schor's forthcoming book is *Plenitude: Economics for an Age of Ecological Decline* (Penguin Press).

CHRISTINE J. WALLEY is Associate Professor of Anthropology at MIT. Her first book, *Rough Waters: Nature and Development in an East African Marine Park*, was published in 2004. She is currently completing a book titled "*The Struggle for Existence from the Cradle to the Grave*": *An Anthropologist's Memoir of Family and Class in the United States*, based on her childhood experiences in Southeast Chicago. She and her husband, Chris Boebel, are also working on a documentary, *Exit Zero*, about the transformations in Southeast Chicago following the demise of the steel industry as well as the increasingly elusive nature of the "American Dream."

JANINE R. WEDEL, an anthropologist, is Professor in the School of Public Policy at George Mason University and Fellow at the New America Foundation. A four-time Fulbright Fellow and recipient of awards from the National Science Foundation, the MacArthur Foundation, the Ford Foundation, the Woodrow Wilson International Center for Scholars, the United States Institute of Peace, the German Marshall Fund, and others, Wedel has written four books. Her latest, *Shadow Elite: How the World's New Power Brokers Undermine Democracy, Government, and the Free Market*, will be published by Basic Books in 2009. *Collision and Collusion: The Strange Case of Western Aid to Eastern Europe* (2001) won the 2001 Grawemeyer Award for Ideas Improving World Order. Wedel has contributed congressional testimony and written for *The New York Times*, *The Financial Times*, *The Washington Post*, *The Wall Street Journal Europe*, *The Nation*, *The National Interest*, *The Los Angeles Times*, *The Washington Times*, *Salon*, *The Christian Science Monitor*, and the *Boston Globe*. An associate producer of three PBS documentaries, she has also appeared on numerous television and radio programs, including BBC, CNN, NPR, and PBS's *Frontline*. Wedel is co-founder and convener of the Interest Group for the Anthropology of Public Policy (IGAPP).

BRETT WILLIAMS is Professor of Anthropology at American University. She has lived and worked in Washington for thirty years, and she has written about gentrification, displacement, homelessness, poverty, credit and debt, and environmental justice. With Jane Collins and Micaela di Leonardo, she co-edited *Landscapes of Inequality* (2008). Her other books include *Debt for Sale* (2004), *The Politics of Culture* (1991), and *Upscaling Downtown* (1988).

INDEX

TEXT
10/12.5 Minion Pro

DISPLAY
Minion Pro

COMPOSITOR
Integrated Composition Systems

PRINTER
Maple-Vail Book Manufacturing Group